PHL

54060000163526

D1348544

THE
**PAUL HAMLYN
LIBRARY**

DONATED BY
THE PAUL HAMLYN
FOUNDATION
TO THE
BRITISH MUSEUM

opened December 2000

HERITAGE AND MUSEUMS

Shaping National Identity

A Book Sponsored by
United Distiller & Vintners

THE
ROBERT GORDON UNIVERSITY
HERITAGE LIBRARY

The convention organisers gratefully acknowledge
generous support from the following sponsors

National Museums of Scotland

National Library of Scotland

Historic Scotland

National Trust for Scotland

Scottish Tourist Board

Scotland the Brand

University of Edinburgh

The Daily Mail on Sunday

Scottish Daily Mail

HERITAGE AND MUSEUMS

Shaping National Identity

Edited by
J.M. Fladmark

Papers presented at
The Robert Gordon University
Heritage Convention 1999

DONHEAD

© The Robert Gordon University, Aberdeen, 2000.
Individual chapters are the copyright
of their authors.

All rights reserved.
No part of this book may be reproduced or transmitted
in any form or by any means electronic, mechanical or
otherwise without prior permission from the publisher,
Donhead Publishing Ltd.

First published in the United Kingdom in 2000 by Donhead Publishing Ltd
Lower Coombe
Donhead St Mary
Shaftesbury
Dorset SP7 9LY
Tel. 01747 828422
www.donhead.com

ISBN 1 873394 41 1

A CIP catalogue for this book is available
from the British Library.

Printed in Great Britain by
Alden Press, Oxford.

This book is produced using camera copy provided by the editor.

THE BRITISH MUSEUM
THE PAUL HAMLYN LIBRARY

069.09411
FLA

CONTENTS

THE SCOTTISH PARTNERS
Towards a National Iconography

INTERNATIONAL EXCHANGE
Learning from Others

FOREWORD

...even though his tongue acquires the Southern knack,
he will still have a strong Scotch accent of the mind.

Robert Louis Stevenson on fellow Scots

Those responsible for planning the event behind this volume started by asking the question: who are the makers and keepers of national identity? The simple answer is that we are all makers and keepers of our own identity, much in the same way that we are makers and keepers of our own destiny. As implied by Robert Louis Stevenson, it goes deeper than the way we speak. It is part history, part what we are ourselves. It is the sum of our past, present and future aspirations which produces that peculiar 'accent of the mind' that is collectively our national identity.

Readers will find much of interest between these two covers. The contributors address issues associated with both identity and destiny, and they do so in some depth and from different angles. For me, the book will stand as a milestone at the crossroads of two momentous happenings. One was opening of the Museum of Scotland, and the other was the reinstatement of the Scottish Parliament. The future interplay between these two key institutions will help to shape both our cultural identity and our constitutional destiny in the next millennium.

The first part of the book is the story of how the Museum of Scotland came into being, from dream to reality. It is told by the staff who worked so hard to create a gateway to our national history that no Scot or visiting tourist can afford to miss. The authors explain why and how it was all done, having first consulted their customer base and raised the necessary money. Whether it might be regarded as a cathedral or as a palace of our material culture, as Mark Jones speculates, is up to us. At a practical level, my hope is that it becomes part of our national life, where all of us will go to recall the past that has made us, and to marvel at our cultural inheritance.

A great strength of this volume, which I applaud, is that it puts the Museum of Scotland in a wider context. I would agree with the underlying argument that there can be no single maker or keeper of national identity. This is addressed in the second part of the book which deals with the inter-agency partnership required if we were to construct a comprehensive iconography embracing all of Scotland's heritage assets. Here we have the Scottish Museums Council, National Galleries of Scotland, Historic Scotland, National Trust for Scotland and the Scottish Tourist Board, all setting out their respective roles in this wider game. The line-up has been extended to include the enterprise sector through a contribution by Scotland the Brand, and the Editor is to be congratulated on this historic bridge-building operation. Indeed, there can be no meaningful progress on this front without close collaboration between the culture and enterprise agencies.

The third part of the book is devoted to international exchange and how to learn from others. If there is any single characteristic of which Scots can be proud, it is our ability to interact with the wider world. Many of our great heroes from the past, whether intellectuals or entrepreneurs, have sustained their native genius abroad: to learn or to stay competitive. In this spirit, we have a set of contributions from Scandinavia with revealing insights into the interplay between cultural policy and nationalism. From across the Atlantic, we learn from Richard West about the Smithsonian National Museum of the American Indian, currently under construction on the National Mall in Washington DC. Like our Museum of Scotland, it is their great cultural millennium project.

To conclude where I started, there is much in this volume to sharpen 'the accent of the mind'. I congratulate The National Museums of Scotland and The Robert Gordon University on the collaborative venture which led to its production. The University of Edinburgh also played a part, along with several other supporters, and this is exactly the kind of partnership action required to keep Scotland at the leading edge of cultural enterprise.

The Rt Hon Donald Dewar, MSP
First Minister for Scotland

ACKNOWLEDGEMENTS

Receiving the invitation to organise an international conference in Edinburgh associated with the opening of the Museum of Scotland was an unexpected pleasure for all of us in Aberdeen, and working in partnership with colleagues at the National Museums of Scotland has been a great privilege. Our sincere thanks go to Mark Jones and his staff for making it possible to add a fifth volume to the University's Heritage Library. We are especially grateful for their support to design a programme extending beyond the museum sector which facilitated consideration of wider questions relevant to the formulation of cultural policy within Scotland's new constitutional framework.

Indeed, it is hoped that the volume will be regarded as an input to deliberations about such policy, and we are honoured by and grateful to The Rt. Hon Donald Dewar MSP for finding time in his busy schedule as First Minister to write the Foreword. We were equally appreciative of the generosity shown by Rhona Brankin MSP, Deputy Minister of Culture and Sport in The Scottish Executive, for allocating time to perform the opening of conference proceedings and to address delegates. The same goes for Sir Robert Smith who kindly agreed to open proceedings on the third day in his capacity as Chairman of the Board of Trustees for the National Museums of Scotland.

The initiative was made possible due to the generous and enthusiastic support of many. We are grateful to United Distillers & Vintners for their sponsorship of this volume. For contributions which enabled us to stage the international gathering in Edinburgh, we are indebted to The Daily Mail and The Scottish Daily Mail, the National Library of Scotland, Historic Scotland, The National Trust for Scotland, the Scottish Tourist Board, Scottish Enterprise through Scotland the Brand, and the University of Edinburgh.

Without contributing speakers there would be no conference and no book, and it is difficult to find words to express adequate thanks to those who entered into the spirit of the operation, first by speaking at the conference, and then to produce manuscripts for publication. This goes for all those who offered home-grown talent, as well as to those who came from overseas, providing the opportunity for international exchange and comparison.

No less important were those who chaired sessions, and here we enjoyed the services of Professor Seaton Baxter, Mette Bligaard, Lester Borley, Lord and Lady Balfour of Burleigh, Jenni Calder, David Caldwell, Ronnie Cramond, Trevor Croft, Professor Ian Cunningham, George Edwards, Dr Howard Fisher, Dr Kåre Hauge, Mark Jones and Jane Ryder. I also thank those speakers who were not able to produce text for publication. They were Peter Eatherley, David Kingsley, Dr Alan Marchbank, Dr Michael Spearman and Vladimir Tolstoy.

The University's home team was again led by Professor Magnus Fladmark, and it is a mystery to us all how he was able to combine the many activities which went into the production of this volume with some other major initiatives. One of these was to negotiate adoption of our MSc in heritage management by a postgraduate school associated with the Russian Academy of National Economy in Moscow, and another was to lead work on establishing a new institute in Norway named after Thor Heyerdahl of Kon-Tiki fame.

I know he would like me to acknowledge the dedicated support given by his own team, especially Rodney Strachan as administrator and editorial assistant, Ian Douglas who designed the conference literature and helped with early planning, and Dr David Silbergh who provided indispensable support throughout. Others to give support were Professors Eric Spiller and Robin Webster, John Donald, Moira Farquhar, Joan Hardie, Dr Stuart Hannabuss, Colin Champion, Katherine Pauling, Jan Flint, Clare Damodaran, Chris Batt and Martin Parker. Help also came from Annabel Bath, David Grant and Erik and Freya Lornie.

He greatly valued the support and guidance provided by Jenni Calder, as well as Mary Bryden and Susan Gray, at the National Museums of Scotland. The smooth running of the conference proceedings was made possible by the excellent service of the technicians, Grant MacRae and Chris Dawson, and the high quality of the catering by Sadie Wastle was much appreciated, as was the help of Professor Duncan Macmillan and Valerie Fiddes and their colleagues at Edinburgh University.

Finally, we would like to record our thanks for active support to John Wastle, to Lord and Lady Balfour of Burleigh and John Foster from our advisory board on heritage affairs, and to Dr Howard Fisher in his capacity as Chairman of our Board of Governors. It should also be said that we are very well served by our publisher, and we are much indebted to Jill Pearce and Dorothy Newberry at Donhead.

Professor William Stevely
Principal & Vice Chancellor

INTRODUCTION

This book is a celebration of what was achieved by those who created the Museum of Scotland. When planning the conference behind it, an early decision was taken to cast the net widely to set these achievements in a broader context of cultural policy. For a new institution concerned with interpreting heritage assets for future generations, it seemed timely to examine the changing context in which museums operate by asking the question: who are the makers and keepers of national identity? With hindsight, this turned out to be a fortuitous decision. Following elections to the new Scottish Parliament, one of the early resolutions of Ministers was to assign high priority to work on a national cultural strategy, an exercise angled very much at the makers and keepers of identity.

In a figurative sense, identity can be likened to the two sides of a coin: one side is the image we have of ourselves, on the other is the image of how we are perceived by others. These two sides are seldom identical, the truth lies somewhere in between. This coinage of identity is shaped by a complex set of forces, frequently manipulated by pontiffs, potentates and politicians. As William Ferguson has shown in his recent book, *The Identity of the Scottish Nation: An Historical Quest* (1998), it has been a central factor in the formation of nationhood since the origin myths that were created in the Middle Ages to unify diverse tribal divisions. The same ingredients are still active, and recent constitutional reforms have again made identity a topical question along with issues of cultural policy.

Indeed, it seems little has changed since these early origin myths and their associated talismanic objects. Collections of material culture seem always to have played an important part in conveying identity. In today's modern nation state, the key moderators in the process of shaping national identity are museums, together with several other categories of heritage agencies. If Scotland is to remain culturally buoyant and commercially competitive, it is clearly no longer acceptable for these individual organisations to work in isolation. Furthermore, it is also argued that there is an urgent need for much closer collaboration between those concerned with cultural activity and wealth creation.

These are examples of the arguments which produced the broadly based conference programme, as now reflected in the main sub-divisions of the book. Few definitive answers are given, but the contributors probe deeply into some of the main challenges facing us in the new millennium. Among these is the issue of whether we are British, Scottish or both. Whichever is the answer, do we continue to 'cringe' over well established stereotypes, or do we proudly embrace these stereotypes along with our rich 'real' heritage? In the dialogue between the holder and beholder, a burning issue is the distinction between fact and fiction, whether this is associated with creative interpretation, or with attempting the quantum leap from cultural iconography to national branding.

PART ONE

Mark Jones starts by invoking the words of the Marquess of Bute. When appealing for funding of the new museum building in 1987, he spoke of Scotland's disgrace, 'having nowhere to tell the full story of its peoples and to show properly its most treasured possessions.' Jones goes on to suggest that the disgrace perhaps did not exist in the first place, as there are relatively few countries with an equivalent museum of national history. He then takes the reader on a journey to retrace the antecedents of today's museums, starting with cathedrals which housed relics to attract pilgrims, and palaces designed to demonstrate the status and taste of owners. The Renaissance was built on re-discovery of Classical Antiquity, and subsequent generations have also sought to bask in the cultural achievements of their predecessors.

Jones is inclined to the view that museums still have a national mission to provide competitive displays that glorify the holder and impress the beholder. However, to remain relevant, museums must respond to the dynamics of changing circumstances and he concludes by saying that 'the full meaning of the Museum is still to be defined – by events still to come and by opinions not yet formed.' By way of a foretaste of such opinions, he provides a spread of public responses drawn from newspaper cuttings.

When explaining how the new building was designed, Gordon Benson dwells on his firm's design philosophy based on the principle that good architecture 'must properly reflect the relationships of context, history and function.' Considering the sensitive setting of the site and its location close to the Old Town of Edinburgh, the city now has a new building which the architect designed to be in sympathy with it surroundings, whilst at the same time reflecting the monumental nature of its content. Interestingly, the sandstone used for the external cladding represents the oldest item on display.

The priority given to marketing, before and after opening of the museum, represents a valuable case study for others facing a similar challenge. Mary Bryden gives an excellent account of how the product was defined and how the Museum developed its marketing strategy. Her story deals with the promotional material used for fund-raising and the market research undertaken, the educational projects carried out to stimulate interest amongst the young, and the consultations undertaken with a wide range of interested parties. She also gives insight into how corporate identity was developed, and how staff and volunteer guides were trained in customer care to ensure that visitors 'regard the new Museum as a gateway, both physically and emotionally, to our national past.'

Development of a strategy for interpretation of this national past fell to Jenni Calder. In her chapter, she explains how the main divisions of material were mapped out by the time of the architectural competition and how the themes and storylines were then developed within a broad chronological framework for the seven floors of the building. Different techniques of presentation were used, and guidelines were produced for script writing. In the next chapter, Rose Watban goes on to describe implementation on Level 6 for *The Twentieth Century Gallery*, where members of the public were invited to suggest objects considered to have had a significant impact on life over the last hundred years.

On the theme of 'objects as evidence', Hugh Cheape undertakes a discursive survey of the antiquarian tradition in Scotland, where he reflects upon the dialogue between the custodians of material culture in museums and the wider community of interested parties. He concludes that it is a function of museums to provide balanced underpinnings for constructs of national identity, but expresses doubts about museologists as begetters of such identity, and warns against allowing 'the perceptible politicisation of museum collections'.

In considering the impact of changing attitudes over time, David Clarke goes on to expose the limitations of a nationalistic stance. He cites an Eastern European example where the constraints of today's national boundaries have clouded the study of prehistoric culture, and goes on to demonstrate how our own antiquarians have wavered in the past between isolationism and pan-nationalism. Clarke clearly belongs to the latter persuasion, saying that 'the absence of England is striking' at the new Museum. He stresses that 'collecting and interpreting within a national framework helps to predetermine to some extent the patterns we are likely to observe and makes the recognition of others more difficult.' He also touches on the thorny question: are museums essentially places of scholarship or of public presentation?

Museologists tend to avoid subjects associated with myths, relics and romanticism, and it is a matter of congratulation that the Museum has had the courage to embrace the Jacobite cause and to give its interpretation prominence alongside the Church and the Enlightenment on Level 3.

George Dalgleish is an acknowledged expert on the subject, and he has provided an absorbing chapter telling the story of the attempted restoration by the Stuarts, as well as how it has been interpreted and presented. In itself, the story is a fascinating case study in skilful brand management by those associated with the cause.

In his chapter on ethnicity and identity, Gavin Sprott is less enamoured of giving the Jacobites 'a place in the sun.' He warns against the twin sins of either ignoring the existence of ethnicity or promoting some specific perception of it, and examines the ebb and flow of what he refers to as 'the idea of Scotland' over the last two hundred years. He draws on parallels from elsewhere in Europe, and also stresses the limitations of isolationism in cultural interpretation. Another dimension of this theme is examined in the next chapter by David Forsyth, who describes the 'Scotland and the World' initiative, which seeks to build stories and networks based on the diaspora in the New World.

The first part is concluded by two chapters looking at the Museum from the outside, in the sense that the authors are not members of staff. The first is by Charles McKean who has written a forthcoming book on *The Making of the Museum of Scotland*. He tells the full story of how the idea for a new museum emerged, how it was translated into an institutional concept and an architectural design brief, and concludes with a descriptive analysis of the end product as we find it today. The last chapter by Fiona McLean and Steven Cooke summarises findings from a study of visitor responses to the Museum, set in the wider context of McLean's work on the marketing of museums and issues associated with perceptions of national identity.

PART TWO

To set the Museum of Scotland in a wider context of cultural governance, contributions were sought from others, representing both heritage and enterprise agencies, to discover potential reciprocity and cross-over of interests in terms of future policy formulation. Those who accepted the invitation to make written contributions were the National Galleries of Scotland, Historic Scotland, the National Trust for Scotland, the Scottish Tourist Board, the Scottish Museums Council and Scotland the Brand on behalf of Scottish Enterprise. There is also a chapter reporting on the outcome of related research undertaken at The Robert Gordon University.

The first two chapters come from the Scottish National Portrait Gallery, starting with James Holloway who provides a fascinating lesson in the skills of reading paintings as a source of cultural interpretation. Using 17th century portraits and carefully chosen texts, he sheds interesting light on the early use of tartans in Highland dress. In terms of demonstrating identity, he also discusses how dress can serve both to heighten and neutralise the political content of a situation, using the visit to Edinburgh by George IV in 1822 as a focus.

Jeanne Cannizzo approaches the subject as an anthropologist, and draws on her work for the 1999 exhibition, *O Caledonia!: Sir Walter Scott and the Creation of Scotland.* In a powerful analysis, combining the use of literature and painting, she shows how Scott made such an enduring imprint on the Scottish coinage of identity, and explains why his 'notions continue to influence how Scots see themselves and how they are perceived by the wider world.' Indeed, her text is recommended as a corrective balance to views expressed in the chapter on 'Highlandism and Scottish Identity' in Tom Devine's most recent book *The Scottish Nation 1700 – 2000.*

The contribution by David Breeze highlights the main operational differences between the museum sector and Historic Scotland, the latter having responsibility for artefacts *in situ* at sites dispersed throughout the country. In contrast to the centralising tendency of national museums, where objects are treated in their own right, Historic Scotland shows artefacts in context for local interpretation. The same goes for the National Trust for Scotland, and Ian Gow explains how the Trust is preoccupied with placing objects in the setting of how people once lived. For both organisations, curation of collections is an integral part of the plan governing interpretation and management policy for each property. In terms of public access via modern information technology, both value their participation in the Scottish Cultural Resources Access Network.

In his analysis of the interaction between culture and tourism, Gordon Adams draws some interesting lessons from the past. Although he acknowledges Sir Walter Scott's pre-eminence, he asserts that Scotland's profile as a tourist destination had been established earlier. He cites Macpherson's *Ossian* of 1760 and Boswell's *Journal* of 1785, and the wider European impact of prominent Scottish Enlightenment figures. He also refers to poets and painters of the period who celebrated Scottish themes, and how all this was reflected in some of the work of major European composers. Later, there was the impact of Queen Victoria's move to Balmoral and the publication of her *Journal* in 1868.

When looking ahead, Adams argues that the Edinburgh Festival and related arts initiatives represent a significant promotional factor, as do a number of recent feature films based on Scottish themes. These and environmental assets, set against the perceptions created by the likes of Scott are, in his opinion, what will draw tourists in the future. However, he expresses concern about the confusion, both in delivery and use of products, caused by the large number of organisations directly involved in tourism. He also asserts: 'Worse still, the cultural institutions of museums, galleries and libraries are inadequately engaged.'

Partnership engagement across the sectors is central to the next chapter by Jane Ryder of the Scottish Museums Council. She reports on her Council's recent work to produce a *National Strategy for Scotland's Museums*. Based on wide consultation, this document articulates an inclusive strategy on behalf of the whole museum sector *vis-à-vis* the Scottish Parliament, and proposes radical new partnership scenarios which include both the National Museums and the National Galleries of Scotland. Her chapter also calls for a national audit of all museums to allow assessment of the level of existing provision against available funding and visitor demand. Referring to a related advocacy document, *Creative Scotland: A Case for a National Cultural Strategy*, she stresses 'the value of arts and culture and their role as agents for social as well as economic development.'

Scotland the Brand was established by Scottish Enterprise in 1997 as a collaborative venture to promote a coherent national image globally. Initial work has concentrated on developing a 'country of origin device', as well a staging events and conferences. For the first time we have an account of this work directed at the cultural sector. Russel Griggs reports on the outcome of a major research study to discover the rate of exchange for Scotland's coinage of identity. The aims of the work are to create a Scottish profile which can be simply but forcefully articulated, reflecting our self-image and how we want others to see us, and to make this profile inclusive so that it is embraced by all concerned in promoting Scotland abroad. For this Griggs proposes the production of a 'brand book' which would set out 'how to refer to and project Scotland to others, structured around a multidisciplinary storyline, providing a generic framework within which each sector can slot its specific requirements.'

Together with John Purser's chapter on music and identity, this section is concluded with an outline of research on practice in the use of heritage assets for interpretation and branding. Although heritage interpretation has traditionally been the preserve of the heritage agencies, it was found that much sophisticated work is now performed in the commercial sector. This is mainly because companies using their heritage asset for branding purposes have developed a more effective process for integrating the functions of interpretation and marketing. The main findings call for less fragmentation of decision-making in the heritage agencies, especially making product development staff listen more to the voice of customers, a closer partnership between those concerned with cultural custodianship and wealth creation, and that higher priority should be given to quality assurance benchmarking to sharpen the competitive edge of Scottish products. Suggestions made by both Ryder and Griggs are supported by the research, which also concludes that there is an urgent need for a partnership framework for the development of a national cultural strategy embracing branding.

PART THREE

Comparative studies of experience in other countries represent a valuable source of insight for both academics and practitioners, and the final part of the book presents contributions from Sweden, Denmark, Norway, Russia, North America and Germany. There are also two chapters by UK authors dealing with philosophical aspects of identity issues.

Stefan Bohman has written extensively on the relationship of museums and nationalism in Sweden, including a much acclaimed book on the subject, and his chapter provides a fascinating insight into the pivotal role played by 19th century museologists in 'the use of history' to shape national identity. In contrast to the UK, where the high culture of national institutions and the ethos of the National Trust movement have governed the national construct, in Sweden it was the ethnology of folk culture and vernacular tradition that dominated the process. He explains how today's intellectual establishment, whose forbears created institutions specifically to shape national identity, are now feeling uneasy about the same institutions being used by 'skinhead nationalists' to promote their own creed.

Denmark would appear to sit half way between the UK and Swedish models, and Mette Bligaard provides an illuminating account of the evolution of national institutions since the 18th century, as a very democratic blend of high culture and ethnology. Many visitors think of the 'mermaid' statue of Copenhagen as the icon of Denmark, but Bligaard points out that Danes themselves look to 'Mother Denmark' as their most powerful national symbol. This is a painting produced at the height of 'Scandinavianism' in the middle of the 19th century, reflecting the perceived essence of Danish history and folk culture. It shows a blonde peasant woman walking through cornfields, wearing national dress and draped in the national flag. She is carrying a sword and is adorned with jewellery, all based on museum pieces well known to the public.

Like Scots, Norwegians have a strong attachment to their national costume, but along with the similarities there are also differences. Costumes exist for both men and women, but it is something which has been worn predominantly by women in the past, although men are now seen using it more frequently. Anne Britt Ylvisåker, who researched a recent international exhibition on the subject, tells how costume fits into the construct of cultural identity, as it has evolved in Norway since the 18th century. She cites two recent events which have contributed to increased awareness and popularity: the Winter Olympic Games and the EU referendum, both of which took place in 1994. As in the past, the wearing of national costume continues to carry both cultural and political significance.

The question of national identity has become a critical issue in countries of the former Soviet Union. The Kazakhs are currently trying to decide whether to adopt Attila the Hun or Genghis Khan as their national icon. The Hungarians have recently moved the millennium-old crown of St Stephen, their first Christian king, into their parliament chamber. It is in the context of such tumultuous change, both cultural and political, that Nikolay Nickishin outlines how Russian museology has evolved, starting with the monastic collections (riznitsas) of the 17th century. Following two centuries of Tsarist rule and one of communism, the main challenge now is to move museums from being overtly political to being institutions of cultural expression.

Richard West then takes the reader to North America, where an Act of Congress was passed in 1989, enabling the Smithsonian Institution to establish a National Museum of the American Indian, now being built on the National Mall in Washington DC. The initiative will fill in hitherto incomplete pages of US museology and help penetrate existing stereotypes. Branded as *The Way of the People*, the museum will depart from conventional practice by treating its constituents as active participants rather than members of a passive audience. In a fascinating analysis of early photographic images, Richard Hill goes on to explain how many Native Americans today live out the stereotyped images of their ancestors created at the time of the 'wild west' shows.

Next comes Stuart Hannabuss, who takes us on a journey around UK heritage sites. Along with an analysis of the complex motivations for visiting such sites, he sets out to look at the many modes of interpretation used to make cultural assets accessible to the public. He returns home with the conclusion that heritage interpretation in its many forms 'is something both provider and consumer should take more seriously as it sets signposts pointing towards the discovery of both reality and the spiritual meaning of identity.' Duncan Macmillan takes a different route, focusing on art, but also travelling widely. His theme is the coinage of identity, as perceived individually and collectively, and he holds up intellectual generalism, free from specialist dogma, as the best weapon against those who seek to manufacture myths for political purposes.

Finally, James Bradburne asks the provocative question: should museums create identity? He starts by arguing that attaching museums to the concept of nationhood and identity 'is dubious, misguided, and possibly dangerous.' Having tested this hypothesis against a wide-ranging review in both time and space, he concludes: 'Museums are for all of us, but to be for all of us, they should not aspire to tell us who we are.' He distances himself from isolationism and advocates a stronger focus on people helping themselves to appropriate culture. Indeed, the most profound museums are those which nourish the local and illuminate the global.

Professor Magnus Fladmark
The Robert Gordon University

THE MUSEUM OF SCOTLAND

Capturing the Spirit of a Nation

1

WHY A MUSEUM OF SCOTLAND?
Aspirations and Expectations

Mark Jones

We owe it to ourselves, our ancestors and our children to provide a lasting display of the cultural heritage of this small but influential Nation and, by so doing, demonstrate that Scotland holds an undisputed historic wealth. Scotland stands almost alone amongst countries of its size in having nowhere to tell the full story of its peoples and to show properly its most treasured possessions. This is a disgrace, long recognised by many.

Thus wrote the Marquess of Bute in 1987, then Chairman of the Trustees of the National Museums of Scotland, in the first brochure printed to attract support for the building of a new museum. It was entitled, *St Andrew will he ever see the light?*, and he was pointing out that the case for a Museum of Scotland 'is obvious'. Looking around there was clearly some truth in this. Denmark has a Museum of National History at Frederiksborg, created after their defeat in the war over Schleswig-Holstein, Sweden has a National Museum of Cultural History in Stockholm, and the Czech Republic has a national Historical Museum in Prague. Hungary, Poland, Ireland and Germany all, to greater or lesser extent, possess institutions that represent their national history through major museums.

In using the phrase 'amongst countries of its size', though, it should be stressed that Lord Bute was uttering more of a qualification than might at first appear. Visitors to the Louvre or the Prado will look in vain for a consistent presentation of the histories of France or Spain. And where are the national historical museums of Italy, Portugal and Wales, or for that matter of England? In short, the creation of a Museum of Scotland is not, as Bute so skilfully suggested, simply the remedy for an evident lack. It is the product of a distinctive choice.

What follows looks at a range of answers to the question posed by the title of this chapter, derived respectively from context, institutional tradition, intention and reception. It is suggested that, though different, each is valid in its own terms, and that we are entitled to draw from any or all of them the construction of our own reply.

Museums are arguably the buildings most representative of the late 20th century. They are the edifices through which communities of all sizes and types represent themselves, both to themselves and to others. Think of the Louvre, a museum which has ejected the Ministry of Finance from the centre of Paris. Thanks to a billion pounds of public money, it has been transformed from a dowdy home for great collections into a glamorous celebration of French, European and Classical culture. Pei's glazed pyramid is the best known and most widely discussed piece of contemporary architecture in France, the new heart of a capital city, gateway to a museum that has had 50 million visits in ten years, a museum that represents France to itself and to the world.

Think of Bilbao. An economically depressed and politically troubled city decided as a conscious act of policy that it would transform its image through the creation of a new outpost of a great international art museum, the Guggenheim, housed in a glamorous building by a famous contemporary architect. And it worked. The way Bilbao thinks about itself and the way we think about it have been radically changed by Frank Gehry's building. Perhaps franchising museums is the way of the future. Every Guggenheim comes with a known approach to art and a guarantee of quality, so the tourist need no longer fear an encounter with the unknown when they venture abroad. Certainly, the Boston Museum of Fine Arts has found that the citizens of Nagoya are willing to pay 50 million dollars for its presence there.

The Getty Museum, clad in riven travertine dominates Hollywood from its hilltop. Accessible only by public transport, in the city of the motor car, it introduces millions of Los Angelenos to communal enjoyment of a common space, and free enjoyment of great art. Te Papa Tongarewa, which dominates the waterfront of Wellington at a cost of £150 million to a population and economy smaller than that of Scotland, has a different mission – to create a space in which to celebrate the histories of Maori and Pakeha in New Zealand, a common asset and meeting place for all the people of that country.

There are many other examples such as the Miho Museum built on a wild mountain to create spiritual enlightenment through the experience of beautiful objects in a beautiful environment, also the Jewish Museum designed by Daniel Liebeskind to commemorate the history of the Jewish community in Berlin. There are the innumerable museums created in the last few decades to preserve and celebrate the history and identity of towns and villages, societies and companies, sports and professions.

Why so many museums? We are all familiar with the view that museums 'are the cathedrals of the late 20th century', implying that they are both the most visibly prestigious buildings of their period and that they have also in some way substituted for the spiritual role of great churches. It can certainly be argued that each age gives birth to public buildings characteristic of their times: museums can also be compared to the great palaces of the 17th and 18th centuries, or to the great municipal buildings of the 19th century.

These comparisons can help us to understand current expectations of museums, and in particular the growing representational function that they fulfil at the end of the 20th century. If we take cathedrals first, it is significant that they characteristically vied for the possession of relics which they elaborately housed and displayed in order to attract pilgrims from near and far. The chief generator of international tourism in the middle ages was pilgrimage, and the motive for pilgrimage was the visitation of relics.

The principal relic-holders of the late 20th century are, of course, museums. Scottish examples are the Monymusk Reliquary and St Fillan's Crozier, kept by abbeys in the Middle Ages and by museums in the 20th century. Others are Mary Queen of Scots' jewels or Bonnie Prince Charlie's canteen. These are what the Maori call 'taonga'. Objects that gain in prestige and power by their association with great people and famous events.

But if museums can be likened to cathedrals, they are even closer to palaces. It is quite misleading to conceive of palaces as overgrown private houses. They were designed and constructed more to demonstrate the grandeur of the ruler, or of the individual who paid for them, than as machines for living in. Carefully thought out programmes of symbolic and literal representation conveyed, through decorative schemes, tapestries and sculpture, messages aimed at a range of visitors from home and abroad.

The collections on display underlined the glory of the states and individuals concerned, through the value of the materials employed: furniture constructed of silver or inlaid with precious stones, or the brilliance of the craft employed in their manufacture, or the variety of the objects concerned. Rarity could be certified by exotic origin: Louis XIV displayed presents from the Shah of Iran and the King of Siam in his private apartments. The status of the maker, as with old master paintings, or the winnowing effects of age, as with classical antiquities, is another. The great municipal buildings of the 19th century were not so different.

Glasgow City Chambers is fitted out with elaborately carved Italian marble and decorated with great murals and mosaics celebrating the history of the city.

In behavioural terms, all of this is competitive display, and it is in the nature of such display that it is aimed at others. But why have museums taken on this role? Indeed, why museums at all? One clue is provided by changes in our attitude to age. In many societies, age in a person demanded respect, but age in a thing suggested that it was obsolete. Now it is the other way round. From the Renaissance onwards the relics of Classical Antiquity have been admired. In the late 18th century, Horace Walpole found romance in the medieval, the Renaissance itself was admired in the 19th century, and the Georgian came into style at the beginning of this century.

Victorian art and architecture was rescued from ridicule in the 1950s and 60s, the 1930s in the 70s, and the 1960s in the 80s. The gap is narrowing as the years go by: history is at our heels. Buildings constructed when the author was already adult, most notoriously Centre Point in London, are regularly listed. In short, the accelerating pace of technological change pushes things ever more quickly into the past. The sense of nostalgia and of loss evoked, even by the more recent objects in the Museum of Scotland's Twentieth Century Gallery, is extraordinary. The faster the world changes, the more we need an anchor in the past: the more we need museums.

So much for things. But the decline in reverence for age in people is also relevant. Old people are a vital source of knowledge in societies dependent on oral communication, but the privileging of textual evidence, the profession of history, the use of photography and film to record both the public and the intimate have devalued reminiscence as a source of information about the past. Social and geographical mobility, the successful search for privacy in the home and in the car, the replacement of compulsory by voluntary human contact have all tended to undermine the traditional ways in which social norms are transmitted, absorbed and upheld. Museums are used by some as a substitute for direct transmission of tradition from person-to-person within a family or community. They have become loci in which to understand who we are and where we come from, and also places in which we can examine the patterns of behaviour of others at other times and in other places and compare them with our own.

In his inaugural lecture as Director of the Institute for Historical Research in 1999, David Cannadine explained and justified the study of history in very similar terms:

...history makes plain the complexity and contingency of human affairs and the range and variety of human experience...it teaches proportion, perspective, reflectiveness, breadth of view, tolerance of differing opinions, and thus a greater sense of self knowledge. By enabling us to know about other centuries and other cultures, it provides, along with the collections housed in our...museums and galleries, the best antidote to the temporal parochialism which assumes that the only time is now, and the geographical parochialism which assumes that the only place is here – there is not only here and now, there is there; and there is then.

The creation of the Museum of Scotland can thus be understood as exemplifying an international, even global trend. However, as suggested at the beginning, it is also specific to Scotland: and not only to a particular moment in Scottish history, but also to a long tradition of regarding the study of national culture as a way of comprehending and valuing Scottish history.

The Museum can indeed be best understood, not as a new museum, but as a new building for an old one. The collections from which it draws its displays derive for the most part from the Museum of Antiquities, founded by the Society of Antiquaries of Scotland in 1780 as part of their mission to 'investigate...antiquities and natural and civil history', the product in turn of a wider scheme by David Steuart Erskine, Earl of Buchan, to reassert Scottish national identity, not only through the study of antiquities but also through the creation of a 'Temple of Caledonian Fame', the publication of a *Biographica Scotica,* and the erection of monuments including a massive statue of William Wallace.

This was the period in which James Macpherson's *Ossian* was widely admired, illustrated and even emulated throughout Europe. It was a time when Tartan was revived, and traditional songs were collected and published by among others Robert Burns. William Smellie, writing about the foundation of the society in 1782, fully recognised the political sensitivities aroused by the study of Scottish antiquities. The need for such an organisation, he recalled, had been felt for many years, but 'till we were united to England, not in government only but in loyalty and affection to a common sovereign, it was not perhaps altogether consistent with political wisdom to call the attention of the Scots to the ancient honours and constitution of their independent monarchy'.

Indeed, this was a thought given renewed expression as recently as 1980 by R.B.K. Stevenson, then Keeper of the National Museums of Antiquities, when he wrote: 'Recently it has again become a practical problem how far it would actually be counter-productive to stress the Museum's Scottishness strongly.' This sense that the Museum had a specifically national mission has seldom been absent. There is no doubting the great late 19th century archaeologist and Director of the Museum Joseph Anderson's strength of feeling, when he wrote:

> We know that the history of Scotland is not the history of any other nation on earth, and that if her records were destroyed, it would matter nothing to us that the records of all other nations were preserved. They could neither tell the story of our ancestors, nor restore the lost links in the development of our culture and civilisation.

This feeling reflects and is reflected in the growth of the collections. Intended from the beginning to cover every aspect of Scottish archaeology and history the Museum became also, in a sense, a national treasure house, inheriting the role of keeper of the relics that played so important a part in the transmission to and conferral of legitimacy on successive Kings of Scots. A house shrine, believed to have contained a relic of Saint Columba, the Monymusk Reliquary has been continually valued and protected by generation after generation from the 7th century to the present day.

Saint Fillan's crozier is another example of such an object. Originally a wooden staff, it was reverently encased in brass in the 11th and in silver in the 13th centuries. In 1785, the Society of Antiquities received a letter from a William Thomson drawing their attention to the fact that he had recently visited the then Keeper of the Crozier, a member of the Dewar family (so named because they were keepers of this relic), who was a day labourer in Killin. This letter, with a later note pencilled on it, both published in 1835, led the great antiquarian Daniel Wilson to search for the crozier in Canada, where he had gone to be Principal of the University of Toronto. On behalf of the Society, he paid Alexander Dewar, the Keeper, 500 dollars for his treasure, of which 200 were remitted on condition that the crozier would remain in the Museum 'in all time to come, for the use, benefit and enjoyment of the Scottish nation'.

More than a century later, the first of a number of small displays went up in the Royal Museum, showing objects destined for the new museum. That same day Nilo Wilson, great granddaughter of Alexander Dewar, was sitting in her kitchen in Canada when she heard a voice saying 'give the money back to the people of Scotland', so she at once sent a cheque for £500. She was there at the opening of the Museum of Scotland to tell her tale to another Dewar, Secretary of State for Scotland at the time.

It is not suggest that the creation of the Museum of Scotland is to be understood or justified in purely national terms. Those who regard it, as did one French journalist, as a 'celebration of Scottish victories over the

English' are surely as wrong as those who imagine that the opening of the new Museum at a time of constitutional change was pure coincidence. It can equally usefully be understood as a purely museological response to a museological problem. How could the great collections in the National Museum of Antiquities be better displayed and enjoyed and understood? A new building certainly. This had been called for with increasing urgency since the 1930s and accepted as a desirable aim by government since 1951. But what structure would make sense? Objects can be displayed in a limited number of ways – for pure visual pleasure, like works of art in an art gallery, or by type – silver in one place, glass in another, by place of origin, size or date, or by theme, however defined.

Objects have many meanings and in different contexts will illuminate different aspects of what they have to say. If they are to be enjoyed and wondered at and understood, they must not only be well shown, but also well placed, within a conceptual structure that engages the viewer and allows each object to reinforce the significance of its neighbours. From this perspective, the decision to order the displays to bring out the value of objects as evidence from which we can learn about the history of Scotland is purely pragmatic. The broadly chronological structure makes it easier to understand the whole. The long themes within it reflect the evidence of the objects themselves, that the material culture of everyday life, and by inference the patterns of existence, remain unchanged for ordinary folk through periods that historians have tended to regard as very different.

The Museum is not, unlike the Museum of Catalan History in Barcelona, a book on the wall, a reproduction of received history illustrated by a few rather embarrassed and irrelevant objects. It starts from the belief that objects themselves have something to tell us about the past and that the evidence which they provide is complementary to, not illustrative of, knowledge derived from documentary sources. This is of course very obvious for prehistory, when everything we know comes from the archaeological record. But it may also be true even for the 19th and 20th centuries. Things which come to us direct from their makers and users may still give us a sense of the past which can not be conveyed by description, whether in words or in pictures.

All of this is about intention and yet the intentions of those involved do not necessarily provide a reliable guide to the reasons why the Museum came into being. Three Unionist Secretaries of State provided the funding that enabled the Museum of Scotland to go ahead. Not one of them intended this decision as a precursor to or a validation of the creation of a Scottish parliament. Yet it would be difficult to argue that the opening of the Museum at a time of constitutional change was pure coincidence. Both will be seen in retrospect as resulting from a single shift in the mood of the times. Indeed, the full meaning of the Museum is still to be defined – by events still to come and by opinions not yet formed. What we can do is to look at its reception so far in the media and elsewhere. From the beginning they made a connection between the creation and content of the new museum in the context of political changes in Scotland. Hugh Pearman, wrote in *The Sunday Times*:

> Normally, where power goes, culture follows. But in this case, culture has anticipated power. So when you get to go round the new Museum of Scotland, consider not so much what it is, but what it stands for. Consider the interesting times that lie ahead for its country. And then consider what those interesting times will yield in the form of materials for a national museum. The collecting is just beginning.

Writing in *The Independent* under the headline *Scots jingoism preserved in glass case,* Ian Jack said: 'Never before, at least in Britain, has a collection of old arrowheads, ship models and teapots been scrutinised so fiercely for their political intent', and concluded, rather surprisingly, 'If a museum of England imitated the Edinburgh Museum's treatment of empire...there would be a lynch-mob at the gates.' Magnus Linklater had this to say in *Scotland on Sunday*:

> By drawing together the evidence of rich and urbane culture with strong links to Europe, reaching back to medieval times, [the Museum of Scotland] challenges head-on the notion that Scotland only began to flourish properly after 1707. Historians and politicians who argue that it was the Union Treaty with England that gave Scotland the means to develop economically and culturally may have some rethinking to do.

Writing in *The Herald* under the headline *Our Nation, our selves,* Ruth Wishart defied:

> ...any visitor not to make connections between discoveries which enhance their sense of where this hybrid nation came from and its adventures along the way to the 21st century...It is a mature person who recognises that they need an accurate sense of self in order to relate comfortably with others; and a mature nation which recognises that self-knowledge is inextricably bound to a sense of self-worth...How strange, how marvellous, that we had the privilege of witnessing the birth of the museum building and that of a Parliament within the space of a couple of years and at the turn of a new century. Those who battled for both can take pride in their bounteous legacy.

This understanding of the Museum as a distinctively different approach towards presenting and undertaking the past was equally reflected, albeit disapprovingly, by Julian Spalding in *The Sunday Times*:

> The Museum of Scotland doesn't tell the history of Scotland. Instead it tells only the part of Scotland's story that can be told through fragments of ancient vessels, buildings, clothes and tools...This isn't a museum for a new Scotland, but Scotland as an old museum.

Dorothy Grace Elder took a different view. While describing the new Museum as 'ace, a joy', she asserted that 'when you find that William Wallace is ignored totally, that smacks either of snooty deadhanding or Establishment feartie factor...'. There were others who, taking the Museum as a definitive representation of Scottish history, were angered by its lacunae. Writing in *Scotland on Sunday* with reference to the 'discovery' of Wallace's letter to Lübeck, Amelia Hill quoted the Scottish historian, Fiona Watson of Stirling University, as saying:

> I think those who made the decisions at the museum had a very anti-Braveheart reaction when deciding what to put into the exhibition. The museum contains a very elite view of Scottish history, chosen by the establishment to reflect the establishment's position...What it boils down to is that Wallace is the people's hero and the elite don't want him in their museum.

Alex Salmond, leader of the Scottish National Party, was quoted in *The Herald* as saying: 'For centuries, members of the establishment have been attempting to eradicate all traces of Wallace from Scottish history. People in Scotland are no longer prepared to accept this persecution of Scotland's greatest national hero', and called on the Director and Curators of the Museum of Scotland 'to hang their heads in shame'. Many individual members of the public wrote to express their own opinion. Lionel Hawes of Glasgow wrote:

> With reference to various letters about the above etc. I would have you note that I will not be visiting the [Museum of Scotland] or the shop therein. From the time I can remember the issue I have suffered from the distortions, omissions and partial glimpses of the wide and intensely varied History of the Country, sorry Colony, I have lived and live in. That obtained in School was a disgrace.

Others had quite the opposite reaction. Sophy Weatherall of Dumfries:

> ...was horrified by the strong political slant that is so evident – I suppose it is a fine line between national pride and support of the Scottish National Party but I do feel most strongly that a museum should be purely educational and in no way political.

The response by Eric V Meulden of Lancashire was:

> Sadly I have to say that I have never been so offended in all my life after visiting the new Museum of Scotland and reading the words on a wall as one leaves the building. You may have seen that to which I refer, namely, 'The Declaration of Arbroath' which states 'As long as only 100 of us remain alive, we will never on any condition be brought under the English rule.'

Many more like Myra Bell of Oxon thought it '...a wonderful museum. We are great museum visitors at home and abroad and this is the best we have visited. It makes me proud to be a Scot, concurring with the view expressed by *The Scotsman* (15 May 1999) that '...the museum which has already come to symbolise the new Scotland...is...a modern monument to Scotland's past.'

But to my mind, the writer who has best expressed the reason for having a Museum of Scotland is Joyce Macmillan who wrote in *The Scotsman*:

> The collections shown in this museum will be a revelation, a magnificent treasure-trove of objects that sometimes confirm our ideas about history, and sometimes...challenge them in seriously important ways...What they have tried to do...is to create a record of Scotland which finally puts Scotland itself, its people and their material culture, right at the centre of the story...It made me feel...somehow more aware of the huge diversity and complexity of Scottish life, and of how each of us, our family, our story, however we came to be here, has a right place in it strongly bound to the rest.
>
> And if the new Museum of Scotland can do that, or something like it, for all the Scots who visit it, then its effect on the life of the nation will not be spectacular or sudden. But it will go deep, in helping to shape a nation fit to make choices on a basis of self-knowledge, confidence and self-respect, rather than on that old superstitious fear of being left behind on the edge of someone else's world. Whichever way our decisions finally fall, that it is surely something to celebrate...for years to come.

The Author

Mark Jones became Director of the National Museums of Scotland in 1992, following eighteen years at the British Museum, latterly as Keeper of Coins and Medals. He has presided over the construction of the Museum of Scotland, which opened on St Andrew's Day 1998. He has published widely on the history of the medal and is President of the Federation Internationale de la Medaille (FIDEM). In 1982, he founded the British Art Medal Society, which promotes contemporary medal art. He is a Board Member of the Scottish Museums Council and the Scottish Cultural Resources Access Network, the Millennium Project SCRAN 2000 which is a collaborative multimedia project to facilitate access to Scotland's cultural resources. In 1996, he gained an Honorary Professorship from the University of Edinburgh, and he became a Fellow of the Royal Society of Edinburgh in 1999.

References

Anderson, R., 'Scotland's in the National Museums of Scotland', in Ambrose, T. (ed), *Presenting Scotland's Story*, HMSO, 1989, pp. 65–74.

Bute, Marquess of, in *St Andrew will he ever see the light?*, National Museums of Scotland, 1987.

Cannadine, D., 'Making History Now', lecture at Institute for Historical Research, 21 April, 1999.

Clarke, C.V., 'Scottish Archaeology in the Second Half of the Nineteenth Century', in Bell, A.S. (ed), *The Scottish Antiquarian Tradition: Essays to mark the bicentenary of the Society of Antiquaries of Scotland 1780–1980*, John Donald, 1981.

Hill, A., in *Scotland on Sunday*, 6 December, 1998.

Jack, I., 'Scots jingoism preserved in glass', in *The Independent*, 21 September, 1998.

Linklater, M., in *Scotland on Sunday*, 29 November, 1998.

Macmillan, J., in *The Scotsman*, 28 November, 1998.

Pearman, H., in *The Sunday Times*, 15 November, 1998.

Salmond, A., in The Herald, 7 December, 1998.

Spalding, J., 'An Object Lesson', in *The Sunday Times*, 29 November, 1998.

Stevenson, R.B.K., 'The Museum, its Beginnings and its Development', in Bell, A.S. (ed), *The Scottish Antiquarian Tradition: Essays to mark the bicentenary of the Society of Antiquaries of Scotland 1780–1980*, John Donald, 1981.

Tramposch, W., 'A Museum Challenge: The Iconography of New Zealand', in Fladmark, J.M. (ed), *In Search of Heritage as Pilgrim or Tourist?*, Donhead, 1998.

Wishart, R., 'Our nation, our selves,' in *The Herald*, 30 November, 1998.

Yeoman, P., *Pilgrimage in Medieval Scotland*, B.T. Batsford and Historic Scotland, 1999.

The Monymusk Reliquary.

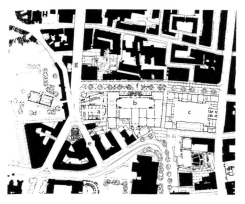

a	Museum of Scotland
b	Fowke's Royal Scottish Museum
c	University Old Quad
d	Greyfriars
e	Bristo Place
f	Chambers Street
g	George IV Bridge

The Museum of Scotland in its urban context as shown in the Nolli plan. *Courtesy The Architectural Review*

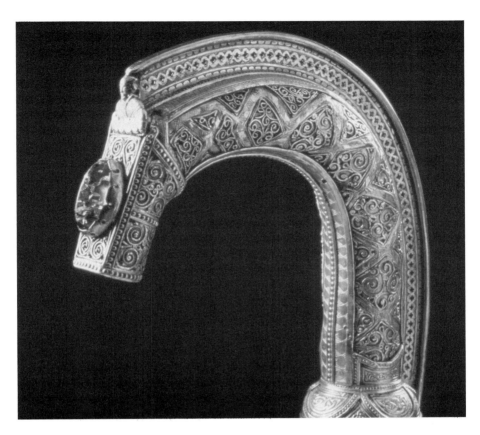

St Fillan's Crozier.

Immediate context approached from George IV Bridge.

2

THE ARCHITECT'S VISION
Designing for Context and Content

Gordon Benson

> The primary purpose of the project is to provide display space for the Museum's collection of material relating to Scotland, creating a Museum environment which will be enjoyable, readily accessible and comprehensible to the public.

This is how the Trustees for the National Museums of Scotland set the tone for the brief of the international design competition in 1990, following the decision to go ahead with a new building to form a fully integrated addition to the Royal Museum in Chambers Street. There were 271 designs submitted for the first stage in 1991, with the author and his partner, Alan Forsyth, emerging as the winners from the second stage shortlist of six more detailed submissions. Although the new building has been eight years in the making, it still displays the strength and clarity which made our entry stand out from the rest of the field. However, it is no longer an extension, as required by the original brief, and now stands in its own right with its own entrance, while still umbilically linked to its neighbour, the Royal Museum.

A strong feature of the building as it now stands is the design and stone used for the perimeter walls. It is a striking Permian period sandstone, about 190 million years old. It was laid down by wind action in dunes when Scotland was located just north of the Equator, in conditions which were similar to those currently prevailing in the Sahara Desert. The oldest exhibit of the Museum is accordingly the material from which its walls are made, and it is the genesis of the stone that is recorded in its surface which gives the building its particular texture and aesthetic flavour. This symbolic connection, between the building's exterior and what it contains, was central to our design philosophy for the project.

Urban context as seen from Castle Esplanade.

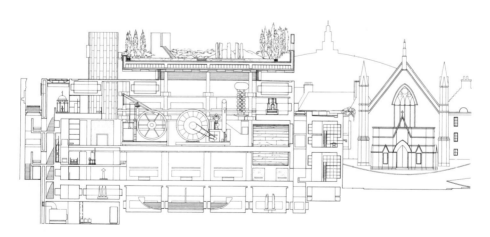

Long section from competition drawing looking south, showing urban context on right. *Courtesy The Architectural Review*

THE PHILOSOPHY

> The architects' search for meaning yields its richest rewards in the way they have embedded this huge new institution in an ancient city, offering new perspectives on the city itself. Indeed, in making these urban connections, the architects suggest the role of geography and history through their representation in the horizontal and vertical axes of the building.

These words by John Allan, in *Architecture Today*, serve as echoes of how we approached the challenge of this commission. The evolution of the design, from competition winning proposal to completed building, allowed us a unique opportunity to explore in practical terms our design philosophy which holds that good architecture must properly reflect the relationships of context, history and function. Our approach to design draws together many diverse strands of thought, reflecting preoccupations which, while they have shifted in emphasis over the years, have remained focused on certain themes. The building is a manifestation of how these strands of thought and themes have been woven together into a coherent whole, yet composed in such a way as to allow many varied and diverse interpretations, but certain ideas have dominated.

The building seeks to be rigorously contextual. Lying on the southern boundary of the city, the Museum is caught between the orthogonal geometry of Chambers Street and George IV Bridge, and the non-orthogonal street pattern outside the former city wall on Bristo Port. The building is contained by the space defined by the façades opposite the site, and the Fowke building adjacent. Within this spatial envelope, the Museum responds dynamically to each edge condition, reinforcing or subverting the existing street pattern to ventilate or compress the spaces contained by the building and its neighbours, as appropriate to their role in both functional and urban terms.

The tower forms a hinge between the north and west façades, acting as a focal point at the convergence of five separate routes into and out of the city, as a sentinel adjacent to the former gateway into the town. The height of the perimeter galleries respects the height of the adjacent buildings to the north. The juxtaposition of prismatic elements along Bristo Port reflects the more organic asymmetry of smaller scale buildings to the south, whilst the central 'keep' or core gallery rises through the perimeter curtain wall. The entire ensemble culminates in the 'boat roof' suspended serenely above the tumult of the city.

In terms of the formal aspirations of the building, it employs an architectural language which, while it displays a certain 'universal characteristic' conventionally associated with the modern movement, it also displays an empathy with the architectural traditions of Scotland: traditions which themselves are often local expressions of broader based architectural phenomena. The broch, the tower house, the architecture of the enlightenment, among other sources, form the provenance of the forms, masses and lexicon of space types assembled on Chambers Street.

Whilst inevitably bound to its Scottish ancestry, and sharing certain characteristics of early modernism, another layer of formal pre-occupation permeates the architecture of the Museum, demonstrated by the evolution of a 'free' or 'organic' form of syntax which punctuates the overall structure of the building. This is focused particularly on elements associated with the act of movement through it. Bridges, balustrades and handrails celebrate in fluid lines and their dynamic forms the progress of visitors. Views are frames – 'postcards'; developed as series of images glimpsed through slots – a 'movie' of sorts; or finely dissected into fragments by rippling metal slats – a 'veil'.

As bridges are crossed and re-crossed, space is dissected, cropped and re-assembled. Images of the building and the objects within it are manipulated and contorted in an exploration of the dynamic interplay between the visitors and the spaces they move through. Static space becomes cubist space. The circulation armature is developed as a series of 'promenades architecturales' which encourages visitors to reflect upon the architecture, its context and content, composing their own journey not only through the building, but through Scotland's history, informing their own unique view.

Wherever possible, the Museum seeks to reconnect the visitor to the external environment, and to recontextualise the artefacts it contains. Having entered via the circular tower, passing through the north wing, a series of windows canted out from the façade reconnect visitors with the street from which they entered. On the second floor, the Lorimer gates are viewed against a window to which Lorimer's extension of the castle provides a backdrop. Adjacent to the Covenant on the ground floor, a window captures an image of the entrance to Greyfriars churchyard where the Covenant was signed. This building could exist nowhere else, and these objects have a unique value in these specific locations.

If the building represents a narrative of which many interpretations are possible, the roof garden represents singular literal and metaphorical conclusion to the story. The spirit of 're-capture' is what is most significant about the Museum as a built artefact and the objects of material culture within it: their connection to the 'stuff' that has defined Scotland as a nation.

For the visitor held aloft, Edinburgh's geography is brought into sharp focus: Arthur's Seat and the North Sea to the east, the Pentland Hills to the south, the Firth of Forth to the north, and the Castle Rock to the west. At the same time, the city itself flows around and below: the Castle, the monuments on Calton Hill, the ridge of the Old Town, the 'artefacts' of human habitation and the places where history has been enacted. This is the source material for the narrative which the boat roof concludes, and it is the pervasive sense of continuity implicit in the building's relationship to its physical and historical context, and the artefacts it houses, which must ultimately be the message it most powerfully conveys.

Writing on the theme of paradoxes, alongside John Allan in *Architecture Today*, Neave Brown had this to say about the building:

> Its first paradox is that it is powerfully 'there', with a strong physical and representational presence, yet it is so inevitably and conformably there as to almost disappear. It is of Edinburgh and of its place, and settles in almost inconspicuously despite its complex fashioning and arresting appearance. You can look up the street which it absorbs without a trace of the offensive intrusion of alien characteristics of most modern monuments. Except that this would be rather like not noticing the Castle itself due to sheer familiarity. Castle and Museum address each other across the void, the one supreme on its hill, the other subordinate and taking its place in the street.
>
> It is also paradoxical in its relationship between solid and void, concrete form and space, positive and negative, the two so integrated as to acquire a simultaneous presence. The big building is composed of a few identifiable major elements: an internal aspidal block almost a nave and aisles. Separate and obliquely set against this is another 'solid', but hollow rectangle. A product of this oblique angle is a high void volume between the two blocks, a residual negative turned positive to become the astonishing central interior generating space. Each block is simple yet supports great complexity within, and in their mutual response, and in the pattern of movement which penetrates and invades and unites them.

THE INFLUENCES

Among those who have had a strong influence on our design philosophy, Le Corbusier ranks above the others. It started with Garches and Roche, and the white houses of the 1920s. In other words, his output that we came to know through books. By the 1960s, when we were looking at his work, its polemical status had been dissolved by historical analysis, and we were fully conscious that Corbusier, far from severing himself from the architecture of proceeding centuries, was using it both to inform his architecture and as a yardstick against which his ideas could be calibrated or assessed.

Roche was clearly derived from the house of the Tragic Poet at Pompeii, being evident from the comparison of the drawings, photographs and sketches of both of these houses in *Œuvre Complète*. There is also the well known comparison between Garches and Palladio's Villa Malcontenta. In addition to the geometrical similarities and formal inversions, figural spaces were being replaced by figural objects within the neutral spatial continuum of the free plan. Comparison of the two elevations is also instructive, showing the iconographic shift between the object placed in front of the 'wall' of the main body of the house (as Greek temple at Malcontenta, and as aeroplane wings and tensile struts at Garches).

When we were students at the Architectural Association, Corbusier was designing the Carpenter Centre and the Venice Hospital and publishing books about them. Needless to say, this was simultaneously an extremely uplifting and depressing experience, comparing one's own fumbling and incompetent efforts with his mature design. If one collages the late work of La Tourette, with the drawings of the Venice Hospital, one can imagine quite accurately what the un-built project in Venice might have been like. It was both an impeccably well organised humane building and a brilliant solution to the problem of absorbing a large homogenous institution into a fragmented mediaeval and idiosyncratic city, which Corbusier loved. It was also an intellectual exorcism of the polemical excesses of his early town planning schemes with which we both could not identify, having grown up in the well ordered and intact 19th century cities of Glasgow and Newcastle.

Our third encounter with Le Corbusier came when we revisited his work with a degree of hindsight and twenty-five years of architectural practice behind us. Our comparison of La Tourette and Le Thoronet (he visited the latter before producing the former), revealed the degree to which 'history and tradition' are re-synthesised and at the very heart of La Tourette. Indeed, he had created something which can be seen as a re-invention of the monastery itself. The most workable material for the Cistercian Monks of Le Thoronet was stone, and this became *in situ* concrete for the Dominicans at La Tourette. But the concrete was used by Corbusier in such a way that its origin in the earth and archaic nature is as visible as are the Roman origins of the Cistercian stone. The sloping cloister which precipitates the visitor into the church at La Tourette equates to a simple cloister following the slope of the hillside at Le Thoronet. Here we rediscovered the unchanging iconography of entry, oratory, vertical circulation and the horizontal framing of the landscape.

In summary, the key principles of design philosophy and practice which we brought to the Museum were: First, from our work on housing, representing precise organisation and planning in which not a millimetre is wasted. It showed us that architecture consists of the irreducible constituents from which the buildings are made and there is no room for a single, unnecessary, redundant or rhetorical component. This may sound like the 'Tenets of Modernism', but the actual trigger for built form in housing was pragmatic and not ideological. Second, from the oratory came the notion of the building having both a spirit and a soul, thereby communicating feeling, which in one sense was 'its purpose', or in other words 'the sense of loss transcended'. Third, from Japanese buildings we learnt that the nature of architecture is a didactic device which comments upon the culture and society within which it is placed. Fourth, from the Victoria and Albert Museum came the idea of a building which mediates between the city within which it is contained and the objects it contains.

Finally, from our teaching experience at the Architectural Association, we saw the need for trying to find a bridge between architecture and town planning. Our standpoint was that, up to the 19th century, all good buildings carried the genes within them from the city of which they were a part. This quality had been lost, willingly during the period of early modernism, in the belief that history was to be written again from the beginning. We were looking for a way of working in which the city could inform individual and contemporary work, and which reciprocally would allow the city itself to be reformed and reinvented through this process.

CONCLUSION

We approached the task of producing the winning competition entry for the Museum of Scotland on the assumption that buildings carry both overtly and covertly the landscape of which they are a part. We believe that through this process, architects unconsciously continue and extend the nature of the land and its influence upon a culture. 'Architects are the last Alchemists' in that they turn the matter of the land into 'spirit'. Accordingly, we tried to design a building which would participate in the city, both at the scale of the city and in its relationship to its immediate surroundings.

Edinburgh, like Paris, is one of those cities where large elements relate to one another like chess pieces: the Castle Rock, the ridge of the Old Town, the extinct volcano of Arthur's Seat. It was imperative therefore that the Museum should participate at an equal level with the other major features in these urban relationships.

The building should also relate in very specific ways to its particular surroundings – urbanistically, where there are specific relationships to the other significant institutions in the city, such as the university and the cathedral, and historically where there are specific relationships between the collections held within the building and architecturally significant elements visible from the building.

Internally, the central idea was to relate the collections to the types of space in which they might originally have been found. We were therefore trying to match architectural typologies and the collections. The type of space would be defined by its height, degree of enclosure, and type and intensity of light so that ecclesiastical objects would be found in a space with a spiritual dimension. We also sought to reflect the development of containing space itself from the Middle Ages to the 19th century so that it could be detected in subtle variations which would parallel the changing characteristics of the exhibits. For example, the medieval church is metaphorically candle-lit, dark and crypt-like, whilst the reformed church is filled with 'God's natural light' and simplicity.

The connective tissue throughout the Museum is freed from the obligations of exhibition and its role is to re-orientate, refresh, define and articulate the different components of the collection. It is penetrated by dynamic sunlight and is framed, deconstructed and reconstructed visually at different levels to enhance the particular moment and heighten the sense of individual place. The journey ends at the roof garden from which one sees the city, the Castle , the extinct volcano of Arthur's Seat, the Pentland Hills, the Firth of Forth and the North Sea.

The Author and Acknowledgements

Professor Gordon Benson was born in Glasgow and educated at the Architectural Association in London, where he has subsequently been a tutor, and he has held Chairs in Architecture at the Universities of Edinburgh and Strathclyde. He established a professional practice with Alan Forsyth in 1979. They have won many major awards and architectural design competitions, including the National Gallery of Ireland which is due to be completed in year 2000, others being the Cowgatehead Library in Edinburgh, Glasgow Auditorium, Glasgow Eurodrome, and they were architects for the Boarbank Hall Oratory in Cumbria, the Morris House in London, and Joyhanna Museum and the Divided House in Oshima Japan. He is a Commissioner of the Royal Fine Arts Commission for Scotland, a Fellow of the Royal Incorporation of Architects in Scotland, and he was Scotland's Architect of the Year 1999.

The author is grateful to the editor of this volume for his input to shaping the above text from a set of speaking notes. They both wish to record their gratitude to the Editor of *The Architectural Review*, Peter Davey, for kind permission to reproduce the drawings.

References

Allan, J. et al, 'Building: Museum of memory', in *Architecture Today*, July 1999.

Architects' Journal, 'Building Study: Museum of Scotland', in *Architects' Journal*, 25 February 1999.

Baker, G. et al, *Le Corbusier: Early Works by Carles-Edouard Jeanneret-Gris*, Academy Editions & St Martin's Press, 1987.

Benson + Forsyth (eds), *Museum of Scotland*, Angus Media & Benson + Forsyth, 1999.

Boesiger, W., *Le Corbusier 1910–60*, Girsberger & Alec Tiranti, 1960.

Le Corbusier, *Towards a New Architecture*, The Architectural Press, 1946.

Le Corbusier, *Œuvere complète*, six vols of work 1946–57, W. Boesiger.

Davey, P., 'National Treasure House', in *The Architectural Review*, April 1999.

The Independent, 'Edinburgh's new stronghold', in *The Independent*, 21 May 1998.

Jenks, C., *Le Corbusier and the Tragic View of Architecture*, Penguin Books, 1973.

Macmillan, D., 'The Museum of Scotland looks set to be Edinburgh's most stunning piece of modern architecture', in *The Scotsman*, 19 January 1998.

Raeburn, M. & Wilson, V. (eds), *Le Corbusier: Architect of the Century*, Arts Council of Great Britain, 1987.

Wilson, P., 'Museum of Scotland: modern history', in *Prospect*, December 1998.

Worsley, G., 'In the Keep of Proud Scots', in *The Daily Telegraph*, 3 December 1998.

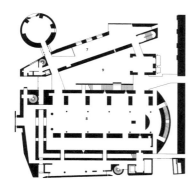
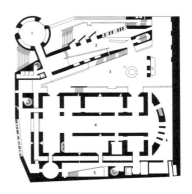

1 entrance	4 Kingdom of	7 Discovery Centre
2 entrance hall	Scotland	8 Industrial
3 Hawthornden	5 Medieval Church	Revolution
Court	6 the Gaels	9 Hawthornden void

Plans of ground floor (right) and first floor (left). *Courtesy The Architectural Review*

The top lit and triangular Hawthornden Court, here looking west, is part of the orientation space with the reception desk behind and the main stair to next floor on left.

Full-height lightwells viewed from basement.

Machine hall on first floor looking east, with display of industrial heritage.

3

SHAPING AND SELLING THE IDEA
How the Product was Presented

Mary Bryden

> The new museum will be one of the most important cultural projects undertaken in the United Kingdom in recent years. It will provide the architect with an opportunity to contribute a significant building to the historic city of Edinburgh and one which will complement the existing Royal Museum of Scotland. The building must be of the highest quality – something of remark and of excellence – which will at last provide a suitable setting for our unequalled collections of Scottish material.

The above is what the late Chairman of the Trustees of the National Museums of Scotland, the Marquess of Bute, once said when describing the kind of building he had in mind to house the Scottish collections. Indeed, his insistence on 'something of remark and of excellence' has been our guiding principle in the development of all aspects relating to the Museum of Scotland. As might be imagined, countless discussions took place, views were expressed, differences of opinion thrashed out, compromises reached and papers written in the years leading up to the opening of the Museum. This chapter is a retrospective look at some of the key ideas we had, how these were developed, and the statements we made, both internally and externally, as the product was shaped and presented.

In the introduction to our marketing strategy, we tried to list the key points about the new Museum. It is, we said, the first purpose-built museum celebrating Scotland's past, its culture, its people and its achievements through the national collections. It is unique. It is, we suggested, the most important cultural project in Scotland in the last 50 years. It will be, we declared, a prime educational resource for students at all levels and of all ages. It will be, we were sure, a focus for the innumerable descendants of Scots around the world. It will be, we guaranteed, a showcase for the nation and a reference point on Scottish identity. And we reminded ourselves it was opening at a time of major constitutional change in Scotland. An exciting list for any marketing person.

The Museum of Scotland had been a very long time in the making. It was more than two centuries since the Society of Antiquaries of Scotland had begun collecting for the nation and half a century since the need for a new museum was first recognised. Its history was chequered. In 1956, the government approved the site at the Southwest corner of Chambers Street in principle. In 1971, the site was cleared, but the building programme was shelved in 1976 because of a standstill in public expenditure.

In its 1981 report, *A Heritage for Scotland*, the Williams Committee recommended that legislation should be introduced to establish a new museum, the Museum of Scotland, based on the collections of the National Museum of Antiquities of Scotland. In 1985, that Museum and the then Royal Scottish Museum were amalgamated and became the National Museums of Scotland, and therefore custodians of incomparable collections of Scottish material. In 1989, the Secretary of State for Scotland announced government support for a new building. I was there at the announcement, and can recall the very moment at the press conference when Malcolm Rifkind quietly made an announcement of momentous importance.

With all this in mind, let me first take the reader back to those early days in the 1990s, when the driving force behind the public understanding of the Museum of Scotland project was inevitably fund-raising. A video about the project was produced to be shown in the boardrooms and offices of directors of external communications round the world.

The emphasis was on the national collections in store, hidden from the public gaze, being brought finally into the light; on the story of the architectural competition and the winners; on the unique dimension which objects bring to an understanding of the past, a dimension totally different from the written document and from oral history, one which had never before had a voice.

A second fund-raising video was quite specifically targeted at the 'Scots abroad' market. Here we emphasised, on the one hand, the diaspora and, on the other, the objects which told the stories associated with Scots emigrating – accompanied by an emotionally charged score with a haunting theme on wind instruments, emphasising the drama and the emotion associated with the return of some of those objects with more than a passing reference to the plight of a nation which until now was not represented in its own 'national history' museum.

How was the development of the Museum being treated in the press during those early days? The headlines in the *Museums Journal* were perhaps predictable: a sober article by Director Mark Jones was headed (not by us), *From haggis to home rule*. An article by our Head of Exhibitions, David Clarke, where he explored the links between museums and national identity, was titled (again not ours), *Me tartan and chained to the past*. *The Times*, in September 1995, introduced a straightforward report on funding the project with the headline, *Home for the Tartan Heritage*. The Scottish press were less concerned with the 'tartan' aspect, and *The Scotsman*, announcing the Lottery Funding decision, used a simple and clear heading: *New National Museum Hits Lottery Jackpot*.

We began to raise the profile of the Museum through education projects, and the hoardings round the site offered an opportunity to work with youngsters from a primary school in a deprived part of South East Edinburgh. They painted the hoardings with their interpretation of the new Museum, producing an intriguing choice of objects from the national collections and figures from the 20th century. A news reporter worked hard to find a critical response from passers-by, but any such view was met with a very vigorous rebuff from one of the nine-year-old boys involved.

And the view from on high? A milestone was the 'topping out' in August 1997, when the then Secretary of State for Scotland, the Rt Hon Donald Dewar, performed the traditional ceremony to celebrate reaching the highest point of the new building. He drew a parallel between the Museum of Scotland and the new Scottish Parliament. He described both as 'symbols for a cultural renaissance in Scottish life which would generate a pride and energy beyond their own walls and into homes in every corner of Scotland'. He described the new Museum as 'a monument to our history and culture and something in which we can take much pride'.

These aspirations and perceptions were the context in which we tackled the job of reaching our potential visitors. In what follows, I look at the consultation processes we went through and the market research we undertook. I take the reader through our thoughts about 'branding' and the promotional campaign we ran, and I finally investigate some of what our visitors are experiencing.

So how would our visitors view the Museum of Scotland? Who were these visitors? What were their expectations? How did we consult them? The public relations work associated with the fund-raising campaign defined the visitors as Scots and those who love Scotland. Our exhibition guidelines identified the Museum of Scotland as a world class attraction for all those with an interest in Scotland's past. We assumed that there would be all sorts of visits and tried to define them: formal education visits, general interest visits, the 'tourist' visit and visits with a narrowly defined focus.

We were fairly certain that the tourists, particularly from North America, could on average be defined as middle-aged and older, and as being strongly influenced by the notion of 'Scotch myths' like *Braveheart* and the Scottish Tourist Board campaigns which encourage visitors who had already 'bought' Scotland as a romantic and historical destination. Others would be looking for cultural destinations to visit, expecting to be able to find a definitive national museum in a capital city.

We were aware of the view held of Scotland and Scots by outsiders, and of their enjoyment even of all things stereotypically Scottish. We also suspected that our Scottish visitors would be committed and keen to improve their understanding of history and find out about their own inheritance, and that they would be interested in asserting their identity in a positive manner. We also expected that they had only relatively recently become aware of the lack of a national museum, and that they might be less interested in the stereotypical presentation.

What did we want our visitors to feel? We hoped they would feel a sense of national pride, a recognition of Scotland's place in the world, and a sense of amazement at the achievements of the past. Furthermore, we hoped to stimulate a sense of fascination at the true, and largely untapped, richness and depth of Scotland's inheritance, and most importantly we wished our visitors to feel inspired to learn and discover more.

How were we going to achieve this? We suggested that staff should imagine they were walking through the exhibitions with a seven-year-old in a family group from somewhere in Central Scotland, a 65-year-old male of Scots descent from the Western Seaboard of Canada, and a middle-aged English couple in Edinburgh for the weekend. We also suggested that they should try to see the whole thing through the eyes of a new Scot, and to imagine taking their own grandmother round the displays.

Our guidelines reminded staff that there should be, to use Robert Louis Stevenson's phrase 'a strong Scotch accent of the mind'. We suggested that, if someone were to be parachuted blindfold into the middle of a gallery, the displays and the language would tell them where they were. We also wanted to make sure that what we had to offer – displays, interpretation, story lines, front-of-house staff, image, promotion, marketing – were integrated and sent out complementary messages.

What was our market research telling us? Our work in this area ranged from qualitative focus groups to questions in omnibus research across the whole of Scotland, as well as an exit survey at the Royal Museum and 100 street interviews were carried out in Edinburgh. It became clear that there was a high level of interest in the new Museum and that people were likely to visit. The respondents were insistent that there should be a chronological route through the Museum, and that information should be available on computer terminals in different locations, especially for children. There was also a desire for programmes of events, including tours to complement the displays.

Other expectations included portable audio headsets which could be carried round telling the story of what is on show, and there should be attendants to 'act as helpers', who should be friendly and approachable and dressed in uniforms with a touch of tartan. Respondents held strong views that the shop should avoid anything which could be considered 'tacky tartan' or poor quality, and that 'Scottish arts and crafts' should be on sale along with books linked to the displays, as well as reproductions of Scottish artefacts. There was also a feeling that the restaurant should offer an element of Scottish food, and that visitation packages might feature whisky and haggis tasting.

This was helpful in planning complementary activities and highlighting differences between tourists new to Edinburgh and the more informed locally based visitors. Indeed, local people seemed happy with a leaflet to help them around the Museum, whilst tourists wanted a trained guide or a portable audio head set. All potential visitors were very interested in the contribution of computer terminals, but regular museum visitors seemed more likely to actually use them. Tourists were as interested in the café, the shop and the attendants, as in the displays.

Much of this confirmed our thoughts. Readers who have visited the Museum will know that we have a chronological framework starting in the basement at Level 0, *Beginnings*, which looks at the geological story of Scotland, and then ascends to the top floor at Level 6, where *The Twentieth Century* is presented. The themes of the displays reflect the strength and distinctiveness of the collections. At the same time, we recognised that to meet public expectation, we needed to tackle some topics where the collections were less strong. We have 21 computer terminals at key points throughout the six galleries to help visitors obtain a quick understanding of objects on display, their purpose and function, their historical significance, and who commissioned and used them. There is a small gallery 'exhibIT' where visitors can interrogate many more programmes as well as our website, and they can access the Scottish Cultural Resources Access Network (SCRAN) for as long as they like.

Our visitor service assistants are well trained in customer care and have all gone through 'Scotland's Best' training. Their uniform was designed by Betty Davies who was asked to deliver a design which reflected the overall image of the Museum and embraced appropriate corporate colours and logos. The tie, made of a newly created tartan (a subtle combination of the corporate blue for the Museum of Scotland and the corporate red for the Royal Museum) is the only part of the uniform which has any tartan in it.

There are programmes of talks, tours, concerts and workshops to complement the displays. We have 40 volunteer guides trained to offer a range of tours, and being brilliant ambassadors for the Museum, they have already introduced 16,500 visitors our new facilities. We have sound guides in English and Gaelic, and will soon also have them available in French and German. These add contemporary words, music and sound effects with a narrative which ties the whole thing together. We have a shop which sells a wide range of material, some of it specifically commissioned to complement the contents of the new Museum. Publications on material related to the displays include titles for children, poetry, biography, and the *Scotland's Past in Action* series. To top it all, we also have the Tower Restaurant which prides itself on serving the best of Scottish food.

We consulted many named people in addition to those who had taken part in the market research anonymously. Academics advised on interpretation and the development of story lines, and language experts advised on the use of Gaelic and Scots. Visitors to the Royal Museum were invited to respond to testbed displays, giving us helpful feedback on specific aspects of interpretation and display. The Curriculum Advisory Group was involved in early discussions about approaches which would support their teaching strategies. A junior board, twelve young people aged between nine and fourteen, advised us on many aspects of the displays and the various services offered to visitors of their age group.

In addition, we worked closely with Scottish Enterprise, the Local Enterprise Company (LEEL), the Scottish Tourist Board, the Edinburgh and Lothians Tourist Board, Historic Scotland and the Scottish Museums Council. We friend-raised and fund-raised with the benefit of support from hundreds of companies, individuals and trusts, their help including donations, sponsorship or in kind.

What about marketing and corporate identity? We were beginning to define the product. We had carried out market research, experimented with testbed displays, and debated with the junior board. The next step was to devise a corporate identity, and then to develop an appropriate promotional campaign to raise awareness of the new Museum which we hoped would create an intention to visit, preferably again and again.

Pentagram was asked to develop an identity scheme for the National Museums of Scotland. We wanted a unifying image for the whole organisation, which would at the same time allow the expression of the individual character and nature of each museum, starting with the Museum of Scotland. The anchor of the design scheme is the letter 'S' for Scotland. This constant, unifying element acts as the chief signifier of

'Scottishness', reflecting the identity of the country, its character and values. The 'S' is not used on its own: for the Museum of Scotland, a motif based on a wood carving of a thistle supports it. We felt that the thistle in this contemporary yet classic and elegant design represented the values we wanted to be associated with: steadiness, determination, sometimes challenging and thrusting, whilst at the same time immediately and recognisably Scottish.

Corporate colours were also part of the new identity, and the colour for the Museum of Scotland is a strong blue. We felt that this 'look' was simple and instantly recognisable. It was the colour to be used for every piece of promotional print such as leaflets, posters, advertising material, postcards, guides and invitations. It was also applied to items on sale in the shop, such as Museum of Scotland chocolate, carrier bags, specially commissioned Bridgewater tea services.

After having established an identity, we began to plan the advertising strategy for the new Museum. What was the Museum of Scotland all about? We reminded ourselves of our 'business': presenting, exploring and explaining Scotland, focusing on a celebration of Scotland's story over 3,300 million years to the present day as told by the national collections. Our mission was to sell the Museum as one of Scotland's top visitor attraction, one with a serious intellectual edge providing access to the nation's rich cultural inheritance.

We wanted to talk to Scots and all those with an affinity for Scotland and who shared a sense of national pride, whatever their origins or place of residence. We also wanted to reach out to domestic tourists, mainly from Northern and South East England, and overseas tourists, primarily North Americans, Germans, Dutch, French and Italians. We also recognised that the campaign would be indirectly influential amongst other important constituencies. In our advertising campaign, we aimed to present the Museum as a unique 'must see' for every tourist, a place of pilgrimage and a place of discovery, and especially self-discovery for every Scot. We wanted the public to think of the Museum as a showcase of enduring focus on Scotland's cultural heritage. We particularly wanted them not just to visit but to participate, and not just occasionally, but often.

The most compelling messages of the campaign were: First, to (re) discover and understand Scotland, you have to visit this unique museum. Second, the Museum of Scotland is the essential starting point for any visit to Scotland.

To support these messages we were confident that the Museum was unique and definitive: it could not exist anywhere else. We knew it was genuine: it contained the original artefacts and real evidence. We could promote it as credible and accurate, since it was developed with the advice of world-class experts. We believed it was essential and enlightening, serving as the necessary starting point for any serious visit to Scotland or understanding of Scotland. In educational terms, it was the key resource for students of all ages.

We also used other features for our marketing agenda. The Museum was to be classical yet contemporary. It would celebrate the cultural and historical life of Scotland, and do it with style. It was historical, located firmly in the Old Town of Edinburgh, with views to the Castle and other major landmarks. It was going to be impressive, being a radical and imposing modern building which made reference to traditional themes. It would be inspiring, a treasury to house the nation's rich inheritance.

A key slogan in our advertising campaign was 'the story so far'. It conveyed the message that the Museum will hold the authenticated story, as far as we know it, but implied that fresh evidence and research may provide a new and challenging slant and the story may move on. The essence of our message was that the Museum would be about the story told by the objects. Most people we were aware of had enjoyed the myths of Scottish history, but with the arrival of the Museum of Scotland it was literally 'time to get real'. A central element in our various campaigns was based on using stereotypes to attract attention, followed immediately by the strong message that the new Museum was going to knock them on the head.

Can the Museum of Scotland realistically aspire to meet the expectations raised by our campaigns? More people are taking increasing interest in who they are and where they came from, which makes the past relevant. Our privilege at the new Museum is to be able to present some of that past, some of the cultural heritage of Scotland. To many, there are surprises. The response of some visitors is 'I never realised...'. Others do ask where the tartan and the bagpipes are. Of course they *are* there in the displays, taking their place alongside other objects in a wider context.

The display which introduces the Kingdom of the Scots on Level 1 is called 'Scotland Defined'. It presents the gradual birth of a nation, with different peoples coming together to take the name of the Scots. Visitors may be surprised at the first object they encounter, after passing the Dupplin Cross. It is the tiny Monymusk Reliquary, an icon of early Scottish identity. Visitors may be expecting the more familiar St Andrew or the Saltire, and will find them further into the gallery. But we chose quite deliberately to open with this portable house-shaped shrine which once held a relic of St. Columba. It was carried as a talisman by the Scottish army at that defining moment, the Battle of Bannockburn, when in 1314 Robert the Bruce defeated the English and secured Scotland's independence. The Monymusk Reliquary was around 600 years old then, and it is nearly 1,300 years old now.

Two ideas produced for our campaign.

Our approach has been to tease out the stories of objects in context. What about those romantic figures tourists have read about? Where is Bonnie Prince Charlie? What about Mary Queen of Scots? They take their place as key figures in contexts that had huge impact on the Scottish people. Mary Queen of Scots is placed firmly in a Renaissance setting in a gallery that parallels the story of the Stewart dynasty told as part of 'Monarchy and Power'. The objects associated with her tell stories of Scotland as one of the nations of North West Europe linked by trade and politics, and by cultural and religious movements. In the gallery called The Jacobite Challenge, visitors will find Bonnie Prince Charlie's sword, his targe and his travelling canteen, all quite genuine, unlike the countless locks of hair.

To tell a story, iconic objects are as relevant to industrial and social developments as they are to romantic heroes. Our key part in Britain's industrial revolution is illustrated by the massive Newcomen Engine, designed by an Englishman, but made and used to pump water out of Scottish coal mines. James Watt's further advancements in the use of steam power were crucial to Scotland's evolution into 'the workshop of the world'. Objects in the Victorian and Edwardian gallery show the effects of this industrial development and success as part of a global phenomenon historically, but experienced in Scotland with particular intensity.

We would like visitors to regard the new Museum as a gateway, both physically and emotionally, to our national past. We want visitors to take away with them a sense of the variety and richness of Scotland's history and its enormous cultural diversity, brought to life by the fascinating stories each object can convey. For example, let us take one particular category of visitors, school parties, and describe how we try to offer them a particular experience. The Museum's Discovery Centre, developed by Sue Mitchell and Maureen Barrie, is a dynamic hands-on area where visitors of all ages can get actively involved in their own learning, using all their senses to find out about Scotland's past. It is a place where museum staff are on hand all the time to provide help and encouragement. The focus of our educational provision for school pupils aged five to fourteen, it is also ideal for other organised groups and families.

In the Centre, visitors develop skills in learning about the past through investigating objects and other forms of evidence, and through that a greater understanding of the displays in the core galleries, and in turn greater knowledge of, and interest in, Scotland's past. The overarching theme of the Centre is to show that Scotland has never existed in isolation, that there has been cultural exchange since the earliest times.

Young people are encouraged to find out about Scotland's national past through different types of evidence and to look at Scotland as a country which for a huge chunk of time has been part of, and therefore influenced by, a larger Europe. Here we hope young people, confronting some of the stereotypes, will make up their own minds and sometimes reject them. However, the Centre is only one route into the displays. There are countless others: sound guides, publications, guided tours, multi-media terminals, working machinery, special events, education packs, workshops and staff. But in the end, the way into the displays is through the visitor, through the visitor's own story, through the engagement of the visitor with the object on display, through awareness and their own imagination.

The Author

Mary Bryden taught history in secondary schools in Scotland for several years before becoming the first Education Officer in 200 years at the National Museum of Antiquities of Scotland. In 1985, she became Head of Education in the newly formed National Museums of Scotland where she introduced the Discovery Room, a project which has toured the length and breadth of the country, and been enjoyed by over 100,000 visitors. She also developed a team of 40 volunteer guides, having started with five in 1991, expanded the talks and lectures programmes and strengthened the schools programme. She became Head of Public Affairs in 1994 and is responsible for the PR, Education and Marketing of the Museum of Scotland, as well as front-of-house and visitor services. She played a leading role in winning a 1995 Charter Mark Award for excellence in provision of services to the public, presented to her for NMS by the Prime Minister, John Major.

References

Boniface, P., *Managing Quality Cultural Tourism*, Routledge, 1995.

Clarke, D., 'Me tartan and chained to the past', in *The Museums Journal*, March 1996.

Davies, S., *By Popular Demand: A strategic analysis of the market potential for museums and art galleries in the UK*, Museums & Galleries Commission, 1994.

Ind, N., *The Corporate Image: Strategies for Effective Identity Programmes*, Kogan Page, 1990.

Jones, M., 'From haggis to home rule', in *The Museums Journal*, Vol 95, No 2, February, 1995.

McLean, F., *Marketing the Museum*, Routledge, 1997.

Runyard, S., *The Museum Marketing Handbook*, Museums & Galleries Commission, 1994.

4

FROM ARTEFACTS TO AUDIENCE
Strategy for Display and Interpretation

Jenni Calder

I often remind myself, and others, of an experience I had many years ago as a museum education officer. A fourteen-year-old had spent half an hour in one of the Royal Museum's galleries. I asked him what he thought of it. 'I don't like exhibitions which make me feel as if I'm not allowed to understand,' he replied.

There is a long tradition, not just in museums, of suggesting to those we tend to refer to as 'the general public' that true understanding is in the heads of people other than themselves. It has for some time now been accepted that this is unforgivable, especially in a publicly funded institution with education as a key objective. Museums have today a much keener awareness of their public and many more means of communicating with them. But language remains crucial, and habits of using language as power rather than communication die hard. A determination to break that habit played a key part in the interpretation strategy that was developed for the Museum of Scotland.

Interpretation begins with selection: of objects and concepts, themes and storylines. In most of the Museum of Scotland, curators made the selection, with some input from education and communication staff and from outside advisers. The process of selection began long before there was a design for a building: the building came in response to the objects. In the old Museum of Antiquities collections there were approximately 200,000 objects. We clearly never aspired to display them all. In addition, material for the geology and natural history displays and most of the industrial material was drawn from the Royal Museum collections. In total, there are around 12,000 items now displayed in the Museum of Scotland.

Many objects selected themselves – it is inconceivable that we would have opened the Museum of Scotland without the Monymusk Reliquary, the Lewis chesspieces or Charles Edward Stewart's silver gilt canteen. People would rightly expect to find quaichs, thistle cups, tartan and claymores. But there were also expectations concerning events in history: even a superficial grasp of Scotland's past would probably include the Wars of Independence, the Union of the Scottish and English parliaments and Clyde shipbuilding, and people such as Mary, Queen of Scots, Robert Burns and David Livingstone. If the process of museum interpretation begins with selection, it continues with the need to bring objects together with two partners: a story and an audience.

THE STRATEGIC FRAMEWORK

By the time the architectural competition for the building was launched in 1991, lists of objects grouped into themes had been prepared; they formed an important part of the brief. The main division of material was mapped out. There were effectively three sections, covering Scotland's geological beginnings and natural history, prehistory, and Scotland in the historical period. Ideas for the 20th century displays were developed later. These lists and divisions were the start of the interpretation process. The exhibition brief evolved over the next five years or so, but the key objects and core messages remained remarkably consistent. Our interpretation strategy was built on that beginning.

At an early stage it was decided that the approach to display would be thematic within a broad chronological framework. The timeframe for geology is obviously very different from that of human history, and the timeframe for prehistory suggests a different kind of narrative from that of the last thousand years. Our collections did not lend themselves to a continuous narrative of Scottish history: few museum collections do. As the objects themselves were the *raison d'être* of the new museum, our responsibility was to present them in a way that allowed them to communicate their stories as strongly as possible. The centrality of the object was a guiding principle.

The next step was consideration of how the exhibits were to be arranged. Every object had potential to be featured in more than one context, to tell more than one story, and indeed during the exhibition development process some objects appeared in several places at the same time. So we had to address the questions: which stories did we want to tell? Which stories best suited the material at our disposal? Which stories would our public expect to find? Again, some stories selected themselves through the strength of the collections. With wonderful objects relating to the pre-

Reformation Church, with extensive Jacobite material, *The Medieval Church* and *The Jacobite Challenge* were themes that emerged naturally from the collections. But others were not so easy. How were we going to make the transition from the early material and introduce the whole idea of Scotland in history? How would we deal with an intellectual movement like the Scottish Enlightenment? What about the Highland Clearances, with virtually no surviving objects? The Trustees were rightly insistent that the Museum of Scotland could not leave these subjects out; it took much longer to develop ways of presenting them.

This stage of development was crucial, often difficult, but always interesting. We sought the views of academic historians, museum professionals, teachers and members of the public. On the Scottish Enlightenment, a number of ideas were debated and abandoned. The objects were the deciding factor. Our collections allowed us to look at aspects of life in Scotland that influenced and were affected by Enlightenment ideas: agriculture, antiquarianism, communications, social and cultural life, for example. By looking at their consequences, we could say something about the ideas themselves without, we hoped, getting too bogged down in abstractions. The resulting theme, which we called *The Spirit of the Age,* is full of links and crosscurrents, which themselves underline the character of the Enlightenment.

This iterative and evolutionary process delivered the arrangement we now have, moving from *Beginnings,* Scotland's geological foundations and early wildlife, on Level 0, to *The Twentieth Century* on Level 6. *Beginnings* is followed by *Early People,* also on Level 0. The link is the last Ice Age, which prepared the way first for repopulation by wildlife and then for colonisation by people. The next hinge is the beginning of recorded history. *Early People* explores the implication of the arrival of literacy. On Level 1 the story is taken up by emphasising how the written word affects our understanding of the past. People are now identifiable, as groups and individuals. *The Kingdom of the Scots* looks at Scotland from around the 8th century AD to the last Scottish parliament in 1707. *Scotland Transformed,* on Level 3, begins with the Union of the Scottish and English parliaments and focuses mainly on the 18th century. Upstairs on Level 4 *Industry and Empire* is introduced by an exploration of Scotland in the 19th century as 'the workshop of the world', and this is followed on Level 5 by galleries which highlight Victorian and Edwardian life. Finally, on Level 6, there is *The Twentieth Century.*

These seven levels incorporate varied approaches to interpretation. In *Beginnings* we believed it was important to explain as well as narrate. Geological time and geological concepts are not easy for the layperson to absorb and the curators were committed to reaching as wide an audience as possible. The information provided is carefully structured, with an emphasis on how geological and zoological evidence can be interpreted. In *Early People* an approach was taken which deliberately cuts across conventional categories. The aim is to challenge the visitor to think not in terms of chronological or ethnic groupings – Bronze Age, Iron Age, Picts, Romans, Vikings – but of the elements of life – food and other resources, travel, social organisation and status, warfare, and spiritual life. The narrative provided is deductive, drawn largely from the surviving archaeological artefacts, but it also invites visitors to use their imaginations to fill in the gaps.

The Kingdom of the Scots signals a new approach, influenced by the fact that the written record now comes into play in the interpretation of objects. Now we have names of people and places, different voices and languages, and documented events and dates and sequences of cause and effect that we can add to the story. In *The Twentieth Century*, the approach changes again, for here the public has selected all the objects, and it is their voices that take over. The curatorial intervention is minimal.

An underlying principle in the interpretation of historic and prehistoric material was to draw attention, not necessarily overtly, to the understanding of the past that can be drawn from material culture. Presentation of the national past to be found in the Museum of Scotland would not necessarily be the same as that found in history books, as our key sources were objects, which tend to be overlooked by mainstream academic historians. Not only that, the means of presentation are different. A good example is *The Reformed Church* gallery. A common perception of the Presbyterian Church is that it is drab and severe and encourages a severe lifestyle. The material displayed, however, suggests something rather different, both through the objects themselves and the interpretation provided by context and explanation. Part of that interpretation lies in the contrast with *The Medieval Church*, which evokes an almost crypt-like space. *The Reformed Church* is lighter and more open. For example, it is not only the style of church silver that has changed, but its context, reflecting the more open environment of Renaissance learning and a democratic church.

Objects can be obscure and remote, and often desperately need help to communicate. But sometimes a single object can deliver significant and relevant impact irrespective of the story in the words. Still within *The*

Reformed Church, the mask and wig worn by the Covenanting minister Alexander Peden is a good example. The story surrounding it relates to a dramatic and distinctive episode in Scotland's history, and we tell that story. But the object itself has its own extraordinary power and, I believe, adds to our understanding of the courage, commitment, fear and fanaticism of the Covenanting wars with an immediacy that words cannot match.

Another example of the way material culture can shift the focus of the historical record is found in two small cases in *The Spirit of the Age.* To understand the Scottish Enlightenment, it is vital to grasp its practical consequences. This was a time not only of intellectual concepts, but also of results on the ground – literally, in the case of agricultural improvement. In one case visitors can see models of some of the new types of machinery that made a huge impact on farming. Opposite, are objects which tell how more productive farming affected the way the improvers lived.

It will already be clear that the selection of themes was a multi-stranded exercise. Some emerged naturally from strengths of the collection. Others were the result of much discussion as to how best to represent distinctive episodes in Scotland's history. The next stage was to think about how material would be sequenced and grouped. Key factors in these decisions were large objects and how and where they would be placed. In the nature of things, there was less choice about how these would be displayed. Space for the Newcomen atmospheric engine, for example, had to be created for the object, and that in turn affected the displays around it. Size does matter, for inevitably something as large as the Newcomen commands attention. Similarly, on a different scale, the Maiden, the beheading machine featured in *Monarchy and Power* on Level 1, dominates the topic on 'Law and order'. It is not only large, but has, since its acquisition in the early 19th century, been considered one of the Museum's star objects.

The next stages in interpretation continued the selection process. How were we going to communicate information about the objects? What sort of information would that be? Let me try to answer the second question first.

There is often a very understandable curatorial tendency to want to tell the public everything there is to know about any given object. But our objects were to be presented as part of a story, so we felt it was important that we confined ourselves to information relevant to that story. We were dealing with a huge amount of material. We were constrained not only by space but also by the amount we could reasonably expect visitors to take in. For example, we decided that we would only explain how a piece of technology worked if it contributed to the overall message. Inevitably, this means that some visitors feel short-changed. The downside of selection is that some aspects are left out.

The big question is how to communicate information. There have been times when we have toyed with the idea of displays without words, and I would still like to devise a wordless exhibition. But not for the mainstream exhibitions of the Museum of Scotland. Words, it was decided at a very early stage, would play a very important role, and so would pictures. These are the traditional display media. We decided against reconstructions and tableaux, for two reasons. We wanted the emphasis to be on the real thing, and we believed that reconstructions could detract from the object. Reconstructions can communicate a great deal and can be a very valuable source of understanding (dioramas are used to considerable effect in *Beginnings*). But they do not necessarily help visitors to understand artefacts. And this underlines the keystone of our approach: we were not telling Scotland's story illustrated by objects. Our aim was to present the stories objects could tell.

What other media did we consider? Sound was fairly high on the list. We decided against ambient sound, but for the use of sound in audio-visual and multimedia programmes. We also decided to develop an audio guide. We were reluctant to overload the displays with fancy technology, but identified at a very early stage the contribution that multimedia could make, and we use that in a number of different ways. Multimedia screens in the galleries feature specific display-related programs, and computers located in the ExhibIT room on Level 1 allow wider on-screen access, including the Scottish Cultural Resources Access Network (SCRAN).

In September 1994, we held a seminar on Exhibition Communication, at which we invited David Anderson, Head of Education at the V&A, and Eilean Hooper-Greenhill, Lecturer in Museum Studies at Leicester University, to comment on current versions of the display briefs. This was open to all staff working on the Museum of Scotland. The seminar was essentially a consciousness-raising exercise, and proved valuable, even though we were aware that many of the suggestions and ideas that emerged could not be accommodated by the architectural vision.

The seminar did help to encourage staff to think about audiences and how to reach them. We decided to develop several topics as testbeds, which were the subject of response from focus groups, NMS staff in general, teachers, disabled groups and the Junior Board. In the event, we tried out two versions of three topics, the second version responding to comment on the first. This was an extremely rewarding exercise. We learned more about our public and their expectations of the Museum of Scotland, and we got feedback on specific aspects of display and interpretation.

Another essential aspect of interpretation is publication of material in support of the exhibitions. The Museum of Scotland publications programme aimed to commission and publish material well before the Museum opened so that on the first day there would be a good range of relevant publications available. An important element of this programme was a series of short and accessible books, called 'Scotland's Past in Action'. The first four titles were published in 1995 and there are now sixteen titles in print with more on the way. This year (1999), NMS Publishing brought out the first four of a parallel series called 'Scots Lives': brief biographies of significant figures. For the actual opening of the Museum of Scotland the main effort was the production of the guide and a guide for children called *On the Trail of Scotland's Past*. Later this year, *Who's Who in the Museum of Scotland* will be published, which provides information on all the people mentioned in the displays.

So these were some of the choices made. Needless to say, the process of making the choices was not quite as straightforward as this may sound, and some aspects of selection evolved in a somewhat convoluted fashion. There was much debate. There was much anguish when objects had to be deleted from the list. And of course there were practical considerations at every stage: issues of architecture, space, circulation, conservation and so on.

SCRIPT WRITING STRATEGY

With the appointment of Benson and Forsyth as architects, the process of refinement of the building's design began, and exhibition development moved into a different gear. My role was as script co-ordinator, and its very existence was recognition of the importance of the text. Although there had over the years been a growing involvement of education staff in producing, or at least commenting on, exhibition text, there had not been a consistent policy. The appointment of a script co-ordinator was a signal that writing and editing skills were considered crucial.

My first task was to draft a scriptwriting strategy. This highlighted the importance of the audience and of a clear, jargon-free style, and recommended that scripts should be written by those with writing skills. Out of this developed 'Guidelines for producing display text' which were intended to act as a general brief for the scriptwriter. The key features were: the need to convey the main message of each display element; the centrality of the object; fitting text to sequence; relevance to the storyline. With so many different people involved in exhibition development it was important to define consistently used terms for the different display elements.

We also felt that it was important to reflect the languages of Scotland. Gaelic should be a presence where relevant, so in *Na Gaidheal* on Level 1, the gallery where we focus on Gaelic culture, we use Gaelic headings and quote from Gaelic literature. Scots words and expressions should be used as appropriate, but we also included, for example, French and Old Norse, as both have contributed to shaping Scotland's language and culture. Above all, we wanted the words we used to reflect what R L Stevenson called 'a strong Scotch accent of the mind'.

SCRIPT WRITING PRACTICE

How did this get translated into practice? The first step was the preparation by myself and Sue Mitchell, who was then Education Officer for the Museum of Scotland, of what we called a communication assessment for each theme. We looked at the curatorial material provided on objects and messages and identified key objects and the central storyline, and produced a framework for the division and sequencing of panel and label information. We suggested the level of background and explanatory information that visitors would look for, highlighted aspects that were particularly relevant to the 5-14 school curriculum, and suggested where additional elements would be useful: graphics (for example, maps and diagrams), sound guide tracks and so on. The guidelines had divided panel and display text into five levels, later amended to four. These were:

> Level A: text introducing each theme, 100 words max.
> Level B: text introducing sections within themes, 150 words max.
> Level C: text introducing a topic, 200 words max.
> Level D: object labels, 30 words max.

Curators were asked to use these frameworks, the guidelines and a stylesheet to provide the raw materials for the display text. What was produced varied considerably. There was raw information which had to be recast as script; there was workable first-draft script which required minimal editing; there was first-draft script which needed radical rewriting; there was minimalist script that needed to be augmented, and lengthy chunks of text that had to be cut down. Most curators did use the frameworks and did write to length. However, it has to be said that most curators did not use the stylesheet and one of the biggest jobs was ensuring consistency.

Aspects that needed most editorial attention were making language and style more accessible and hitting the right level of information and reference. I often use the analogy of a train journey in explaining the gap that frequently occurs between the points at which curators and visitors begin. If you want to travel from Edinburgh to Glasgow, it doesn't help if the train starts at Falkirk. As communicators, we have to ensure that we are starting at the same place as our audience, which is why it is so important to understand who our audiences are.

Another issue was that of gender. Our collections are largely the result of the interests and activities of men. Our male-oriented society has ensured that the material that survives reflects mainly that orientation. We can try to redress the balance in the material we collect to reflect society now, but there is little we can do about the distant past, except fortuitously. Nevertheless, we have consciously tried to draw attention to the lives of women, to bring them into the foreground where there is a genuine opportunity. It is, however, an issue that I believe needs more research, more debate and more focus.

My main involvement as script co-ordinator was with those texts that related to the historic period. The aim was to ensure that all the text on Levels 1 to 5 communicated what we had intended. As I have indicated, the level of intervention on my part varied considerably. Some scripts I wrote myself, including researching more information where I felt the visitor would want to know more, or where I felt something was needed to provide links in a sequence. I brought in an outside scriptwriter to do some rewriting. The process of rewriting, cutting and refining was lengthy and often frustrating, but it was also, like many other aspects of exhibition development, a source of creative challenge. A final version of the text was agreed with the curator concerned, and was then copy-edited by a professional, before another final check.

Display text can be used to achieve many diverse goals. Our aim was the elucidation of objects in the context of a storyline that was part of the larger story of Scotland. But both objects and storylines have links across the Museum, and many themes are generated which are not specifically identified. How do we encourage people to recognise these links and pick up the secondary themes, without overloading them with information and instructions?

There are some secondary themes which we hope visitors will pick up without specific help. An example is religion. Visitors can follow the theme of religious belief in Scotland, from *In Touch with the Gods* in *Early People*, through the *Medieval Church* and *The Reformed Church* on Level 1, on to *The Church* on Level 3 and *Daith Comes In* on Level 4. Their relationship is underlined by the fact that they are 'stacked' above each other – visitors will find religious themes in the same place on Levels 1, 3 and 4, and there are visual links between levels. The industrial theme is linked visually, across Level 3 and up to Level 4.

We have also included some specific cross-referencing between displays, pointing out to visitors where they can find related material or where a different aspect of a topic is looked at. In addition, there are links with other museums, historic sites and places of interest that relate to our displays. For example, in the Renaissance gallery we tell visitors about Renaissance style buildings which they can visit: the royal palaces at Stirling, Falkland, Linlithgow and Holyrood, among others. The topic on coal mining refers people to the Scottish Mining Museum and on iron and steel to the Bonawe ironworking site. It is not necessarily that we expect people to rush off and visit these places, although we have produced a 'Treasure Trails' leaflet which encourages them to do just that, but that by creating these links we signal the Museum's role as part of a much larger network. We aim to stimulate interest as well as to satisfy curiosity; the Museum of Scotland provides an ideal opportunity to show how the material in the national collections relates to the whole country.

As we were working on the texts, the building was taking shape and exhibition layouts were being refined. Unexpected space constraints emerged, on wall panels and inside cases, and locations of panels sometimes had to change because of other requirements. This has left us with a few instances where the position of panel information in relation to objects is not ideal. Where cases had large numbers of small objects it was clear that there would not be room for 30-word labels for every object, so we produced group labels and sometimes had to cut to the bone the information we were able to provide.

The ground floor presented a number of problems, as many of the cases are very small, with correspondingly narrow panels and rails inside the cases for the object labels. Our word counts proved too generous for some of these, and we had to cut. Sometimes changes in case sizes had us cutting text on the final proofs. Many images had to be deleted. In some areas newly acquired objects were accommodated, which meant adding text, and that in turn could mean taking it away somewhere else. We became highly skilled in juggling text, although it can be a high-risk strategy, especially when engaged in at a late stage in the process.

The contract for graphic design for Levels 1–5 went to Millhouse, who also took on the graphic design for *Early People*. They proposed sizes for different types of panels and for type, which conformed to NMS guidelines (type sizes ranged from 18 point for object labels to 24 point for panels). A strategy was agreed for dealing with texts, which included a consistent format identifying the different levels of text, headings and captions, and allowed for three stages of proofs. A symbiosis between text co-ordination, graphic design and layout design was vital. We had to be flexible and we had to be able to respond rapidly to each other. Last minute changes were inevitable: for weeks there were problem solving phone calls on a daily basis. While the text was being drafted, the huge task of accumulating graphic images had been going on, and all captions and copyright acknowledgements had to be checked.

AUDIO GUIDE

In the meantime, we were producing an audio guide. We wanted to use sound to provide something generic to that medium. In the testbed on coal mining, we had included an audiotape with seven minutes of 19th century accounts of conditions in the mines. We used professional actors, but there were just words, no sound effects or music. The focus groups liked it. We decided to take this further, and developed an audio guide which added words contemporary to the displays, plus music and sound effects where appropriate, with a linking narrative to tie it all together and relate it to the objects.

The aim was to enhance the narrative of the exhibits, to allow visitors to hear contemporary language, and to evoke experience in a more immediate way than was generally possible through the displays. It was a major task, and a major collaboration between curators, research assistants, myself as scriptwriter, the production company Heritage Productions, the BBC and Antenna Audio. The BBC partnership allowed us access to their archives, which provided most of the music and sound effects.

The audio guide means that visitors can hear not only Gaelic and Scots, but also Old Norse and Anglo-Saxon. They are introduced to archive material, some of it not widely accessible, and can get the flavour of contemporary comment and reaction. We are also developing sound guides in several foreign languages. We already have published guides to the Museum of Scotland in French, German, Italian, Spanish, Japanese and Gaelic, as well as in English.

I began by saying interpretation is about selection. I have tried to suggest something of that process and the factors that influenced it and to describe some aspects of production. Interpretation can also be described as a process of building bridges between objects, which are often accidental survivals with obscure relevance to what most of us understand of the past, and visitors. Those visitors may not share our culture or our language or our assumptions about significance and value. But even if they do, the process of interpretation does not stop with the opening of an exhibition, or indeed of a museum.

In fact, our task has only just started. We are continuing the bridge building in many different ways: through the Discovery Centre, which gives children and families hands-on access to museum material, and its child Discovery on the Move which will make its first tour in spring 2000; through a broad spectrum of education programmes and public events; through temporary displays; through new research and making new knowledge available; through publication; and through working with other institutions to augment and enhance a wider experience of the Scottish inheritance.

The Author

Jenni Calder joined the then Royal Scottish Museum as an education officer, and became Head of Publications in 1992. She was Script Co-ordinator for the Museum of Scotland and has written, compiled and edited a number of books for NMS, including *The Enterprising Scot* (1986), *The Wealth of a Nation* (1989) and the *Guide to the Museum of Scotland* (1998). She is also author of over a dozen books on literary and historical subjects, including *RLS: A Life Study* (1980) and *The Nine Lives of Naomi Mitchison* (1997). She is currently Head of the Scotland and the World initiative launched by the National Museums of Scotland in 1999.

References

Calder, J., *Guide to the Museum of Scotland*, NMS Publishing, 1998.

Calder, J. (ed), *The Wealth of a Nation*, Richard Drew, 1989.

Hooper-Greenhill, E., *Museums, Media, Message*, Routledge, 1995.

Hooper-Greenhill, E., *Museums and the Shaping of Knowledge*, Routledge, 1992.

Kavanagh, G., *Museum Languages, Objects and Texts*, Leicester University Press, 1991.

Kentley, E. and Negus, D., *The Writing on the Wall*, National Maritime Museum, 1989.

Lynch, M., *Scotland: A New History*, Century, 1991.

McKean, C., *Creating the Museum of Scotland*, NMS Publishing, 1999.

Mitchell, S. and Wade, M., *On the Trail of Scotland's Past*, NMS Publishing, 1998.

Nolan, G., *Designing Exhibitions to Include People with Disabilities: A Practical Guide*, NMS Publishing, 1996.

Rayner, A., *Access in Mind: Towards the Inclusive Museum*, INTACT, 1998.

Smout, T.C., *A Century of the Scottish People 1830–1950*, Collins, 1986.

Smout, T.C., *A History of the Scottish People, 1560–1830*, Collins, 1969.

Sorsby, B.D. and Horne, S.D., 'The Readability of Museum Labels', *Museums Journal 80 (3)*, 1980.

Vergo, P., *The New Museology*, Reaktion, 1989.

5

PUBLIC PERCEPTION OF HISTORY
The Twentieth Century Gallery

Rose Watban

If you, the reader, were to choose one thing from the 20th century, what would it be? Sean Connery chose a milk bottle, Elaine C Smith selected her washing machine, and Irvine Welsh suggested Jim Baxter's shirt from the 1967 Scotland versus England football match at Wembley. These are among the suggestions selected for display to tell the story of the 20th century.

Rather than curators selecting objects for an exhibition, it was decided to ask the public to choose things which, in their view, have made a major impact on life in Scotland over the last 100 years. Alternatively, a more personal memento, which related to an individual's life story, could be chosen. Taken together with the reasons for these choices, we were able to create a unique 20th Century Exhibition on Level 6 of the Museum of Scotland.

We asked people living in Scotland, and Scots living elsewhere for their suggestions. In September 1997, leaflets were distributed to museums, libraries, universities, colleges and schools throughout Scotland in the hope of reaching as large an age range and geographical spread as possible. The initiative was also advertised in the press and on the radio. Some well known Scots, at home and abroad, and some well known people with Scottish connections, were also specially invited to participate.

The outcome of this exercise is what you see in *The Twentieth Century*, and it is very different from that which is displayed in the rest of the Museum. In the other galleries, history is being represented through objects from our diverse collections relating to Scottish history. Behind our approach to the exhibition were questions such as: Can we really understand the past through objects? Will people in the future understand life in the 20th century through the objects displayed in the gallery? Have the wide range of people represented chosen typical objects, and for representative reasons? Were the choices dictated by cultural identity, geographical location, age, sex, social and economic position? Or, as we reach the end of the 20th century, has a global culture started to emerge?

In all about 1000 suggestions were received, but due to restricted space, only about 350 are displayed. Many objects were chosen by more than one person, and in some cases more than one reason accompanies the display. All suggestions and accompanying reasons have been entered into a database which can be accessed by visitors to the gallery. The majority – including the celebrities, who represent no more than ten per cent of the contributors – chose objects of personal significance rather than objects of national importance. Most of the choices fell easily into the following broad themes: home, leisure, war, health, education, working life, communication, technology and transport.

The exhibition sections, although untitled, more or less follow the structure of these themes. The gallery also contains a small cinema where a programme of short film clips, from the Scottish Film Archive, on subjects relating to the exhibition themes, is shown throughout the day. A programme of longer Scottish films and documentaries is shown on a Tuesday evening when the Museum has late night opening.

Some objects appear in more than one section depending on the reasons given. For example, the radio appears in both leisure and technology, the biro in education and technology and the fax machine in both working life and communications.

In most cases, apart from some very personal mementoes, the objects themselves are familiar, often mundane, and could arguably have been chosen as representative of many western cultures in the late 20th century. So do the reasons given identify the contributors as Scottish?

Not surprisingly perhaps, television was chosen by 56 people, mainly for its entertainment and educational value. In 1936, the BBC opened the first full scale British television service, but few had TV until the 1950s or 1960s. By the 1960s, satellites made it possible to link the television networks of Europe and the USA, and by the 1970s, satellite links could be made to most parts of the world.

Television, along with cinema, cheap foreign travel, and, increasingly, the internet have broadened our outlook and given the majority access to a wide range of cultures only imagined or read about earlier this century. According to Lisa Ann Robertson who lives in Shetland and who was born in 1987:

Television is very good entertainment for all ages, in the old days you had to make your own entertainment. I think television is important in the 20th century because it lets us see all kinds of things. I can watch television in Shetland and learn all about people and animals all over the world.

Some slightly older contributors were less enthusiastic about television, Anne Nimmo, born in 1953 and from Edinburgh said:

The television set has widely superseded the fireplace as the focal point of the living room. The ability to see live pictures from all over the world still amazes us! However television has generated a lot of controversy thanks to its huge viewing figures and influence; the creation of the couch potato, censorship and broadcasting of biased views. As well as the promotion of a nation of 'channel hoppers' with short attention spans. In the near future you will be able to dictate what you view. Television will be used for banking and shopping. It will be computer, videophone and Internet linked and be even more central to home life.

Radio was chosen by many of the older generation, not because they had no access to television but because they remember a time before television. This was said by Maurice Carmichael, born in 1935 and from Edinburgh:

As a four-year-old, at the beginning of World War II, I remember seeing, and hearing, my first radio when my father bought one. I have been a fan ever since, and still have a radio 'on' at home most of the time...

In the case of Margaret Gourley who now lives in Canada, it reminded her of the Scotland of her childhood:

...some of the programmes I listened to as a child were Just William, Dick Barton Special Agent, The McFlannels, Scottish Country Dance Music (Jimmie Shand's band), Workers' Playtime, Sandy MacPherson at the Organ and Music from the Palm Court of the Grand Hotel. Any time I think of rainy Sundays in Kirkcaldy, in the Scotland of my childhood, playing in the background is music from the Palm Court of the Grand Hotel!

Air travel has revolutionised transport and made the world a smaller and more accessible place. Jeanne Cannizzo, a native North American now living in Edinburgh, said of the aeroplane:

The jet engine, by making long distance travel fast, safe and affordable, lets me see my family in North America at least once a year...It works the other way too: Dewars, Dippies, MacKenzies and Cowans come here in search of ancestral roots. Vancouver to Inverness is nothing by jet...

And Jennifer Walker from Edinburgh had this to say:

The aeroplane opened up the world, making travel easy for all, regardless of class or financial background. It brought access to new attitudes and religions, and opened up a pathway for new and deadly diseases to travel freely. Air travel changed people's 'places' especially women who were no longer limited to the 'village' or the nation...Free Boundaries for everything to mix.

Sixteen people chose the washing machine for its labour saving qualities. Indeed, many of the objects chosen have made our lives easier or more comfortable. Microwaves, vacuum cleaners, dishwashers, duvets, fridge freezers and frozen foods were all chosen. Technological advances are very important to many of the contributors to the exhibition and there are more objects from the present and recent past than from early in the century. The telephone, mobile telephones, computers, e-mail, the internet, compact discs and CD players were all popular choices.

Throughout the exhibition there are objects which demonstrate Scottish heritage and reflect both pride in achievement and a sense of loss. A pharmacist from Perthshire, D.W.M. Davidson, nominated the new medicines being developed in Scotland, in particular the advances being carried out at present in cancer research. Two people chose the Scottish biologist Alexander Fleming's discovery of penicillin. Professor Malcolm Baird, son of John Logie Baird, praises his father's invention.

A poster from the film Braveheart was chosen by Alex Salmond, leader of the Scottish Nationalist Party, and D.J. Macleod from Aberdeen chose the HMY Iolaire disaster:

The rejoicing over the end of the war turned to grief in Lewis on the first of January 1919 when HMY Iolaire sank and over 200 islanders who had survived the war were drowned, yards from their native shore...

Some contributors' choices were related to their experience of the Scottish climate and landscape. Helena Kennedy QC remembers that: 'As a child brought up in Scotland, with no central heating, I recall being frozen. I could not live without central heating now.' And to Mrs J. Skelligan: 'A tumble dryer is a boon in Scottish winters.' For Paul Munro: 'The tractor has changed work on farms and crofts in Scotland. It makes

life easier and is quicker than walking miles with a horse up hills...'.
Adam Scott from Dumfries offered this opinion:

> Before they had quad bikes, they either had to take a tractor, which
> was slower and couldn't get to as many places as the quad,
> especially on steep ground; or in some cases they had to walk the
> fields, which was slower still and took up a great deal of the
> farmers valuable time.

Some suggestions focused on Scotland's past industries, as did Murray
Grigor, film director and writer:

> The Queen Mary was the culminating achievement of Scotland's
> integrated industries of coal extraction, steel production,
> engineering innovation and shipbuilding design which had sent
> over half the world's shipping out from the Clyde...

Fiona Salveson: 'My grandpa, Hugh Allison, helped construct this ship
(the SS Olympia), one of the last cruise ships built on the Clyde, in 1939...'
In relation to the car industry, Simon Clegg explained:

> I chose a personal memento of the Hillman Imp, which I have in the
> form of an ashtray made from the metal of a Hillman Imp engine
> case and inscribed: *Manufactured by Rootes Craft Apprentices,
> Linwood.* For me, no other piece of manufacturing sums up the
> cynical and self-deprecating nature of the Scots nation. I was
> reminded of this when I met someone who used to work on the
> shop floor in Linwood. I said during conversation: 'So what became
> of the Hillman Imp then, I wonder?' To which the reply came:
> 'Well, would you buy a car made in Scotland?'

The final section in the exhibition contains the objects felt to be
particularly Scottish. Although unnamed, like the other sections in the
gallery, it was given the working title 'Cultural Identity' and includes: a
sash of Royal Stuart tartan, given by HM Queen Elizabeth The Queen
Mother; a copy of the Scotland Bill signed by The Secretary of State
Donald Dewar; and a 'Yes Yes' poster, badge and a ballot box used in the
1997 devolution referendum.

Barr's Irn Bru was chosen by three contributors including G.J. Moonan
from East Kilbride, Lanark who said of the drink:

> As a country partial to the odd libation, could this amber antidote
> for a hangover have been invented by anyone else? This sweet

nectar must have saved more lives on a Sunday morning than the chickenpox vaccine.

There is a figure of *Oor Wullie* and a cartoon of *The Broons*, thought of by many as Scottish cultural icons, and which still appear in *The Sunday Post* newspaper. Visitors can listen to a recording of the song *Flower of Scotland* written by Roy Williamson in 1968 and considered to be the people's choice for Scotland's National Anthem.

It would seem to be the case that, as we become increasingly globalised, objects relating to identity become more important. This can have a specifically national Scottish expression, or it can be an expression of personal identity relating to an individual's specific experiences or memories.

The perfume chosen by a child because it reminded her of her deceased grandmother. The pebble found on a beach which became a 'lucky stone' for a Shetland schoolboy, or the coloured optic sheet chosen by Bill Thompson from Glenrothes, Fife who said:

Something wonderful happened in my life that was to turn my world upside down in my early 50s. I discovered that I am dyslexic and have Scotopic Sensitivity Syndrome. Up until then using white paper and blue or black ink disorientated my eyes and mind – they would not work well together. When I was given my golden rod optic sheet (a yellow overlay sheet) everything came into focus and I was able to see words that had evaded me all my life. I now use pink ink and yellow paper and enjoy a new found freedom...

Possibly the most poignant choice of personal memento, however, came from Greta Dyer, a retired teacher from Edinburgh:

My husband Roy trained as a wireless operator and air-gunner in World War II. In 1942, at the end of his training, he joined 228 Squadron, Coastal Command, flying on the Atlantic patrol in Flying Fortresses. After he received his 'wing' he asked me to embroider a similar one for him. I was deeply touched that he wore my less than perfect wing throughout. In doing so, I liked to think that my prayer for his safe return was always with him. When I look at it now, I remember vividly the pain of so many partings and the great joy each time he returned home on leave.

The last example is from the cultural identity section of the exhibition. It came from Lewie Peterson who was born in 1985, and who expressed a strong sense of national pride:

The Stone of Destiny was used for Scottish Kings and Queens to sit on during their coronation ceremonies for hundreds of years before Edward I, King of England from 1272 to 1307, stole it and took it to Westminster Abbey. In 1950, on Christmas day, the stone was stolen by a group of Scottish Nationalists. It was recovered four months later. In July 1996, the Prime Minister, John Major, announced that the Stone of Destiny should be returned to Scotland. I think that the Stone of Destiny is a symbol of Scotland and its Spirit. Whenever I think of the stone and its past I feel very Scottish and proud of it. There have been arguments over where the stone should finally go but I think that it should go to Edinburgh, our great nation's capital, and I can't think of anywhere better than the new Museum of Scotland.

Since the Museum of Scotland opened to the public on 1 December 1998, it has attracted an international audience and visitors to *The Twentieth Century* have been encouraged to choose their 20th century object. Many Scots have suggested items related to the setting up of the new Scottish Parliament, but perhaps surprisingly, the majority of visitors have chosen very similar objects to the original contributors irrespective of age, sex or nationality. One difference in the choices is that there is a much larger number of people, places and events now being nominated.

All visitors' suggestions will be entered into a database, and when the exhibition closes at the end of December 2001, it will be interesting to compare choices and reasons with the backgrounds of the contributors. Until then, it seems that the majority of Scots who have contributed to the display have chosen objects which could just as easily have been chosen by people living anywhere in the developed world. These objects, while able to give visitors of the future a glimpse of 20th century life in Scotland, would not necessarily give many clues as to a national identity.

The Author

Rose Watban holds a degree in European Humanities from the Open University and has been with the National Museums of Scotland since 1970. She is currently Assistant Curator of European Glass & Ceramics in the Department of History and Applied Art. In 1996, she was asked to curate *The Twentieth Century* Exhibition for The Museum of Scotland.

References

Glennon, L. (ed), *Our Time: The Illustrated History of the 20th Century*, Turner Publishing, 1995.

Harris, P., *Scotland's Century 1900–2000: 100 years of Photography*, Lomond Press, 1999.

Harvie, C., 'Modern Scotland: Remembering the People', in Mitchison, R. (ed), *Why Scottish History Matters*, Saltire Society, 1991.

McCrone, D., *Understanding Scotland: the Sociology of a Stateless Nation*, Routledge, 1992.

Paterson, L., *The Autonomy of Modern Scotland*, Edinburgh University Press, 1994.

Sampson, A., *Anatomy of Britain*, Hodder & Stoughton, 1962.

Smout, T.C., *A Century of the Scottish People, 1830–1950*, Collins, 1986.

Turnock, D., *The New Scotland*, David & Charles, 1979.

Underwood, R., *The Future of Scotland*, Croom Helm, 1977.

Vergo, P. (ed), *The New Museology*, Reaktion, 1989.

Bessie Watson, 'the youngest suffragette', 1909. *Courtesy City of Edinburgh Museums.*

6

OBJECTS AS EVIDENCE
The Evaluation of Material Culture

Hugh Cheape

We know that the history of Scotland is not the history of any other nation on earth, and that if her records were destroyed, it would matter nothing to us that all the records of all other nations were preserved. They could neither tell us the story of our ancestors, nor restore the lost links in the development of our culture and civilisation.

These were the words of the second and longest serving Keeper of the National Museum of Antiquities of Scotland (a remarkable 44 years), when he delivered his first Rhind Lectures in October 1879. This patriotic warning by Anderson was published in the first volume of his *Scotland in Early Christian Times*. It sounds a claim to which many Scots and visitors, expecting to see the records and memorials of Scottish history in Scotland, would doubtless subscribe, without perhaps appreciating its deeper meaning. He was first and foremost an archaeologist, and his message refers principally to material culture records rather than the more obvious written records which had, as Scottish scholars knew, suffered such catastrophic and even avoidable depredations at the hands of hostile powers in past centuries. As Keeper of the Museum, he presided over collections of prehistoric and historic material which had grown rapidly in the course of the 19th century, and which he and others such as Daniel Wilson (1816–1892) had been systematically arranging and classifying.

In these circumstances of accumulation and definition, Anderson and his colleagues were keenly aware of the constructive efforts of Scandinavian scholars since the late eighteenth century to locate, conserve and evaluate their prehistoric and historic records. As early as 1787, the Icelandic scholar, Grímur Thorkelin, befriended by the Society of Antiquaries of

Scotland and elected a member in 1783, had visited Scotland to research the remains of Viking settlement. In their reiteration of patriotic purpose, Scottish antiquarians used the example of Scandinavia where, in Denmark for example, the collection and preservation of antiquities was a concern of the state rather than merely of private bodies. This then was a plea for increased public awareness of and support for the role of a national museum in Scotland and the Society of Antiquaries of Scotland as its parent body. Nevertheless, Anderson offered a challenging concept, not only in his appeal to patriotic purpose, but also for a potential exclusivity and central role for objects as historical evidence.

In the development of historical studies, at least in the English-speaking world, there had rarely been any serious consideration of objects as evidence. Even in medieval studies, where conventional sources were notoriously uneven, fragmentary or absent, material culture had been largely ignored and clearly had never been part of the British historiographical tradition. In contrast, continental historians were more wide-ranging in their use of evidence. For example, French historians enthusiastically embraced quantitative methods and the emerging social sciences. Co-operative and interdisciplinary research became a hallmark of the *Annales* school in the early 20th century, and the historian Marc Bloch developed historical synthesis effectively in his studies of feudal society and of medieval village communities. Even in times of methodological change, such as the Rankean revolution in research techniques, and when economic and social models supplanted political and constitutional theories and heroic interpretation, material culture might have been, but rarely was, thrown into focus by such paradigm shifts.

Significantly, when Scotland could boast of a broad school of history under the tutelage of Enlightenment scholars, historians such as William Robertson (1721–1793) threw the net wide in their survey of source material and set new standards in scholarly technique. But the latter provides a telling note which gives an insight into contemporary attitudes, which was that material culture belonged to the antiquarians and should be considered as the antithesis of conventional record evidence. In his *History of Scotland* (1759), he structured Scotland's past in four periods and dismissed the early period of Scottish history as '...the reign of pure fable and conjecture, and ought to be totally neglected, or abandoned to the industry and credulity of antiquarians.'

A museum exists for the collections housed in it; and investigating and evaluating material culture is a primary purpose of museums and is perceived as an important and legitimate activity. There is therefore an *a priori* assumption in museums that objects constitute evidence and in effect the primary sources in the respective fields of study. To offer and provide a safe repository for objects is the corollary of collecting, constraints on such purpose being prompted by collecting policies and the collecting activities of other museums, national or local, areas of activity for which there exist professional guidelines on the 'ethics and practicalities of acquisition'. Acquisition policy will also be shaped by the processes of explanation and interpretation pursued by a museum, which in turn will influence how collections are organised and recorded, and such practices normally form the parameters within which objects are considered as evidence.

The success of a museum or gallery may be measured in terms of accumulation, and such obvious performance indicators are as old as museums themselves. Historically, with the accumulation of relics and treasure, this would reflect status-building activity or be more discriminating as in the 'cabinets of curiosities' of Renaissance scholars. Observation and collection of facts was part of the new learning of the Renaissance with the exploration of the natural world and discovery of the New World. The investigation of natural history and geography, human history and antiquities began to supply detailed insights into material culture. Sir Robert Sibbald, natural scientist and polymath, was a Scottish example of the scholar who assembled information and observed facts to form an absolute and constant corpus of knowledge; Aristotelian classifications allowed 'curiosities' to confirm or depart from a preconceived order and taxonomies.

Though there were likely shortcomings, an orderly accumulation of material supplied information and evidence in an epistemology belonging most obviously to the sciences. Antiquarian interest in the 18th century had tended to depart from this epistemology, an intellectual state which was ultimately caricatured by Scott in his novel of 1816, *The Antiquary*. Scott constructs his satire on dilettante and eccentric individual behaviour and it may be unfair to impute the characteristics of Jonathan Oldbuck esquire of Monkbarns to the corporate persona of the recently founded Society of Antiquaries of Scotland. Though methodology took time to develop and began to adopt scholarly disciplines from England and Scandinavia, history and the study of the past was still a social activity. When it came into being at the end of the year 1780, the new Society drew inspiration and example from the London Society of Antiquaries and the first published volume of its learned papers in 1792 reflects the varied and ambitious projects that were being pursued. The founding father and first vice *praeses*, the quixotic David Erskine, Earl of Buchan, was clear about the aims of the Society and its patriotic purpose; he wished to encourage a wide range of activities and antiquarian enquiry in the pursuit of the archaeological and historic record of Scotland.

Though object collection was not at first seen as the only or even necessary purpose of the Society of Antiquaries, a museum devoted to the national history could conserve and record all that was perceived as contributing to the distinctive identity of Scotland. Buchan's attitude is exemplified by his own contribution to the Society's published transactions, *Archaeologia Scotica*, and was the outcome of a plan to survey all the parishes of Scotland, first formulated by Buchan as early as 1761 and prefiguring the Statistical Account of Scotland later instigated and carried through by Sir John Sinclair. If any single influence persuaded the new Society of Antiquaries to embark on a systematic acquisition of objects, apart from the more obvious acquisitive predilections of its members, it was likely to have been the investigation of 'northern antiquities' which touched Scotland and Edinburgh in the late 18th century. Antiquarian studies were comparatively well advanced in Denmark (particularly with the national collections in Copenhagen), Sweden, Norway and Iceland and scholarly and fieldwork visits of northern scholars in those years, following in the footsteps of Thorkelin, showed the relevance and importance of their work to early Scottish history.

The accumulation of collections and a museum in which to house them were, as Buchan believed, of first importance for the new Society and the first recorded accession was a collection of 53 pieces of broken up bronze weapons and scrap dredged from Duddingston Loch, Edinburgh, almost all still extant in the National Museums today. Buchan in developing the concept of objects as evidence cited the examples of earlier (17th-century) collections, those of Dr Andrew Balfour and Sir Robert Sibbald, which had been bequeathed to Edinburgh University, but were later dispersed because of neglect and lack of curatorship. A property acquired in Edinburgh in 1781 was intended to provide a home for objects as well as proper meeting-rooms for the Society, Buchan himself bearing most of the cost.

Museum collections are built up through a process that is *sui generis* and, within the terms of contemporary circumstances, methodical and rational. The material culture collections now displayed in the new Museum of Scotland, while including many of the earliest acquisitions of the Society of Antiquaries of Scotland, do not give a true picture of the collecting activities of the Scottish antiquarians. Scottish prehistoric material was clearly a priority, but foreign prehistoric and ethnographic material was collected in quantities as a natural concomitant to activity in the widening sphere of the empire. Subsequently, large amounts of objects have been transferred to other museums in bids to rationalise the collections, not least to bring them more into line with the patriotic purpose of completing the record of Scotland's past. Though termed a museum of 'antiquities', it is important to recall that this concept was more widely interpreted; from the earliest days of the society, 'modern' or contemporary material was also collected. Some of this included natural history specimens that were also considered as curiosities, for example an unusually shaped branch of Scots fir and the 16ft long jawbone of a whale. Other objects were collected for insights that they might give into historic or prehistoric societies and also in the prevailing spirit that times were changing and that the familiar would soon be an irretrievable thing of the past.

This prefigured the beginnings of a more philosophically devised plan, formulated by Dr (later Sir) Arthur Mitchell (1826–1909), to collect comparative ethnological material, then disregarded and overlooked, within Scotland itself in order to throw light on prehistoric material and techniques. In essence, this process characterised objects as a new form of evidence – the survival of 'the past in the present' – and related to the contemporary Darwinian debate on theories of evolution and concepts of progress. From the 1860s Mitchell began to add a new stratum of material, what he called the 'neo-archaic', to the archaeological collections of the Museum of Antiquities. In his travels as a government commissioner, he observed and collected pottery, ploughs, spades, looms, querns and cruisie lamps which had been recently made and whose manufacture could still be observed and were still in use though apparently prehistoric.

The process of collecting is shaped by the purpose and constitution of the institution itself: for example, whether the museum is primarily an archaeological or a history museum, whether there is a distinction maintained between history or social history and the fine and applied arts. The different criteria may produce the exhibition paradox of the visually attractive or aesthetically pleasing, but ultimately trivial versus the mundane and visually unappealing but historically significant.

The origins of a museum are of course highly significant. Many public museums have evolved from private collections and Glasgow's Burrell Collection is an obvious case in point. The impetus that has created what is undoubtedly a remarkable museum was no more or less than the considerable resources and strongly marked tastes of Sir William Burrell. The assembling of objects for taxonomic or other scientific purposes and the construction of an epistemological base are criteria that may be low on the agenda or absent in a dynamic driven by fashion and conspicuous consumption. Such collections of course usually supply matchless evidence in the wider schemes of scholarship and are generally very familiar to the competent curator who naturally includes in his calculations of the evidence supplied by the object record the self-evident fruits of private patronage.

The scholarly and curatorial responsibilities of local and national museums are generally distinct. In considering the potential of objects as evidence, the sum total of material culture held in museums and galleries in Scotland for the benefit of her people would take account of all such repositories wherever they are in city, burgh or countryside. It is clear that outstanding and important collections of materials such as ceramics, glass, furniture, woodwork, tools and implements, quite apart from extensive archaeological collections exist in abundance in other, non-national, museums in Scotland.

The potential of knowledge maximisation and data capture from such widespread known deposits might be imagined to be an endeavour which has only recently been realised with electronic cataloguing. Awareness of this and serious consideration of its potential was a by-product of Joseph Anderson's period of office and of the patriotic purpose of his stewardship. In 1887, the Society of Antiquaries was made the beneficiary of a monetary gift 'to help experts to visit other Museums, Collections, or Materials of Archaeological Science at home or abroad, for purposes of special investigation or research'. This gift was in line with the example set by some Continental museums which had as a consequence published some remarkable monographs prepared by young scholars who had been given the opportunity to travel widely and to gain international perspectives of their own material culture. Typically at the time, the most successful of these scholars came from Denmark, Sweden and Norway.

The Society of Antiquaries inaugurated their grant-aided travel scheme by sending Anderson and his Assistant Keeper, George Black, to inspect and report on the condition and contents of the archaeological and ethnographical sections of local museums in Scotland. They visited 32 local and university museums and a detailed report subsequently filled about 90 pages of the *Proceedings of the Society of Antiquaries of Scotland.* Their observations on these local collections were illuminating and they recorded a considerable amount of information apparently unknown even to the custodians themselves of these collections. Dr Anderson in particular was unequivocal in his comments on such sins of omission as failing to localise and provenance finds, and delivered the odd rebuke. For example, in Perth, besides the prehistoric collections, he noticed '…a good old Scotch candlestick and a taper-holder misnamed a pair of snuffers'.

Anderson and Black were critical, not surprisingly perhaps, of local museums and their comments suggest a large measure of disappointment. They found the archaeological collections poor and fragmentary, and it was evident that none of the collections was adequately representative of the archaeology of its respective district or of Scotland as a whole. They continued:

> In point of fact, the case may be even more strongly and yet truthfully stated. If the National Museum were non-existent, and if all the contents of all the local Museums (so far as these contents are known to be Scottish) were brought together, they would fail to

furnish the materials for a systematic archaeology of Scotland as we now know it. To take a striking instance. In the Museum at Forres, which is the nearest to the Culbin Sands, I found that extraordinarily rich locality represented by a dozen arrow-heads; while the result of the systematic effort made by the Society of Antiquaries of Scotland to ascertain the capabilities of the Culbin Sands as an archaeological index, has been the accumulation in the National Museum of upwards of 15,000 specimens, chiefly of Flint and Stone Implements; while from another sandy district in the south of Scotland, which is scarcely represented in any local museum, we have amassed about 10,000 specimens.

His comments were, in spite of such strictures, generally brief and to the point; of a piece inspected in the Hunterian Museum, for example, he wrote:

A beautiful bowl of Samian ware, perfect, found 7th October 1876, in an excavation in the Flesher's Haugh, in Glasgow Green. This is the finest specimen of Samian ware known to have been found in Scotland.

Other curious details emerge such as the enormous wealth of imported exotica and ethnographical material, reflecting the extent to which Scots had travelled from all parts of the country to all corners of the globe and in the spirit of enlightenment had bequeathed their personal relics and spoils of empire for the benefit of their fellow countrymen. Another curiosity is that nearly every museum collection inspected possessed a pair of *rivelins* from Shetland, these being a type of homemade laced shoe of rawhide. The authors marched on without fear or favour:

The principal defects of local museums are (1) that they are not sufficiently local in character, and (2) that they have not been systematic in the formation of their collections. They have not made it their business to tell any particular story from beginning to end, either of science, or history, or locality, and the fragmentary stories they do try to tell are so incompletely and unsystematically set forth, that they are unintelligible to the public.

What may have been prominently in the authors' minds' eye, for example, was the collection displayed in the Burns' Museum, Kilmarnock:

The Museum is fortunate in possessing the valuable collection of archaeological relics found during the excavation of the Crannog at Lochlee. It must be mentioned, however, that the Managers of the

Museum seem to be unaware of the importance of these objects, with the result that they are piled on the shelves, or laid in the cases in a way that renders them neither instructive to the student of archaeology nor attractive to the general public.

Predictably, there was a collection of Burns' relics, consisting principally of a library of about 600 volumes, and then, enigmatically, an ethnographic selection from Zululand including such obvious rarities as 'beads of blue and white worn by Cetawayo's wife'. Anderson's report illustrates how well-developed the concept of objects as evidence already was, how this was perceived as an indicator of national, regional and local significance, and how these concepts were part of the mental furniture of the curators of the National Museum and being consciously, if exceptionally, fostered by them.

It is clear from the foregoing that the keepers of the national collections regarded object collections as part and parcel of the documentation of a fragmentary record of a fragmented past. As experience shows, the assembling, presentation and stewardship of museum collections is essentially a practical exercise and documentation and research is often inevitably a secondary (and luxury) option for the curator. This process is itself an unpredictable one in spite of established and accepted methodologies.

The ways in which a curator engages with his material is often highly subjective, the opportunity for in-depth research being unevenly available in circumstances where purposes of exhibition and audit generally take precedence over academic investigation. Predictable shortcomings in assessment however prompt reassessment, a process that must be applauded. The collections of the National Museums of Scotland readily demonstrate such potential and the reassessment implicit in the organisation of the collections for display in the Museum of Scotland has thrown up many topics in which objects offer unusual and new perspectives in the evaluation of evidence. The briefest selection is offered here, almost to tease or challenge the scholarly mind that further reassessment is possible and desirable, that the validity and effectiveness of objects as evidence can be further tested, and that conventional historical sources could usefully take account of material culture in their analysis and interpretation of the past.

In the prevailing atmosphere of national self-examination and debate over Scottish identity, the Museums' collections of Highland dress and tartan offer extraordinary opportunities to come to grips with the topic of the creation or misappropriation of imagery and identity; using the evidence of material culture, it rapidly becomes apparent that the 'invention of tradition' thesis cannot be applied to 19th-century Scotland without substantial riders and qualifications. The paradigm of the 17th century as cultural desert which has always been the traditional pabulum of historical texts and teaching might be readily challenged by the impressions and message conveyed by the 'New Horizons' Gallery in the Museum of Scotland. This was the violent age of the Thirty Years War and the English Civil War, the destructive collision of old church with new state, the emergence of institutionalised brutality on a vast scale (which incidentally is also addressed in the Museum of Scotland), and the practice and European-wide acceptance that the individual should be instantly despatched for their beliefs and in the name of the Christian religion. Few crave murder as a career and the paradox is available in the material culture of the 17th century which more obviously prefigures the Enlightenment than betrays that Scotland might ever have been a race of bigoted thugs. In surveying his own handiwork, the earl of Strathmore mused in 1684:

> Who can delight to live in his house as in a prison?…Such houses truly are worn quyt out of fashione, as feuds are,…the cuntrie being generally more civilised than it was.

The earlier eras of the Renaissance and Reformation similarly offer challenges to conventional teaching and even hint that a single graphic of Scottish material culture might offer as much as several chapters of closely argued prose. The mass of Reformation silver plate and carved and painted woodwork of the late 16th and 17th centuries belie the notion that Scotland after John Knox was a bleak Calvinistic theocratic wilderness. Earlier carved woodwork on display suggests that there are important and specific messages evident in Scottish traditions of Renaissance decorative art.

The 'Montrose Panels' for example represent sections of oak wall panelling and a door, richly carved in Renaissance styles, possibly from the hall of a hospital founded in Montrose by Abbot Patrick Paniter. Conventional styles of decoration with patterns of thistles and roses, vines and grapes, oak leaves and acorns suggest distinctively Scottish Renaissance carving, characteristic perhaps of an east-coast port open to Continental styles and workmanship yet working within its own traditions.

Particularly noteworthy are two panels each showing a pair of foxes dressed as friars; one panel shows the pair walking in procession, each holding a staff, and the other shows them holding up a goose between them while their staffs are crossed in front of them saltire-wise. This appears as vivid, dimensional satire on the proverbially unpopular mendicant orders of medieval Europe, recalled vividly in Sir David

Lindsay's *Ane Satyre of the Thrie Estaitis* in which the Vices of Flattery, Falsehood and Deceit masquerade in the habits of friars as Devotion, Sapience and Discretion. It is known that the Dominicans or Black Friars were also referred to in a medieval Latin pun as *Domini canes* or 'dogs of the Lord'. If this then can be interpreted as the Scottish version of the joke, surely the woodcarvings throw significant light on the attitude of the founder of the revived house of Friars Preachers in Montrose, Parick Paniter himself, under a Writ from James V in 1516. Additionally it has always seemed part of the Scottish 'democratic intellect' to reconcile irreconcilables, the sacred with the profane, the solemn with the riotous, the sublime with the ridiculous.

Examples can be multiplied but two will suffice. The richly carved Beaton Panels, possibly from premises of Arbroath Abbey, show the Royal Arms and thistle and rose symbols representing James IV and Margaret Tudor. The 'marriage of the thistle and the rose' was a popular contemporary metaphor, used for example by William Dunbar in his 'The Thrissel and the Rois' and it is refreshing to learn how the contemporary Renaissance (and poetic) eye might visualise natural objects and transform them into icons in an age which set great store by visual images.

A more homely and human view of contemporary society is offered in the carved oak panels from Greenlaw, Kirkcudbrightshire, showing a pageant of figures including men-at-arms, acrobats and musicians. Assuming a unity in this figurative carving, we may have a unique depiction of a phenomenon of great social and cultural significance, the itinerant bardic and minstrel band, customarily performing in court, castle and burgh and labelled, often pejoratively, as *Joculatores* in medieval Latin and delightfully as 'Jockies' in the vernacular.

The claim can be made that objects as collected and displayed in a museum – in the Museum of Scotland for example – are both valid and essential historical evidence. They may be considered as evidence per se, and also as a measure of the range, quality and diversity of Scotland's material culture. Objects also, as we have suggested with a limited number of examples which might be liberally expanded in Scottish history, are often the unrealised potential for a challenge to a thesis or historical perspective. Scotland's experience might be regarded as noteworthy in that through the creation of the National Museum of Antiquities and the vigour and views of the Society of Antiquaries in the late 18th century, a Scottish dialectic may be identified, that is, in a rationalisation of the accumulation of national collections for patriotic purposes.

This expression of patriotism supplied an ideological imperative which in Scotland's case was grafted onto evolving museological practice such as scientific method, taxonomy, comparative ethnology and other methodological trends observable in the 19th century. It finds definition and direction for example in Sir Daniel Wilson's *Archaeology and Prehistoric Annals of Scotland* of 1851, where it was stressed that the Museum was to be a focus of patriotic interest and feeling. The success of this is questionable in circumstances of persistent underfunding and lack of support for the concept of a new home for the national collections until the building of the Museum of Scotland in the 1990s.

Assuming that we can sustain an argument for a Scottish dialectic, we may assume that any such patriotic feeling was distinctive and arose from a particular sense of identity. What is now considered a strong sense of national identity among Scots has history as a strong component; at the simplest level, there is an implicit belief in the antiquity and continuity of Scottish nationhood. Following research and revisionism and new and vigorous directions in Scottish historical studies, there has in recent years been a more lively and self-conscious pursuit of the concept of Scottish identity and the new Museum of Scotland has consciously addressed this issue, though not in assertive or polemical mode.

It must be the duty of a 'museum of Scotland' to supply balanced information for the 'Scottish identity' construct while, arguably, not necessarily being the creator or begetter of identity. This avoids topical issues such as the perceptible politicisation of museum collections in the late 20th century, and begs the question whether the National Museum was creator or begetter of national identity in the past. From the words and actions of past antiquaries, it is suggested that the National Museum saw itself as custodian rather than architect or creator of national identity, and that the pursuit of patriotic purpose effectively fell short of begetting national identity.

The imagery of national identity, retailed in populist rather than museum sources, or the stigma of its misappropriation has gone far to satisfy cravings and, whatever its virtues, Scotland's material culture has been too long omitted from the dialectic. A potential for objects as evidence in patriotic discourse may never be fully realised, in spite of the Museum of Scotland, while, more typically, we engage with the issues of living in Scotland secure in the knowledge of where we have come from and who our ancestors are. The sight and sound of Scotland always inspire an instinctive recognition and we readily identify with the words of one of the most famous of international medieval schoolmen, John Major or Mair (1469–1550), when he wrote from Paris in the nostalgia of self-imposed exile:

> Our native soil attracts us with a secret and inexpressible sweetness and does not permit us to forget it.

The Author

Hugh Cheape is curator of Modern Scottish Collections in the National Museums of Scotland. He joined the National Museum of Antiquities of Scotland in 1974 after Edinburgh University and worked in the Country Life Section until transferring to work in the applied and decorative arts in 1982. He has been closely involved in the establishment of the Angus Folk Museum, the Scottish Agricultural Museum, the Museum of Piping and, since 1989, the Museum of Scotland. He has worked on 35 exhibitions both at home and abroad and has published widely. He is author of *Tartan:: The Highland Habit*, 1991, second edition 1995, and *The Book of the Bagpipe*, 1999, and co-author of *Periods in Highland History* (with the late I F Grant), 1987, paperback 1997, and *Witness to Rebellion* (with Iain G Brown), 1996. He is editor of *Tools & Traditions: Studies in European Ethnology presented to Alexander Fenton*, 1993 and *'A Very Civil People': Folk, History, Literature and Language in the Hebrides* (forthcoming).

References

Anderson, J., *Scotland in Early Christian Times*, Edinburgh: David Douglas 1881

Anderson, J., and Black, G.F., Reports on Local Museums in Scotland, in *Proceedings of the Society of Antiquaries of Scotland* Vol, 22 (1887–8), pp. 331-422.

Anderson, M.L. (ed), *The James Carmichael Collection of Proverbs in Scots*, Edinburgh University Press, 1957.

Archaeologia Scotica. Transactions of the Society of Antiquaries of Scotland, Vol I, Edinburgh, 1792.

Bell, A.S. (ed), *The Scottish Antiquarian Tradition*, Edinburgh: John Donald 1981

Bloch, M., *Feudal Society*, 2 vols, second edition, London, 1967.

Caldwell, D. (ed.), *Angels, Nobles & Unicorns. Art and Patronage in Medieval Scotland*, National Museum of Antiquities of Scotland, 1982.

Catalogue of the National Museum of Antiquities of Scotland, Edinburgh, 1892.

Cheape, H., *Tartan. The Highland Habit*, second edition, National Museums of Scotland, 1995.

Constable, A. (ed), *A History of Greater Britain by John Major, 1521*, Edinburgh: Scottish History Society, 1892.

Cowan, I.B., and Easson, D.E., *Medieval Religious Houses. Scotland*, second edition, London, 1976.

Ferguson, W., *The Identity of the Scottish Nation*, Edinburgh University Press, 1998.

Mackay Mackenzie, W. (ed), *The Poems of William Dunbar*, Edinburgh, 1932.

Maxwell, S., 'Carved Oak Panels formerly at Greenlaw, Kirkcudbrightshire', in *Proceedings of the Society of Antiquaries of Scotland,* Vol 82 (1947–8), pp. 290–292.

Millar, A.H. (ed), *The Glamis Book of Record,* Edinburgh: Scottish History Society, 1890.

Mitchell, A., *The Past in the Present. What is Civilisation?,* Edinburgh, 1880.

Robertson, W., *History of Scotland during the Reigns of Mary and James VI,* London, 1759.

Wilson, D, *The Archaeology and Prehistoric Annals of Scotland,* Edinburgh and London, 1851.

Joseph Anderson (1832–1916), Keeper of the National Museum of Antiquities of Scotland from 1869 to 1913, whose writings articulated how he saw the Museum as an agent in shaping cultural identity. Oil on canvas by Henry Wright Kerr.

George Fraser Black, Assistant Keeper, examining a bronze spearhead in the Museum of Antiquities' collections in 1890, shortly before their move to the new building in Queen Street. The display reflects the efforts of the Museum in collecting, classifying and arranging the Scottish material record.

A corner of the displays in Edinburgh's Royal Institution at the Mound in 1890, showing the density of material both from Scotland and overseas, often collected too indiscriminately by the early antiquarians.

7

BUILDING COLLECTIONS
Constraints of Changing Contexts

David Clarke

The Scottish collections of the National Museums have been assembled over more than two centuries. In that time the ambitions of those undertaking the collection have varied considerably, as indeed have the purposes for which the task was pursued. These variations are my subject here: or more accurately, those played out in the last century or so, but even this will be more a series of images than a fully worked out fugue. My comments are rather heavily biased towards the issues that might in the broadest sense be thought to relate to archaeological collections. It is, of course, the area that I know best, and it helps to provide some sort of focus for my observations. But archaeological collections were the dominant concern of most of those collecting Scottish material until after the Second World War. However, before we venture into word pictures of aspiration and intent, it is worthwhile to spend a few moments considering what exactly we understand by the term 'Scottish collections' and some of the implications that arise from that understanding.

At first sight, the idea of the Scottish collections seems so straightforward as to merit no serious discussion. And, I suppose, if one concentrates on using a simple geographical description as the basis for defining the subject matter that is largely true. But even this approach is not problem free. Can we, for instance, necessarily assume that an area of land defined by relatively recent nationalist perceptions has validity for our understanding of the more distant human past? Perhaps such an approach might even obscure rather than enlighten the situation. The problems posed are increased by an order of magnitude when one tries to use what we might describe as a national geographical approach as an explanatory base for geological and natural history events before the arrival of human groups.

Particularly good examples of the difficulties that can arise are found in eastern Europe. Two groups of the 5th millennium BC have been recognised in areas adjacent to the Danube where it forms the border between Bulgaria and Romania.[1] On one side, in Bulgaria, we have the Karanovo complex and on the other, in Romania, the Gulmenitsa group. But few looking at these two groups without the distortion of the spectacles of nationalism can detect any meaningful difference between them. Alas, this particular prehistoric group did not understand that living on both banks of a particularly significant river like the Danube would mean that their integrity as a group had to be sacrificed to defend 20th-century perceptions of group identity. But before we slide into an unvoiced sense of western European superiority we might consider the late Ruadhiri de Valera's determined attempts to maintain separate groups of Neolithic tombs in northern Ireland and south-western Scotland.[2,3] Perhaps with a name like de Valera it would be too much to expect that he could embrace an acceptance of close links between Britain and Ireland even in prehistory. Defended differences in prehistory often provide clear justifications for today's attitudes.

Yet even now the mind-set in Britain and Ireland is still very much one that sees the North Channel as a boundary or an edge, rather than as a main street with essentially the same community living on either side of it. This is not the place to argue about what patterns might be discernible with different perceptual starting points. Nor am I suggesting that our current interpretations are necessarily incorrect. I raise these matters only to make the point that collecting and interpreting within a national framework helps to predetermine to some extent the patterns we are likely to observe and makes the recognition of others more difficult.

But collection cannot usually be undertaken without more parameters being invoked than just geographical area. The most common additions are to say that the Scottish collections represent items made or used in Scotland. But this is not without its problems. Is a knife, made and used in Scotland but taken to Canada when its owner emigrated there, an object that should be in our Scottish collections or in Canada's national collections? Usually, the key element is geographical location at the moment of collection, so that the knife I have just mentioned would normally be regarded as a Canadian object rather than a Scottish one.

Even this approach is not necessarily applied in the case of exotic material. A Roman bronze pan discovered in circumstances comparable to the one found in Dowalton Loch[4] would undoubtedly be treated as a Scottish object, whereas a painting by Canaletto long in a private Scottish collection might well not be, should it become available for collection. This might well be the case, even though the pan was made in Italy and perhaps used there and elsewhere in the Roman Empire, before passing into the hands of the individual who deposited it in Dowalton Loch. Indeed, the pan might have been used in Scotland for only a very short time, whereas a painting might have remained in use for a couple of centuries following its acquisition by Scottish owners.

A fine example of the way Scottish and non-Scottish considerations intermesh in the case of relatively recent objects is provided by the terracotta sculpture of Hercules and Antaeus made by Stefano Maderno in Rome in 1620 (Evans 1990, to whom the author is grateful for information about this sculpture).[5] The piece is described by Sir John Clerk in the mid-18th century as 'A fine statue of Hercules and Antaeus in clay being a model by Michael Angelo..., brought from Italy by my son James. A most curious figure'. The attribution is a curious piece of wishful thinking when the piece is inscribed with the name of the artist and the date.

Sir John was one of the first Scots to undertake the Grand Tour and his son, James Clerk, was in Italy following in his footsteps between 1733 and 1736. It is unclear whether he sent the piece ahead or brought it with him when he returned from the University of Leiden in October 1739. Which ever is the case, the piece had been in the ownership of the Clerk family for almost 250 years when the National Museums of Scotland acquired it in 1981. Its acquisition was as an outstanding piece of Italian Baroque sculpture and as a documented piece collected by a Scot on the Grand Tour. The balance of emphasis though has been towards it as a piece of sculpture so that it is currently displayed in our 'European Art 1200–1800' gallery. In other words, different criteria are used to define whether an object is considered Scottish and how important that attribution of Scottishness is relative to other considerations in the museum's fields of interest.

In the case of archaeological objects the situation appears to be the most straightforward. The act of deposition within the geographical area of Scotland makes an object liable to be claimed as Treasure Trove.[6] Such a claim means that the object is regarded as being Scottish and having importance for the nation. Of course, this apparent reliance solely on the fact that the object is buried in the ground, rooted as it is in legal considerations, runs contrary to current archaeological thinking. This sees objects as having individual histories in which function and role varies through time and the acts of deposition and recovery are not necessarily the most significant features in an object's history.

What is equally interesting is the way that this simple concern with the object having been buried in the ground is in actuality overlain by other considerations. To be claimed as Treasure Trove, an object has in practice to be from Europe or a country bordering the Mediterranean. A

Polynesian stone axe found on the shores of a Scottish loch, or Zulu iron spearheads found close to a Roman fort would not, and were not, claimed as Treasure Trove. Nor was a recently reported discovery of an iron spearhead near Auchtermuchty. It has been identified as a product of the Ngombe people living in the People's Republic of Congo, and it seems to be about one hundred years old. Some of my more radical colleagues would see this as overt discrimination, maintaining Scotland's established origin stories firmly rooted in western European traditions, but seeking to avoid recognising one of the less welcome sides of British imperialism. Certainly, there appear to be limits on the level of exotic objects which are acceptable as fundamentally important in Scotland's story.

But at the other end of this spectrum of criteria are financial considerations. This is, at least in its present form, a relatively new phenomenon. It arises from the fact that finders of objects declared Treasure Trove are rewarded with payments representing the full market value of the object. Now we do not have to be concerned here with how these values are determined or whether full market value is an appropriate level of reward for what is often a piece of happenstance. The key point is that the reward has to be provided by the museum to which the object is allocated. This reward system has generally worked well in the past, although the difficulties that might arise from the discovery of another Hunterston Brooch, Monymusk Reliquary or a treasure like that found at Derrynaflan in Ireland are hard to imagine.[7]

Nevertheless, it is not the really big rewards that have so far produced the problem. Following a recent sale of a carved stone ball, the market value of these quintessential Scottish items has now to be measured in the low thousands whereas previously, without saleroom evidence to the contrary, valuations had been in the low hundreds. Perhaps as a result of these increased values carved stone balls have recently begun to roll off the mantelpieces of north-east Scottish farmhouses into the Treasure Trove system. In so doing, they have exposed a serious weakness in what is generally regarded as the best antiquities system in Britain. Despite the fact that carved stone balls are by any criteria an exclusively Scottish type, no museum is prepared to devote scarce resources to enlarging their collection of them. The problem is that they are uncommon but not rare, and the valuations placed upon them, though not large by art standards, are too high for something only judged to be uncommon. Their return to the private domain and dispersal through auction sales, possibly in the United States, means that some knowledge of Scotland's past will become temporarily, perhaps permanently, lost to those studying that past.

Yet a further perspective on the variability of treatment for Scottish material in the Treasure Trove system is provided by coins. Such finds, particularly when found as hoards, are one of the normative definitions of treasure. But the way they are usually treated as Treasure Trove differs from every other type of object because it introduces the concept of the duplicate. This is not something that regularly figures in Treasure Trove thinking because the system essentially deals with objects dating from before industrialisation or which have certainly not been the product of that process. Numismatics curiously transports the idea back into pre-industrial times and is able to do so by regarding collection as solely for the purposes of academic research on coin types. If the type is already in the collections it need only be noted for the purposes of recording the contents of the hoard and then returned to the finder to do as he will with it. Only if it is not in the collections will a numismatist recommend its acquisition. This is not an approach which is applied to any other kind of material found in hoards.

One might expect that prehistory and early history and their collection systems might be the least burdened with ambiguities of what Scottish meant and what should be collected. Unfortunately, the situation does not align with these expectations. Nor can it be said that attitudes towards collecting are well integrated with the academic approaches used to study the objects.

In these circumstances it will surely come as no surprise that the problems of definition and the achievement of consistency of approach become ever more difficult the nearer one comes to the present. It may perhaps seem paradoxical to suggest that collecting Scotland's present or recent past is the most difficult task facing its museum community, but that is certainly the case. Nobody has yet set out a coherent agenda for collecting the 20th century in fields other than art. We are aware of the wealth of opportunities, but what form will a comprehensive Scottish collection for the last century or century and a half take? Made here or used in Scotland provides little guidance. The levels of materialism, largely without the limitations imposed by survival through time, challenge the paradigms that have controlled our collecting attitudes for all previous periods.

It is hoped that I have offered enough comments to suggest that collections are not fixed entities. And the efforts of previous generations and their beliefs about what it was appropriate to collect place limitations on the interpretations we can attempt now. Every generation has sought, largely unconsciously, to create their own version of the Scottish collections. None succeeds because of the straightjackets fashioned by their predecessors. But the attempts to achieve success, are what have given the national collections the quality that they now have. In turning now to the aspirations that have motivated collecting through the last century or so, it is important to realise that collection and access have always been different sides of the same coin.

In exploring the issues my main interest will be with the Scottish collections in the 20th century. Of course, the early decades of the century were no more than a continuation of 19th-century attitudes. It was not, Stuart Piggott felt, until after the Second World War that thinking about the Scottish collections emerged, to use an image from that war, from its Anderson Shelter.[8]

But the phrase could with equal force, as Piggott well knew, apply to the influence of Joseph Anderson. Anderson was Keeper of the National Museum of Antiquities from 1869 until 1913. His expertise embraced most of Scotland's prehistoric and historic material culture. Early in his Keepership, Anderson gave four seminal series of Rhind Lectures, subsequently published as pairs of volumes under the titles Scotland in Early Christian Times and Scotland in Pagan Times. His views fill over 1200 pages and at the end of it all he says:[9]

> ...it may have become evident to those who have followed the whole of the four courses of these Lectures, that, taken together they are parts of one continuous demonstration, the outcome of which is that Scotland has an Archaeology – disclosing a succession of manifestations of culture and phases of civilisation peculiar to her own area; and that she must therefore of necessity create and maintain her own school of investigation.

Even by Victorian standards, these volumes cannot be described as popular works. And Anderson's conclusions reflect both his purpose in emphasising the individuality of Scotland's past, and the central role that academic research would play in fulfilling that purpose. Throughout his career, he published extensively on Scottish material culture. In these pieces he always used his remarkable knowledge of European finds to demonstrate that Scotland's individuality was not a product of backwardness, but due to its particular responses to wider issues.

But how was Scotland's own school of investigation to be created? Anderson opened his Rhind Lecture series with a lecture entitled: *The means of obtaining a scientific basis for the archaeology of Scotland.* This was to involve the 'exhaustive collection of materials' from which could be extracted 'the story of human progress on Scottish soil.' Certainly, collection had to be properly organised:[10]

> ...for it is obvious that if the observations by which comparison and induction are accumulated have not been scientifically made, the conclusions drawn from them can have no scientific value, and that the first necessity in every scientific enquiry is accurate observation, exhaustive in its range, and recorded with the requisite precision and fullness of detail.

This is a world committed to social evolutionary thought, with key words like progress, and key methods like induction. Once the information had been assembled, it could be subjected to a 'natural method' that is 'nearly akin to the scientific method.' Anderson goes on:[11]

> By following this natural method, and interrogating each of the implements separately as to its purpose, we find no difficulty in getting out all the edged-tools and arranging them in separate heaps, consisting of different types of tool – such as axes, chisels, gouges, saws, knives, and so forth – or types of weapons such as arrow-heads, spear-heads, daggers, and so on. During this process of getting out the edged-tools and arranging them by their typical forms, a singular fact will have disclosed itself. In the first of sorted heaps we shall have nothing but axes but we have axes in three materials – stone, bronze and iron. Every group has the same triple repetition of the tool in the same three materials. This, then, is the second problem – What is the meaning of the fabrication of the same tools in these three materials?

> The testimony of universal experience tells us that the less suitable and effective material is always supplanted in time by that which is more suitable and effective, after it has become generally procurable. The more unsuitable implement may maintain the struggle for existence for a longer or shorter period, according to circumstances; but when it comes to be a competition of materials, the law is, that the fittest shall survive, and the less fit dies out…

It is from this unity of function and typology that Anderson's sense of sequence comes. But equally it is not difficult to see that Anderson's wider purpose of demonstrating and detailing that sequence could only be achieved by the collection of everything. It is, said J Y Simpson:[12]

> …only by collecting, combining, and comparing all the individual instances of each antiquarian object…all ascertainable specimens, for example, of our Scotch stone celts and knives; all ascertainable specimens of our clay vessels; of our leaf-shaped swords; of our metallic armlets; of our grain-rubbers and stone querns, etc, etc; – and by tracing the history of similar objects in other allied countries, that we will read aright the tales which these relics – when once properly interrogated – are capable of telling us of the doings, the habits, and the thoughts of our distant predecessors.

There is no doubt that Anderson felt that the appropriate place for these all embracing collections was the National Museum. If it did not exist, he wrote, '…and if all the contents of all the local Museums (so far as these contents are known to be Scottish) were brought together, they would fail to furnish the materials for a systematic Archaeology of Scotland, as we now know it.' He cited the fact that the museum at Forres had only a dozen arrowheads from Culbin Sands, whereas the national collections held upwards of 15,000 specimens from the same area.[13] Nor was this an exceptional case. George Black noted in 1887 that 'few things of any Archaeological or Antiquarian value have been added since [the original donation of material in 1851]' to the Arbuthnot museum in Peterhead.[14]

I have spent some time discussing Anderson's approach because he is fundamentally important to 20th-century developments. Piggott felt that Scotland conferred secular canonisation upon him after the publication of his Rhind Lectures. That may be a little extreme, but Piggott's claim that 'his influence continued to loom large for decades after his death' is not.[15] Indeed, one wonders sometimes whether it is even now fully dissipated.

The problem was that those who controlled the collections in the National Museum of Antiquities after Anderson retired aged 81, Graham Callendar and Arthur Edwards, transformed his views into an isolationist position that saw Scotland as somehow separate from the rest of Europe. As Piggott notes, this view was not restricted to Scotland, but developed widespread currency in England.[16] Distribution maps stopped at the English border – a phenomenon not at all uncommon today. But these attitudes were not universal. Gordon Childe produced some radical interpretations of Scottish prehistory in the 1930s and 1940s.[17,18] And some Scandinavian scholars ventured to believe that Scotland might have relevance to areas other than itself. Grieg's survey of Viking material and Roussell's study of building techniques in the Scottish islands reinforced Childe's implicit message that Scotland could be integrated with northern Europe.[19,20] Yet those within the museum, controlling the collections, remained both hostile and sceptical. There the research agendas remained those articulated by Joseph Anderson in the late 19th century, although they were pursued by individuals without his flair or appreciation of the importance of the European dimension.

But it would be a mistake to see the situation as totally caught in a time-warp. Callander's lack of Anderson's vision and commitment to the development of the national collections through the acquisition of everything seems to have created in him a very fuzzy view of why he was collecting at all. I do not wish you to infer from this statement that Callander was not engaged in enlarging the Scottish collections, quite the contrary. But before his appointment as Director of the National Museum of Antiquities, he had been an active collector of Scottish material. Whether he continued to collect after becoming Director is unclear, but he certainly continued to hold material. The ambiguities involved in his attitudes are well illustrated by his handling of the material from the rich

Iron Age burial at Waulkmill, Tarland, Aberdeenshire discovered in 1898:[21]

> The relics were acquired by a policeman at Aboyne, but they were claimed and recovered by Mr J A Milne, proprietor of the estate..., who afterwards presented them to the National Museum [in 1905].

> Some years ago [Callander is here writing in 1915] I called on a policeman in central Aberdeenshire to see a very good collection of prehistoric antiquities which he had gathered together, chiefly from the Buchan, Garioch, and Deeside districts of Aberdeenshire. Amongst other things noted were a small cup of cast bronze [now interpreted as a model of a cauldron], the crown of a human molar tooth found in the cup, a disc of translucent blue glass broken in two, and twelve pebbles of brown, grey and whitish quartzite. The owner said that the glass disc was all that remained of a number of similar objects and other relics found in a sand-pit near Tarland, which were once in his possession but which he had been compelled to give up to the Laird; that he had kept the glass disc, it being broken, and that the cup, tooth, and pebbles had been found afterwards in the same sand-pit and he had secured them, their discovery having been kept secret. After the death of this man I bought the relics from his representatives, and they are exhibited to the Society to-night.

Accordingly, there is a curious sequence of events. The landowner gives what finds he can recover to the national collections in 1905. Somewhere in late 1909 or early 1910 Callander becomes one of the Society of Antiquaries' two honorary curators in the Museum. Quite when he visits the policeman is unclear, but his purchase of the material is likely to have been in late 1914 or early 1915, since he is by then Secretary of the Society and can presumably control the exhibition of material at their meetings. What is even more remarkable is that Callander subsequently gave the finds he had to the Marischal Museum in Aberdeen.

Nor was this in any way exceptional. Callendar appears not to have been interested in maintaining the integrity of assemblages or even in trying to ensure that all material from excavations was acquired. For instance, the material from Skara Brae was shared with the British Museum and perhaps other places, and the extensive assemblages from Erskine Beveridge's work on North Uist are clearly incomplete. Nothing demonstrates better than Treasure Trove the poverty of Callander's approach. Among the last objects claimed during Anderson's Keepership are a stone axehead and a stone pounder. Such objects never appear as Treasure Trove while Callendar was in control. Most of the material he claimed are coin hoards, with most of the coins returned to the finder, and objects of precious metal.

Of course, Anderson was the last Keeper who could expect to display everything in the collections. The 1892 catalogue, written to coincide with the move to Queen Street, was both a list of everything in the collections and a guide to the displays. Callander was probably the first to face the problem of a new phenomenon, the study collection. Certainly, it can be convincingly argued that Anderson's displays were a form of open storage. Neither the displays nor the catalogue offered much in the way of guidance to the uninitiated visitor. This was not necessarily considered a drawback by Anderson as he clearly regarded the museum as a research institute. This attitude was certainly maintained by Callander and Edwards. Not until Robert Stevenson took over, after the Second World War, were even the most tentative steps taken towards establishing displays that might have some meaning for the non-specialist. But this never got very far because Stevenson's principal aim was to get out of Queen Street altogether into a new building on the site at the end of Chambers Street now occupied by the Museum of Scotland. That project died in 1976, but it has always seemed to me that it was the beginning of the belief that a Museum of Scotland was both desirable and achievable.

However, Stevenson's contribution was much more fundamental. He was the person that began to bring Scottish artefact studies back from the self-congratulatory wilderness where Callander and Edwards had left it. Stevenson and his small staff, together with people like Childe and Piggott, began to re-integrate Scottish material with the wider European community. This was no easy task. Certainly, Piggott soon found Scottish topics far from congenial to work on because of residual attitudes among members of the academic community. Thirty years of isolation had created a sense of 'otherness' about Scottish material still with us today.

But it did not fall to this group to create the Museum of Scotland. Piggott, writing in 1983, summed up the dilemma of his generation saw as:

> All museums whether those specifically concerned with antiquities or with other collections in their care, face a common problem which has grown in intensity in recent years, the degree to which they can effect a satisfactory compromise between their services on the one hand to scholarship, and on the other hand to the instruction of the general public.

It is not a coincidence that Piggott places scholarship before 'instruction of the general public'. He went on to say that 'What makes the history of the National Museum of Antiquities of Scotland so interesting and unusual…is that it was by definition a museum dedicated primarily to research from the beginning, as an integral part of a learned body, the Society of Antiquaries of Scotland'.[22]

This world that Piggott describes was overturned in the amalgamations that led to the creation of the National Museums of Scotland in 1985. Perhaps, although no-one offered it as a serious comment at the time, it needed this break with a research tradition stretching back over 200 years to make today's Museum of Scotland possible. Only then could the relative positions of scholarship and the general public be transposed in importance.

The great legacy, of course, was not the approaches but the collections. Whilst in academic and intellectual terms one can criticise the maintenance of versions of late-19th century thinking, the desire to collect everything continued much longer than one might have expected. Realising the desire was often a very shaky affair in practice, but the national collections have retained a pre-eminence for most areas of Scotland's past other than perhaps recent times. Anderson's comments on the weaknesses of local museum collections remained as valid a century later as they were when he made them. All of this ensured that when the Museum of Scotland became a reality, collections sufficient to tell many stories already existed. And the result is that criticism when occurring has been directed at the absence of topics or individuals for which no artefacts exist, like William Wallace.

In the Museum of Scotland, it was always our intention that the collections should be dominant. Our topics were to be restricted to those that could be told with three-dimensional material culture and we happily sacrificed any claim that our story might seek to be comprehensive. Nor did we seek to impose a uniformity of approach to the presentation of Scotland's past. The quality and range of the surviving evidence and the interpretations that might reasonably be imposed upon it varied significantly through time. Although we have gone a long way towards removing that sense of 'otherness' hanging over Scottish material, it is not yet wholly eliminated. The absence of England is striking. Although perhaps not a balanced presentation of past realities, it reflects a welcome attempt to define Scottish identity in terms other than those of comparison with the bigger country next door.

Naturally, the building of a national history museum is expensive and that alone imposes restraints and limitations. The conceptual structures of major museums, like the Museum of Scotland, have to last for a generation even though we know that academic interpretations will not stand still for that length of time. The hope is, of course, that the structure will be flexible enough to accommodate change, but only time will tell. What we do know is that these restraints naturally encourage established, some might say conservative, solutions to the presentation of the collections.

What I have tried to suggest above is that the Scottish collections are outstanding because they were acquired not for communication but for research. And in a research ethos that endorsed the collection of everything, even if in practice that was not achieved. Forty years ago, Christopher Hawkes observed that the role of the old Department of British and Medieval Antiquities in the British Museum was from its foundation in 1886 'to collect antiquities of national importance and used the knowledge gained from them to guide...the public understanding of the country's...archaeology.'[23] The collectors of our national collections did not feel the least bit restricted to objects of national importance, although inevitably they collected them avidly. The creation of the Museum of Scotland has forced on us, certainly for the first time since Anderson, a comprehensive review of the collections now assembled over 200 years. The radical aspects of the project may well turn out to be, not the displays in the new museum, but the stimulus that it provides for the renewal and development of material culture studies in Scotland.

The Author

Dr David Clarke read archaeology at University College Cardiff and received his PhD from the University of Edinburgh. Having worked in the National Museum of Antiquities and at the National Museums of Scotland since 1968, he became Keeper of Archaeology in 1985 and was Head of Exhibitions for the Museum of Scotland Project 1992–98. A prolific writer, he was elected a Fellow of the Society of Antiquaries of Scotland in 1969 and of the Society of Antiquaries of London in 1981.

References

1. Bailey, D.W., 'Bulgarian archaeology: ideology, sociopolitics and the exotic', in Meskell, L (ed), *Archaeology under fire: Nationalism, politics and heritage in the eastern Mediterranean and Middle East*, London & New York, Routledge, 1998, p. 90.
2. de Valera, R., *The Court Cairns of Ireland*, Proc Roy Ir Acad, 60, 1959–60, 1960, pp. 9–140.
3. de Valera, R., *The 'Carlingford Culture': the long barrow and the Neolithic of Great Britain and Ireland*, Proc Prehist Soc, 27, 1961, pp. 234–52.
4. Curle, J., *An inventory of objects of Roman and provincial Roman origin found on sites in Scotland not definitely associated with Roman construction*, Proc Soc Antiq Scot, 66, 1931–32, 1932, pp. 277–397.

5. Evans, G., 'Italian Baroque sculpture', in *The Antique Collector*, 61, March 1990, pp. 71–77 (to whom the author is grateful for this information)
6. Carey Miller, D.L. & Sheridan, A., 'Treasure Trove', in *Scots Law, Art, Antiquity and Law*, 1(4), 1996, pp. 393–406.
7. Youngs, S. (ed), *'The work of angels', Masterpieces of Celtic metalwork, 6th–9th centuries AD*, London, British Museum Publishing, 1998.
8. Piggott, S., 'The National Museum of Antiquities and archaeological research', in O'Connor, A. & D V Clarke, D.V. (eds), *From the Stone Age to the 'Forty-Five: Studies presented to R.B.K. Stevenson*, Edinburgh, John Donald, 1983, p. 6.
9. Anderson, J., *Scotland in pagan times – the Bronze and Stone Ages: The Rhind Lectures in archaeology – 1882*, Edinburgh, David Douglas, 1886, p. 387.
10. Anderson, J., *Scotland in early Christian times: The Rhind Lectures in archaeology – 1879*, Edinburgh, David Douglas, 1881 p. 21.
11. Anderson, J., *Scotland in Early Christian Times: The Rhind Lectures in archaeology – 1879*, Edinburgh, David Douglas, 1881, pp. 17–18.
12. Simpson, J.Y., *Archaeology: its past and future work*, Edinburgh, Edmonstone & Douglas, 1861, p. 42.
13. Anderson, J. & Black, G.F., *Reports on local museums in Scotland*, obtained through Dr R.H. Gunning's Jubilee Gift to the Society, Proc Soc Antiq Scot, 22, 1887-88, 1888, p. 421.
14. Anderson, J. & Black, G.F., *Reports on local museums in Scotland*, obtained through Dr R.H. Gunning's Jubilee Gift to the Society, Proc Soc Antiq Scot, 22, 1887–88, 1888, pp. 365.
15. Piggott, S., 'The National Museum of Antiquities and archaeological research', in O'Connor, A. & D V Clarke, D.V. (eds), *From the Stone Age to the 'Forty-Five: Studies presented to R.B.K. Stevenson*, Edinburgh, John Donald, 1983, p. 5.
16. Ibid.
17. Childe, V.G., *The prehistory of Scotland*, London, Kegan Paul/Trench/Trubner & Co, 1935.
18. Childe, V.G., *Scotland before the Scots: the Rhind Lectures –1944*, London, Methuen, 1946.
19. Grieg, S., 'Viking antiquities in Scotland', in Shetelig, H. (ed), *Viking antiquities in Great Britain and Ireland*, Part II. Oslo, Aschehoug, 1940.
20. Roussell, A., *Norse building customs in the Scottish isles*, Copenhagen & London, Levin & Munksgaard/Williams & Norgate, 1934.
21. Callander, J.G., 'Notice of a bronze cup and other objects found apparently in a sepulchral deposit near Tarland, Aberdeenshire', in *Proc Soc Antiq Scot*, 49, 1914–15, 1915, pp. 203–206.
22. Piggott, S., 'The National Museum of Antiquities and archaeological research', in O'Connor, A. & Clarke, D.V. (eds), *From the Stone Age to the 'Forty-Five: Studies presented to R.B.K. Stevenson*, Edinburgh, John Donald, 1983, p. 4.
23. Hawkes, C., 'The British Museum and British archaeology', in *Antiquity*, 36, 1962, pp. 248–51.

The silver knife, fork and spoon presented to Dr Murdoch Macleod by Prince
Charles Edward Stuart, 3 July 1746.
Courtesy Trustees of the National Museums of Scotland

8

OBJECTS AS ICONS
Myths and Realities of Jacobite Relics

George Dalgleish

This chapter seeks to explore the relationship between the notions of icon and relic, and in turn their relationship to the vast array of objects associated with the Jacobite cause, both as a live political force and a 'romantic lost cause'.

In museums, use of the term icon has sometimes taken on an additional definition to that of most dictionaries. Within the Museum of Scotland display planning process, it has also come to denote a object or group of objects that formed a focus of a display round which the physical and intellectual orientation of the content was centred. This is nowhere more obvious than in the 'Jacobite Challenge' displays, where yet further layers of complex meaning came into play. The nature of the Jacobite cause, and its central characters, meant that certain objects associated with them took on aspects of the standard definition of an icon: 'a representation of some sacred personage in painting, bas-relief or mosaic, itself regarded as sacred and honoured with a relative worship or adoration'.

The other term which has been used most frequently in the past to describe this material is 'relic'. There has been an enormous pendulum swing in the public and academic attitude to the acceptance of Jacobite relics. One hundred years ago, virtually everything associated with the Jacobite cause and its main characters was accepted as genuine by the public and contemporary historians alike. Today, the pendulum has swung to the other end of its arc, and there is a high degree of scepticism, at least in mainstream history, about so-called relics. I would argue that perhaps the truth lies somewhere in the middle, and what follows looks at both genuine and 'romantic' relics, the reasons for their existence, and seeks to identify several phases in their production.

Definitions of the term relic emphasise '...some object...an article of personal use, or the like, which remains as a memorial of a departed saint, martyr or other holy person and as such is carefully preserved and held in esteem or veneration' or an object 'held in reverence as a incentive to faith and piety'. It can be argued that the very nature of the Jacobite cause itself fostered such interpretations. A combination of the political and religious convictions of the Jacobites produced a movement whose pseudo-religious nature gave rise to a rash of 'devotional' relics associated with the heroes of the cause.

The Stuarts in exile propagated this themselves, as a very effective form of propaganda, but with a deeper meaning as well. Both James Francis Edward and his son Prince Charles commissioned large numbers of portraits and miniatures for distribution to their followers, and here one can reflect on the traditional representational properties of icons. It was extremely important for the exiled figureheads of the cause to keep images of themselves before their supporters: to foster loyalty, to give the impression that something was happening and, perhaps most importantly, as a means of emphasising the need for continued faith in the rightness of their cause.

Two of the most important portraits of Prince Charles Edward Stuart and his brother Henry, Duke of York are those done by Antonio David in 1732, when the boys were twelve and ten respectively, now in the collections of the Scottish National Portrait Gallery.[1] These were just two examples of this artist's work for the exiled court. He had been appointed as an artist to the court as early as 1718, and from 1720 onward he produced numerous miniatures of James's children, including two of Charles aged eighteen months and about four years which were presented to Sir John Hynde Cotton MP, parliamentary leader of the English Jacobites.[2] Incidentally, Sir John also possessed in his collection of miniatures, one of the Hanoverian monarch George II, as many Jacobites were equally adept at sitting astride the political fence.

Many other artists were employed by the Stuart court, and a steady stream of images of the Royal family were produced, until well after the defeat at Culloden. In 1742, a portrait by Dominic Dupra of 'King' James was sent to Lord John Drummond, brother of the 3rd Duke of Perth and an influential commander of the French Royal Scots during the 1745 Rising. James's secretary, James Edgar adds an interesting comment in his letter to Lord John: 'Dupra was at all the pains he could about it, and I took care that it should be of the same size with their Royal Highnesses you already have'.[3] Drummond already had portraits of the two princes, having mentioned two years earlier in a letter to Edgar that 'they are just now making at Paris Printes of the Two Young Gentlemen upon my pictures which I hope will turn out very well, the Eldest is almost

Finished'.[4] The 'printes' were obviously engravings based on the original portraits and this exchange of correspondence is a fascinating commentary on how the propaganda value of portraits was enhanced by the dissemination of large numbers of engraved prints.

One of the best likenesses of Prince Charles was said to be the bust of him by Jean Baptiste Lemoyne, produced sometime after 1748.[5] Lemoyne was paid 1400 livres for some unspecified work that year, possibly the terracotta model, and in 1750 he was paid a further 1400 for a 'marble bust'.[6] This bust, a plaster replica of which is in the Scottish National Portrait Gallery,[7] was the model for a whole series of images of the Prince, including some very fine gold insets for rings, which may have been produced by the Scottish goldsmith, Adam Tait, who had fought for Charles at Culloden and had escaped to Paris. One of these gold insets was given to the Museum of the Society of Antiquaries by an Edinburgh goldsmith, Alexander Gardner, who later became goldsmith to the Prince Regent. Interestingly, this donation was made in 1783, five years before the death of Prince Charles.[8] Many other cameos and medals were also based on the Lemoyne bust.

Medals were a very important and popular way of spreading propaganda and were used by both sides from the 17th century onwards. The political significance of issuing medals has a long history, and the Stuart court did not underestimate their value. The Stuart Papers contain many references to payments for the production of medals. For example, in May 1748, Charles's banker was authorised to pay the engraver Roettiers for 400 silver counters and 300 bronze medals,[9] while in September of the same year he paid for ten silver and 200 bronze medals (*ibid*). These are only two of dozens of similar references, but they give some impression of the numbers in circulation. The Stuarts were not alone in appreciating the political importance of medals, and the House of Hanover was fairly adept at producing rival medals. A recent publication on medals of the Jacobite period lists some 249 different issues, produced by both sides.[11]

One can argue that these contemporary 'iconic' representations of the Stuarts had more than a simple propaganda function as mementoes of the exiled royal family. It is possible they were intentionally imbued with something of a mystical quality, which probably derived from the more metaphysical aspects of the interpretation of kingship by the Stuarts. The position of the King from time immemorial had a significant religious and mystical element in it, and the Stuarts, particularly in the person of James VI, used this in the development of the theory of 'Divine Right'.

One interesting illustration of the mystical power of the King was the Stuart promotion of the ceremony of 'touching' as a means of conferring the mystical Royal powers of healing to the sufferers of scrofula (glandular tuberculosis), known as 'the Kings Evil'. All the later Stuarts practised the ceremony. Originally, a gold coin (an 'angel') was given to those who had been touched. As this ceremony became more popular, Charles I was said to have touched 90,000 people during his reign, small medalets, known as 'touchpieces', were introduced to reduce the cost. The last ruling British monarch to perform the ceremony was Queen Anne. The Hanoverians rejected it, but the exiled Stuarts continued to perform the ceremony on a large scale.

I would argue that something of the significance of this mystical element was deliberately fostered by the exiled Stuarts to produce a cult of relics of their cause, which was akin to and connected with the cult of religious relics propagated by the Roman Catholic Church. I would say there is a direct link between the relics of Mary Queen of Scots, the Martyr Queen of Catholic mythology, through those of the Martyr King, Charles I, and on to the vast array of objects associated with the exiled Royal House of Stuart, the Jacobite cause and its heroes, such as the Marquis of Montrose and Bonnie Dundee. These relics, which include everything from bits of tartan to bits of Montrose himself, were a deliberate part of Jacobite political ideology. They served to bolster the nature of their kingship and therefore the insistence on their indefeasible hereditary right to the thrones of Great Britain.[12] Jacobite relics are, therefore, an important part of the philosophy of the movement, and should not be dismissed totally as a product of an over romantic imagination.

However, one should be wary of taking a completely uncritical view of the vast range of objects currently associated with the Jacobite cause, as many of them have a very dubious legitimacy. It is clear that not every lock of Bonnie Prince Charlie's hair which is lovingly preserved today came from the royal head. There are, it can be argued, at least two main groups of Jacobite 'relics'.

The first of these are the contemporary items: those which were produced at or near the time of the events to which they relate. These may, of course, not all be 'genuine', in the sense that they are not all tangibly connected with a member of the royal family, or one of the figureheads of the cause. This was not crucial, because of the nature of the cult of the relics did not have to be genuine to have the required political effect. It was only necessary for the recipient or owner to believe they were genuine for them to have served their purpose. Accordingly, there are many items of memorabilia still in existence which date to the Jacobite century: from wine glasses to rings, from fragments of tartan to pistols. But far fewer can be proven to have a direct connection with the Stuarts.

The second spate of relics is as interesting as the first, and indeed constitute a far larger numerical group than the first. These began to make their appearance when Jacobitism had lost its political teeth. This process started with the defeat of the '45, but was accelerated in the second half of the 18th century, when it became obvious that there was no chance of the Stuarts being restored. This was partly due to Charles's decline into a drunken old age, but more was the result of the changed political climate which made the Hanoverian grip on the throne unbreakable. With this developed the romanticisation of the Jacobite cause, particularly among the gentry, as part of the general upsurge in interest in all things Scottish at the end of the century. With the Jacobites no longer a real threat to the establishment, it became acceptable and indeed socially advantageous to possess ancestral links with the heroes of the '45.

Robert Burns, who at other times espoused radical republican views, was one of those who held a romantic attachment to the House of Stuart. He was invited to attend a dinner to mark Prince Charles' birthday on 31 December 1787, a month before his death. These dinners were held in the Edinburgh house of James Stuart, a prominent advocate, and were attended by a wide range of the nobility and gentry of the city. Thomas Erskine, later 9th earl of Kellie, was one guest, and he is said to have commissioned a set of wine glasses for the dinner, enamelled with portraits of the Prince. Also used to drink the Prince's health was an 'amen' glass (so called because they were engraved with the Stuart version of the national anthem and incorporate the word 'amen'). This is dated 1743 and bears an inscription commemorating David Drummond, the Treasurer of the Bank of Scotland from 1700–41 and a Jacobite supporter.

The ruling royal house were no exception to this interest, and both George III and especially George IV were fascinated by their exiled cousins. He actually paid both Charles and his brother pensions. On his death, Cardinal Henry bequeathed the remains of the British Crown Jewels, still in Stuart possession, and the Stuart Papers to George Prince Regent. In return, the Prince Regent also arranged for the magnificent marble monument to James, Charles and Henry to be erected in St Peters, Rome, where they are buried.[13]

Another member of the Royal family who was fascinated by the Stuarts was Augustus, Duke of Sussex, George IV's brother. He actually visited Cardinal Henry in Rome in 1792, calling him by the title of Royal Highness, and arranging for an increase in the old man's pension. Sussex was so keen on all things Scottish and Highland that, on being elected the President of the Highland Society of London in 1805, he ordered a Highland outfit, complete with a replica of the silver hilted sword which had belonged to Prince Charles Edward and then in George IV's collection, having been lost at Culloden.[14]

The pinnacle of this process of Romanticisation of Scotland's past was undoubtedly the visit of George IV to Edinburgh in 1822. This romantic jamboree, engineered by Sir Walter Scott, produced a welter of mementoes of Bonnie Prince Charlie and the cause, and it is to this occasion that one can trace many of the locks of hair, pieces of tartan and particularly weapons that still exist today. Certainly, virtually every Highland chief who marched behind the King's carriage up the High Street from Holyrood to the Castle, carried a sword or targe or pistol that had been carried at Culloden, even if we still have the evidence that many of them were provided by outfitters such as George Hunter & Co of Edinburgh, a few weeks before the visit. For example, Sir Evan Macgregor bought 28 broadswords, three dozen dirks and 40 pistols from John MacLeod, outfitter in Castle Street, Edinburgh, to equip his Highland followers. The chief himself had his grandfather's legendary sword carried during the '45.[15] It is relatively easy to understand how legitimate provenances and associations of genuine 'relics' could be transferred to other items specially produced to mark the Royal visit.

The middle and late-19th century saw further outbursts of relic display. The early visits of Queen Victoria from 1842 onwards, and her obvious love for the Romantic version of Scotland's history, gave an impetus to the 'discovery' of further relics. She was presented with ever increasing numbers of mementoes of the Prince and the '45. For example, Victoria records that on 13 September 1873, when returning from a visit of Glencoe: 'As we came through Ballachulish the post-boy suddenly stopped, and a very respectable, stout-looking old Highlander stepped up to the carriage with a small quaich out of which he said Prince Charles had drunk and also my dearest Albert in 1847, and begged that I do the same...'.[16]

This was also the era of exhibitions and displays on historical themes, and of course Jacobite relics figured prominently. In 1889, to mark the bicentenary of the Revolution, an exhibition called the *Royal House of Stuart* was held in London. It contained 104 items or groups of items said to be associated with Prince Charles alone, and that does not include portraits, miniatures, medals or documents. They included no fewer than fifteen locks of hair and eleven pieces of tartan, ranging from small fragments right up to complete outfits. If one multiplies these by the numerous other exhibitions that took place in the late-19th and early-20th centuries, one must come to the conclusion that the gentry of Scotland were awash with Jacobite memorabilia, and if all of the items were indeed genuine relics of Prince Charles, then he must have been a particularly threadbare and ill-groomed young man during the '45. Obviously, many of these 19th century relics are completely spurious, and one can take the case of the vast number of so-called Jacobite glasses which exist as a cautionary example.

Many examples of this type of glass are found today, complete with the typical Jacobite symbols of rose and buds. Some may indeed be 18th century in date, but a catalogue of the Edinburgh and Leith Flint Glass Works (produced between 1906 and 1920 and openly advertising 'Jacobite Glasses'), must serve as a warning that not all such glasses are what they seem. Here one can see at its starkest the pendulum of acceptance. Some glass historians have argued that virtually every so-called Jacobite glass is a 19th or 20th century creation. Many are, but again one should be cautious about sweeping statements. Glasses engraved with likenesses of Prince Charles were certainly produced at the time of the '45. One of his staunchest supporters, John Drummond, the exiled titular 5th Duke of Perth, wrote in 1750 to his kinsman Drummond of Logiealmond that 'I have sent...a glass...which is the more valuable that it came from Manchester it is adorned with the Princes figure – with a suitable motto & with a rose and thistle...this fancie I thought would be agreeable to you'.[17]

THE KNIFE, FORK AND SPOON

I wish to conclude by looking at a series of objects in the National Collections that are so intimately connected with the central figure of the Jacobite cause, Prince Charles Edward Stuart, that they have in effect become 'icons' within the Museum of Scotland's displays. One is a simple set of silver cutlery, being perhaps the most interesting since it very graphically demonstrates the process of elevation from workaday utensil to the status of 'relic' and treasured family heirloom.

Because he lost all his personal possessions at the battle of Culloden, many of the people who helped Prince Charles during his wanderings and escape provided him with clothes and utensils. What became known as Prince Charles' silver knife, fork and spoon were in fact made in Paris in 1739, where they were bought by Ranald MacDonald, heir to the Chief of Clanranald, when he was at university there. He brought them back to his home in Uist. When on Benbecula, Charles and his companions were helped by the Chief, who presented the Prince with this cutlery and a silver cup. These were welcome and necessary, as they had all been forced to use whatever was at hand to eat their meals. One of Charles's companions, Colonel O'Sullivan commented that it was '...a cruel thing to see him drink brochan at his turn in the only wooden vessel we had...One shell served him as a spoone and the other a dram cup, but now...he was like a Prince, he had a silver cover [i.e. knife, fork and spoon], a silver cup and a couple of napkins...'.[18]

Charles later presented these pieces as mementoes to Dr Murdoch MacLeod, who had fought for the Prince at Culloden, and who had helped him during his wanderings round Raasay and Skye. Murdoch brought the cutlery to Edinburgh in 1747 to show Bishop Robert Forbes, a collector of

Jacobite accounts and information. It was then that Murdoch had the pieces engraved with 'Ex Dono C P R, July 3 1746' (The Gift of Charles, Prince Regent).[19] Although they had only belonged to Charles for about six weeks, the fact that they swiftly became 'relics' of the Prince, ensured that they were proudly preserved by the MacLeod family and their descendants until 1984, when they were acquired by the Museum.[20]

THE SWORD AND TARGE

Like many of his troops, Prince Charles was armed with the traditional weapons of the Highlanders, including a basket-hilted sword and a targe. However, Charles' weapons were much more elaborately decorated than most and were presented to him by James, Duke of Perth in 1740. He also gave Charles and his brother, Henry, a complete tartan outfit each. He advised the Prince that the only place in Britain where he could recruit troops for the rising was the Highlands. During the campaigns of 1745–46, Charles made the Duke of Perth Lieutenant-General of the Jacobite army. There are numerous references to the Princes wearing their 'Highland Clothes' to balls, carnivals and the opera in Rome. Curiously, while these references are quite clear about the clothes being of tartan, there is no direct mention of kilts or plaids. It seems fairly clear, therefore, that when the correspondents mention the Prince as being 'dressed in the manner of the Scottish Highlanders' they mean in tartan trews and jacket, as surely the appearance of a kilt in Rome would have excited even more detailed comment.

The sword, which has a silver basket-shaped hilt, was made in London in 1740, by a goldsmith called Charles Kandler. After the defeat at Culloden, Charles's Sword was captured by the government commander, the Duke of Cumberland, along with most of the Jacobite baggage train. It remained in the Royal Collection of Arms and Armour, until 1820 when George IV presented it to his friend Reginald MacDonald, Chief of Clanranald. Clanranald showed it to a meeting of the Society of Antiquaries of Scotland in 1831, and his descendant Angus, the 23rd Chief presented it to the Museum in 1944. This was of course the sword used as the model for the Duke of Sussex's sword in 1805.

The targe, although made in the same way as other Highland targes, with overlapping wooden boards covered in leather, is much more elaborate, with a series of decorative silver mounts, probably added in London or Paris in 1740. After the disastrous defeat at the battle of Culloden (16 April 1746), Charles had to make such a rapid escape, that all his baggage and personal belongings were abandoned on the battlefield. His targe was rescued by one of the Jacobite officers, Cluny MacPherson, who had not been present at the battle itself. On the night of the battle, he managed to recover one of the baggage wagons which he 'found on the high road desserted by every person.' The targe remained in the MacPherson collection until 1928, when it was sold to a Mr Murray of Clava, who later presented it to the Museum.[21]

THE CANTEEN

Prince Charles Edward's Canteen is simply a fancy picnic set, containing beakers, knives, forks and spoons for two people, as well as a salt and pepper cruet and a combined corkscrew and nutmeg grater. All these fit into a beautiful Rococo style outer case, which is only nine inches tall.

The outer case is decorated with emblems of the Prince. The front panel is engraved with the badge of the Prince of Wales, as in Jacobite eyes, Charles became the 'True Born' Prince of Wales on his birth on 31 December 1720. The lid and rim of the canteen are chased with the St Andrew Badge and Collar of Thistles of the Order of the Thistle. (Charles was made a Knight of this Order shortly after his birth). It was made by an Edinburgh goldsmith called Ebenezer Oliphant in 1740–41. Oliphant was a younger son of the staunchly Jacobite Laird of Gask in Perthshire. Both his father and brother were 'out' with Prince Charles during the '45.

Although it was ideal for a military campaign such as the '45, it was made in 1741 and it is much more likely that it was given to the Prince as a 21st birthday present. As he was very fond of hunting and outdoor pursuits, this would have been a most appropriate gift. Along with all his other personal belongings, Prince Charles was forced to abandon his canteen on the battlefield. It was captured by the Duke of Cumberland, and given by him to his aide-de-camp, George Keppel, later Earl of Albemarle. It stayed in his family until 1964, and was finally purchased by the National Museums of Scotland in 1984.[22]

All these objects, by virtue of their proven associations with Prince Charles Edward have survived the vicissitudes of the intervening 250 years to become not only relics of the Jacobite cause, but also iconic objects within the Museum of Scotland displays. For example, the examination of the structure of the Jacobite army and the military events of 1745–46 is centred round the Prince's targe and sword, while the canteen forms the centrepiece of the case investigating the life and character of Prince Charles. Here, as elsewhere in the Museum of Scotland real objects have primacy as another form of evidence of the nation's past.

It is hoped that the above has shown that the study of items associated with the Jacobite cause is one which can give an intriguing insight into, not only the history of the people and events of the period, but also into the mythology which grew up around the developing romance of a lost cause. Both are, after all, ingredients of the historical melting pot from which national identity emerges.

The Author

George Dalgleish read Scottish History at the University of Edinburgh, and was appointed a curator in the National Museum of Antiquities of Scotland in 1980, following training as an archivist at the Scottish Record Office and the University of Glasgow. He is currently Curator of Scottish Decorative Arts in the History & Applied Art Department of the National Museums of Scotland, and was involved in the creation of the 18th and 19th century displays of the Museum of Scotland. His special interests include Scottish ceramics, clocks, Jacobite relics, pewter and silver on which he has published widely. A former Council Member, he has served on the Editorial Board and as Deputy Editor for the Proceedings of the Society of Antiquaries of Scotland. He is an Expert Adviser to the Reviewing Committee on the Export of Works of Art, and is a Member of the Incorporation of Goldsmiths of the City of Edinburgh and the Incorporation of Hammermen of Edinburgh.

References

1. Smailes, H. (comp) *The Concise Catalogue of the Scottish National Portrait Gallery*, PG 888 & 889, Edinburgh, 1990.
2. NMS Collection H.NT 244 & 245.
3. Stuart Papers, Vol 226/87, Edgar to Lord John Drummond, 20 September 1742, Royal Archives, Windsor Castle (referred to by gracious permission of Her Majesty the Queen).
4. Stuart Papers, Vol 244/69, Lord John Drummond to, 17 September 1740, Royal Archives, Windsor Castle (referred to by gracious permission of Her Majesty the Queen).
5. Nicholas, D., *The Portraits of Bonnie Prince Charlie* , Privately published, 1973, p. 30–31.
6. Stuart Papers, Vols 289/97, Nov 16 1747; 296/161 March 10 1748; 454/111 1st Oct 1750, Royal Archives, Windsor Castle (referred to by gracious permission of Her Majesty the Queen).
7. Smailes, H. (comp) *The Concise Catalogue of the Scottish National Portrait Gallery*, PG 594, Edinburgh, 1990.
8. NMS Collection H.R. 129.

9. Stuart Papers, Vol 296/161, Prince Charles' Accompt with George Waters, Jan 1748–Jan 1749, Royal Archives, Windsor Castle (referred to by gracious permission of Her Majesty the Queen).

10. ibid.

11. Woolf, N., *The Medallic Record of the Jacobite Movement*, London, 1988.

12. Lenman, B., *The Jacobite Risings in Britain 1689-1746*, London, 1980, pp. 19–27.

13. Marshall, R., *Bonnie Prince Charlie*, Edinburgh, 1998, p. 206.

14. Marshall, R. & Dalgleish, G.(eds), *The Art of Jewellery in Scotland*, Edinburgh, 1991, p. 63.

15. Prebble, J., *The King's Jaunt, George IV in Scotland, 1822*, London, 1988, pp. 134–135.

16. Duff, D. (ed), *Queen Victoria's Highland Journals*, Exeter, 1983, p. 78.

17. Scottish Record Office, Murthly Castle Papers GD 121/104/3/112.

18. Dalgleish, G., 'The silver knife fork and spoon given by Prince Charles Edward Stuart to Murdoch Macleod, 3 July 1746', in *Proc Soc Antiq Scot*, 118(1988), p. 298.

19. Paton, H. (ed), *The Lyon in Mourning,*), Forbes, R. (comp), 3 vols, Edinburgh., 1886 [=*Scot Hist Soc*, 21–23], i, 77n.

20. Dalgleish, G., 'The Silver Travelling Canteen of Prince Charles Edward Stuart', in Fenton & Myrdal (eds) *Food and Drink and Travelling Accessories*, Edinburgh, 1988, pp. 168–184.

21. Dalgleish, G. & Mechan, D., *I am come home: Treasures of Prince Charles Edward Stuart*. Edinburgh. 1985, pp. 8–10.

22. Dalgleish, G., 'The Silver Travelling Canteen of Prince Charles Edward Stuart', in Fenton & Myrdal (eds) *Food and Drink and Travelling Accessories*, Edinburgh, 1988, pp. 168–184.

Further Reading

Hawkins, E., Franks, A. & Greuber, H., *Medallic Illustrations of the History of Great Britain and Ireland*, 2 Vols, London, 1885.

The silver canteen of Prince Charles Edward Stuart, by Ebebezer Oliphant, Edinburgh, 1740–1. *Courtesy The Trustees of the National Museums of Scotland*

9

JOCK TAMSON'S BAIRNS
Ethnicity and Identity

Gavin Sprott

Weil, fat about Jock Tamson's Bairns? Who is Jock Tamson, and the long suffering Mistress Tamson, by whom, we assume, he had all those bairns? Is Jock a sub-rural version of Rab C. Nisbit with his Mary Doll? Well, Rab has a strong cultural identity: Scottish to people outside, but really Glasgow. If you are talking about 'ethnic' character, the reality is that Scotland is a land of regions. That regional character is strong enough to throw national organisations such as the Scots Language Society into despair. This is not some bone-headed local patriotism, but something different: a natural peasant distrust of theoretical fabrication.

Now, I use the word 'peasant' advisedly and cheerfully, because I have a personal sense of identity with the peasant's ungrateful and curmudgeonly attitude to all these theoretical constructs of national character and attributes. We have heard much about identity and how it is formed, and the various national experiences of that. In certain respects, I suspect the 'heritage industry' is the bargain basement of the 'identity industry'. This identity industry has become something of a happy hunting ground for academics and journalists in search of a bit of rough fun to cheer up their lives. They pull the entrails out of 'heritage' and 'nationalism', Hobsbawm as the Grand Inquisitor,[1] and Robert Hewison as the first among various puritan prophets upending the money-changers' tables of the heritage industry.[2]

A countervailing line is taken by Raphael Samuel in *Theatres of Memory*.[3] This is a kindlier, anti-elitist bottom-up look at popular perceptions of history, and he gives what he calls the 'heritage-baiters' a severe thrashing for what amounts to rampant and, paradoxically, rather unthinking academic snobbery. Well, I suppose that some contributors to this volume will agree with Samuel on that point.

In a different category we have the late Ernest Gellner, a lively thinker, whose 1983 book, *Nations and Nationalism* was a much-translated best seller.[4] His views were summarised in the succinct *Nationalism*, published posthumously in 1997.[5] Gellner does not pass judgement on nationalism and the related questions of 'identity' (although his family suffered severely from it), and he analyses it not as some false creed, but as a fact bred of industrial society. Here we have a substantial scholar's playground of our own dealing with identity, heritage etc. The popularity of this academic pastime is shown in that four fairly recent anthologies dealing with Scotland and identity include 27 separate authors.[6,7,8,9]

This preoccupation tells us something, but nothing about Jock Tamson. Let no one be so foolish as to presume on being some self-appointed advocate for Jock Tamson, a vain Tribune of the Plebes fantasy. Because Jock Tamson's only identity is that he is human. He and Mistress Tamson are Adam and Eve, hiding their shame not behind fig leaves but a skeppit bunnet and a fish supper. They are not 'ordinary' as Mrs Thatcher used to talk about 'ordinary people' because the very meaning underlying the saying that 'we're a Jock Tamson's bairns' is that we are all of the same clay. The watchwords of 'heritage' and 'identity' take us in a different direction as the means we choose to distinguish one cultural community from another.

Let me take a good bash at this word 'heritage': not the snooty academics' distaste for the rabble enjoying themselves, or the Jeremiads warning how such preoccupation with the past is corrupting our ability to live in the present. The very word heritage implies ownership and possession, validated by the fact that it is there from the past. In *The Rights of Man*, Tom Paine complained bitterly about the way old and dead interests dominated the present in the Britain of his day, and that it is only those who live in the present who have an interest in it. We might turn that on its head, and rail at the absurdity of people feeling that they 'own' the past, when they talk of 'our heritage'.

An interesting touchstone of this is the mine-ridden landscape of *spachpolitik*. No sooner had the honest endeavours of the Ulster-Scots Heritage Council (*The Ulster-Scotch Heirskip Cooncil*) got European minority language status recognition for that tongue than various other interests started politicising the issue by speaking of the language of 'Protestant heritage' as reported in the *Sunday Herald*.[10] To continue the Irish parallel, did St Patrick have a beard? That depends whether your 'heritage' is a Catholic or Protestant one. It is this sense of owning the past that has caused more trouble than we can even imagine. The only thing that might be said for the more recent interest in heritage is that it has given people such as Australian Aborigines and native Americans a better notion of themselves.

Nor can the question of ethnicity be avoided, because it is there. To avoid its existence is as much a deliberate act as to promote some perception of it. I am frequently surprised at just how different outside observers consider Scottish ethnic character to be, because the record shows that we have been busy destroying it ourselves for the last two centuries: not some devilish English plot, as some cultural nationalists would have it.

But is it what we think it is? A certain sector of museums is involved, which brings us to the folk museum. There are three so called in Scotland: the Highland Folk Museum, The Angus Folk Museum, and the Fife Folk Museum. They are all related in that the one was inspired by the other starting with the extraordinary labours of Dr Isobel Grant in the inter-war years. Also, there is the Ulster Folk Museum and the Welsh Folk Museum. One way or another, the trail leads back to Skansen (1891) and Dr Artur Hazelius, and the parallel re-creation of characteristic country buildings or even whole villages at various international exhibitions from the late 19th century onwards.

All these museums are blameless and respectable, with the 'ethnic' being interpreted as community character rather than some mysterious genetic attribute. But some had close shaves. The Dutch Open Air Museum (Nederlands Openluchtmuseum) was founded at Arnhem in 1912. In the 1920s, it narrowly avoided being taken over by proto-Nazi theorists, who wanted to stage jolly national folk moots and what have you. It did not happen, but when the Nazis did move in, the struggling museum was nationalised, and by default stayed so after the war was over. But the memory of the Nazi 'ethnic' drumbeat was enough to cast a serious shadow over the museum's development for three post-war decades.

In terms of *sprachpolitik*, the same fate befell the Breton tongue, because rather unfairly, its advocates were tarred with the brush of courting Nazi sympathy during the occupation. Iowarth Peate, the guru founder of the Welsh Folk Museum (1948), verged on near mystical glorification of pure Welsh culture as an antidote to the barbarities of the 20th century. The attachments of certain pre-Revolutionary Russian visionaries to the land, and the canonisation of peasant wisdom could convert into the insane Nazi farrago of *blud und boden* – blood and soil. Nazi art is a dreich catalogue of humourless praise for sturdy men and infant-toting blondes among plentiful farmlands peopled by *das Herrenvolk*.

The paradox is that what we might perceive as regional or local community character and national cultural constructs do not necessarily go together. In the Italy of 1945, some 60–65 per cent of the people spoke a dialect that was hardly intelligible to their regional neighbours. In the 1990s, the polarity is reversed, in that 80 per cent speak a standardised Italian based on the Florentine tongue, besides some continuing to speak their native dialects among themselves.[11] But this is also the land of Umberto Bossi and his Northern League and Lombard nationalism. Or consider the Basques. They are busy standardising the dialects of that tongue out of existence, because they perceive that only a standardised tongue will survive. In the by-going they will have destroyed one character to construct another. Such are the choices people face. But when they speak of 'Euskera: the symbol of a historical identity', it will indeed become a symbol of a created identity.[12] Nor can they have any certainty of achieving their objective of a new standard language, as nearly a century of linguistic experiment in Norway has shown.

This re-processsing is not without its problems. It is like cutting off limbs, but not knowing what to do with the nerve-endings and the confused messages that result. A familiar example is our own. The 1999 exhibition *O Caledonia!* at the Scottish National Portrait Gallery, shows just how Scott created a homogeneous and standardised image of Scotland, in which Highland and Lowland identities were conflated to produce the kilted Lauderesque heiderum hoderum that is recognised as Scots all over the world.

This image is the subject of quite strong like and dislike among Scottish people. We are not all happy with it. But the standardising element is both explicit and comical. Look at kilt-makers' catalogues of 'Highland dress'. They do not just describe their products, but devote text to what is 'correct', often illustrated by fashion drawings that are themselves stylish throwbacks to 50 ago.[13] If anything, this Highlandising process is gaining ground. I do not know of any statistics, but if the weddings page in the *Scottish Farmer* can provide a crude index, it is now common for the groom and best man to wear a kilt, where before that was rare. Central Edinburgh on the day of a rugby international is now like a Hollywood set for a battle of the clans.

Under this lies a strange paradox. In the Scotland of 1707, English was spoken by only a handful. The population spoke Scots and Gaelic in almost equal proportion, and the Norn tongue was still spoken in Shetland. Now English is universal, the Norn is long since dead, and Scots and Gaelic exist in a kind of sub-culture. A foreign visitor looking at newspapers or the TV or the average bookshop would not know that Scots existed and would have to go off the tourist track, and perhaps further, to hear it spoken. Yet this is a country with a new parliament, and if the English Nationalists do their stuff, it will be heading for independence.

This paradox can breed the unreal. Occasional letters appear in the posher newspapers written in a Scots that nobody ever did or does speak. It is usually English dressed up in Scots words, with no understanding of grammar, word order or idiom. Semantically, there is nothing to distinguish it from Standard English.[14] In one sense, this is nothing new. The best example dates back to Burns: *Scots wha hae wi Wallace bled?* *Scotch 'at his bleedit wi Wallace* would be nearer the mark. But there is a vital point that flows from this. Burns was pitching Wallace not as some grim ethnic warrior saint representing a 'pure' culture, but as a surrogate George Washington. He would use or invent any linguistic formulation that would serve this purpose. His Wallace represented civil liberty, not some bogus tribal virtue.

Not that civil liberty had always been high on the list of Scottish community politics, and that is part of the reason why intellectual and spiritual liberty was such a prize to Burns and like minded contemporaries. The 18th century saw a steady crumbling of social restrictions that we may know about, but the personal effect of which is really hard to imagine, because we are so far removed from the atmosphere of the times. The nearest we can get to it is Burns' striking passage in a letter to Mrs Dunlop. He paints a vivid contrast:[15]

> The first Sunday of May; a breezy blue-sky noon some time about the beginning, & a hoary morning and calm sunny day about the end of Autumn; these, time out of mind, have been with me a kind of holidays, – Not like the Sacramental, Executioner-face of a Kilmarnock Communion...

That Kilmarnock Sunday was the least of it. The high tide of Covenanting theocracy in 1649 was incredibly destructive, and I have often wondered what Scotland would have been like had Cromwell not defeated the theocrats at Dunbar. But that is not how it appeared to the generation after Burns. The 18th century distaste for 'enthusiasm' was being elbowed out by a rising tide of evangelical fervour that turned the question of Kirk patronage into a touchstone of 'attitude', so the Covenanters became re-invested with an aura of justified romance.

There was one exception: Walter Scott. *Old Mortality* combined an admiration of the moral courage and character of the Covenanters with a direct criticism of the fanaticism that went with it, and that got him into hot water with the retro-Covenanters in the Kirk. 'But I am complete master of these times,' he retorted, 'and I trust that I have come decently off.' *Master of these times!* What he imagined he was doing was replacing myth with history, and significantly writing in the same decade as Leopold von Ranke, who was also trying to see it *as it really was – Wie es eigentlich gewesen.*[16] Now, indeed he was doing so after a fashion. Scott's years of burrowing in the Register House gave him a command of original sources that he turned to formidable use in recreating an almost filmic sense of time and place. But in terms of identity, the communal and public myth of the Covenanted Nation from which both Burns and Scott were running from was first and foremost one of spiritual community.

The reformed Kirk in its various manifestations had no strong ethnic locus. John Knox and his successors were Anglicisers, and no one thought ill of them: except Ninian Winyet, who twitted Knox that he had forgotten 'our auld plane Scottis quhilk your mother learit you'. Jennie Geddes, the stool thrower (another myth), was not objecting to so-called English church usage as such, but the subordination of Kirk to state. When they had a chance, the theocrats were ruthless in introducing English puritan usage, as in the *Westminster Confession,* to this day the standard of orthodoxy in the Free Church, the Free Presbyterian Church, and the Reformed Presbyterian Church. Scotland in general got stuck with much of it, including the unspecified add-ons, which led to the destruction of whole bodies of traditional music and the forbidding of dancing and so on: all the stuff of 'ethnic' character that we can now only guess at. The English sensibly dumped Puritanism when they got the chance.

Now, here is a force which helped shape what we perceive to be Scottish character, but to interpolate modern national identity questions into a different age is nonsense. Sir Roy Strong recently suggested that 'the English sank their own identities to bring other people in', to accommodate the accession of Scotland to the respective unions of the Crowns and Parliaments.[16] Such batty notions would never have occurred to people then, as that was not the way they thought, and the idea is enough to make a horse laugh.

But come the early 19th century, Scott had covered a vast literary canvas with what we would now call 'ethnic' character. Both he and Burns were avid collectors of old songs and ballads, but with Burns (and with his predecessors such as Alan Ramsay), often we cannot tell where the originals end and Burns begins, because they were part of his cultural furniture. With Scott, the 'minstrelsy' is consciously set apart as an Ossian-like fragment, a literary folly of magnificent cultural ruins. And now the technology of industrialisation would have far-reaching effects. Widespread literacy was matched by cheap print and effective distribution. Although Burns was born in the old world of peasant Scotland, his fame was promoted by the new industrialising culture. And with this we are also approaching the land of identity issues and nationalism, as they are commonly understood. The National Association for the Vindication of Scottish Rights was founded in 1853, and although it was hardly a forerunner of the SNP, it was the sign of something different.

Yet so much of what we now think of as 'Scottish character' was the creation of the 17th century. By then, the country was without the focus of what we might term her own metropolitan culture. Historians have usually dwelt on the loss of the court in 1603 rather than on the often fruitful developments that filled the vacuum. And the loss is usually represented in purely cultural terms. There is no understanding of the broader function of the court, where play was intermingled with the work of running the country. The court was the milieu from which those that headed the executive organs of state were appointed. When that milieu went south, however much James might rule his kingdom with the pen, some of those executive mice began to play behind his and his successors' backs.

I think that it is from this point that the 'idea of Scotland' began to grow in a different direction, or perhaps even began to grow. And that growth was and is to do with ideas – religion and law – and was not ethnically based in a cultural sense. Thus many of the opponents of what they conceive to be Scottish 'nationalism' have often found it hard, indeed impossible, to locate their target. They have sought haggis-bashers to ridicule, but where are the haggis-bashers? They are an endangered species, because the people who derive most fun from bashing the haggis-bashers are the Scots:

> *Kiltie kiltie cauld dowp*
> *Three hackles up yer dowp:*
> *Ein for you and ein for me*
> *And ein for kiltie cauld dowp.*

Yet what happened once the substrate of religious-based ideas and the interests of Empire began to recede in the first half of this century? One thing was that a significant proportion of the native Scottish population began to turn its back on the Kirk, because after the Great War the Kirk itself took a political lurch to the right as socialism increasingly devoured the traditional liberal vote. Reinforced by the Catholic Labour vote, this was in effect a new and secular religious identity. The myth of Scotland as a nation of firebrand revolutionaries was born, and it persists, notwithstanding the fact that most people were and are pretty conservative with a small c. Then there was a growing intellectual rejection of the religious and cultural constructs of the post Reformation centuries. In *Scotland 1941*, Edwin Muir fells several dogs at one go:

But Knox and Melville clapped their preaching palms
And bundled all the harvesters away,
Hoodicrow Peden in the blighted corn
Hacked with his rusty beak the starving haulms,
Out of that desolation we were born.

Nor is Muir kinder to the people who did much to undo this legacy:

...mummied housegods in their musty niches,
Burns and Scott, sham bards of a sham nation...

Now, Muir was writing in a Scotland brought desperately low by the depression, but there is a resonance there which is still utterly familiar. One does not have to agree with Muir to admire his noble effort of honesty. But are we chasing an infinite regression of perception? Is 'reality' a perpetual chimera, an ever-vanishing rainbow? Do we just leave people with 'their own reality' for which read 'heritage'? And does that condemn the National Museum to tip-toe in a sweat of historico-political correctness between the rock of Braveheart and the hard place of dishonest journalism? Because as soon as William Wallace becomes more than a brave and remarkable (and also a cruel and rather terrifying man), and is turned into one of those grim warrior saints to whom we are expected to pray, then we are on a downward path.

My view is that we have to lift ourselves beyond what we imagine to be the national, into a fresh framework of reference that reflects the world we live in, and at least think in terms of the Scottish experience of European history. You can see in the Museum of Scotland symbols and signs of many of the great changes that affected much of Europe over the centuries. The instances are too numerous for me to expand on here. I will give just one example. There are various memorabilia that relate to what the wretched heritage copywriters call Scotland's colourful and 'turbulent' story. Why were we always so turbulent, or is it a kind of historical machismo?

Here you have a symbolic sequence starting with the Reformation and a sovereign being forced to abdicate at the instance of her subjects, causing a European-wide row at the time. What were the duties a people owed to a sovereign? The same arguments resurfaced with the fate of Charles I. Meanwhile, all those Calvinists, not just Scottish ones, but Dutch ones, English Puritans, French Huguenots, they were ransacking the scriptures for examples of a contractual relationship between creator and created, in which the sovereign must necessarily have some locus. So here you are on the road to a written view of a constitution, in the case of Scotland, the National Covenant, and to some extent, the *Institutes* of Stair and

MacKenzie. It would end up with the American and French Revolutions, to which there were plenty of interesting connections in Scotland.

Then there is Bonnie Prince Charlie: can he have a real place in the historical sun, or was he just a romantic irrelevance with no significance outside 'Scotland's story'? His focus was on the prize of London and England. He did not stand for Scotland in particular, but for patriarchal kingship. As the title of the great MacCrimmon pibroch composed on the eve of the battle of Worcester symbolises: *Fhuair mi pòg ò laimh an Righ* (I got a Kiss of the King's Hand). Prince Charles Edward's defeat presaged that of the House of Bourbon in France. By the time he died in his bed, a sad devotee of what his brother called 'the nasty bottle', Louis had already perished on the scaffold, but for the same reason as Charles Edward had failed: most people with influence had grown far beyond the notion of patriarchal kingship. All that precious memorabilia has survived precisely because it is a symbol of some magic quality embodied in a royal person, the 'divinity that doth hedge a king'. Now, this may all sound a rather intellectual way of looking at this chunk of European (and American) history, but that is just the wiring behind it. Whether these things were 'ours' or started here or not is irrelevant. They are part of Europe's, and by extension, America's history, represented in near perfect microcosm.

Seeing things in microcosm is allied to fusing material and record scholarship, and what I am getting at might be illustrated best not by a museum, but a fictional chronicle or novel, *The Bridge over the Drina (Na Drini Cuprija)*, by Ivo Andric during the Nazi occupation of Belgrade. It is the tale of the bridge at Višegrad in eastern Bosnia over four centuries, the symbol of the coming and twilight of Ottoman civilisation in the Balkans. Every sort of observation is grist to his mill: food, clothing, the shape and disposition of buildings, crime and punishment, religious observance, technological innovation, political change, all coupled by the conversation of the participants, which usually takes place on or near the bridge.

What really drives the book and its characters is the relationship between the local and an ever widening world, but all centred round a principal object, the bridge. The book starts with its construction and ends with its destruction. We start with something that is a pinpoint on a map, and end in what is recognisably modern Europe, in this case on the verge of monumental tragedy. What is of particular interest is the way Andric handled the ethnic question. Remember, this was a man born a Croat and a Catholic, who lived close to the *Bosniak* or Muslim community, who got involved in Serb nationalism before the Great War, and saw his country totally wrecked twice by war. Yet he went through some process of getting wisdom in which he could distance himself from the constructs and write a book that could see inside differing sub-cultures with an uncanny sure-footedness and humanity.

This same purpose of seeing a larger world in microcosm underlays John Galt's *Annals of the Parish*. In one sense, Galt was too ingenious, because many readers will never see beyond the whimsical musings of the charming and slightly dottled old minister. Yet great events of the time such as the Industrial Revolution and the American and French Revolutions are all carefully reflected in the characters and their physical context. The difference is that *The Bridge over the Drina* has a much broader historical sweep, and is underpinned by a formidable effort of scholarship.

The outstanding character of these two examples is their integration of the physical and intellectual. And that is the answer to the question, why museums at all? Because those physical remains are just as important a clue to the past as written records. Not so long ago, museums were just zoos of relics and grisly curiosities: collections of bygones, complete with that strange animal, a 'Keeper of Bygones'. But the original concept was of a house of the Muses, a place of spiritual and creative inspiration. Now, try and explain an exhibition brief to a modern professional, and she or he will snap back at you, 'and what is the story-line?' So still we end up with 'creation', but sometimes of an unwitting and dull sort, the worst of the heritage industry. My question is not, why museums? – but why do professional historians not take more interest in material culture as evidence, instead of their self-imposed confinement to the motte and bailey of written record scholarship?

How do we put this into practice? The new *Museum of Scottish Country Life* at Kittochside near East Kilbride will open fully in the Spring of 2001. It will not be a 'folk' museum. The folk will be there, not *das Volk*, nor Mrs Thatcher's one-dimensional 'ordinary people', but as part of a social picture that has various layers and changes in different places at different times. We will show how the old peasant Europe (which is still here in some degree) was changed by the Agricultural Revolution and evolved into present-day farmers, country tradesmen and professionals.

We will show aspects of environmental history and the development of agricultural technology and science in equal measure. This is the classic historical geographer's triangle of environment, technology and society. But we are interested in history in order to see how we have got to where we are now. Not 'The Way We Were' but 'Here Comes the Present'. And flowing from that, how does modern agriculture fill the supermarket shelves? An attempt to close with the facts, to root about like pigs in a wood if you like, to figure things out: through demonstrations, experiments and analysis that are infinitely more interesting than nostalgia. Here we are using an important part of Scotland's history to answer questions that apply throughout the Western world. I am prepared to risk that this will be of far greater interest to the public than some fake 'experience' of – what?

That does not mean that we ignore or abandon an interest in cultural character. Rather, we show that character in a broader context that does it justice and that conveys a sense of the bigger historical landscape in which it exists. If we are to develop the community of this place we call Scotland as fresh and civilised and sane, those of us who are entrusted with the collective and institutional memory have a real burden or responsibility. Without getting too solemn and carrying all of the world's burdens on our shoulders, at the same time we cannot afford to be casual in our scholarship or careless of the use to which it is put. It is not just that Jock Tamson looks to us to provide a view, for the most part he pays us: through the Heritage Lottery Fund, various European Community funds, Landfill Tax Credits, the Grant-in-Aid that keeps the National Museums going, quite apart from the many private benefactions. At the end of the day, the service he asks of us is the same he would ask of a professional such as an advocate: an opinion, in this case our opinion of the past. The picture we provide must not be some *ersatz* two-dimensional caricature of national or class identity. If we are to deal in 'stories', they must be about the connections between things, the whys and the wherefores, the ifs and buts and maybes. Easier said than done, but I still reckon that will knock all your heritage stuff into a cocked hat.

The Author

Gavin Sprott is Keeper of the Department of Social and Technological History of the National Museums of Scotland, and one time curator of the Scottish Agricultural Museum. His interests include 19th and 20th century European history and ethnology. He has had various articles published on the history of rural Scotland, and wrote *Pride and Passion: the Life, Times and Legacy of Robert Burns*, the companion book to the National Burns Exhibition in 1996. He has had various short stories published, some in tongue of his native Tayside.

References

1. Hobsbawm, E., *Nations and Nationalism since 1700*, Cambridge University Press, 1990.

2. Hewison, R., *The Heritage Industry: Britain in a Climate of Decline*, Methuen, 1987.
3. Samuel, R., *Theatres of Memory*, Verso, 1994.
4. Gellner, E., *Nations and Nationalism*, Blackwell, 1983.
5. Gellner, E., *Nationalism*, Phoenix, 1997.
6. Broun, D., Finlay, R.J. & Lynch, M. eds. *Image and Identity: The Making and Re-making of Scotland Through the Ages*, John Donald, 1998. Andric, I., *The Bridge over the Drina*, translation by W.H. McNeill, Harvill Press, 1995 (*Na Drini Cuprija*, 1945).
7. Jackson, R. & Wood, S., *Images of Scotland*, Northern College, 1997.
8. McCrone, D., Morris, A. & Kiely, R., *Scotland – The Brand*, Edinburgh University Press, 1995.
9. Rosie, G. (ed), *The Manufacture of Scottish History*, Polygon, 1992.
10. *Sunday Herald*, 6th May, 1999.
11. Marianacci, D., Director of Italian Institute of Culture, information obtained via Italian Consulate in Edinburgh, 1999.
12. Padania, in *Europa Newsletter, www.europadania.org*.
13. Kinloch Anderson, Kiltmakers of Edinburgh, trade catalogue, 1998.
14. Scots Language Society, statement on taking of the oath of loyalty in the Scots Parliament, 1999.
15. Mackay, J.A., (1987) *The Complete Letters of Robert Burns* (letter of 1st January 1789), Alloway Publishing, 1987, p. 163.
16. von Ranke, L., *Geschichte der Romanischen und Gemanischen Völker von 1494 – 1533, vol I, appendix: zur Kritik neuer Geschichtsschreiber*, 1824.
17. *Scotland on Sunday*, 23rd May, 1999.

Further Reading

Hobsbawm, E. & Ranger, T. (eds), *The Invention of Tradition*, Cambridge University Press, 1994.

10

SCOTLAND AND THE WORLD
Building on the Diaspora

David Forsyth

Emigration has long been central to Scottish historical identities.

This statement neatly sums up the importance of the 'Scotland and the World' gallery in the Museum of Scotland, and our decision to develop a network of international connections through the initiative.[1] It is founded on the fact that Scots have always been on the move, whether the motivation was to trade, to go to war, or to seek asylum from persecution. A major theme of this culture of mobility has been the phenomenon of emigration, an experience which has been central to Scottish society from our initial contribution to the 17th century plantations in Ulster and right up to the present day, when most families have kinfolk overseas through their part in joining the great diaspora.

The most commonly quoted statistic, which provides an indication of the scale of Scottish emigration, shows that rather more than half of the natural increase of the population left the country of their birth in the eight decades immediately prior to the First World War.[2] In absolute terms, one estimate puts the number of people leaving Scotland between 1825 and 1930 at over 2.3 million. For such a relatively small country, judged by any standard, this represents a large figure. Indeed, the true total might still be masked, as available government statistics for the period from 1825–52 had a tendency to underestimate the number of emigrants.[3]

The late Professor Michael Flinn described Scotland as being locked in an 'unenviable championship' of emigration which took place among the major European nations. This league of countries witnessed Scotland in competition with Norway for second place behind Ireland, the latter being consistently Europe's leading country for relative propensity to emigrate.

All this took place in the context of a huge European-wide diaspora which was marked by around 52 million people leaving their country of birth for destinations in the New World during a period from the end of the Napoleonic Wars in 1815 to the economic depression of the 1930s.[4] What made Scotland unique among the European countries to experience such a mass out-migration during this time was the fact that Scots were a people who had opted to leave a society which enjoyed the twin dynamics of industrialisation and economic growth.

There is a large body of evidence, much of it anecdotal, which chronicles the large extent to which Scots have been successful in spreading themselves across the globe. One commentator considered that 'the proverbial Scotchman had not long to be looked for'.[5] David Macrae, a well-known United Presbyterian minister from Gourock, while making his first trip to the United States in 1867, remarked that 'I begin to think that either the world was very small or Scotland very large'.[6] Indeed, this comment could easily be extended to summarise the position of Scots, not just in the United States, but also in the other popular destinations for Scottish emigrants such as Canada and the Antipodes. For example, there are areas with particular concentrations of Scottish settlement such as at Otago and Waipu, located respectively in the South and North Islands of New Zealand.

SCOTLAND AND THE WORLD GALLERY

In the development of the 18th and 19th century displays of the Museum of Scotland, migration was identified as a theme for a special gallery to be known as 'Scotland and the World', one of fifteen themes within the Industry and Empire galleries of the Museum of Scotland. They are situated in a pivotal position on Level 5, between the displays showing the industrial output of 19th century Scotland and the social and domestic life of the Victorian and Edwardian periods.

As part of their contribution to the Museum of Scotland Campaign, United Distillers & Vintners (UDV) generously sponsored a curatorial assistant's post dedicated to work on the research and development of the Scotland and the World displays, which range over four display cases and an entire wall given over to a montage of images on three large wall panels entitled *The Scottish Homeland*. The order of the displays were designed to encourage visitors to follow a preferred circulation route and viewing sequence. The starting point for following the emigrant trail is the case entitled *Reasons for Leaving*, which illustrates the variety of triggers (economic, social or political), which prompted so many Scots into seeking their fortune or improvement in a new life overseas.

The Scottish Homeland strives to encapsulate the experience of rural and urban life during the 18th and 19th centuries, touching on Scottish enterprise and exports, and considering the Scotland that was left behind. The visitor is then encouraged to turn around and view. Two cases illustrate the destinations many Scots left for. The first considers the Scots in North America, with material from earliest colonial times until the opening up of the Pacific coasts of the United States and Canada, often through the enterprise, ingenuity and frequently the sheer muscle power of Scots. The displays show a range of material which was either taken out to North America, or made and used by emigrants once they had settled in their new home.

The second case illustrates the varied life and activities of the Scot in India, Africa, and the Antipodes. There is a colourful range of material including a ceremonial feather gorget from Tahiti presented by the widow of Captain James Cook to Sir John Pringle, which he in turn donated to the collection of the Society of Antiquaries of Scotland in 1781.

These displays highlight the integral part that Scots played in the British Empire as soldiers, missionaries and explorers. From a scimitar belonging to Tipu Sultan who was captured by General Sir David Baird's troops at Seringapatam, to the silver tea and coffee service presented to a Scottish Presbyterian minister on his retirement from his church in Calcutta. This second destination case reveals the great diversity of the Scottish experience. Material collected by, or associated with pioneers of African exploration, like David Livingstone and Joseph Thomson, is also represented.

To deal comprehensively with the historiographical phenomenon of migration, the displays had also to take account of the equally important dynamic of internal migration within Scotland, especially in terms of seasonal employment. This culture of mobility was easily extended into Scots taking a decision which ultimately led to the enormous step of moving overseas. In terms of material culture, this was one of the more challenging themes to illustrate. To ensure a comprehensive picture of Scottish migration, the question of immigration into Scotland also had to be addressed. It is one of the great paradoxes of Scottish history that as Scotland experienced a great haemorrhage of people through emigration, Scottish society also displayed a marked propensity to attract inward migrants, especially from Ireland.[7]

BUILDING ON THE DIASPORA

If the Scotland and the World initiative was to be successful, then one of our tasks was to develop and cultivate an international network of contacts, be they individuals or institutions, with an interest in the Scottish diaspora. This network was identified as a vital means of tracing and securing material for the displays, as a basis for further research, and as a medium through which awareness of the Museum of Scotland could be projected to an international audience.

The network identified three key loans for the opening displays. These objects were obtained from three very different institutions situated in three geographically disparate areas of North America. Each object was an appropriate metaphor for the area of Scottish influence or settlement from where it was taken or used. The objects were also very distinct, such as a pair of Luckenbooth style brooches from the Royal Ontario Museum in Toronto, a teapot by the Aberdeen silversmith Robert Cruickshank from the American Decorative Arts and Sculpture collections of the Museum of Fine Arts in Boston, and a Gaelic Bible taken to North Carolina by a Scottish emigrant and now kept in the archives of the Presbyterian Church at Montreat in North Carolina.

The teapot in question was originally owned by an Elspeth Burnet, who in 1705 married Alexander Middleton, a collector of customs from Aberdeen. The teapot passed to their son Alexander Middleton Jr who took it to Boston, when he emigrated to British North America around 1735. The Middletons had been a prominent family in Aberdeen, both the father and grandfather of Alexander Middleton Sr having served as principals of King's College, whilst Middleton's father combined this position with that of Dean of the Diocese of Aberdeen.[8]

The heart-shaped brooches of silver used for trade purposes became highly sought after by native Americans during the early years of the fur trade from around 1760 to 1821. However, once the Hudson's Bay Company had established a virtual monopoly of the fur trade (which covered a staggering one-quarter of North America after its amalgamation with the North West Company in 1821), silver was no longer used as a trade commodity. During this golden age of fur trading, such was the popularity of the heart-shaped Luckenbooth brooch among the Iroquois, that it became widely viewed as the national symbol of the Iroquois people.[9] In a description, published in 1795, of the early commercial exchange between Europeans and native peoples, one is presented with the range of equivalents for bartered trade goods and skins. This account detailed the rate of exchange for one beaver pelt as '6 small silver brooches'.[10]

Brooches of this design might have been consciously introduced into British North America, as exemplified by the work of the Montreal based silversmith Robert Cruickshank. Perhaps the distinctive design was adopted after native Americans had made contact with Scottish fur traders or settlers who might have been wearing similar brooches made in

Scotland and brought over the Atlantic. Either way perhaps the knowledge of the Luckenbooth as a love token struck a chord with the Iroquois and fed into elements within their own popular culture and folk tales. As a point of interest, contemporary Iroquois silversmiths appear to have continued the limited production of such brooches, and they have occasionally been seen for sale at native Canadian craft centres in Ontario.

The Gaelic Bible from Montreat, North Carolina, was published by the British and Foreign Bible Society and belonged to Alexander Leach (1784–1886) who along with his family emigrated to North Carolina in 1802, following one of the well-established routes within North America for Scottish emigrants, especially those with Highland origins. After landing at Wilmington, the major port of disembarkation for previous generations of newly arrived Scottish emigrants, Leach journeyed further up the Cape Fear River to Fayetteville, centre of one of North Carolina's earliest Highland emigrant communities. Many of the original settlers here had been resolutely loyal to King George III during the American War of Independence, and it was still a recognisably Scottish community.

Leach finally settled in the farming country of Moore County some 40 miles northwest of Fayetteville. During a recent investigation on the internet, the writer discovered a website containing census data for Moore County, the census of 1820 included the name of Alexander Leach. The Bible was presented to the Presbyterian History Society at Montreat by Leach's grandson and granddaughter.

THE MULTIMEDIA PROGRAMME

The full Scotland and the World multimedia programme can be viewed at two points in the gallery, and the programme of short essays can also be interrogated in 'EhibIT' (the Museum of Scotland multimedia resource room). The initial panel to the Scotland and the World gallery is a large revolving map of the world presented on a screen. This acts as an introduction to the visitor by providing them with a highly visual presentation of the spread of Scots across the world through place-names of Scottish provenance. Although it is not a scientific means of quantifying numbers, it does provide a highly effective means of showing the international presence of the emigrant Scot. This is on a revolving world map, alongside which are two other smaller screens. The first shows captioned images of the places in which Scots settled, with some of the classic romanticised views of Scottish emigration, including Thomas Faed's *The Last of the Clan,* and J Watson Nicol's *Lochaber No More.* Most of the images are from overseas institutions and had not been previously published in this country, and the international network was critical to the success of this programme.

The second level of the programme is a series of short multimedia essays, which complement and expand some of the themes addressed in the displays. For example, although we have only one object associated with the explorer Joseph Thomson, his Royal Geographical Society Founder's Medal, the multimedia essay augments the information by using images from his travels in Africa and pictures of both the waterfalls and gazelle which were named after him.

Future plans for this aspect of our work include the development of the map of place-names into an interactive gazetteer which could be interrogated for more information about each place. A number of pilot examples have already appeared in the multimedia essay section of the existing programme, where we have included entries on New Glasgow, Nova Scotia, Guelph, Ontario and Dunedin in New Zealand.

THE INTERNATIONAL NETWORK

The Scotland and the World initiative was formally launched on 30 April 1999 with the declared aim to further our understanding of the life, work and influence of the Scots overseas. It would seek to harness the energy which went into the development of the Museum of Scotland, and it has been described as a 'bold attempt to look out from Scotland and make links throughout the world', as well as 'a springboard with enormous potential for the future'.[11]

The initiative will build on the contacts made to date through the development of the displays, and draw on available expertise within all the curatorial departments of the National Museums of Scotland. It is the intention to promote programmes of collaborative exhibitions, study exchanges, and conferences. In this way, it is hoped that the initiative will become a focus Scottish diaspora studies. Indeed, a major symposium and a conference on cognate themes are already planned, the first being on the theme of *Colonial Baggage*, to focus on links between Scotland and New Zealand.

It was particularly significant that this symposium grew out of an initial proposal by a visiting researcher from New Zealand, who was attached to Scotland and the World while conducting a comparative study of national museums and national identity in Scotland and New Zealand. By the end of 1999, we will have been hosts to a total of four visiting researchers and student attachments. A number of these young scholars have actively sought a placement through hearing about us through the network of contacts.

120

The poetry competition sponsored by the National Museums of Scotland, *Present Poets*, had as its theme for 1999: 'the experience of people who have emigrated and the effects of emigration on Scotland itself.' There was an excellent response from around the world, and interestingly a number of the contributors included with their entries their family's genealogy. This is an indication of an as of yet untapped source of material which is intrinsically relevant to the scope of Scotland and the World. Indeed, much material both documentary and graphic has been collected during the course of developing the displays and the multimedia programme.

With the Museum of Scotland now open, and a number of new major projects by the National Museums of Scotland being carried out at the Scottish United Services Museum at Edinburgh Castle and the new Museum of Scottish Country Life at Kittochside, there has never been a better time to take the national collections to the world. Given that Scotland now has a Parliament of its own, there is a great deal of interest, not least among the Scottish diaspora, in all aspects of the 'New' Scotland. The author is confident that the programmes associated with the initiative will make a significant contribution to a more effective presentation of Scotland to the World and of the World to Scotland.

The Author

David Forsyth became the first Research Assistant for the Scotland and the World initiative in 1998, following two years as Curatorial Assistant on the Museum of Scotland Project when he worked specifically on the Scotland and the World display and the in-gallery multimedia programme. He previously worked in public libraries, and in 1992 became a research student and teaching assistant in the Department of History at the University of Strathclyde, his research interests being Scottish national identity and the Empire 1800–1914, Scottish unionism and early home rule demands.

References

1. Harper, M., *Emigration from Scotland between the Wars: Opportunity or Exile?* (quoted from J.M. Mackenzie's introduction as general editor), Manchester, 1998, p. ix.
2. Flinn, M. et al, *Scottish Population History from the 17th Century to the 1930s*, Cambridge, 1977, pp. 488.
3. Ibid, p. 447.

4. Baines, D., *Emigration from Europe, 1815–1930*, Cambridge, 1995, p. 4.
5. Cage, R.A. (ed), *The Scots Abroad: Labour, Capital, Enterprise, 1750–1914* (quote in the editor's introduction from 'Scottish Capital Abroad', in *Blackwood's Edinburgh Magazine*, Vol 136, October 1884), Beckenham, 1985.
6. Macrae, D., *American Presidents and Men I have Met*, Glasgow, 1908, p. 121.
7. Devine, T.M., 'The Paradox of Scottish Emigration', in T. M. Devine (ed), *Scottish Emigration and Scottish Society*, Edinburgh, 1992, pp. 2–3.
8. Falino, J. & Ralli, T., they work at the Museum of fine Art in Boston and the author is grateful to them for supplying the results of their genealogical research into the various owners of the Cruickshank teapot.
9. Frederickson, N.J., *The Covenant Chain: Indian Ceremonial and Trade Silver*, Ottawa, 1980, pp. 52–53.
10. Ibid, p. 92.
11. National Museums of Scotland, a statement by the Board of Trustees, in *Museum of Scotland Prospectus*, Edinburgh, 1998, p. 30.

11

A HOUSE BUILT FOR IDENTITY
National Shrine or Distorting Mirror?

Charles McKean

A national museum, if it is to represent more than a passive title, appears to contain the seeds of schizophrenia. Traditionally, museums are about the amassing, curation and communication of collections: a scholarly activity arguably at odds with the historical and political undertones implied by a 'national' agenda. This paper studies the impact that a national agenda might have had on the making of the Museum of Scotland.

Ironically, the two most significant issues in the emergence of the museum, namely its site and the nature of its institutional locus, arose not from a national agenda, but from a contingent and expedient response to a political problem. The nation's jewel casket, seemingly so inevitably in the right place emerging at the right time, was nonetheless the product of happenstance. The pendicle of land, which it occupies at the western end of Chambers Street, had been the subject of a tussle between two competing, dissimilar and mutually suspicious museums for most of the 20th century. For decades, both the Royal Scottish Museum in Chambers Street, and the National Museum of Antiquities of Scotland in Queen Street claimed *droit de seigneur* over the piece of unoccupied and variably valuable residual real estate cast up by the creation and subsequent widening of George IV Bridge.

After sixteen years of tortuous design development examining the extent to which both museums (whose original ambitions had extended to perhaps four times that space) could satisfactorily be squeezed into the same structure on the same extremely constricted site, it was finally accepted that the site simply could not accommodate two separate organisations. In summer 1983, the Secretary of State for Scotland announced that the two museums were to be married and joined in a single museum organisation, solemnised by the 1985 National Heritage (Scotland) Act. The creation of a Museum of Scotland was to be one of the new organisation's principal tasks. It is not often that a major public institution representing a nation is created pragmatically by the spatial limitations of a plot of ground.

A MATTER OF TITLES

Being the embodiment of ideas about Scotland and how to portray them, the concept of a 'Museum of Scotland' has been subject to continuous discussion ever since the founding of the Society of Antiquaries of Scotland and its museum in 1782. Yet the concept of a national museum has not always implied a museum of national identity. In 1849, the Lord Provost of Edinburgh was informed that 'by a national museum is meant a museum in a capital city open to the public gratuitously independent of private, collegiate or society.'[1] Things moved on, for when the Williams Committee sought to revivify the NMAS collections by rechristening them the 'Museum of Scotland' in 1981, its agenda was specific, and the committee was rather smug about it:[2]

> This name should have immediate appeal...The new Museum should be more than a repository for collections satisfactorily catalogued, conserved and researched. We expect it to contribute greatly to the interpretation of Scottish culture, and to be a magnet for visitors to Edinburgh, and educational groups of all ages who want to learn about Scottish history...Accordingly...the status of the renamed NMS should rise correspondingly.

Accordingly? Simply as the consequence of a change of name? The Committee members must have considered that some power must reside in the name of Scotland. By rank coincidence, the concept of a Museum of Scotland emerged in the same year that Barbara and Murray Grigor astounded Edinburgh with their celebration of what they regarded as Scotland's true culture, namely kitsch, in an exhibition entitled 'Scotch Myths', with the climax of a pianola, against the background of a Scots panorama, foaming to the strains of Mendelsohn's Fingal's Cave. It was a suitable warning.

The matter of Scottish identity knocked against almost every aspect of the generation of the new building: the relationship between the new museum and the Royal Museum of Scotland, between Scotland and England, and indeed between Scotland and the world. Lord Perth, an enthusiastic proponent of the name 'Museum of Scotland' ever since his membership of the Williams Committee, fought tenaciously in the House of Lords both for the title (their Lordships indulged his 'particular interest in the name') and for the requirement that the NMS should 'have regard for things Scottish' in the Act itself, even though the Government itself considered such amendments superfluous.[3] Some peers were concerned that such a title might encourage a chauvinistic approach, but were persuaded that since the Scots were such sensible folk, it should not: particularly in the light of Perth's further amendment emphasising that the new Museum would include any or all objects in the collections of *both* museums, rather just from that most closely associated with being Scots.[4]

A group of senior staff from both museums wrote to the Scottish Office to welcome the opportunities provided by a single museum, and aspired to a building that could relate 'the achievements and aspirations of the Scots in all disciplines.'[5] Its coded message was that there was a need to broaden the concept of the Museum of Scotland to embrace objects of Scottish relevance, engineering, technology and industry, from far beyond the NMAS collections.

At a time when the curators were contemplating how the Museum of Scotland might broaden out from the reformatting and relocation the collections of the NMAS to include other Scottish-connected collections, the title came to life. It began to attract a tidal wave of emotion and ideas revealing aspirations of a national identity that went far beyond mere collections. Perhaps inadvertently, when the Secretary of State referred to the notion of a Museum of Scotland as 'the prime repository for artifacts representing the cultural history of Scotland,' in his decision to form a single museum under a single Board of Trustees in 1983, he endorsed the emerging idea that the museum should somehow represent the country's culture, a point observed with much approval in the House of Lords two years later.[6] Representation of a national history to its people signifies a considerable conceptual shift from a scholarly research institute making residual provision for the 'ordinary sightseer and visitor', as had been the proposal back in 1951. Furthermore, a museum with a specific cultural agenda implied the organisation of its displays along a thematic storyline pattern.

Opening the John Michael Wright exhibition in July 1982, Lord Bute referred to the proposal as 'a sanctuary of national pride', thereby considerably upping the stakes for a mere museum. It was now to be a cultural Valhalla. Such populist and political overtones tended to distress curators and museum buffs, so it was not unexpected that the Council for Museums and Galleries in Scotland might propose that the intended museum should confine itself to the sublunary task of presenting 'distinctive or outstanding aspects of the national culture.'[7] The very title of the new museum organisation proved prickly. Some Lords desired the title 'Museum of Scotland' to embrace the entire Government funded Scottish museums operation. This idea of Scotland was getting out of hand and frightening the horses. The National Museums of Scotland proved a smart compromise.

With the establishment of the Secretary of State's creature, the Museums Advisory Board, which first met on 2 May 1984, priorities shifted from a national agenda. Lord Bute pointed out that 'the new Museum is neither a title nor a building, but a concept to be developed,' and before they could create a new museum, they had first to create a new museum structure from two institutions of fundamentally different personalities and philosophies.[8] For the time being, the pibroch strain of the 'sanctuary of national pride' had been overlain by the more prosaic one. But the national issue would not lie 'doggo'. It surfaced in even the least exciting of administrative documents, for after all: what was the new building to do? It was never going to be a complete museum in a holistic sense, with its own staff, its own direction, its own identity, its own curation, conservation and research. It was instead destined to be a display and interpretation centre using borrowed staff with the mission to 'develop a coherent display of material illuminating Scottish culture and history,'[9] or be a 'major new building [with] displays focusing on the history and culture of Scotland.'[10]

Once the NMS had settled down as a single organisation, the latent national purpose of the proposed building burst through and came to dominate work on exhibition development. The Director, Dr Robert Anderson boasted that 'no museum has presented a national history in Scotland or indeed in the United Kingdom,' implying that the new one would be proud to do so.[11] When Michael Forsyth was appointed Minister of State for the Scottish Office, Lord Bute wrote to him to inform him that 'we all consider that a new building in which to proclaim Scotland's past and present is absolutely vital.'[12]

The implications of 'proclaim' were emphasised in the John Richards' Feasibility Study, published in August 1989: 'a new national museum will be seen as a symbol of national identity.'[13] The greater the rhetoric, the more difficult it would become to design a museum in line with curators' natural desires: namely a flexible black box. The metaphorical implications for the country would be too profound. That Robert Anderson could in 1990 state that 'we considered every Scottish or Scottish-orientated object as a potential resource,' was an indication, on the one hand, that the passage toward unity within the NMS was being won; equally it signalled the emergence of a much stronger Scottish dimension to the project than had been the case six years earlier.[14] From the brief issued for the architectural competition in 1991, it was reasonable to infer that a comprehensive history of Scotland was to be fashioned by and within the new building.

THE MUSEUM BRIEF

The first expression of the new building was contained in the instructions to a 1986 Working Group 'to express the philosophy underlying the new building which will influence its form and which will animate what it contains.'[15] This rare and remarkable requirement that the building's form should 'animate' the artifacts within was a strong marker to all those involved that a 'black box' museum would not be acceptable. Implicitly, icons of Scottish history would be selected for key locations and curators were soon tasked to identify them. The working group was also expected to devise ways 'to persuade the people of Scotland that the new building, and what it could do, was something they absolutely must have.'[16] What it could do, indeed. What are museums meant to do? Display, curate, conserve and interpret collections...or perhaps more in this case.

Although the proposed building was still conceived as an extension of the existing Royal Museum within the NMS' institutional umbrella, and indeed entered only through the original Royal Museum entrance, the competition brief implied a new hesitation. Reading like a Guardian editorial, the brief required the new building to 'have a distinct identity', and yet 'complement the existing Museum buildings, and avoid compromising their qualities.'[17]

The earlier insistence upon the single entrance emphasising museological unity was wobbling: the Trustees 'saw merit in having a single main entrance to the Museum complex, probably retaining the present principal public entrance.' What the competitors took from this, as indicated in the winning scheme, was a building that was easily convertible to a stand-alone design with its own entrance. Coincidentally or not, between conception in 1986 and implementation in 1992, all non-Scottish components of the proposed building – galleries for Chinese Lacquer and the Ethnographic material, the library and the Information Centre – were excised from the new project one by one.

THEMATIC DEVELOPMENT

The Museum of Scotland developed not as a museum of collections so much as a thematic museum, intended to convey 'the story of a whole nation.'[18] A narrative approach to museum display was certainly not unknown, but what distinguished the project was the scale of it. In most

127

galleries, items selected for display were those that both supported the story, and from which it was derived, and curators, designers and visitors were required to make novel and occasionally surprising connections.

Jenni Calder, who had edited the exhibition catalogue for The Wealth of a Nation, later the Museum of Scotland script co-ordinator, had strong views about likely visitor perceptions. For example, was it right to ignore critical periods of Scottish history, if the collections tended not to support them? For example, should Mary Queen of Scots' jewellery be in a display about Renaissance jewellery or in one about Mary Stewart? She had the support of the Director: Robert Anderson himself was a collections man who yet nonetheless veered toward narrative even where the collections did not appear to sustain it. Responding to an exhibition proposal focused on themes of how people lived, traded and sheltered themselves, he wrote: [19]

> ...have we moved too far away from history? I can detect huge historical events, even periods, in the [draft exhibition brief]. I frequently mention the problem of the Enlightenment, saying that at least it must be mentioned. But where would that be?...We are missing out. We are not treating the history of Fine Art and architecture. There is a distinctiveness in architecture. Recent RIAS exhibitions bring this out clearly...

He was referring to the then current Edinburgh Festival exhibition, The Architecture of the Scottish Renaissance.

So, despite the reiterated intention that the national narrative would emerge from the selected objects themselves, rather than one imposed upon them from a historical perspective, there was sustained pressure for a more overarching approach. In time, it extended even to Trustee pressure for the Museum to 'answer public expectations by covering, for example, the Clearances and immigration, the growth of Glasgow, and the importance of Edinburgh in the Scottish Enlightenment.'[20] However, collection-focused curators were reluctant, fretting that if the themes of a chronological national narrative were not adequately sustained by the collections, the resulting displays might stray from the strict presentation and interpretation of the hapless objects. As one testy memo put it, 'the difference between a Heritage Centre and a Museum is that the latter does not attempt to make bricks without straw.'[21] In a contribution to the exhibition brief, The Keeper of Archaeology had made a special case for the archeologists:[22]

> Our main messages are: (1) that people in prehistoric and early historic times are not to be regarded as squat grunting savages

leading squalid brutish lives. (2) That for 90%, in terms of time, for the human occupation of the geographical area of Scotland, the concept of a Scottish nation, as we now understand it, is now meaningless. (3) Our view of Scotland as a relatively impoverished country at the extreme edge of Europe is merely a modern map projection that provides no universal template for understanding pre-history and early history.'

The message was clear. Archaeology would have no truck with any narrative based upon something that it regarded as meaningless in terms of pre-history. Approximate chronology upstairs, perhaps (albeit difficult given that the Keeper was Head of Exhibitions for the Museum of Scotland) but in the basement things would be different.

In any case, how could a museum of objects cope with one of the pinnacles in the country's intellectual history, the Scottish Enlightenment, which on the face of it, was not well represented by material artefacts? Even if a pickled Enlightenment brain had been available, how would it be displayed and what could it communicate? Generally, it would be either by examining the application of ideas, as in medicine or science, or by the display of books and manuscripts which only rarely makes a vivid or popular exhibition. In fact, that is what had been attempted in 'A HotBed of Genius' exhibition. Reviewing it retrospectively, Anderson had this to say:[23]

> A good deal of thought has, on occasion, been put into how to present an historical account by means of exhibited objects...The ambition of the exhibition was to tell the story of the Scottish Enlightenment in a popular way...But the process of development of the exhibition was somewhat agonising. Clearly there are going to be problems in an exhibition on this theme central to Scottish history: how does one present Hume's views on causation, Smith's economic theory, or even Black's work on latent heat? The exhibition itself developed as a series of portraits, memorabilia and personalia backed up by the books which dealt with these intangible matters. It was an excellent experience, but, again, the well-prepared scholar would derive considerably more from it than the curious but uninformed member of the public.

Other aspects of Scots history stumbled on the same obstacle. The original proposal for 'Modern Times', for example, was criticised as an unsorted collection of unconvincing items unable to sustain the weight of its story. 'Keir Hardie's silver tea service, the only significant item for the period, seems unlikely to give a representative picture of radical politics in the twentieth century.'[24] Moreover how would items pass the Scottishness test: made in Scotland, made for Scotland, bought by Scotland, stolen by Scotland or made by Scots abroad? An irritated Director memorialised:[25]

> ...the fact that the Boulton & Watt engine was made for an English brewery is not that important. Surely we are not intending to be that racially pure in the Museum of Scotland? Watt is one of Scotland's greatest sons...To show the Boulton & Watt elsewhere than in the Museum can be intellectually justified, but to the public it would seem capricious.

There were gaps in the collections: very little on post-reformation Catholicism; only a certain amount of heavy engineering, very little significant on Clyde shipbuilding since that had been encouraged to go to Glasgow, and only a few spare items of furniture by those renowned for furniture design: Francis Brodie, Robert Adam, Charles Rennie Mackintosh and Sir Robert Lorimer.[26] Moreover, there was insufficient space upon the site for even a representative summary of Scotland's history. 'This apparent weakness we have sought to turn into a benefit. We have quite deliberately constructed our presentations around the idea that much of the evidence is available elsewhere in Scotland...Our hope is that the Museum of Scotland will create in visitors the wish to explore more.'[27]

Curators summarised the contribution they thought their collections might make to the national story, with the exception of the adamant archeologists who sought, instead, to communicate how ancient peoples lived, and the themes gradually emerged by a form of consensus. The exhibition text was thus assembled, reworked, and reassembled in an iterative process until an object-based narrative emerged. However, at this point the design of the galleries emerged as a potential problem. Displays that were over-dependent on chronology or too didactic in theme would prove difficult to arrange in a gallery with multiple entrances. Any display based upon the accretion of knowledge in a specific sequence became vulnerable to the thrawn visitor who, human and contrary, might enter at the wrong end of a sequence; or, worse, graze at random. Conversely, such a difficulty could be turned to an advantage in these post-modern, deconstructed days of multiple themes. The proposal to address the 18th century as 'the Jacobite Century' was soon defeated by the monstrous regiments of the Church, the Improvers, the industrialists and the Enlightenment. As Gavin Sprott put it: 'Displays should avoid the sense of the past inevitably leading to the present, because that is the fodder of myth. History is full of blind alleys and unexpected breaks, and that is what makes it exciting.'[28] Multiple entrances, disconnections and cul-de-sacs would do very nicely.

National identity beetled equally upon the selection of an architect. Determined that the Trustees of the National Museums of Scotland should emerge as patrons, Bute strongly supported the appointment of a designer by architectural competition. It proved improbably controversial once HRH the Prince of Wales accepted a role as President of the Patrons of the new museum. His dramatic attack on the short list for the architectural competition for the National Gallery in Trafalgar Square in 1984 led to the process being abandoned, as had a further foray into the rebuilding of the Paternoster Square area around St. Paul's. The ghost of extra-national intervention haunted the entire procedure.

Scots architectural competitions were organised by the Royal Incorporation of Architects in Scotland from their base in Rutland Square, Edinburgh. Unhappy about the Director's inclination toward a limited architectural competition, the Incorporation was ready to resist publicly a contest where no Scot could enter. In February 1990, rumours swept through Edinburgh, and the RIAS and the museum were beleaguered accordingly. Bute sidestepped a direct approach by focusing on a matter of common agreement: 'Like yourself, I hope that a Scottish architect may emerge as a winner.'[29] Visiting the Royal Institute of British Architects (RIBA), the Director found that it would not contemplate even a limited competition that was closed to English architects, and nominated a few for consideration. The RIAS was much more international, more open and more bullish. It faced Anderson with 'a strong case for a two-stage competition with an open first stage providing the basis for a restricted second stage.'[30] The Trustees chose the latter, and requested the RIAS to clear the competition brief with the International Union of Architects. However, the museum found their rules for competitions almost impossible to administer and grossly uneconomic to run. To have followed them could have doubled the timescale and the cost of the competition. The museum duly determined to reject the Union's involvement.

The RIAS then had to choose between upholding the Union's regulations and thereby lose the competition, or ignoring the international community, and agree to organise the competition. It chose the latter. Two days after the launch of the competition, the RIBA Competitions Officer, Ian Shaw, wrote to the RIAS:[31]

> As we are party to the UIA, it follows therefore that you could not say that the competition is RIBA-approved. I recall that the last Scottish international competition of significance, that in Iona, was

also not RIBA approved. I wonder why this is? Does Scotland simply not bother, or deliberately disregard the UIA?

Reworking the Scots ballad 'The Miller of Dee', the RIAS Secretary dispatched a quick response: 'the UIA will not recognise the RIAS; and, as a consequence, it does not seem incumbent upon us to seek UIA approval for our competition.' Two days later, Shaw retorted:

> The UIA recognises the United Kingdom. Scotland, as Wales and Northern Ireland, is a part of the UK...As a fellow Scot, you know that I appreciate the Scottish interest and position...What I am not clear about, again as a Scot, is whether you believe that, at the most, Scotland should be a separate EEC member...

In May 1991, the International Union of Architects anathematised the contest with commendably little effect upon the international enthusiasm to enter it.

Over 700 competition briefs were dispatched worldwide. 371 designs were received, eventually reduced to a shortlist of six. The short list of architects caused equal trouble north and south. To the personality-dominated London press, they were relative nonentities. To the Scottish press, that five firms were from London and one from Northampton was inflammatory. Project Scotland lamented the absence of any Scots on the short leet: only to receive a riposte from Colin Mackenzie (an architect from Clydebank who had been job architect on the Linn Products factory in Eaglesham by Richard Rogers) that Ulrike Wilke had studied in Scotland (the Mackintosh School), had married a Scot and worked for a Scot in London, whereas Gordon Benson was not only Professor of Architecture at Strathclyde University but had 'as filthy a Scottish accent as you could wish for.'[32] Nor was discontent confined to the media. Unhappy with the result, Edinburgh architect Ben Tindall wrote to the RIAS:[33]

> It is true I find it upsetting, strange and wrong that five out of the six finalists out of 360+ entries to an international competition should come from London. Is London really the world centre of architectural excellence? Is it a pure mathematical fluke? I think not. The only logical explanation is that the entries were judged against the mores of London architecture. When architecture is to be judged against London mores, then the attempts of Scottish/foreign architects will be in vain...If there is any conspiracy, perhaps it is the Museum who appeared to want Richard Meier in the first place and chose the nearest they could get.

The day of the announcement of the winner, the Scotsman carried exclusive coverage of the Prince of Wales's resignation as President of Patrons, published at a time and in a manner designed to pre-empt the press conference to announce the winner of possibly the largest international architectural competition to be staged in the United Kingdom. The Prince withdrew on the grounds that 'he did not feel that the process was consistent with his hope that as much weight be given to interested lay opinion as so-called experts.'[34] Since, as it happened, Bute had been peculiarly sensitive to the Prince's views on this matter, and had arranged an overall balance between architects and others, the reason given may be taken as camouflage for the fact that the design did not suit the tastes of the Prince's set. The world media had been so diverted by the Prince's resignation that there was a danger that the announcement of the winner would be overshadowed, in spite of any calm assurance that might be offered by Bute and Perth. On the way into the press conference, Bute reassured a Trustee 'since when did the House of Windsor rule taste in this country?' and altered his course by neither jot nor tittle.[35]

Three weeks later, Henry Porter wrote in the *Independent* Magazine:[36]

> It is difficult to avoid the feeling that the Museum authorities in Edinburgh are pretty pleased with the outcome of this now famous dispute…They have, after all, defeated the great supervening amateur of the Eighties, and they will now build their Museum of Scotland as they want it…The Prince had become used to obeisance in architecture, and like many princes before him, he had failed to watch his northern border.

It was the national agenda that enabled the Scots to sidestep the constraining influence that the Prince had wielded in London. Those who had contemplated the lineage of Crichton Stuart (Bute) and Drummond (Perth) concluded that the decision to proceed was the final act of Culloden.

DESIGN

The implications of national identity upon architecture are more complex. Architecture, traditionally, is the locus where nationalism can be expressed with least adverse consequence: indeed, where residual nationalism can appear satisfactory in the most international of countries. Such had been Scotland's case, for example, during the 19th century. However, national implications are difficult. By analogy, consider the inflated Roman imperialism preferred by Albert Speer for public manifestations of the regime, as compared to the preferred *heimat* implications of Teissenow's designs for suburban estates. Nationalism, in short, is not always expressed by having the principal public buildings being overtly nationalistic. What you did in the privacy of your own home was a different matter. With its emphasis upon respect for location, the Museum of Scotland's brief implied some Scottish reference, and some entries were duly bizarre.

The Indian Royal Gold Medal-winning architect Charles Correa has suggested that 'architecture is about a kind of transformation of the past. You have to understand the mythic images of place.'[37] The competition-winning architects, Benson & Forsyth, understood perfectly the implications of constructing a building to encapsulate national identity, but had no intention of copying historic styles. Gordon Benson's philosophy was that 'architecture from the past touches the heart. The next step is how to continue it.'[38] His preferred approach was that of abstraction and appealing to historic resonance: national identity oozed from their competition entry drawings. The new museum was shown not just as anchored to its site, emphasising the views to the Castle and Chambers Street, but adorned with iconography of intensely Scots inspiration: tower houses, brochs, the standing stones of Callanish, views and details of Edinburgh. Vignettes of the Highlands and the view across to Eigg alternated with photographs, the most significant being that of Dunstaffnage, indicating its broad formal resemblance to their design. They also provided tempting indications of how the icons of Scottish history identified in the brief – water wheel, the Hamilton Palace drawing room, the steam engine and some standing stones – might be incorporated within the fabric of the building itself.

Their design was adjudged winner for four reasons: its imaginative response to its location in Edinburgh, at the hinge between the rational, orthogonal educational boulevard of Chambers Street, and the mediaeval idiosyncrasies of Candlemaker Wynd, the Grassmarket and the Castle; to its appealing proposal to pedestrianise and plant Chambers Street, adorned with open-air auditoria; to its clever plan of a tower of flexible galleries enfolded by a less flexible curtain wall of study galleries; and by the use of icons from collections at charismatic points in the museum journey. The Scottishness of the design also embraced the use of stone, albeit deployed in a manner wholly uncharacteristic of traditional Scottish buildings (the stone walls of the Museum of Scotland take the form of a rain screen with open rather than mortared joints, in place of the solid masonry promised in the competition entry).

The expression of these functions was resolved into a plan implying far deeper-seeming nationalist intentions. A building formed of a higher tower of stacked galleries enclosed by a lower 'curtain-wall' of side galleries, ancillary uses, stairs and open orientation spaces, produced something close to a Gaeltachd mediaeval curtain-walled stronghold. The resemblance to Dunstaffnage, whose accommodation had lain against the wall with space at the centre, until a fashionable tower house had been added in the late 15th/early 16th centuries, was emphasised in the competition drawing. In addition to the plan, the massing of the museum, and the relationship with its drum tower, and the detail of some of the windows also conveyed abstraction from Scots precedent. The beautifully smooth Clashach stone echoed the ashlar, the polished squared stone, of the principal facade of the most important Renaissance structures such as Parliament House, George Heriot's Hospital, or Holyrood; and the contrast between the stone curtain and the white concrete or harled mass behind (best appreciated from Bristo Port) echoed the Renaissance contrast between dressed stone facades and harled flanks. It was less a 'Scottishness' of spurious crowsteps or corbels in the Lorimer tradition so much as a Scottishness of abstract geometries in the tradition of Charles Rennie Mackintosh.

These explicitly 'Scottish' characteristics were to become the principal selling point of the Museum, both to the public and to the Heritage Lottery Fund, in January 1995:[39]

> The design derives in part from castle architecture: the main core galleries forming the keep, and the outer building with its heavy external stonework a surrounding curtain wall. The circular tower in the northwest corner echoes the form of Edinburgh Castle's half-moon battery, which will be visible from the tower rooms, and from the roof of the new Museum.

Despite the curious architectural interpretation (there are few 'keeps' in Scotland: did they mean a tower-house? – and there is scant resemblance between the low billowing thickset rubbly Half Moon Battery and the formidably smooth drum tower) the Lottery was persuaded to contribute £7.5 million toward the fitting out costs. Was it really convinced that a contemporary museum should self-consciously take the form of a castle? It seems improbable. By implying that the character of the building was composed of an eclectic build-up of pieces from Scottish architectural history, such descriptions mislead. The Museum of Scotland is a late 20th century museum building. Its design is the logical consequence of function, site, sightlines, levels and townscape; such 'Scottishness' as exists is a matter of expression.

It is difficult to imagine how the interior of a contemporary museum could, in any overt way, be nationalistic. There was nothing historic about the structural grid of 7.5 metres recommended by its (English) engineer,

Tony Hunt. The conditions within the museum were a particular variation on museum norms, but for forefront ecological reasons. Air conditioning, light levels thermal controls, Health and Safety requirements are independent of cultural historicism. The colour, typeface size, length and location of the captions were all the consequence of intensive testbed studies. The exception was the captions themselves. Exhibition guidelines drawn up by Mary Bryden and Jenni Calder emphasised that, in Robert Louis Stevenson's words 'there should be a strong Scotch accent of the mind.' The guidelines stated: 'our presentation, language and tone should all contribute to conveying the material and cultural environment of Scotland and Scots. Someone helicoptered blindfold into the Museum of Scotland should at once have a sense of where he is.'[40]

DISPLAYS

The Museum of Scotland's first composite exhibition brief, produced finally four months after the competition was concluded in December 1991, stated that:[41]

> It would neither be possible nor desirable to fashion this material into a comprehensive 'History of Scotland'. The unique nature and strengths of the Scottish collections suggest different approaches, based on particular kinds of evidence…The aim of the new museum is to stimulate the visitor to explore Scotland's culture, to enjoy and appreciate what has contributed to the making of Scotland…our aim, also, is to ensure that the exhibition relates to the environment outside, both to the immediate environment of Edinburgh, and to Scotland as a whole. We expect there to be many opportunities to do this, literally through windows, visually through photographs and graphics, and metaphorically through context and information.

The displays were, therefore, to be organised in a fundamentally site-specific manner within the overarching concept of exploring the nation's culture: a marginally different approach to that of exploring the culture of the peoples who live there. The exhibition brief also anticipated that displays would:[42]

> …stimulate the visitor to explore Scotland's culture, to enjoy and appreciate what has contributed to the making of Scotland…We want to create a variety of experience for the visitor, in terms of message, means of display and interpretation, and pace…We want our visitors to feel at home in the museum, but we also want to

stimulate and surprise them...The visitor could take a chronological path through [the three sections], tracing sequence and consequence, or sample according to interest and inclination...Striking variations in scale will be as significant a feature as variations in material. Diversity, richness, and contrast will be the keynotes.

Robert Anderson hoped that 'striking and intriguing' galleries would bring out the full significance of the objects on display, and relate them to their place in history or pre-history. The collection, being superb, had no need of 'acres of plastic, or designs that shout, or serried ranks of videos, or computers by the score. We don't want labels restricted to thirty one-syllable words.' He wanted sensitive, low-key, high-quality interior design, with changes of pace and variety of experience.[43]

Since the Museums Advisory Board had concluded that the displays associated with Scottish history should be multi-disciplinary, with objects grouped 'in period' rather than in the 'discipline dominated arrangements' back in 1985, the decision to favour a chronology over collections had been made long before the concept of the Museum of Scotland had entered development.[44] However, Testbed surveys of public response ten years later indicated overwhelming public support for a chronological presentation. It gave Jenni Calder the framework to challenge widely held myths about Scotland's past. 'Visitors, be they from Scotland or from other countries, almost certainly arrive with preconceptions about Scotland and the Scots. Though powerful, these myths are comparatively few in number and have tended to impoverish perceptions of Scottish culture.'[45] By including a lodging house booth, a bothy, a croft and perhaps a 20th-century public sector house, the Museum could stimulate reaction from visitors by displaying material with which they would already be familiar (sic). By presenting a concentration of objects that existed nowhere else, it would make visitors question their own perceptions of Scotland, and open up a dialogue as to the real nature of Scottish national identity. The strength of the collection lay in material that illuminated forgotten aspects of Scottish culture and its interaction with international cultural forces. 'Where else would you find anything about the colour and aesthetics of the Reformed Church?'[46]

The curators shared the almost Messianic desire to deploy the objects, many never having been seen before, and none ever having appeared before in this context, to transform the opinion of Scots about themselves and their history. Their agenda was to demonstrate how the country's culture was richer and more complex, as well as more colourful, than had hitherto been appreciated. However, order and context still had to be given to 20,000 potential exhibits, over 200 of them large and uncased, and varying in scale from roof bosses, crosses and endless timber panels to spinning machines, power looms, X-ray machines, 'Robot Freddie', a diorama, gaming machine, the Albion travelling shop, and a saurian footprint. Even once combined in sequence, all these potential exhibits, in their glorious complexity might not sustain a narrative of national history. There is no necessary reason why they should.

Then there were the growing problems of space and curatorial ambition. Back in 1987, when curators were first invited to reel out their ambitions for their galleries, there had still been a notional 8,500 square metres of display space; and their aspirations had swelled far beyond. Reality provided less than 7000 square metres, and a structure whose column grid had had to be set at 7.5 metres long around the larger objects long before final visions for displays had emerged.[47] The process of design development became, inexorably, a reductive one.

There was then the architect's contribution. Objects have many different potential stories, and the one deduced by the architect may not have coincided with the one selected by the curator or desired by the educationalist. In traditional museums, curators had control, and design should have been a service provided under curatorial direction. It was clearly difficult for curators to come to terms with a building that expected to contribute so much to the interpretation. Sir Philip Dowson, chairman of the competition assessors, and latterly architectural adviser during construction, suggested that:[48]

> The careful construction of display ideas wedded to a design predicated upon the power of the objects themselves, should produce a correct synthesis. Visitors should be confronted with great works, in circumstances that are both formal and informal...All parts should relate to each other, and authority and authenticity should run right through it.

It was the national agenda that predicated a national narrative; and the exigencies of that narrative greatly influenced the contents on display. Take for example the case of the Hamilton Palace Drawing Room. The Hamilton Palace display was intended to comprise three 'impressive major exhibits'. The setting was to be the panelling from the drawing room of Hamilton Palace, designed in the late 17th century by James Smith, who had trained at St. Luke's in Rome. Robert Anderson had gone to the Bronx stores of the Metropolitan Museum of Art, New York, to open the boxes in which it lay, as indeed it had done since its purchase by William Randolph Hearst some seventy years earlier. Within the re-erected room were to be exhibited the travelling service of Napoleon's favourite sister, Princess Pauline Borghese, bequeathed in 1825 to her lover, the 10th Duke of Hamilton; and half of the tea service of Napoleon I purchased by the 10th Duke of Hamilton in 1830.[49] Anderson thought that the conjunction of the silver with the drawing room would show that 'we do not want the boundaries of our new national museum to be too sharply drawn...What we are displaying is Scotland as it relates to the rest to the world.'

When the Drawing Room was first inspected, Anderson enthused to Scotland on Sunday that it was exactly the kind of artifact the new museum required. 'It is wonderful to think that we can rebuild it and unveil it in Scotland, in our new national museum in the country where it originated.'[50] As the concept developed, the museum intended to purchase a 1774 portrait of the eighth Duke of Hamilton by Prud'homme, for it would complete an ensemble intended to demonstrate to the world the hitherto unrecognised level of sophistication that had once been achieved in Scotland.[51] But upon inspection after arrival in Scotland, only the superlative armorial mantelpiece proved to be of the requisite late 17th century period. The remainder was almost entirely 19th century, dating from between 1818 and 1833 and David Hamilton's stupendous transformation of the palace into the largest and finest country house in North Britain. Its quality was not in question: but it was unable to sustain the emerging history of 17th century Scotland. It had been trapped in the wrong chapter of the story, and there was no room for it in the 19th century. The Museum contains no other interior of that supreme quality.

The design of the spaces within the building have no overt nationalism, but they are overwhelmed by cultural memories, exemplifying Benson's frequent references to the Edinburgh close when explaining the design rationale behind either the Hawthornden Court or the full-height lightwells which surround the core galleries; but to infer something uniquely or deliberately Scottish would require a novel sophistication, particularly given the architects' rejection of the possibility.[52] Nonetheless, when pressed, certain spaces had been designed with Scots prototypes in their mind's eye. The little meeting room at the foot of the round tower was compared to the Lecture Theatre in the basement of Mackintosh's School of Art; and the Board Room, three storeys above was designed as the conclusion to the building: 'The Board Room is unquestionably one of the most important spaces in the building, and in our view is critical to the totality of the Museum, as is the Director's Office in Mackintosh's Glasgow School of Art'.[53]

The carefully detailed white American ash panels, the brilliant, unpainted right-handed plasterwork and the stone floors are not ethnic decisions. Nor, given the love affair Scotland has enjoyed with technology, is the architect's persistence in concealing the technology of the building wherever possible. It is conceivable that the architect's principal interior device, that of the thick wall, could be classified as 'Scots' given the inheritance of the brochs; and two of them in the museum do indeed contain curving staircases. However, those thick walls have practical purposes: they embrace the display cases as though they were niches, and provide a home for relocated lintels, doors, and other building bits. Their very thickness allows the main entrances through them to be emphasised, as though with 'orders', to highlight procession.

The clean, spare spaces have no nationalist implication, save that some freestanding objects had to be omitted since there was no room. Some curators felt that the bare approach to gallery display inhibited their desire to communicate the 'richness' of previous Scots cultures.[54] The displays themselves follow a logical rigour of 'object in case' or 'object freestanding'. But it was the deployment of the latter that impinged upon a Scottish agenda. As freestanding artifacts they inevitably became icons, and these the architects celebrated. The desire to make the museum object-specific in this way had originated with the Trustees, and probably from Bute himself. The curators were initially very doubtful. They considered that it removed the object from its context and transformed it into an art object rather than an object with social or national information to convey. That the architects came to see the conjunction of a particular object and a particular location as an 'aria' (Benson's term) or high point.[55] Others regarded it as elitist.[56] The Trustees never wavered: the architecture was to inform the contents, and the selection and placing of objects was a principal means of doing so. The narrative of the museum would enhance the narrative of the object.

Perhaps the most striking example is the Newcomen engine. By the device of locating it concealed at the head of the great stairs in the Hawthornden Court, to be discovered accidentally by the visitors who are led to believe that they are entering an attic rather than an immense turbine hall, gives an overwhelming industrial feel to the 18th century, relegating Culloden to a relatively insignificant corner. Given the narrative, the engine is in the only place it could have been; but a deconstructionist could conclude legitimately that the gallery presented an Improver's perception of the century.

CONCLUSION

So what influence did the concept of a 'House for Identity' have upon the Museum of Scotland? But for the nationalist agenda, it is unlikely that the Museum would exist at all. It would have remained dead after 1976, or cut in 1995. Equally, that agenda played a critical part in the competition, in its organisation, in the result, and in the Museum's ability to withstand the pressure of Prince Charles' resignation. However, it is far too early to say whether the evident nationalist context of the project distorted the Museum itself and its displays. It had no bearing on the location of the building, nor really upon its institutional context. Indeed, it is properly regarded solely as a thematic display location, since it has neither an exclusively dedicated curatorial staff nor a dedicated director, as might have the National Museum of Denmark.

To what extent were the displays and, for that matter, the overall museum experience influenced or distorted by the debaters over identity or over Scottishness? The process bent over backwards to prevent it, but notions of identity have a habit of seeping through the cracks. The fact that it emerged a museum of largely chronological national narrative highlighted by selected icons is certainly a consequence of a national consciousness, and that structure had strong implications for the displays, such as the excision of the Hamilton Palace Drawing Room and the prominence of the Newcomen engine. The somewhat acrimonious dispute between the archaeologists and the others hinged upon whether a 'national' concept was appropriate. In archaeology at least, there is little perception of whether an 'early person' in this island was much different from an 'early person' from the Steppes. Whether, in the galleries above, adequate objectivity has been maintained will be judged by posterity. It is always possible that too much significance might have been given to an object that, in world terms, might be insignificant. Beyond the matter of iconography, the interior designs are only 'Scottish' by monumental inference, and by the deliberate interaction of the skies and the light.

The exterior of the Museum, with its skin of russet Clashach sandstone panels offset by cream-harled monolithic walls, and its striking geometries, is Scots in that it is unlikely that it could have fitted so well anywhere else in the world. It is also Scots, in the resonance that its forms might have, to those who know Scotland. Yet the influence of Le Corbusier is, if anything, more obvious than that of Charles Rennie Mackintosh. It is only possible to state that it is a building of international quality that could only have been built in Scotland.

The Author

Professor Charles McKean holds the chair in Scottish Architectural History at The University of Dundee. He was formerly Secretary and Treasurer of the Royal Incorporation of Architects in Scotland. A prolific author, he was founder and series editor of the popular RIAS/Landmark Trust illustrated architectural guides to Scotland, several written by him. He has contributed chapters to *Glasgow – the Making of a City, The Scottish Country House,* and a volume about Alexander 'Greek' Thomson. Other works include *The Scottish Thirties (1987), Architectural Contributions to Scottish Society since 1840 (1990)* and *Edinburgh: Portrait of a City (1991).* The above is based upon researched for *The Making of the Museum of Scotland,* to be published by the NMS.

References

1. Charles D Waterston, *Collections in Context,* 1997, pp. 83–5.
2. Williams Committee, *A Heritage for Scotland,* HMSO, 1981, Appx. IV, para 6.
3. Hansard, 12.3.1985 pp. 844–927.
4. Ibid.
5. Joint letter to Miss J.L. Ross at the SED from Hugh Macandrew, Charles Waterston, Dale Idiens, David Clarke and Allen Simpson, 12.5.1983.
6. Stated in the Secretary of State's decision 21.7.1982, in Royal Scottish Museum Trustees file 2.1.9.
7. NMS Williams Committee Miscellaneous Papers, file 5.6.6 (1980–84), letter 2.9.1983.
8. Lord Bute to the introductory meeting of the Museums Advisory Board 12 May 1984.
9. Museums Advisory Board Report to the Secretary of State , Scottish Education Dept, para 1.9, p. 4.
10. *Scotland's History in the National Museum of Scotland* in Ambrose, T., (ed), Presenting Scotland's Story, (Edinburgh 1989), p. 65.
11. Ibid.
12. Lord Bute to Michael Forsyth 3 July 1987 (New Building Working Group Part 1, correspondence).
13. Richards, Feasibility, Introduction, p. 1.
14. Anderson, R.G.W., *Meeting Public Needs* in 'A new Museum of Scotland', 1990, p. 41.
15. A phrase within the New Building Working Group's brief, drafted by Lord Bute on 7 November 1986. (NBWG files Part 1, 7.11.1986.)
16. NBWG Part 1, 1.12.1986.
17. Competition Brief, 3.26.
18. Interview with Jenni Calder.
19. Anderson, R.G.W., memorandum 1.4.1991. (RIAS Competition files 2.3 Comp.a.)
20. NMS Trustees Minutes, 18.10.1991, items 18 and 19.
21. D Bryden to Jenni Calder 4.11.1991. Curators had reacted adversely to he second draft exhibition brief which appeared to move from chronology toward a more thematic pattern. MoS Exhibition sub-committee files.
22. Clarke to Calder 27.8.1991.

23. *Scotland's history in the National Museum of Scotland,* in Ambrose, T., (ed), 'Presenting Scotland's Story', 1989), pp. 71–2.
24. John Shaw to Jenni Calder, 12.6.1991.
25. Anderson, R.G.W., memorandum to Dr. David Bryden 30.6.1990 (Museum of Scotland Exhibition sub committee minutes, 1990–91).
26. Information from Dr Allen Simpson.
27. Clarke, D, in *Society of Antiquaries of Scotland Newsletter,* 10.1, Sept. 1998, p. 2.
28. Gavin Sprott to Jenni Calder, 23.6.1991.
29. Tindall to Bute 25.7.1990, BT 009 File B 212.1; Bute to Tindall 8.8.1990.
30. MOS (90) second meeting. Item 3c minutes 5.2.90. The meeting had been with McKean and Bill Jessop, the pro-active RIAS Competitions Convenor.
31. Ian Shaw to Kate Comfort, RIAS Head of Public Affairs, responsible for the competition, 17.1.1991; McKean to Shaw 22.1.1991; Shaw reply 25.1.1991.
32. Project Scotland, 13.6.1991 and 27.6.1991.
33. RIAS 2.3 Comp.a. Ben Tindall to McKean, 22.8.1991. Tindall had been 'outraged at the disparity between the short listed designs and the brief requirements for prominence, respect for the street and that the contents should dominate'. He judged that the assessors had chosen by fashion, media and their own prejudices. If the results had been preconceived, months of work had been wasted. Worse, there was no planned exhibition and no feedback. He considered that the RIAS had been exploited. Since he was then doing up an office off Johnston Terrace, he obtained the names and addresses of the competitors from the RIAS, and wrote to them all, offering to hang a drawing each for £20. He exhibited over 100, and it took days to hang. The number of visits from Museum staff was notable.(Interview)
34. *Independent* 14.8.1991.
35. Interview with Ronnie Cramond.
36. *Independent,* 7.9.1991.
37. Speaking at the RIAS Convention, Glasgow, June 1999.
38. Interview with Gordon Benson.
39. Application to Heritage Lottery Fund, (January 1996), p. 8.
40. Museum of Scotland – Exhibition Guidelines, 1.2.1996.
41. Exhibition Brief, second stage draft, (n.d.) Introduction.
42. Anderson, R.G.W., *Meeting Public Needs* in 'A New Museum', p. 45.
43. Ibid.
44. Museums Advisory Board Report to the Secretary of State , Scottish Education Dept, 1985), 4.7.
45. *Social history in the Museum of Scotland,* 25.1.1991 by Jenni Calder. She stated to David Clarke, in memo 21.8.1991, 'I feel that both Mary Queen of Scots and 'Scotland and Europe' need some kind of specific focus...although I think it would be better if Mary Queen of Scots, at least, had something separate, however small.'
46. Interview with Jenni Calder.

47. The grid was determined on 24.1.1992, MoS Client Committee Minutes, 1992–5.
48. Stated at the Cultural Tensions seminar, 20.9.1997.
49. Memo from Godfrey Evans to Jenni Calder, 26.9.1991, 'Hamilton Palace Display'. Calder, MoS Early Exhibitions folder.
50. *Scotland on Sunday*, 18.8.1991.
51. Godfrey Evans. op.cit.
52. Interview with Gordon Benson.
53. G. Benson to M. Jones 15.5.1998.
54. Interviews with Hugh Cheape and George Dalgliesh.
55. Interview with Gordon Benson.
56. Interview with Dr David Clarke.

Further Reading

Ambrose, T. (ed), *Presenting Scotland's Story*, HMSO, 1989.
Bercedo, I., Puyuelo, A. & Sen, I., *The architecture of museums*, 1997.
Clarke, D.V., 'Scottish Archaeology in the second half of the 19th century', in Bell, A.S. (ed), *The Scottish Antiquarian Tradition*, 1981, pp. 114–142.
Clarke, D.V., 'Presenting a national perspective of prehistory and early history in the Museum of Scotland', in Atkinson, J.A, Banks, I. and O'Sullivan, J. (eds), *Nationalism and Archaeology*, 1996, pp. 67–77.
National Museums of Scotland, *A new Museum of Scotland*, NMS, 1990.
Newhouse, V., *Towards a New Museum*, 1998.
Philip, J.R., *The Philip Report*, Command 8604, HMSO, 1951.
Stevenson, R.B.K., 'The Museum, its beginnings and its development', in Bell, A.S. (ed), *The Scottish Antiquarian Tradition*, 1981, pp. 31–86, and pp. 142–212.
Williams Committee, *A Heritage for Scotland*, HMSO, 1981.

NMS Archival Documents

Museums Advisory Board Report to the Secretary of State , Scottish Education Dept, 1985.
The Proposed Museum of Scotland: Report of the New Buildings Working Group (the Cramond Group), March 1987.
John Richards, Feasibility Study The Museum of Scotland, August 1989.
Museum of Scotland Competition Brief, (1991).
Exhibition Brief , Museum of Scotland (1991).
Conceptual brief – The Museum of Scotland project: May 1992.
Application to Heritage Lottery Fund, January 1996.

NMS et al Committee Papers

Royal Scottish Museum: Steering Committee file 1.6.0, 1961 ff.

RSM: Joint Steering Committee files, 1965 ff.

Williams Committee Miscellaneous Papers, RSM, 1980–84.

Museum Advisory Board Miscellaneous Papers 84.1, NMS, 1984–5.

Museum Advisory Board Correspondence files 2.1.9/5.6.6, NMS, 1984–5.

New Building Working Group Part 1, (NMS (87),7, 1986–7.

Working Group Part II, MoS, 1987.

Working Group Part I, MoS, 1986–7.

Museum of Scotland Committee & Working Group Parts 1 & 2, NMS, 1988–90.

Development Committee Minutes, MoS, 1989–90.

The Museum of Scotland Trustees Committee parts 1 & 2, NMS, 1989–90.

Museum of Scotland Exhibition sub committee minutes, 1990–91.

The MoS Policy Development Committee Minutes, MoS, 1990.

The Board of Trustees Client Committee Minutes, NMS, 1992–5.

NMS Trustees Minutes, 1990–98.

Architectural Institute of Scotland, Proceedings, 1857–62

RIAS Competition files 2.3 Comp a, 1998–1991, Royal Incorporation of Architects in Scotland

Benjamin Tindall Architects box 0009 files 6–8, 1990–91.

12

COMMUNICATING IDENTITY
Perceptions of the Museum of Scotland

Fiona McLean and Steven Cooke

A national museum can be regarded as a place where the nation tells its story to itself and others. However, this does not mean that narratives can simply be 'read off' the museum displays. Rather, ideas of the nation are mediated through the complex interrelationships between exhibition and viewer. This paper explores these relationships within the context of the conceptions that the visitors have about the role of a national museum in contemporary Scotland. It argues that both the consumers' reasons for visiting and their conceptions of the Museum of Scotland's representations of Scotland are multiple and often contradictory. It ends by raising a number of issues relating to the challenges posed to museums through changing notions of both national and individual identity.

After a long and somewhat contentious history, the new Museum of Scotland opened to popular and critical acclaim on 30 November 1998. 'Presenting Scotland to the world', the museum houses the Scottish collections of the National Museums of Scotland. The opening of the museum was heralded in the media and by promotional literature issued by NMS itself as a place where the story of Scotland could at last be told, fulfilling a perceived lack that had been identified as long ago as the 1920s.[1] The Museum of Scotland is thus placed within a discursive framework common to museums from the mid-18th century onwards: it is a place where narratives of the nation are made manifest through classification and display of artefacts and specimens.[2,3]

With ongoing debates over the political, economic, social and cultural future of Scotland, the building of a new National Museum at this time gives a fascinating opportunity to explore the relationship between museums and national and individual identity. This paper explores these issues through an investigation of visitor perceptions of the role of a national museum in Scotland at the end of the 20th century. It suggests that the visitors have a number of different conceptions of the story that the Museum is trying to represent but that this is complicated by their desires to create their own meanings, articulated through their understandings and use of the spatial layout of the Museum.[4]

MUSEUMS AND NATIONAL IDENTITY

Given recent cultural and political developments, the Museum of Scotland has opened at a crucial time in Scottish history. The Scottish cultural renaissance is manifested in the increase in cultural production and calls for Scottish cultural institutions. The growth of Scottish museums has far outpaced the growth of museums throughout the rest of the UK,[5] conceivably reflecting Scotland's reassertion of its national identity, culminating in the devolution referendum and the re-creation of Scotland's own Parliament. When the idea of Scotland is itself in a state of flux, the stories of the nation told in the Museum, which give a sense of location, a connection between the individual and the nation as an 'imagined community' are especially important.[6]

Anderson's work describes the concept of 'nation' as being imagined, because 'members of even the smallest nation will never know most of their fellow members, meet them, or even hear of them, yet in the minds of each lies the image of their communion'.[7] National identity is thus 'a particular kind of collective identity...it is an identity constituted at a given strategic level of society'.[8] Nationalists are often drawn to the dramatic and creative possibilities of the arts and media, through which they can celebrate or commemorate the nation, evoking emotional responses from the community.[9] However, Schlesinger contends that national cultures are not simply the repositories of shared symbols to which the entire population stands in identical relation. Instead, there is competition over the defining of such symbols. National culture then is a discourse,[10,11] a way of constructing meanings which influence not only our actions, but also our conceptions of ourselves. As Hall has argued: 'It follows that the nation is not only a political entity but something which produces meanings – a system of cultural representation'.[12] This is often articulated through 'legends and landscapes, by stories of golden ages, enduring traditions, heroic deeds and dramatic destinies located in ancient or promised home-lands with hallowed sites and scenery'.[13]

With the concepts of national and individual identity 'under erasure',[14] one of the ways in which the concept of identities can be reformulated is by thinking in terms of 'routes' not 'roots'. Within this there is an understanding of the inter-relatedness of production and consumption within identity formation:

> Though they seem to invoke an origin in a historical past with which they continue to correspond, actually identities are about questions of using the resources of history, language and culture in the process of becoming rather than being: not 'who we are' or 'where we came from', so much as what we might become, *how we have been represented and how that bears on how we might represent ourselves* [emphasis added].

Identities are produced and consumed within discursive sites and practices by the articulation of 'specific enunciative strategies'.[15] Within this conceptualisation, museums can be seen as sites of discursive formation, a space where the 'legends and landscapes' of the nation are presented and represented and where identities are made and re-made.

Scotland is an interesting and much studied case of a 'stateless nation' which supposedly suffers from a 'deformed culture'.[16,17] This is because of a dislocation between nationhood and statehood, and (perceived and actual) English political, economic, social and cultural dominance. For a discussion of how this concept originated and was taken on board by Scottish intellectuals, see *The Eclipse of the Scottish Culture*.[18] With the limited political autonomy brought about by devolution, the changing narratives of Scotland will be a source of debate and contention. It is to a discussion of the role of the museum in such narration that we now turn.

MUSEUMS AND NARRATING THE NATION

Museums are the display cabinets of national heritage, presenting the artefacts of a nation to itself and others. Initially created as private collections by elites through conquest and exploitation, they relate to the world view of the 'Prince' or the 'Scholar'.[19] Drawing on the work of Foucault, Hooper-Greenhill has examined the role of the museum in the 'disciplinary society'. She refers to the growth of museums in France after the Revolution being related to an increase in the 'disciplines...methods that divided and controlled times, spaces and movement', embodied in institutions such as the hospital, the asylum or the school. These can be viewed as techniques of power: through hierarchical observation, normalising judgement and (self) examination.

The linkage of 'nation' and museum is thus readily apparent. The founding of the Victoria and Albert Museum, created from the exhibits of the 1851 Great Exhibition, represented the pride of the nation in its industries and in its colonisation of others.[20] In addition, Coombes has argued that such Imperial exhibitions were spaces for inculcating various sections of the population with certain values concerned with Empire, by constructing spectacles of the 'other'. During the early years of the 20th century museums became an issue of regional pride and instruments for inculcating attitudes of social responsibility as a significant number of museums were opened by municipal authorities.[21]

Since then, museums have developed their role in conserving cultural heritage and educating the public. However, Hooper-Greenhill suggests that elements of the 'disciplinary society' are still evident in contemporary museums. She argues that:[22]

> Now, with the concept of the museum as an instrument for the democratic education of the 'masses', or the 'citizen', a division is created between knowing subjects, between producers and consumers of knowledge, expert and layman [sic]. In the public museum the producing subject is located in the hidden spaces of the museum, while the consuming subject is located in the public spaces...The seriated public spaces, surveyed and controlled, where knowledge is offered for passive consumption, are emblematic of the museum as one of the apparatuses that create 'docile bodies' in the disciplinary society.

Although 'offered for passive consumption', this does not mean that they will be received passively.[23,24] As Silverstone has argued, museum visiting is a social activity. The visitor to the museum connects the personal to the museum's account through spun narratives. The visitor gives the museum object a personal expression, one that is unique to that individual. Visitors bring their own preconceptions to the museum that shape the nature and perceptions of their visit.[25] The museum offers the visitor 'a heritage with which we continually interact, one which fuses past with present'.[26] Visitors give complex, often contradictory meanings to museum objects, meanings that are representative of their identities.

Within the reconceptualisation of identity formation put forward by Hall, du Gay and others, the museum can be seen as a place where people go to actively make and remake their identities, to selectively select and reject and manipulate the images and identities found within. Therefore, the consumer's active role in identity formation needs to be held in tension with the symbolic and institutional power of the museum to tell 'authoritative' stories of the nation.

What follows explores this relationship between the production and consumption of stories of the nation. We start by examining the ways that consumers conceptualise the museum as a site of narration, to provide an indication as to what stories they think that the museum might be telling. The final section explores the ambivalence on the part of the consumer in the desire to be told, and to construct his or her own, narratives of Scotland.

VISITOR PERCEPTIONS OF THE MUSEUM OF SCOTLAND

Given the theoretical focus on the relationship between museums and national identity formation, the consumer interview schedule contained a number of questions designed to explore whether the consumers conceived that the museum was attempting to define or narrate Scotland. First, the visitors were asked the reasons why they visited the Museum that day. A recent study undertaken by MORI for the Museums Association found that 40 per cent of those interviewed suggested that general interest in the collections was their motivation for visiting.[27] The authors' research on the Museum of Scotland gave similar responses. General interest was indeed cited by many people as the reason for their visit. For example:

> Just interested. I'd been in the first week, but it was so crowded and decided – there was so much to see.
> I just think it looks quite interesting.

However, other stated reasons were more mundane. Many visited the Museum just 'because it was there', or because they were looking for some way of filling their time:

> Just because it was close at hand.
> Um, basically I had an hour to spare, and I quite often come in at lunchtime.
> Em, I had some time on my hands and I thought I would like to walk around the new part of the museum.
> I must confess I'm in between two things and I have got a season ticket anyway.
> Eh, nothing to do [laughs]. We were just walking past and we said 'right, we'll come in here'.

It seems evident that, at least on the surface, the Museum is not just a place for education or for the inculcation of Scottish history. Different people use the museum in different ways and for a variety of reasons. For example, one visitor interviewed came to the Museum of Scotland most weekdays. He and his two-year-old daughter used the spaces of the

151

Museum as a giant 'play-school', his daughter choosing where in the Museum she would like to explore that day. Although an interest in the exhibits was present, the main factor was the 'exciting spaces' of the Museum and the friendliness of the staff towards his daughter which made the Museum the ideal choice to spend time and 'get out of the house'. Whether this particular visitor viewed the museum as an explicit space of identity formation is therefore open to question.

Although the visitors did not seem to explicitly conceptualise their visit in terms of an educational experience, to explore these issues further the visitors were also asked during the interview whether they thought that the museum was saying anything about Scotland, and whether the museum portrayed a defined image. A number of themes can be identified within their responses. These relate to the perceived role of the museum, its core brief of 'presenting Scotland to the World' and the inability of the museum to tell stories of Scotland.

One of the most common responses was related to the perceived general role of a museum in contemporary society. Despite not necessarily coming to the Museum for educational purposes, for many the Museum of Scotland was a space for the telling of *history*. Thus:

> It's showing what we have historically in artefacts.
> (laughs) I suppose it is outlining its entire history, its heritage.
> How much time have we got? Well, I suppose it is just laying before you the varied history of Scotland from very earliest times through to modern times.
> It's just telling its history.

Others seemingly related it to the museum's logo – 'presenting Scotland to the world'. Further, this was identified as presenting a positive image of Scotland, acting as an 'ambassador' for promoting Scotland to the world:

> What an interesting place it is basically, that it has an interesting history that sort of thing.
> Mm, em, what a wonderful place it is.
> Oh, crikey. Em a wealth of culture throughout the ages.
> Em, basically I think it's just showing Scotland at it's best.
> Em, it's trying to give a decent sort of proud energy, Scotland and its history, that's what it says to me.

A number of people argued that the museum had an important role to play in 'defining' Scotland itself. Apart from a few instances, however, this did not translate into an identification of the museum with overt nationalism. Those that did read this into the museum, referred almost exclusively to the Declaration of Arbroath, which is written on the walls within the 'Scotland Defined' gallery:[28]

> Well, I was quite kind of bowled over the first time I came into the Museum and saw the quotation from the Declaration of Arbroath, em, just around the corner there, and I thought, gosh, it's so strongly nationalistic in its, em, sentiments.
> What it does – it's got a strong feeling, you know, it's got the writing on the wall about the anti-English, which maybe at the moment isn't such a good – oh it is part of our heritage but at the moment, the way things are, it maybe wasn't a good idea having that written on the wall, em, that one thing, that did strike me.

Other visitors denied that the museum was telling a prescriptive story about Scotland:

> (pause) you are free to make up your own mind
> I think there is so much and too many people will come at it from a different perspective that you can really choose what you take out of it. That is no one specific message.
> Oh, I don't think that the museum is making any particular case.
> Now that's difficult. I would reserve judgement at the moment on that one
> I haven't really, you know, formed an opinion as such.

In general then, it can be argued that the visitors interviewed had a wide range of ideas about whether the museum was presenting a particular story of Scotland and, if so, what that particular image or story might be. One of the ways in which museums construct narratives is through their spatial layout and through the construction of relationships through and between objects. So how does the architectural space of the Museum building influence the narratives that the visitor 'reads'? The architecture of the Museum of Scotland has attracted a wide variety of positive comments in the media, and a number of visitors commented both on their admiration for the architectural design and on the relationship between the architecture and the displays themselves:

> Well, I think the architecture is very exciting...I mean it's, it's having a competent, forward looking building housing, you know, artefacts from the past – it's obviously trying to isolate and promote the kind of pride that Scotland has in, you know, it's past, historically and aesthetically.
> Em, I don't know, I think that the architecture is really important, in fact maybe even more important than the objects in that it's saying

something about Scotland and about its em, well, about design and sort of style and stuff like that.

Others found the internal spaces of the museum problematic. When asked at the conclusion of the interview whether there was anything in general that they would like to add about the Museum, many suggested that they found it difficult to find their way around. Here are two responses:

> It's too much for one day. They should warn people at the door that they need to come back several times to take it all in…It's very hard to follow the map. We just couldn't work it out at all. I mean, yes, it shows you the different levels, but it doesn't show ways…I think more maps of the displays and where you are would be a lot easier to follow, because this doesn't really show you where the stairs are, where you are.

> Um, slightly difficult to find your way around. I think it's a wonderful use of space but it's like a warren [pause]. The architecture is wonderful, and I know lots of people like it, but I personally find it extremely difficult to find my way around. So if you are up on the upper floor and somebody says you have got five minutes to get out of here, dear God, especially if you have two small children, it's difficult to steer and navigate your way around. I know there is less space than the old museum but the old museum you could, was very easy to take yourself around, whereas this one is very difficult.

Part of the design of the museum is the inclusion of a number of 'cul-de-sac' galleries, relating to specific themes such as 'The Church and the community' within the Medieval Church on level one. Again, this proved problematic for one visitor who commented:

> It's an interesting building! [in a slightly ironic tone] It's difficult to find one's way around I find. You keep going in to dead ends as it were, and there are so many of them, I know they are special little rooms, but you know, the first time I came I almost panicked, you know, how do I get out!

Some visitors took this 'warren-like' layout of the museum a stage further and related it to the relationship between the role of the Museum and the stories that it attempted to tell about Scotland:

154

It's impressive, I don't find it easy to walk around and I don't know whether that is deliberate or not. [pause] I don't know whether that is deliberate or not. I don't know whether they deliberately don't want you to feel you are following a definite plan...or whether it would actually be better to have more of a plan because I find you tend to stray from subject to subject without realising you've done it.

Ummm, better sign posting maybe...the people who designed it obviously had some ideas about how it should be laid out, or how they'd lay it out. Some sort of better way of guiding through their preferred route, let's say. Obviously people want to go where they want, they've got a [unclear] way that they've laid it out, it would have been nice to know.

The other thing that struck me, and I know you can get the audio sets, which would [unclear], but I think you are coming in and going into the gallery, and even with the plan, it's very difficult to find, I don't mean from level to level, but within that, to find your way around the sequence, and there's so much information...And I know that it's not always good to have a set path, because it allows you to choose, but I think it would be helpful if there was at least *some* visual and other ways of thinking, well, suggested routes that you might take. [original emphasis].

We felt lost on the second floor and because of that everything seemed a bit disjointed. You wouldn't want to have it too set, but I mean there could be a happy medium.

I don't get an overall message, I feel that the building is more important almost than the contents and I felt that the places were full of interesting things should have been a magnet to draw you towards them and I felt that the lighting within the place is too dull and the lighting within the room consequently too bright. If the balance was shifted I think it would highlight each exhibit more, em, we both felt it was – *there was no progression, no natural progression* – the building imposed on you wherever you were moving within it and you know, series of straight lines just seems to be everywhere and somehow out of context with the old things it's displaying. We just felt the logic wasn't there you know, we were missing something, *we didn't feel a progression through time* [emphasis added].

For some visitors, the architectural design seemingly disrupts the ability of the Museum to tell the story of Scotland by not giving a set route to follow: there is 'no natural progression'. The visitors' desire 'to be told' was held in tension, however, with the desire to create their own journey through the displays and to construct their own narratives of Scotland. The Museum is thus perceived by both producers and consumers as a place where Scotland's story can be told, but little agreement exists on 'what that story should be'. Many of those interviewed argued that the museum should be non-prescriptive in the narratives it tells about Scotland. In other words, they called for a multi-vocal space where consumers can explore their own identities. The Museum of Scotland uses both thematic and chronological displays to present the artefacts of the nation, and the deliberate lack of a structured route through the museum is seemingly an important component in this multi-vocality.[29]

CONCLUSIONS

By relating museum visiting to the conceptions that the visitors have about the ability of the Museum to present narratives of Scotland, this paper has sought to problematise the relationship between Museums and national identity. Although museums in general have been theorised as spaces where the nation is made manifest through the articulation of narratives of the nation, the reception of such narratives is little understood.

Following calls by Pearce, Macdonald and others to reject the notion of a unitary public who passively receive the poetics and politics of display within the museum, our research would seem to suggest that the relationship between museums and the visitors is indeed not one of non-reflective inculcation of the narratives of the nation. The visitors interviewed had many and varied responses to the exhibits in the Museum of Scotland and critiqued the representations that they were given.[30]

It would also be wrong to overplay the importance of the museum as a space of identity formation. Although the museum does have a role in national identity construction, as a location where the narratives of nation are displayed, it is apparent that visitors use the museum in a variety of different ways and for a variety of different reasons, not all of which seem to have a role in 'national' identity formation. Although the Museum can play a part in individual identity, as a space where one can be, or act as a 'heritage enthusiast', a 'collector of cultural capital' or even a 'good parent', the relationship between these discursive frames, and the negotiation between them and ideas of national identity needs further exploration.[31]

Further, the research has highlighted how many of the visitors articulated ambivalence, both in the ability of the Museum to tell the story of Scotland, and the desirability of actually being told. In other words, for many of the visitors, the link between the Museum and construction of their own sense of a Scottish national identity is not readily apparent. By commenting on the layout of the museum, the visitors seem to be arguing for a fluid relationship between themselves and the museum. The museum is still seen as a source of authority and whose assertive voice is looked for, but which is now subject to critique and renegotiation. The authorial voice should be present but should be decentred and non-prescriptive, allowing the visitors to negotiate between their own 'routes' and the 'routes' presented for them by the Museum.

To continue with the travel metaphor suggested by Hall and du Gay, the relationship between museum and visitor can be conceived, albeit somewhat glibly, as similar to that between travel operator and (potential) traveller: the traveller desires an itinerary with which to work, but also demands a greater or lesser amount of leeway to improvise around its central locations and themes. This raises questions about the 'itinerary' that the visitors are presented with: the journey through Scotland that the visitor is encouraged to make. Ongoing research by the authors is investigating these issues, exploring the politics and poetics of the Museum, especially with respect to the 20th century gallery.

As debates over the future of Scotland continue, the Museum will also be the focus of continued debate as to the narratives of Scotland that it articulates, the face of Scotland that it 'presents to the world'. As both the idea of 'Scotland' undergoes change and our theories of national and individual identity formation become increasingly 'messy', how does the Museum, as a place traditionally where visions of the nation are made material, respond to such increasing heterogeneity? How does the Museum reflect the plurality of our collective memories of the nation, whilst being coherent and accessible? With the relevance, and even the desirability, of such concepts as national identity under critique in an age of globalisation, the question perhaps becomes: what is the future of a National Museum?

The Authors

Dr Fiona McLean is a Senior Lecturer in the Department of Marketing at The University of Stirling. She graduated in Politics from the University of Edinburgh, undertook postgraduate studies at Moray House Institute, and gained a doctorate in museum marketing from the University of Northumbria at Newcastle. She continues to develop her research interest in the museums field, and has published widely on the subject in a number of journals. She is the author of *Marketing the Museum*,[32] and is currently writing a book which takes a critical approach to heritage marketing. She was awarded a grant by the Leverhulme Trust in 1998 to direct research on the construction of national identity at the new Museum of Scotland.

Dr Steven Cooke is a research fellow working with Dr McLean on the Leverhulme study. After an undergraduate degree in Human Geography from University of Wales, Lampeter, he undertook doctoral research at Cheltenham and Gloucester College of Higher Education investigating the origin and development of Holocaust museums and memorials in the UK. His research interests focus principally on the relationships between memory, place and identity.

References

1. For example, in the Preface to the Reference Manual to the Museum of Scotland Project, the Board of Trustees of NMS commented that 'Scotland stands alone amongst countries of its size in having nowhere to *tell the full story* of its people and to show properly its most treasured possessions. This is a disgrace, long recognised by many' (June 1996, emphasis added). The inadequate space for the display of the National Museum of Antiquities of Scotland's collections was first identified by the Royal Commission on National Museums and Galleries in 1927, (see the 'Phillip Report': *Report of Committee on the National Museum of Antiquities of Scotland*, 1952) and has since been the subject of ongoing debate.
2. Bennett, T., *The Birth of the Museum*, Routledge, 1995.
3. Hooper-Greenhill, E., 'The Museum in the Disciplinary Society', in Pearce J. (ed), *Museum Studies in Material Culture*, Leicester University Press, 1989.
4. The visitor responses were drawn from a series of in-depth, semi-structured interviews with visitors to the Museum of Scotland during early 1999. The authors would like to thank the trustees and staff of NMS for their support and help in undertaking this and other research connected with the Museum. The research was funded for a period of two years by the Leverhulme Trust, which is gratefully acknowledged.
5. McCrone, D., Morris, A. and Kiely, R., *Scotland – the Brand. The Making of Scottish Heritage*, Edinburgh University Press, 1995.
6. Anderson, B., *Imagined Communities*, Verso, 1983.
7. Ibid.
8. Schlesinger, P., *Media, State and Nation: Political Violence and Collective Identities*, Sage, 1991, P. 173.
9. Smith, A.D., *National Identity*, Penguin, 1991.
10 Bhabha, H.K. (ed), *Nation and Narration*, Routledge, 1990.
12. Hall, S., 'The Question of Cultural Identity', in Hall, S., Held, D. and McGrew, T. (eds), *Modernity and its Futures*, Polity Press, 1992, p. 292.

11. Samuel, R. (ed), *Patriotism. The Making and Unmaking of British National Identity, Vol. III: National Fictions*, Routledge, 1989.
13. Daniels, S., *Fields of Vision: Landscape Imagery and National Identity in England and the United States*, Polity, 1993, p. 5.
14. Hall, S. and du Gay, P., 'Who Needs Identity?', in Stuart Hall and Paul du Gay (eds), *Questions of Cultural Identity*, Sage, 1996, p. 1.
15. Ibid., p. 4.
16. McCrone, D., *Understanding Scotland: The Sociology of a Stateless Nation*, Routledge, 1992.
17. Nairn, T., *Faces of Nationalism*, Verso, 1997.
18. Beveridge, C. and Turnbull, R., *The Eclipse of Scottish Culture*, Polygon, 1989.
19. Hooper-Greenhill, E., 'The Museum in the Disciplinary Society', in Pearce, J. (ed), *Museum Studies in Material Culture*, Leicester University Press, 1989, p. 61.
20. Billinge, M., 'Trading History, Reclaiming the Past: the Crystal Palace as Icon', in Kearns, G. andPhilo, C. (eds), *Selling Places: The City as Cultural Capital, Past and Present*, Pergamon, 1993.
21. McLean, F., *Marketing the Museum*, Routledge, 1997.
22. Hooper-Greenhill, E., 'The Museum in the Disciplinary Society', in Pearce, J. (ed), *Museum Studies in Material Culture*, Leicester University Press, 1989.
23. Pearce, S., 'A New Way of Looking at Old Things', in *Museum International*, Vol. 51, No. 2, 1999, pp. 13–17.
24. Macdonald, S., 'Theorizing Museums: an Introduction' in Macdonald, S. and Fyfe, G. (eds), *Theorizing Museums*, Blackwell Publishers, The Sociological Review, 1996.
26. Lowenthal, D., *The Past is a Foreign Country*, Cambridge University Press, 1985, p. 410.
27. See *Visitors to Museums and Galleries in the UK: Research Findings*. Study conducted for the Museums and Galleries Commission, May 1999.
28. The section of the Declaration of Arbroath quoted within 'Scotland Defined' reads: 'for as long as but a hundred of us remain alive, never will we on any conditions be brought under English rule. It is in truth not for glory, nor riches, nor honours that we are fighting, but for freedom - for that alone, which no honest man [sic] gives up but with life itself'. The declaration was in fact a letter to Pope John XXII, written in 1320, in response to an English attempt to have Robert the Bruce excommunicated (see Mackie, J.D., *A History of Scotland*, Penguin, 1991).
29. However, it must be remembered that although there may not be an explicit discourse on the development of Scotland, a Museum, by its very nature, embodies certain ideological assumptions about the world, and about attempts to make the world 'knowable' through classification and display (see Bennett, T., *The Birth of the Museum*, Routledge, 1995).
30. The role of stereotypical signifiers of Scotland within the museum is a case in point, with criticism of the Museum for its 'silences' on William Wallace and the film *Braveheart* (see Cooke and McLean, *Narratives of Scotland: the*

production and consumption of national identity in the Museum of Scotland,
paper presented to the Critical Management Studies Conference, July 1999).
31. The authors are at present setting up further in-depth interviews with visitors to the Museum of Scotland in order to examine these issues, and to investigate the relationship between the Museum and the negotiation of a whole range of visitor identities, such as gender, class, ethnicity, religion and so on.
32. McLean, F., *Marketing the Museum*, Routledge, 1997.

Further Reading

Bagnall, G., 'Consuming the Past' in Edgell, S., Hetherington, K. and Ward, A. (eds), *Consumption Matters*, Blackwell Publishers, The Sociological Review, 1996.

Brown, A., McCrone, D. and Patterson L., *Politics and Society in Scotland*, Macmillan, 1996.

Calder, J., *Museum of Scotland Guidebook*, NMS Publishing Limited, 1998.

Coombes, A.E., 'The Franco-British Exhibition: Packaging Empire in Edwardian England' in Beckett, J. and Cherry D. (eds), *The Edwardian Era*, Oxford University Press, 1987.

du Gay, P., Hall, S., Janes, L., Mackay, H. and Negus, K., *Doing Cultural Studies. The Story of the Sony Walkman*, Sage Open University, 1997.

Fyfe, G. and Ross, M., 'Decoding the Visitor's Gaze: Rethinking Museum Visiting', in Macdonald, S. and Fyfe. G. (eds), *Theorizing Museums*, Blackwell Publishers, The Sociological Review, 1996.

Hetherington, K., 'Museum Topology and the Will to Connect', in *Journal of Material Culture*, Vol. 2(2), 1997, pp. 199–218.

Kaplan, F.E.S. (ed), *Museums and the Making of 'Ourselves': the Role of Objects in National Identity*, Leicester University Press, 1994.

Macdonald, S., 'Cultural Imagining Among Museum Visitors', in *Museum Management and Curatorship*, 11, 1992, pp. 4019.

Mackie, J.D., *A History of Scotland*, Penguin, 1991.

McCrone, D., *The Sociology of Nationalism*, Routledge, 1998.

Roosens, E., 'Interest Groups with a Noble Face', in Costa, J.A. and Bamossy, G.J. (eds), *Theories of Modernity and Postmodernity*, Sage, 1995.

Smith, A.D., *National Identity*, Penguin, 1991.

Tomlinson, A. (ed), *Consumption, Identity and Style: Marketing, Meaning and the Packaging of Pleasure*, Comedia and Routledge, 1990.

THE SCOTTISH PARTNERS

Towards a National Iconography

King James III (1452–88) and his son by the Flemish artist Hugo van der Goes.
Courtesy Scottish National Portrait Gallery

13

IMAGES AND IDENTITY
The Cultural Context of Portraits

James Holloway

Whilst every portrait is a record of the physical presence of the person portrayed, many provide considerable information on the status, profession and interests of that person. Usually, the signs and symbols employed by the artist to convey that information were easily recognised and correctly identified by the sitter, their friends and contemporaries. However, often later viewers, looking at early portraits, even to some extent at contemporary portraits, need help to reveal the significance of detail and by doing so correctly interpret the cultural context of the portrait.

Heraldry is an early and obvious means of providing information about identity. It came into use as a means to identify knights, heavily armoured and therefore invisible, on the battlefield. It developed into a highly sophisticated system of coded identification, which could be read at a glance, rather like shorthand, to provide very detailed information on family and family relationships.

In the portrait of King James III and his son, by the Flemish artist, Hugo van der Goes, the arms of the King of Scots are prominently displayed.[1] Described heraldically, they are 'Or, a lion rampant Gules, armed and langued Azure, within a double tressure flory, counterflory Gules.' At a time when most of his subjects would not have been able to recognise the King of Scots, but when almost everyone would have recognised the King's coat of arms, heraldry was a crucial component of portraiture. Not just for royalty but for anyone: knight, bishop or any of the other pieces on the chessboard of medieval European portraiture.

But, while identification is crucial to the purpose of a portrait, there are other important factors as well. The jewellery in de Critz's portrait of King

James VI sends several signals to the viewer.[2] The badge suspended from the King's neck is the badge of the highest order of chivalry, the Order of the Garter. This alone indicates the sitter's high status. The jewels in his hat are again crucial to this portrait which was painted in 1604, the year after James, who had been King of Scots for many years, succeeded Queen Elizabeth to the English throne.

The hat jewel, known as the Mirror of Great Britain, was made up from parts of Elizabeth's jewels combined with items from the Scottish crown jewels. The Mirror of Great Britain was both one of the most splendid pieces of European jewellery and a unique symbol of the new union of the two countries in the person of the King. De Critz's portrait is a celebration of that union.

As a child, James had had the great Latin scholar, George Buchanan, as his tutor. Learning, rather than ancestry or high status, are what Arnold Bronckhorst wanted to convey in his modest portrait.[3] The open book is the means he used. It is the book as a symbol of learning rather than any particular book which conveys the point. This is not a portrait of a man reading, Buchanan is not in fact looking at the book, but it is the portrait of someone for whom books are an essential component of life. The Latin inscription reinforces the visual message. In translation it reads: 'So were Buchanan's features and countenance. Seek his writings and the stars if you wish to know his mind.'

Much fuller of significant details and harder to decode is John Campbell's portrait by William Mosman, painted in Edinburgh in 1749.[4] Campbell was an interesting and unusual man in that he was one of the few Gaelic speaking Highlanders who had managed to make a successful career in the expanding economic climate which was a feature of both Edinburgh and Glasgow in the mid 18th century. He was feted in Gaelic poetry of the time as someone who had made the successful transfer between Highland Gaelic life and the Lowland mercantile world. Campbell proved it could be done. As cashier of the pro-government Royal Bank of Scotland at the time of the Jacobite Rising 1745–46, Campbell saved the bank's assets by transferring them to the safety of Edinburgh Castle. The banknote on the table, signed by him as the Bank's Signatory, is an indication of his professional role.

So too is the table itself. It has a handsome marble top and is almost certainly an example of one that Campbell himself had produced. He had a business interest in the Netherlorn marble quarry at Ardmaddy in Argyll. He also had a factory in Leith which produced such tables. The one in his portrait is there to indicate this aspect of Campbell's business interests. The view from the window in the portrait is not just any view, it was chosen by Campbell to underline his ancestry, his home territory and family history. John Campbell was descended from the Campbells of

Argyll, one of the greatest and most powerful of all highland clans. His father was Colin Campbell of Ardmaddy and it is Ardmaddy Bay with its three rocks pointing out into Seil Sound which Mosman depicts through the window.

Just visible on the original canvas is the cave in the cliff where Neil Campbell of Ardmaddy had hidden in times of danger. This, as well as Campbell's elaborate and traditional highland dress of belted plaid, decorated cross belt, targe and weapons, would have confirmed to an informed viewer of his portrait John Campbell's status as a senior member of an ancient and powerful family.

A portrait by a still unidentified artist shows Sir Alexander Macdonald of Sleat.[5] The way that Artist has used apparently insignificant details to make highly important points about the interests and aspirations of his sitter is very similar to the way Mosman portrayed John Campbell a generation earlier. Just as the view from the window behind John Campbell contained clues to the banker's ancestry and his pride in his native land, so one of the most telling details in the Macdonald portrait is the only building in the picture, the castle of Duntulm, shown some distance behind Sir Alexander.

In 1773, when James Boswell and Samuel Johnson visited the Macdonalds on the Isle of Skye, they recorded that Sir Alexander Macdonald's principal home was at Mugstot, and this is confirmed by Thomas Pennant writing just before this portrait was painted. It might therefore be thought odd for a man whose family had abandoned Duntulm half a century earlier for more comfortable and convenient quarters elsewhere on Skye to choose not even the old castle itself but a fairly nondescript hillside in its neighbourhood as the location for this very imposing and formal portrait.

There was a reason for Sir Alexander's choice, and it can be found in Pennant's Tour of Scotland. Pennant illustrated the castle (and it was the print of the castle in Pennant's volume which Macdonald's artist copied), and described at some length the significance of the piece of ground on which Sir Alexander stood for his portrait.[6] It was known in Gaelic as *Cnoc an Eireachd*, 'The Hill of the Assembly'. It was the place where the Lords of the Isles had formerly held their courts and dispensed justice. Still maintaining a gaelic bard and piper, Sir Alexander made a deliberate choice to present himself to his contemporaries and posterity as the legitimate heir of the Lords of the Isles, by having himself depicted, standing where his forebears had once stood in the traditional heart of their territory.

These significant details, a castle, a table and a piece of jewellery to use some examples in portraits I have just described, had a particular importance for the artist and sitter which are not difficult to interpret given the cultural context of the time. More difficult to evaluate is an object or accessory the significance of which changes from one period to another.

Nowadays tartan is synonymous with Scotland and the kilt has become the national costume; but, as the following portraits show, the significance of tartan has had different meanings at different times.

In the early 1680s, John Michael Wright painted the portrait of Lord Mungo Murray, a younger son of the Marquis of Atholl.[7] It is the earliest known portrait of anyone in Highland dress. From contemporary literature we know that it was the custom in the Highlands to wear such costume for hunting. Indeed, it was considered bad manners not to:

> For once in the yeere, which is the whole moneth of August, and sometimes part of September, many of the nobility and gentry of the Kingdom (for their pleasure) doe come into these Highland countries to hunt, where they do conforme themselves to the habite of the Highland men, who for the most part speake nothing but Irish (Gaelic)...

The English writer goes on to describe in detail the Highland dress worn by those hunting and their weapons and he concludes:[8]

> As for their attire, any man of what degree soever that comes amongst them, must not disdaine to weare it; for if they doe, then will they disdaine to hunt, or willingly to bring in their dogges; but if men be kind unto them, and be in their habit, then they are conquered with kindnesse, and the sport will be plentifull. This was the reason that I found so many noblemen and gentlemen in those shapes.

Lord Mungo is dressed exactly as described by the writer and he is armed for hunting. What little that is known of him, he died in Panama trying to establish a Scottish colonial empire in Central America, confirms that tartan and Highland dress were seen by him and his contemporaries as appropriate wear for hunting or fighting. In 1697, the family chronicle described Lord Mungo as pursuing Simon Fraser, Lord Lovat, marching 'in a belted plad to admiration which did encourage the men much.'[9] Highland dress was seen as local to the Highlands, but a costume that outsiders as much as locals should wear if they wanted to take part with Highlanders in Highland activities.

Half a century later, in 1743, the artist William Mosman had the difficult task of painting a posthumous portrait of Sir Robert Dalrymple of Castleton. There was a small oval portrait by William Aikman to help but the family wanted something much more ambitious and so Mosman had to invent a portrait and for costume chose tartan. The Dalrymples were, still are, a Lowland family. They were very recent supporters of the union of Scotland with England. They sided politically with the German House of Hanover rather than the exiled Stewarts. And yet, Mosman put Sir Robert in tartan and it had nothing to do with hunting or fighting. The real reason he explained in a letter to Sir Hew Dalrymple in 1744:[10]

> Please herewith receive Sir Robert's original picture by Aikman with the half length coppy I have done from it. I have been at more then ordinary pains with it as I wish nothing more then to please you in what you are pleased to employ me for. As I understand Sir Robert's character was of more than ordinary love for his country and a great encourager of the manufactures. I have clothed him therwith and given him a plan of the estate before him to indicate his great love & abilitys for agriculture.

Tartan for Mosman and the Dalrymples in 1744 was associated not with the Highlands, as it had been fifty years earlier, or with a political faction as it was soon to be, but with national and mercantile patriotism.

The Jacobite Rising the following year changed that. Tartan as a national patriotic symbol was appropriated by one side for its own use. Portraits of Prince Charles Edward Stewart, Bonnie Prince Charlie, and the widely circulated engravings after them, often display tartan as a symbol of Scotland and as an anti-government symbol. This was so powerful and pervasive that the British Government passed an Act of Parliament in 1747 banning the wearing of Highland dress.

Tartan was only permitted to be worn as a component of British army uniform, an act of state policy which began the transformation of tartan from a badge of political dissent to one of loyalty. Portraits which include tartan and which were painted between 1747, when the proscription act was passed, and 1782, when it was repealed, have to be interpreted according to whether the sitter is challenging the act of parliament or rather, making a loyalist statement.

The difference is nicely confused in a portrait of a veteran of the Battle of Culloden. Patrick Grant was a Jacobite soldier who had fought for Bonnie Prince Charlie in 1746, but who lived long enough to survive well into the 19th century. In 1822, George IV came to Scotland on a state visit carefully planned as an occasion for national reconciliation. Grant was found, over a hundred years old, and presented to the King as 'His Majesty's Oldest Enemy'. At the same time, his portrait was painted.[11] The artist, Colvin Smith, took particular care with the costume, buying it himself to make sure it looked authentic. William Maule, on whose estate the old soldier lived and who commissioned the portrait, wrote to the artist: 'I have no doubt you have made a good picture of the veteran of Culloden, you did quite right in ordering him a suit of clothes. I hope you have been particular as to his costume in the Highland garb etc.'[12]

By 1822, even a former rebel was allowed, even encouraged, to wear what had become national and picturesque costume. More interesting even than Patrick Grant being dressed up in tartan for the occasion was the attitude of King George IV himself. The King's visit to Scotland for a few weeks in the summer of 1822 was potentially disastrous. The King was unpopular throughout Britain, in large part due to his treatment of his wife, his extravagance and his dissolute lifestyle. No member of the House of Hanover had visited Scotland since the Duke of Cumberland had crushed the Jacobite army in 1746 and had pursued the remnants of the army with a ruthlessness and barbarity which had shocked even an 18th century audience.

It was Sir Walter Scott who persuaded the King to come, and it was Scott who largely masterminded the state visit. Tartan was to be the symbol of the whole of Scotland, not one region of it as it had been at the end of the 17th century, or just of one faction as it had been at the time of the Jacobite Rising. Nor was the wearing of tartan to be seen as an encouragement of local products, as it had been for the Dalrymple family. Instead, it was to be the national dress, a symbol of all Scotland, Lowland as much as Highland, Hanoverian as much as Jacobite.

The King himself wore the kilt on one more memorable occasion. He was lampooned at the time, but his intention was very serious. Much of the pageantry of the state visit involved the King resuming his ancestral role of King of Scots. Sir Walter Scott and the thousands of spectators present at the royal appearances realised that, while the King's tartan gesture not only made the claim for King George as King of Scots, it also reinforced Scotland's position, under the King, as part of Great Britain.

There is a modern parallel. In 1995, South Africa won the Rugby World Cup. At the end of the victorious match, in a gesture very similar to that by George IV in Edinburgh, President Mandela put on the jersey and cap of the Springbok team, signalling that in the new South Africa the team which had been considered the pride and symbol of white apartheid South Africa, was now the truly national team. Just as the King had neutralised the political content of tartan in Scotland in 1822, so Mandela took apartheid out of the Springboks and made them heroic figures in which the whole new rainbow nation could take pride.

The significance of tartan can be shown to have altered several times in only a hundred and fifty years. Details in all portraits need to be interpreted in the cultural context of their period. It is critical to our correct understanding of the men and women presented in them.

The Author

James Holloway is Keeper of the Scottish National Portrait Gallery, and has worked on Scottish art since graduating from the Courtauld Institute of Art at London University in 1971. He was formerly employed at the National Gallery of Scotland, as a Research Assistant, and as Assistant Keeper of Art at the National Museum of Wales. His major projects include the exhibitions *The Discovery of Scotland* and *Patrons and Painters: Art in Scotland 1650–1760*. In addition to writing many published articles, he currently edits the National Galleries of Scotland's series of booklets, *Scottish Masters*, for which he has written the volumes on James Tassie, Jacob More, William Aikman and the Norie family. He continues to lecture frequently on Scottish art and collections, and has also acted as adviser to the National Galleries of Australia.

References

1. Thompson, C., and Campbell, L., *Hugo van der Goes and the Trinity Panels in Edinburgh*, National Gallery of Scotland, 1974.
2. Scottish National Portrait Gallery, PG 561.
3. Scottish National Portrait Gallery, PG 2678.
4. Holloway, J., *Patrons and Painters: Art in Scotland 1650–1760*, National Galleries of Scotland, 1989, no 83, pp. 109–112.
5. Scottish National Portrait Gallery, PG 2609 (possibly by Sir George Chalmers).
6. Pennant, T., *A Tour in Scotland and Voyage to the Hebrides*, 1774, p. 304.
7. Scottish National Portrait Gallery, PG 997.
8. *Colectanea de rebus Albanicis* (Iona Club), Edinburgh, 1847, Appendix, pp. 3940.
9. Chronicles of the Atholl and Tullibardine Families, Edinburgh, 1908, vol 1, pp. 441–442.
10. Letter in private muniments of Sir Hew Hamilton-Dalrymple, Bt. The two portraits referred to of Sir Robert Dalrymple of Castleton are still in family ownership.
11. Scottish National Portrait Gallery, PG 2924.
12. Colvin Smith, R.C.M., *The Life and Works of Colvin Smith, RSA 1796–1875*, University of Aberdeen Press, 1939, p. 59.

King James VI (1566–1625) by unknown artist. *Courtesy Scottish National Portrait Gallery*

Lord Mungo Murray, a younger son of the Marquis of Atholl, painted by John Michael Wright in the early 1680s and is the earliest known portrait of anyone in Highland dress. *Courtesy Scottish National Portrait Gallery*

Patrick Grant (1713–1824), a Jacobite soldier who fought at Culloden, painted by Colvin Smith at the time of George IV's visit to Scotland in 1822. *Courtesy Scottish National Portrait Gallery*

14

MONUMENTAL IMAGES
Scott and the Creation of Scotland

Jeanne Cannizzo

In the political scale of nations, we may rise, or we may fall.
In his pages we are a glorious people, and a favoured spot for ever![1]

This chapter explores the use and interpretation of two portraits of 'Highlanders' on display in the 1999 exhibition *O Caledonia! Sir Walter Scott and the Creation of Scotland,* curated by the author. The exhibition is neither biographical nor literary in nature; rather, it explores the problematic concepts of ethnicity, nationalism and nation. The anthropological approach to ethnicity is not quite the same as that often voiced in popular opinion. The 'primordialist' view is one in which individual and collective ethnic identity is often defined by a list of characteristics deemed 'essential'. There is also an 'instrumentalist' interpretation in which ethnicity, based upon an appeal to shared blood or race, is used in pursuit of a political agenda. The 'constructivist' approach, in which ethnic identity is always contingent, changeable and which emerges from or within particular chronologies and social circumstances, is the one which underlies the exhibition and this paper.

Here the emphasis lies less on essential, non-changing characteristics, or concepts of relatedness based on blood, but on subjective experience.[2,3] This revival of interest in ethnicity has coincided with another in cultural production and the consumption of ideas, representations of the past, and social memory. These ideas are applicable outside of the academy, including in the Scott exhibition, although words such as ethnicity do not actually appear in the exhibition. But *O Caledonia!* is indeed about how, through his novels and poems, Sir Walter Scott created a particular vision of his native land, its peoples and their collective past. The exhibition explores Scott's imaginative construction of cultural identity through his own writings and the work of those who found in him inspiration for their visions of Scotland.

In the 1822 painting by Sir Henry Raeburn, Scott is portrayed in the year that he stage-managed the visit of George IV to Scotland. He was at the height of his literary fame; the great French novelist Balzac called him 'one of the noblest geniuses of modern time.' His influence in 19th century Europe and America is hard to overestimate but can be described in many different ways. He is often credited with the invention of the historical novel. He also penned the first sequel novel in English and helped define the short story as a genre. Even a partial list of fellow writers whose works were informed by Scott's writing must include Balzac, Dumas, Fenimore Cooper, Hawthorne, Hugo, Manzoni, Pushkin and Thackeray. The first novel Queen Victoria ever read was by Scott. His particular vision of Scotland acquired mythological status, as did the living author himself.

It is here appropriate to look at image and identity with reference to Highlanders, real and imagined, as conveyed by Scott. Sir Leslie Stephen had this to say on the matter in *Cornhill Magazine* (1871):

> Scott invented the modern Highlander. It is to him that we owe the strange perversion of facts which induces a good Lowland Scot to fancy himself more nearly allied to the semi-barbarous wearers of the tartan than to his English blood-relations.

How did Scott create his Highlanders, and how was this act of cultural imagination to be presented in the exhibition?

The publication of *Waverley* in 1814 is often heralded as the birth of the historical novel. The story of the 1745 Jacobite Rising also placed Highland culture firmly in the past and infused the values which had governed it with an elegiac melancholy. To Scott's critics this betrayed those he described by creating a romanticised myth palatable to the British body politic. To others, however, the same act created what one scholar has called 'a modern kind of national subjectivity',[4] through which readers may still gain aesthetic access to the fictionalised people of the Highlands. The following is a quotation from *Edinburgh Evening Courant* of 24 September 1832:

> The Waverley Novels will be prized as permanent depositories of the genuine Scottish character, which is fading away before the fast encroaching tide of southern refinement.

In his attempts to demarcate and strengthen the distinctiveness of Scottish society in comparison to England, Scott succeeded in imposing an homogeneity which obscured significant cultural differences within Scotland. Although he wrote about the Lowlands and Scottish cities as well as mountain glens, Scott's worldwide readership found in the Highland novels the 'essential' Highlander, an honoured, but powerless, figure in a timeless past rather than an active agent of recent history. For many, this Highlander came to represent all Scottish peoples.

Writing in the introduction to the 1829 edition, Scott claimed he was inspired by the novelist Maria Edgeworth whose depictions of the Irish he believed 'have done more towards completing the Union than perhaps all the legislative enactments with which it has been followed up.' He chose the year of 1745 and invented the story of young Waverley, an Englishman serving in a Hanoverian regiment who travels north where he is so overwhelmed by love and the romance of the Highlands, that he joins the Jacobite Army. He eventually becomes disillusioned, returning to his 'proper' place in society and a peaceful life with the right woman.

Scott was a committed participant in and beneficiary of post-Union Scotland, but seems in this novel to mourn the failed rebellion, not as a political act, but as the final expression of the old virtues of loyalty, courage and chivalry. Scott wrote in 1806 that 'I became a valiant Jacobite at the age of ten years old; and, even since reason and reading came to my assistance, I have never quite got rid of the impression which the gallantry of Prince Charles made on my imagination.'

In seeking images to convey Scott's complicated views and feelings about Highlanders, I decided to use, among several others, two portraits of Highland veterans: namely, survivors of the Battle of Culloden. The first is by David Wilkie, 1785–1841, who was by training a history painter but who became one of Britain's most distinguished genre painters.

In 1817, Wilkie had undertaken a sojourn through the Highlands; convinced that a unique traditions and communities were vanishing, he sought to document their lifeways and collect objects revealing in their physical forms the values and customs under threat. Those values were probably those which were praised in a postscript to *Waverley:*

> This race has now almost entirely vanished from the land, and with it, doubtless, much absurd political prejudice; but also, many living examples of singular and disinterest attachment to the principles of loyalty which they received from their fathers, and of old Scottish faith, hospitality, worth and honours.

Wilkie met Scott through the publisher John Murray in 1809 and was certainly impressed by the Wizard of the North's fictional vision, although he only rarely illustrated scenes and characters from the novels or took up the history subjects suggested by the novelist's works. Scott himself recognised the compatibility of Wilkie's vision and his own, suggesting through the pages of *The Antiquary* in 1816 that, 'In the inside of the cottage was a scene which only Wilkie could have painted, with the exquisite feeling of nature that characterizes his enchanting productions.' It is not surprising then that Wilkie sought Scott's advice on people and places he might pursue on his Highland tour.

He notes with pleasure in a letter home on 15th August 1817 that 'I wrote to Mr Walter Scott from Edinburgh, and have had a most kind answer, giving me various directions about what is to be seen and inviting me to come for a few days to see him at Abbotsford, where he says he will tell me some old stories, and show me some interesting ruins in his neighbourhood.'[5]

However, Scott had been unable to actually suggest the names of any veterans of 1745 as is clear in his letter to Wilkie dated 2 August 1817: 'I cannot, now-a-days, pretend to point out any good Highland originals, to be rendered immortal on your canvas, for the old Forty-Five men, of whom I knew many in the days of yore, are now gathered to their fathers.'[6]

Somewhere Wilkie, it is presumed, found his veteran highlander and sketched him during the travels of 1817. The portrait was probably painted for a sale rather than as a commission: the price was thirty five guineas framed. It was exhibited in 1820 at the British Institution. The artist first entitled this character study 'Veteran Highlander, who served at the Battle of Minden'. It was the King's Own Scottish Borderers, a Lowland regiment, who fought in this battle of 1759, one of the more notable of the Seven Years War; but it is certainly possible that Highlanders were present in the British infantry which fought under Ferdinand of Brunswick against the French cavalry in what became a famous British and Hanoverian victory. He seems to have brought out for the artist/viewer his sword and belt, and retrieved part of his uniform, but is still wearing a craftsman's leather apron. The whole seems infused with a near but totally eclipsed past presented without and disjunction or discontinuity.

This portrait then becomes the embodiment of 'loyalist' form of Scottish nationalism,[7] appropriate and acceptable to a Whiggish patron of the art and founder of the British Institution which was devoted to the promotion of native painters. It was bought at the asking price by the numismatist and noted collector of bronzes, Richard Payne Knight. A vice-president of the Society of Antiquaries, he wrote on ancient art, owned hundreds of drawings by Claude and was an occasional poet. He was also elected MP for Leominster in 1780 and was a follower of Fox. Wilkie's politics were described by his friend and contemporary, the history painter Benjamin Robert Haydon (whose own paintings were admired by Scott) as 'a cautious Tory'[8,9] but others found Wilkie apolitical.

He was to describe Scotland as like a 'volume of history' and 'a land of tradition and poetry', writing to his patron, Sir George Beaumonte in 1818 that: 'every district presents some memorial of the past, the scene of some remarkable event of history or of fiction.' However, Errington has noted:[10]

> Since the highlands were to the Fifeshire Wilkie territory as foreign as Italy, Spain, Ireland and Syria, he grasped at some of the most obvious points-tartan, bagpipe music, and a propensity for slaughtering red deer. These, in novels from Scott's *Waverley* up to Compton Mackenzie's *Monarch of the Glen* have been, and are still, made prominent features in most portraits of the highlands.

Although Scott claimed a sentimental attachment to the Jacobites throughout his life, he had a keen appreciation of what he believed were the benefits that accrued to Scotland after the Act of Union in 1707. No reigning monarch had been in Scotland since 1651. Scott, who was personally acquainted with the Prince Regent, conceived of a state visit that would express and enhance a sense of unity. In 1822, George IV undertook what Scott called 'the King's Jaunt', which those less enthused by the spectacle derided as a 'plaided panorama'.

Such a visit would accomplish a number of political aims: it would boost the King's popularity after the debacle of Queen Caroline's trial; it might deflect attention from Radical protests about the state of the economy; it would offer Scottish landowners the possibility of improving their public image as their policies spread human misery. The King had visited Ireland in 1821, and needed to reaffirm the unity of his crown, which fitted perfectly with Scott's vision of reconciliation between the past and present in Scotland.

Once the last Stewart in a direct line had died, in 1807, the Hanoverians could assert their claim to be rulers of both England and Scotland. By being offered and then accepting the Honours of Scotland, the symbols of the state at Holyrood, George IV is acknowledging his obligations and asserting his rights to the nation. Something similar is happening in the meeting of the Monarch and this man.

Patrick Grant (1713–1824) was rumoured to have been one of the seven 'outlaws' who hid Bonnie Prince Charlie in their cave and saw him off to France. Certainly he was a Jacobite survivor of the Battle of Culloden. An inscription in black oil on the back of the canvas reads: *Patrick Grant: the Veteran of Culloden.* He was Sergeant Major in the Highland Army in 1745 and one of those who escaped over the walls of Carlisle to fight among his 'native mountains': this portrait of Grant, at the great age of 109, was painted by order of the Hon Wm Maule of Panmure, on whose estate he then resided, in the Parish of Lethnot County of Forfar. He lived two years afterwards, and enjoyed a pension of one guinea per week granted to him with remainder to his daughter (aged 65) by His Majesty George IV, Brechin Castle, June 1822, W.M. 'W.M.' is undoubtedly William Maule, later Lord Panmure. Beneath this inscription is an old label which describes his death and funeral, emphasizing, in a way Wilkie would have appreciated, the Highland traditions:

> This Extraordinary Man, with scarcely any Previous illness Died Easily in his Chair Feby 11.1824 in the 111 Year of his Age. His Funeral was Conducted in old Highland fashion, Three pipers being Placed at the head of his Coffin, playing what wadna fight for Charlies Right, while an anker of whisky was consumed by The Assembled company, Three hundred in Number, by whom His body was Carried to the Grave, Patrick Grant resided in the Parish of Lethnot Forfarshire when this Portrait was taken 1822.

Grant, a crucifix on his broad chest, in bold plaid and tartan trousers with a sporran, rests on the hilt of his sword which bears the weight of his body, and it seems, his reflections. With his introduction in 1822 to George IV as His Majesty's 'oldest enemy', Grant became the embodiment of acceptable cultural nationalism within the framework of the Union: namely, a Highlander loyal to the Hanoverians. Perhaps that is at least part of what appealed to the man who commissioned this portrait from the artist Colvin Smith (1795–1875) who was himself from Brechin, in Angus. As early as 1821, he appears to have been working on a portrait of William Maule (later Lord Panmure) MP and Patron as well as President of the Forfarshire Agricultural Association. Maule, the second son of the 8th Earl of Dalhousie, was said to have been a generous and liberal benefactor in his public acts which included building a hall and library for the local Mechanics Institute and bestowing an annuity upon the widow of Robert Burns.

Although from a Tory family, Maule was a Whig MP from 1796 until 1831. A subscriber to the principles of orator and statesman, Charles James Fox, he provided a pension for his widow. He commissioned the portrait which was exhibited in 1826 at the Institution for the Encouragement of the Fine Arts in Scotland. A late 19th century critic of his work suggested that 'Colvin Smith's portraits are generally reckoned faithful likenesses, well drawn and simply treated.'[11] It would seem that this sentiment was shared by William Maule, whose letter of 17 April 1822, to the artist begins: '[I] have no doubt you have made a good picture of the veteran of culloden, you did quite right in ordering him a suit of clothes. I hope you have been particular as to his costume (italics) in the Highland garb, etc...'.[12] In 1852, thirty years after the original portrait was painted, Colvin Smith made a copy for Lord Panmure.

Scott was to write in a postscript to *Waverley* that:

> There is no European nation which, within the course of half a century, has undergone so complete a change as this kingdom of Scotland. The effects of the insurrection of 1745 (the destruction of the patriarchal power of the Highland chiefs; the abolition of the heritable jurisdictions of the Lowland nobility and the barons; the total eradication of the Jacobite party, which, averse to intermingle with the English, or adopt their customs, long continued to pride themselves upon maintaining ancient Scottish manners and customs) commenced this innovation. The gradual influx of wealth, and extension of commerce, have since united to render the present people of Scotland a class of being as different from their grandfathers as the existing English are from those of Queen Elizabeth's time.

These images of two veteran Highlanders embody the reconciliation between past and present sought by Scott; they provide pictorial evidence of an encompassing identity for the future in which it would be possible to be a Highlander, a Scot and a Briton.

Sir Walter Scott's productivity, even in comparison with the most prolific of his contemporaries, was phenomenal, as was the public response to his novels, many of which became best-sellers. It was estimated that by 1840 two million copies of his books were circulating in French translation alone. Byron claimed to have read Scott's books 'fifty times over'. Ten thousand copies of *Ivanhoe* sold in two weeks. Such was his saleability that as early as 1807 his publisher paid 'one thousand guineas' for a poem which he had not yet begun. The immense popularity of his works over many generations ensured that for millions of readers Scotland became, in the words of the poet Alexander Smith 'Scott-land; he is the light in which it is seen.'[13] These notions continue to influence how Scots see themselves and how they are perceived by a wider world.

The Author

Dr Jeanne Cannizzo is an anthropologist at the University of Edinburgh where she teaches material culture and the anthropology of art. She was co-curator of *David Livingstone and the Victorian Encounter with Africa*, which opened at the

National Portrait Gallery in 1996 and continued at the Royal Scottish Academy in Edinburgh. Her most recent exhibition, *O Caledonia! Sir Walter Scott and the Creation of Scotland*, opened the day after the election of the Scottish Parliament in May, 1999.

References

1. *Glasgow Herald* 24 September 1832
2. Smith, A., 'The Politics of Culture: Ethnicity and Nationalism' in Ingold, T. (ed), *Companion Encyclopedia of Anthropology*, Routledge, 1994
3. Sokolovskh, S. and Tishkov, T., 'Ethnicity' in Barnard, A. and Spencer, J.(eds), *Encyclopedia of Social and Cultural Anthropology*, Routledge, 1996
4. Duncan, I. (ed), Introduction to *Rob Roy*, Oxford University Press, 1998
5. Cunningham, A., *The Life of Sir David Wilkie*, John Murray, 1843, Vol 1, pp. 469–70.
6. Ibid. pp. 470–71.
7. Craske, M., *Art in Europe 1700–1830: a history of the visual arts in an era of unprecedented growth*, Oxford University Press, 1997.
8. Ibid.
9. Marks, A., *The Paintings of David Wilkie to 1825*, PhD thesis, Courtauld Institute of Art, 1968.
10. Errington, L., *Tribute of Wilkie*, National Galleries of Scotland, 1985, p. 24.
11. R. Brydall quoted in Colvin-Smith, R., *The Life and Works of Colvin Smith, R.S.A. 1796–1875*, University of Aberdeen Press, 1939, p. 55.
12. Colvin Smith, R.C.M., *The Life and Works of Colvin Smith, R.S.A. 1796–1875*, University of Aberdeen Press, 1939, p. 59.
13. *Scotsman* 17th February 1866.

Further Reading

Chiego, W. et al, *Sir David Wilkie of Scotland (1785–1841)*, North Carolina Museum of Art, 1987.

Colley, L., *Britons: Forging the Nations 1701–1837*, Yale University Press, 1992.

Gold, J. and Gold, M., *Imagining Scotland: Tradition, Representation and Promotion in Scottish Tourism since 1750*, Scolar Press, 1995.

Haldane, K., *Imagining Scotland: tourist images of Scotland 1770–1914*, UMI Dissertation Information Service, 1992.

Hardie, W., *Scottish Painting: 1837 to the Present*, Studio Vista, 1994.

Harvie, C., *Scotland and Nationalism: Scottish Society and Politics 1707–1994*, Routledge, 1994.

Hobsbawm, E. and Ranger, T. (eds), *The Invention of Tradition*, Cambridge University Press, 1983.

Kerr, J., *Fiction Against History: Scott as Storyteller*, Cambridge University Press, 1989.

Lang, T., *The Victorians and the Stuart Heritage: Interpretations of a Discordant Past*, Cambridge University Press, 1995.

Lenman, B., *The Jacobite Risings in Britain, 1689–1746*, Eyre Methuen, 1984.

Lockhart, J.G., *Memories of the Life of Sir Walter Scott*, Bart, R. Cadell, 1837–38.

Lynch, M. (ed), *Jacobitism and the '45*, Historical Association Committee for Scotland and the Historical Association, 1995.

Macmillan, D., *Scottish Art 1460–1990*, Mainstream, 1990.

Miles, H., *Sir David Wilkie 1785–1841*, Feigen, 1994.

Pittock, M., *The Invention of Scotland: The Stuart Myth and the Scottish Identity, 1638 to the Present*, Routledge, 1991.

Prebble, J., *The King's Jaunt*, Collins, 1988.

Shaw, H. (ed), *Critical Essays on Sir Walter Scott: The Waverley Novels*, Prentice Hall International, 1996.

Sutherland, J., *The Life of Walter Scott: A Critical Biography*, Blackwell, 1995.

Womack, P., *Improvement and Romance: Constructing the Myth of the Highlands*, Macmillan, 1989.

Woosnam-Savage, R. (ed), *1745: Charles Edward Stuart and the Jacobites*, HMSO Edinburgh, 1995.

King George IV on his visit to Edinburgh in 1822 by Sir David Wilkie. *Courtesy Scottish National Portrait Gallery*

Sir Walter Scott (1771–1832) by Sir Henry Raeburn. *Courtesy Scottish National Portrait Gallery*

'Veteran Highlander, who served at the battle of Minden' by Sir David Wilkie (1785–1841), probably sketched during his travels in 1817. *Courtesy Paisley Museum and Art Galleries*

15

ARTEFACTS AND MONUMENTS
The Building Blocks of Identity

David Breeze

Historic Scotland is an executive agency within the Scottish Executive, being responsible for undertaking duties in relation to the protection of the built heritage. This includes the scheduling of ancient monuments, the listing of historic buildings and the offering of advice and grants. Another major responsibility is management and presentation of the 300 properties in its own care. The author contributed a chapter on marketing to an earlier volume in this series, and readers may also like to consult Macinnes, Macniven and Munro on different aspects of work by the agency.[1,2,3]

Historic Scotland seeks to present each property in its care through the provision of one or more site interpretative boards. All staffed properties have a guidebook, in colour where justified by visitor numbers. At about 40 properties there is a visitor centre which provides further information and where artefacts are displayed. Several series of books seek to place individual monuments in wider contexts. These include the *Scotland BC* series, the Batsford/Historic Scotland books and the recently launched Canongate series.

Historic Scotland is most closely associated with the care and protection of the archaeological and architectural elements of our cultural heritage – the built heritage – but in fact it has in its care many artefacts and detached architectural fragments. Historic Scotland owns, has in its care, or retains temporarily archaeological and historical artefacts and architectural fragments for three reasons. First, objects, mainly sculptured or moulded architectural fragments, are retained at properties in Historic Scotland's care because they are part of the monument, though now detached from it. Second, some objects are retained at properties in care in order to be displayed there and thus help interpret the monument. And third, any archaeological artefacts discovered during work sponsored by Historic Scotland are retained until they are passed to an appropriate museum through the Finds Disposal arrangements, with the exception of those artefacts claimed through the Treasure Trove procedures.

In this discussion, objects within the third category will be ignored as they are only in Historic Scotland's care while en route from an activity such as an archaeological excavation to their final location in a museum. Historic Scotland either owns or cares for about 50,000 artefacts.

The range of these items is very wide. It includes archaeological artefacts, arms and armament, books and documents, building components, carved stones, costumes and textiles, furniture, militaria, numismatics, paintings, drawings and prints, the Honours of Scotland and the Stone of Destiny.

The range of architectural fragments is particularly large. It includes the tombs of nobles and lords, bishops and clergymen buried in our mediaeval cathedrals and churches, a wide range of sculpted fragments detached from mediaeval cathedrals, abbeys and castles, ranging from some of the most important carved fragments to survive from mediaeval Scotland to ordinary pieces of moulded stonework, and objects which were created to sit within our mediaeval buildings. This one group makes up about 50 per cent of the whole collection.

Our primary aim in relation to artefacts, is to maintain them in their context, that is at the building or monument at which they were found or with which they are associated. This is because the artefact aids both the visitor's understanding of the physical remains and its historical, cultural and social context. Such objects used either to form part of the monument, like a fragment of sculpture, or were once placed within a structure, like a tomb, or were used within it, like pottery, tools and weapons. English Heritage has recently emphasised that its aim is to 'continue to bring collections back to their historic sites so that they may be appreciated in context'.[4] This is also is the aim of Historic Scotland, and in 1998, we published two documents on interpretation at properties, one sets out our operational policy, the other is a manual on operational practice.[5,6]

Some individual collections may be substantial. The Seafield Collection at Fort George, on loan to Historic Scotland from the Scottish United Services Museum, is one such item, an outstanding collection of arms and military equipment mostly dating to the Napoleonic Wars. On a different scale, Kinnaird Head Lighthouse retains the furniture and fittings in use when it was taken into care.

A special programme of recording every item in Historic Scotland's very large collection of detached carved and moulded fragments from its mediaeval properties is under way. To date inventories have been prepared of the sculptural fragments at nearly thirty monuments including Aberdour Castle, Arbroath Abbey, Craignethan Castle, Dunfermline Abbey, Crossraguel Abbey, Elgin Cathedral, Melrose Abbey and Stirling Castle Great Hall. Work is in hand to improve the storage of such fragments on site. These are fragments which are already detached from the individual monuments. In some cases, Historic Scotland has itself acted to detach sculptural fragments from buildings. This is undertaken in very rare instances and only where it is felt that the item will deteriorate to an unacceptable level if left *in situ*. At Melrose Abbey the principal statues and the inscription recording work by Jean Morrow have been removed: the latter is now displayed in the Commentator's House and a replica erected in its place. The statue on Bishop Reid's Tower at the Bishop's Palace, Kirkwall, has similarly been removed and replaced. There is considerable concern about other *in situ* sculpture, such as the door at Brechin Round Tower. A further concern is vandalism, and it is as a result of such activities that the effigy of Princess Margaret at Lincluden Collegiate Church has been removed for safekeeping. In such cases, although the sculptural fragments have been removed from the most immediate context, it is still Historic Scotland's aim to retain each item at the monument from which it was detached.

At some of the monuments in its care Historic Scotland has established visitor centres – the first was at Skara Brae in the 1920s and the programme of improving them continues. The purpose of these is to help visitors, who number in excess of 2.9 million annually, understand the monument better. In most cases, this aim is sought through the display of a relatively small number of artefacts. At some sites, replica prehistoric pots have been made for display in a tomb, such as the cairns at Cairnpapple and Unstan. Elsewhere the amount of material surviving at the monument and worthy of display is so great that the visitor centre can more appropriately be termed a museum. Examples of this are at St Andrews and Melrose Abbeys; the *lapidaria* such as at Meigle and Kilmory Knap, perhaps falls into this category but have not been included in this discussion for they are separate collections of carved stones not associated with an existing building.

Most of the artefacts other than worked stone recovered from excavations at properties in Historic Scotland's care have been passed to museums. In the past, many finds have been deposited with the National Museums of Scotland. This is as might be expected because, almost by definition, the sites in state care form part of the best surviving ancient monuments in Scotland, in effect the core of the national archive of ancient monuments and historic buildings. It could, of course, be argued that many artefacts retained at individual properties in care could take their place in the National Museums of Scotland in view of their national importance. Here is the central tension of this discussion, between Historic Scotland's aim of retaining artefacts within their intended context at nationally important buildings in state care, and acknowledgement of their national importance which would render them eligible for display in the National Museums of Scotland. There is also a clash between different cultures. On the one hand, there is the traditional centralising tendency of a national museum which is generally associated with the country's capital. On the other, by its very nature, the national collection of the built heritage is de-centralised and still in its original locations and this ensures that some nationally important artefacts will remain with nationally important monuments in dispersed and local contexts.

Yet not all artefacts retained at monuments are of national importance: many relate to the more ordinary aspects of life. We should note that there is a distinction to be made between Historic Scotland and a national museum's collection, for it is the aim of Historic Scotland to display not just the 'best' artefacts, however they might be defined, but artefacts which aid interpretation of the monument. This includes objects which might not normally be displayed in a museum. Indeed, some of these more 'ordinary' artefacts might be better interpreted within their original context.

The central tension detailed in this paper between a centralised national museum wishing to display artefacts of national importance and a decentralised national collection of the built heritage can be eased by loans. The National Museums of Scotland, for example, have loaned to Historic Scotland the Jedburgh comb, the splendid early 12th century ivory comb found during excavations undertaken by Historic Scotland at Jedburgh Abbey; and it is now displayed in the abbey's visitor centre along with those artefacts found with it. The comb was claimed as Treasure Trove and allocated to the National Museums. In other instances, for example at Skara Brae, objects discovered during excavations carried out by Historic Scotland's predecessor were given to the National Museums' predecessor, the National Museum of Antiquities. Again material has been loaned back to Historic Scotland for display in the new visitor centre at the site. Loans can flow both ways. Historic Scotland recently loaned artefacts from Jedburgh and Glenluce Abbeys and St Andrews Cathedral, as well as the Dupplin Cross, to the Museum of Scotland, and short-term loans have been made, including the St Andrews Sarcophagus to the British Museum and the National Museums of Scotland. The Macdonald Collection formerly at Arbroath Abbey mainly relates to the social history of Arbroath town and has therefore been placed on long loan to the Signal Tower Museum in the town.

The National Museums of Scotland has emphasised its willingness to co-operate with Historic Scotland in the display of appropriate objects in the national collection at properties in state care and discussions are in progress concerning the loan of artefacts to the new visitor centre planned for Urquhart Castle.

Developments in the field of Inheritance Tax and Capital Transfer Tax are also relevant to this discussion. 'Objects – pictures, prints, books, manuscripts, works of art, scientific objects etc. – may be accepted in satisfaction of tax...[and] in the case of an object accepted on condition that it...remains *in situ*, formal ownership will normally be vested in an appropriate public body...'.[7] This is a clear acknowledgement of the importance of context as is specifically noted by the Inland Revenue.

Although the main focus of Historic Scotland's activities relate to the protection of the built heritage, we naturally wish to ensure that the highest standards are also applied to the curation of the artefacts in our care. Accordingly, Historic Scotland is applying for Museums and Galleries Commission Registration. Historic Scotland remains content in general to continue to pass material recovered from excavations at its own sites for retention in the most appropriate place, namely a museum. Material relevant to the interpretation of the monument, however, we do wish to retain on site. Indeed, as I have indicated, Historic Scotland seeks to return more artefacts to monuments. Hitherto, Historic Scotland when offering finds from its own excavations to a museum has not indicated which objects it intends to retain at monuments, but it now intends to do so, through 'TAK TENT' the Scottish Museums Council's newsletter. Furthermore, Historic Scotland intends that the computerised catalogue of its collections of artefacts should become more publicly accessible and is exploring ways in which this might be achieved.

Since this paper was written, there has been a significant organisational change in that Historic Scotland has become an Executive Agency of the Scottish Executive Education Department, and more specifically has joined the Culture Group of the Department which sponsors the National Museums of Scotland. This change offers the opportunity for further fruitful collaboration between two bodies responsible for the care of important aspects of Scotland's cultural heritage. As an indication of this, a Statement of Intent governing relations between Historic Scotland and the National Museums of Scotland was signed on 28 September 1999.

The Author and Acknowledgements

David Breeze is Chief Inspector of Ancient Monuments in Historic Scotland and a past President of the Society of Antiquaries of Scotland. He is a graduate of Durham University where he is now a Visiting Professor of Archaeology.

He is also an honorary Professor of Scottish History in the University of Edinburgh. He has written several books on Roman frontiers, is author of a book on the buildings associated with Mary Queen of Scots and is co-author of the guidebook to the Stone of Destiny.

The author is grateful to Richard Emerson, Dr R. Fawcett, Mrs D. Grove, Graeme Munro, Mr B. Naylor, Mr C.J. Tabraham and Mr R. Welander for reading and commenting on an earlier draft of this paper.

References

1. Macinnes, L., 'Towards a Common Language: The Unifying Perceptions of an Integrated Approach' in Fladmark, J.M. (ed), *Heritage: Conservation, Interpretation and Enterprise*, Donhead, 1993, pp. 101–111.
2. Macniven, D., 'Presenting Historic Scotland' in Fladmark, J.M. (ed), *Cultural Tourism*, Donhead, 1994, pp. 225–236.
3. Munro, G.N., 'Sense of Place in Towns: Historic Buildings as Cultural Icons' in Fladmark, J.M. (ed), *Sharing the Earth:: Local Identity in Global Culture*, Donhead 1995, pp. 325–331.
4. Bryant, J. (ed), *Collections Review*, Volume Two, English Heritage, London, 1999.
5. Historic Scotland, *Operational Policy Paper No 6: Site Interpretation at Properties in Care*, 1998.
6. Historic Scotland, *A Manual for Site Interpretation at Properties in Care*, 1998.
7. IR 67 *Capital Taxation and the National Heritage* 11, 12 and 17.
8. Ibid., 11, 3 and 12.

Further Reading

Breeze, D.J., 'Marketing our Past' in Fladmark, J.M. (ed), *Cultural Tourism*, Donhead, 1994, pp. 237–247.
Connely, D., 'The Work of the Historic Buildings and Monuments Directorate', in Ambrose, T. (ed), *Presenting Scotland's Story*, HMSO, 1989, pp. 55–64.

One of the 'Stirling Heads', made in the mid-16th century for the Palace at Stirling Castle, where they are still displayed.

The St Andrew Sarcophagus displayed in the Great Hall of the Royal Museum of Scotland in 1997.

16

HOLDING HERITAGE IN TRUST
Curating the Diversity of a Nation

Ian Gow

As the new Curator of a long established body, the National Trust for Scotland was founded in 1931, allow me to begin with an object to have featured in my work since starting: the Culloden Sampler. This began as a very conventional young girl's sampler, but became an extraordinary artefact as she worked down the cloth and the Jacobites started to appear. I have dealt with few objects more redolent of an historical event and of such gossamer fragility. Handling it unframed, as we had to recently, you feel that it might disintegrate were you to sneeze. Indeed, when it came up for auction in Bond Street two years ago, there was perhaps an expectation that it would go to a museum, but thanks to the Heritage Lottery Fund, it came to the Trust. This poses the question: if it qualifies as a museum exhibit, with me as its Curator, should the Trust be regarded as a museum?

This chapter explores the rather paradoxical relationship between the varied activities of the Trust and more conventional museum endeavours at national level. At the outset, it should be stressed that we are committed to registering our collections, where appropriate, under the Museums and Galleries Commission registration scheme. As a new Curator, you learn fast that there is no purchase fund, because we do not actively collect. We acquired the Culloden sampler, not for itself, but because we hold part of the Culloden battlefield. We wanted to show it alongside our collection of relics, many of which are on loan to the Trust, including many from the National Museums of Scotland, and we house it in the visitor centre near the historic battlefield.

The special circumstances under which the Trust operates are perhaps the more obvious to a new curator who had spent the previous 21 years in national collections both in London and Edinburgh. But I was reasonably well prepared, as prior to my appointment, I served for two terms on the Trust's Curatorial Committee under the convenership of the late Lord Bute who was also Chairman of the Trustees for the National Museums of Scotland.

The unusual nature of our collections was brought home to me, almost in my first week, when I met Jim Broughton and the staff of Broughton International who had come to see us from the US. They had approached the Trust with the intention of putting together, for their very extensive new Wilmington exhibition facility in Delaware, a didactic travelling show intended to introduce Middle America to the history of Scotland from earliest times to the particularly exciting moments of recent constitutional events. They specialise in exhibitions where historical themes unfold through carefully chosen objects and art works.

It was obvious to me that the Trust, in spite of its enormous collections, could simply not deliver what they had reasonably expected from our name and reputation. It would certainly have been possible for us to piece together a story of the development of Scottish Architecture, confining ourselves to our own fine jigsaw pieces. After all, we hold Craigievar, Robert Adam's Culzean, Mackintosh's Hill House, and now Greek Thomson's Holmwood. We have a collection of paintings which include many that would be equally eligible for the National Galleries of Scotland, or even the National Gallery in London. At Fyvie we hold a complete art collection built by an American millionaire industrialist, which just happens to be in Grampian rather than Pittsburg. By consulting George Dalgleish's chapter in this volume, it can also be seen that we have Jacobite icons worthy of a mention.

Looking rather more widely, we hold the birthplaces of such famous Scots as Thomas Carlyle, one of our handsomest buildings in my view, and J M Barrie, the creator of Peter Pan. We have a surprisingly extensive portfolio of industrial archaeology, including several mills and a working printer's shop at Innerleithen, where they have just designed a bookplate for our bequest books (yes, they *did* have a thistle colophon). We even hold properties that have conventional museums, of which the star is the Angus Folk Museum. Our Georgian House in Charlotte Square paints a picture of life in the New Town of Edinburgh, and has its obverse at Gladstone's Land, which presents life in the Old Town: both are created from synthetic collections of appropriate antiques to invoke particular historical periods.

The Trust's portfolio certainly reflects the 'Diversity of Scotland' (there is a Japanese garden in the shadow of Craigievar), and it embraces innumerable separate stories and experiences rather than having been collected deliberately to form a coherent historical pattern in the way that the new Museum of Scotland unfolds its storyline. Our properties and collections represent a kaleidoscope of Scotland, frequently shaken up by new accessions. For example, our new Edinburgh headquarters will bring together a gift of 20th century Scottish paintings and a loan of a spectacular collection of English Regency furniture, coming with the strongest of Scottish connections. Rather than a neatly fitting jigsaw offering a coherent picture, the Trust can be viewed as 'a cultural federation of individual places, people and objects'.

Returning to Broughton's team, we inevitably had to point them in the direction of colleagues in the National Galleries and the National Museums of Scotland, while expressing our willingness to serve as junior partners. Our counterparts in the national institutions have been seeking out objects over a long time to develop a deliberate national story illustrating cultural development both at home and abroad. The Trust by contrast, rather than manipulating its properties and collections to create this kind of national narrative, is striving to articulate the special character and idiosyncrasies of individual places. It would be only too easy to flatten their individuality into the blandness of a misguided corporate identity.

Another factor of difference with its own associated problems is this: whilst it is conventional museum practice to acquire objects and put them into a controlled environment of increasingly complicatedly serviced buildings, we always leave things *in situ*, sometimes outside like Historic Scotland. Although we have an excellent record of lending to others, both nationally and internationally, we have to explain politely but firmly that we prefer to lend over the winter when our properties are resting. During the open season, people may have travelled long distances to see our collections, say at Brodick on Arran. Visitors from the US wishing to see a particular painting would be perturbed to find that they had passed it while over the Atlantic and that the said painting was currently on show back in St Louis.

Extensive though Mr Broughton's premises in Wilmington are, we hold so much of Scotland's beautiful countryside that this aspect of our work could only be brought to their museum through paintings, photography and film. No less readily moveable are the fauna and flora that diversify this landscape, although I never cease to be amazed at what my gardening colleagues achieve at Chelsea each year.

In turning now to our acquisitions policy, I can confirm that it is based on the conventional tests such as quality, threat and availability of resources. Needless to say, we can not afford to add a new acquisition that has the potential to create a financial burden that might imperil the stability of our existing responsibilities. In basic terms, we have what people have wanted us to have, and this is essentially the key to our passive, rather than active acquisitions policy. We are not really in the normal curatorial business of seeking out attested masterpieces, filling gaps or trying to make up sets of similar artefacts. Quite often properties come at the end of a particular line, or in order to frustrate the otherwise inevitable action of some perceived threat to their survival.

Accepting what people have wanted to give, and are prepared to endow, may sound like a conventional museum curator's worst nightmare. However, the human dimension is important to us, and because we generally leave things where they are, they tend to remain emotionally charged. We actively encourage the involvement of donor families and, in contrast to normal museum practice, this will continue down succeeding generations. If these families live far away and the properties are thus out of their sight, this will often enhance their passionate attachment and concern for the well-being of their gift. Our volunteers and staff usually become equally attached to the charm and individual idiosyncrasies of their properties.

People tend to think of the scale of the Trust's collections in terms of its larger properties, and I am keen to give a greater focus to the many very generous individual gifts and bequests of particular collections to be given a home at one of the properties. My ambition is to have a modest published list rather than a catalogue, which would run to volumes to include such lively individual collections as the Mazarines (fancy term for ceramic drainers). This is the example that always springs instantly to mind, as it happily graces the Tea Room at Haddo. There is also the astonishing 'Mr Riach's Performing Theatre of Arts': an enchanting model theatre that must sometimes startle visitors in the basement offices at the end of their tour of the House of Dun.

Administratively, these bequests have tended to be sent to whatever house we have been working on when they were gifted, although a few collections over time be moved to more suitable settings. Sometimes they take on a local colouring because of the selected setting they have been given, one such being the Steele Bequest of Scottish Pottery on display in a most elegant case designed by Bill Cadell at Culross Palace. However, this bequest turns in reality out to be a much more diverse and exciting collection than originally taught, as Mr Steele was attracted to a very wide range of porcelain figures and had an amazing eye for striking coloured enamels. It is my intention to reunite the entire collection, which includes a glorious Louis Napoleon clockcase, and eliminate the current *salon de refuses* of Continental things at Mar Lodge.

Unlike most museums, the Trust is a membership organisation, which has a strong bearing on our collecting policy. Our Members are very generous, and this inevitably means that we accept things that a conventional museum would not consider. As an example, I recently took on a cabinet of glass and two cabinets of china, collected with pin money from charity shops, by Jenny Campbell who took an amateur's interest in antiques. In accepting these from her widowed husband, I was influenced by the fact that I had had the privilege of meeting her as a frail invalid and that, unlike a conventional museum, we have thousands of square feet of holiday flats at Mar Lodge to enliven. But I am not ashamed of preserving this modest collection which has the additional interest of being a woman's collection and, if Jenny Campbell lacked the resources of Isabella Stewart Gardener, who is to say if her modest cabinets will not be of future interest.

That is briefly how we have built up our portfolio of places, individual collections and artefacts. Next I turn to describe how we manage the collections, as this is again different to conventional museum practice. The significant point to appreciate here is that the properties are managed at regional level, the Curator being effectively curatorially passive in that I and my colleagues are called in by the regional staff and individual Property Managers as expert advisers from headquarters.

The Curator is concerned with contents, and by extension interiors, but not with entire buildings because my immediate colleagues in headquarters include the Senior Buildings Adviser and the Head of Gardens. All three of us report to the Director of Buildings and Gardens, Charles Strang. Although most of the content come with a gifted property, some collections and artefacts are retained or sold by donor families. This means that we are regularly in negotiations to add to the original content, often seeking to return things that had left the property years before coming into our care. Last year, with the help of the Heritage Lottery Fund and a purchase grant from the National Museums of Scotland, we returned a number of things to Kellie, and we are currently trying to bring back to Craigievar a small collection of modern studio pottery and some ordinary Meissen with the most glamorous of histories. It was allegedly bought new from the factory by our Ambassador to Frederick the Great who then left everything to the Laird of Craigievar in the 18th century.

In dealing with the problems of opening houses to the public, I am most fortunate to be the first Curator to benefit from the advice of the Trust's own Conservator, Wilma Bouwmeester. With a background in textile conservation, she was appointed six months before me in 1997. Like all good conservators, Wilma would probably be happier if the houses were not open to the public. Indeed, visitor pressure had already forced us to take diversionary tactics at Craigievar where the granite steps were allegedly wearing away and fragile plaster ceilings put at risk (Croft, 1994). This was done by limiting its advertisement and banning any reproduction of its image for a few years. At Crathes, we operate timed tickets because of the disproportionately large number of visitors attracted to a very small scale Castle.

When required to make changes at properties, I am frequently bombarded with informal advice from our volunteers who say firmly that they do not want the houses to 'look like museums'. At present there is little fear of this, as more museums seem to be dismantling their period rooms. In a museum, it is relatively easy to divide objects by material categories into specific custom designed storage and display zones to ensure that each has the optimum conditions for long term survival. In the Trust, we cannot hope to achieve this degree of environmental control, as we have to cope with rooms that are the most exotic salads of every conceivable fragile material tossed together.

Although there have been recent warnings about the effects on historic glass, we have put UV filters on some windows. We have also installed conservation blinds, politely restrain visitors from sitting on upholstered chairs, and we monitor the conditions of sensitive artefacts. Textiles are especially vulnerable and, for purely practical reasons, they have all too often in the past been replaced, at best, with facsimiles, or more often, with modern chintzes, and far too many busily patterned oriental rugs have been introduced.

Although the Trust is pledged to provide access to its properties, it is not easy to decide how to facilitate full visitor enjoyment of the varied paintings, ceramics and furniture in the drawing room at Brodie without imperilling one of our most important and precious historic carpets that was allegedly made for the room and is now very frail. At Culzean, my predecessor solved the access issue by re-weaving the saloon carpet, although when the castle came into our care in 1946, it was regarded as one of its most important treasures attributed to Robert Adam himself. The access problem may have been solved, but it does not cure my own headache over what to do with a huge circular carpet which belongs to one particular property.

At Haddo, the morning room was designed in 1880 to display a collection of water-colours. The National Gallery of Scotland would unframe these, place them in conservation mounts in solander box darkness, and only show them for six weeks in carefully controlled conditions every ten years or so. Not only does this room at Haddo have a huge Victorian bay window, but to add to the challenge, the present Dowager Lady Aberdeen and her late husband opened up two further windows. As she has repeated frequently to me: 'drawn blinds during the day look funereal, and Haddo is *not* a Museum'.

In this context I am again fortunate to have help, as our Living Memorial to the late Lord Bute takes the form of internships to bring innovation to conservation practice. Our current intern, Monica Ronaldson, is a paper conservator who has been asked to study the problems raised by this room and to find a suitable compromise. We plan that our next internship will look at our ordinary furnishing textiles rather than tapestries or oriental carpets, this being our most urgent priority. The findings of such work may change traditional practice by the Trust, as we normally do not use guard ropes and druggets wherever possible to enable free movement by visitors.

If our display practices, from a museologist's point of view, could be said to leave objects at risk, our conservation practices must also take account of the overall effect. At Newhailes, the atmosphere is imbued with an overall mellowness (the suspended animation of the Sleeping Beauty effect), and I shall be deservedly lynched, if the necessary repairs overstep the mark and stray into a shining-up that will effectively destroy the current visual balance and bloom. Similarly, with regard to our works of art, while it was common conservation practice to reduce built-up canvases to their original artist's intention, allegedly recovering their aesthetic, there are few circumstances when we would contemplate interfering with the appearance of any item as it has come down to us, since it has now become part of a greater totality.

It would be wrong for the Trust to introduce museum-style exhibition techniques. Our best exhibition at any property must be the Military Exhibition at Leith Hall. The owners of this rather deceptively ordinary country house had played a rather extraordinary part, in common with many Scottish families, in the military prowess on which the British Empire rested. As a result of these activities they brought home as souvenirs a remarkable range of loot, including Napoleon's sash, the King of Oudh's throne and a particularly long-lived parakeet. To explain the origins of these resplendent items, and to show off the many military uniforms that the collection holds, the Trust has created a quite exemplary museum display in former bedrooms on the second floor which is beautifully lit and shows a particular flair for colour. However, by removing these things from the family living rooms below, a particular ethos of this extraordinary house has been eliminated. To rectify this, we have ended up introducing another collection of family portraits to the living rooms.

A more positive way of looking at this issue might be to simply accept that museums can display costumes better than the Trust. I am increasingly taking the view that the paraphernalia of labels, spotlights and approved modern conservation cases tend to strike a jarring note in our houses. There is an exceptionally offending modern case holding some of our finest Beckford and Hamilton ceramics at Brodick that is more akin to suddenly stepping into the china department of a retailing chain.

As a rule, the Curator's Department has always tended to work under pressure to meet the demand of houses requiring a quick turn-round time, and staff have developed skills to meet looming opening days within tight deadlines. The sense of almost indecent haste has been the product of complex funding packages where the money would vanish at the end of the financial year. The old approach was ad hoc and unstructured with the emphasis on 'making something of the house'. Collections were rearranged, related objects scattered throughout a building were reunited and many items were enthusiastically restored. With limited resources, and as a result of the inspiration of my colleague, John Batty, a great deal was achieved through the Government's successive Job Creation Schemes. Many of the craftsmen thus trained by the Trust, like Rodney French of Londsdale and Dutch, have subsequently set up in business on their own account and continue to help us.

An important part of my brief is to undertake research to learn from the past and improve practice. Knowing precisely what one is dealing with helps to target scarce resources with greater precision. There have been some very expensive mistakes as a result of a faulty understanding of the history of some suites of room. Brodick is a case in point, where Gillespie Graham's approach to architectural decoration has been lost on the Trust, the result having been elimination of the all-important graining from the woodwork of the main reception rooms and suppression of the gilding on the Library ceiling.

I have been trying hard to catch up with this backlog of research, and sometimes it seems as if several *Country Life* articles are to be written each week. Sadly, the conclusion of even the most superficial research all too often questions the wisdom of much that has achieved in haste. At Kellie, the Trust was simply incapable of tuning-in to the sophisticated 1950s Francophile *chic* of Hew and Mary Wylie Lorimer, who were both artists. Their children use words like 'Victorian' and 'heavy' to characterise the tenor of our changes. Over the coming winter, we are going to rework the Blue Room with its almost Doris Day voile curtains and Gothic chairs from Crawford Priory, which were rather foolishly exiled to the Chapel.

At Craigievar, where the Trust, from 1963 onwards, placed stress on the earlier periods, members of the family now remind us rather firmly that we are in severe danger of destroying the particular post-war atmosphere which was so characteristic of the property. After looking into this matter in some detail, the Curatorial Committee was inclined to agree with the family's criticism, and we are now engaged on reversing a series of previous changes. We were half way through this process last month when Gabriel Forbes Sempill, who was brought up in the Castle, returned to help with some final tweaking. It was particularly gratifying when she did not even notice we had put back the original humble withdrawing room carpet, retrieved from storage in the stables.

The Sempill family had always played up the atavistic character of Craigievar, but its current visual flair can be attributed to the late Cecilia, Lady Sempill. Like the Lorimers at Kellie, she was a trained artist. Before the war and her marriage, she had been a partner in Dunbar-Hay Ltd, a shop that had been founded in London to encourage links between artists and industry and to sell their commercial designs: Eric Ravilious designed both the furniture and her trade card.

With her artist's eye, Cecilia edited and added to the collection at Craigievar and, as her creation re-emerges by degrees in some of the smaller spaces, there is a sense of stepping into a three-dimensional painting by Anne Redpath. But such an approach is often much less visually rewarding, as the concern is not so much with the immediate visual effect, as with the more reflective interest in trying to establish how such houses and their furnishings worked and was used in daily life. This brings us full circle back to museological ideas, as the approach is close to the material culture studies that lie at the core of America's historic house museums.

But there are losses as well as gains at Craigievar. We have now introduced electricity to a house that had none because the Sempills actively resisted modernisation. To those people who can remember, the infinitely romantic experience of seeing the castle by lamplight at the end of the day has been lost.

At Newhailes, the Heritage Lottery Fund has been anxious to see that we have both the time and the resources to undertake the necessary research before any work starts, perhaps reflecting a concern over some of the Trust's previous efforts. Although it was an hotel when we it came into our care, I believe that House of Dun was no less important than Newhailes in terms of the survival of its complete material culture. But the Trust was then clearly ill at ease to find that such an attractive 18th century house possessed rather less immediately visually appealing 19th century furniture. As a consequence, the saloon with spectacular stucco was refurnished with introduced Georgian Revival contents. The result is that important drawing room furnishings (at the top of the domestic hierarchy in terms of expense and elaboration) are now encountered in unimportant spaces, instead of being located in positions for which they were specifically designed. As a new Curator, bringing a fresh eye to such under-researched collections every day is like a continuous Christmas celebration.

At Culzean, I bumped into a Canova in a back corridor, although it originally held pride of place in the saloon, because it did not fit in with our mono-maniacal cult of Robert Adam at this property. At Leith Hall, there is a table in the morning room by the cabinetmaker Bullock. It probably narrowly escaped exile to the Military Museum, as it is likely to have come to Leith Hall by way of Napoleon's St Helena. Earlier this year, we recovered Mackintosh's drawing room chairs from the Hill House in a facsimile of the original fabric. There was every conceivable reason to believe that they had lost every last stitch of their original upholstery. It was only by the merest chance that we discovered that a previous upholsterer had been lazy and merely covered over the original backs. The fabric just happen to look like the kind of stuff that upholsterers use under the top cover to prevent the horse hairs sticking through.

In our management of such large collections, we are fortunate to have a computerised data base. The Trust made an early foray into computers, and there are now some 38,000 records. However, the actual quantity of material held is much greater due to sets of objects: ceramics come in bulk rather than as single cups and saucers, each set being given a single number and then individual piece sub-numbers. There is a great deal that we can do to improve our data base, and the dream is that visitors will eventually be able to be quiz the data base directly on terminals at the properties.

A significant flaw of our current data holding is that object values are based on auction house valuations, as the Trust (unlike national collections) insures everything in its care. Because the financial criteria has to be saleability in the marketplace, it is an approach which snobbishly tends to overlook the value of an item as material culture. Recently, I had to stress the importance of a superficially mundane table (made of kindling) in the attic at Newhailes, with a tattered remnant of pink glazed lining material barely attached. Superficially it could date from 1750 or 1950, but it is in fact an extremely rare survival of the underskirt for a lace-draped dressing table, likely to be the sole survivor of several mentioned in the 1873 inventory, and now exceptionally rare even for Britain.

In the longer term, we must wean the database away from tedious antique trade description (we are already digitising images), and try to fill in details gleaned from earlier inventories, and where possible attempt to tie objects back to original bills in family muniments. Our Conservator, Wilma Bouwmeester often quotes a Trust saying: 'It is likely that in future, we will be the only resource for the study of certain categories of object which are considered to be of little significance today.'

The preparation of property management plans are crucial to the Trust's holistic conservation management. After a variety of experiments, it seems that the most useful curatorial contribution we can make is to supply a furnishing plan. Because of a tendency to become quite bulky, it is perhaps best attached as an appendix. These furnishing plans take the form of a room by room tour, summarising the various periods of activity that have conditioned the appearance of the room and its current contents. From documentary and visual evidence, missing elements are taken into account and the plan concludes with a prescription that will either guide us towards making the most of a room visually or explain why its current altered state should be maintained. The format of these plan has undoubtedly been influenced by North American practice, which suits the Trust's current needs, and the discipline of setting our present perceptions down on paper is an important part of the decision making process. In museum terms, it is essentially a cataloguing process and encourages us to look closely at our interiors.

The Trust's collections can only take their proper place in national cultural life when we have this research and evaluation in place and can disseminate information as an educational resource. At present, our only means of communication, other than through guided tours, is the guidebooks. Although their appearance and square format has remained the same for some years, their content and quality is changing through each successive edition. The best guide to a house is often the Property Manager and the excellent recent guidebooks to the Tenement House and Hill House, by Lorna Hepburn and Anne Ellis respectively, bear this out. They are complemented by the Studio's design so that, if read away from a property, the successive illustrations give a vivid impression of the experience of a tour. The intention is that our productions should serve to complement those of the national institutions concerned with art and material culture.

I personally wrote the new guidebook to Craigievar, but I had so much to say that it needed Hilary Horrocks, our Editor, to compress it into the standard format. This new guidebook gives much more space to the relatively recent history of the castle and the family rather than the remote and undocumented past. I am sure that the compressed version is more than adequate for the patience of most of our visitors, but I would like to see the fuller version in print. It would provide a more detailed evaluation and discussion of the extent to which the survival of Craigievar was a function of the family's modernisation of their much larger seat at Fintray which was demolished after war-time requisitioning.

Publications are the responsibility of our Commercial Division rather than Education so there is little enthusiasm for competing titles in an area that is not especially profitable. We have to find some other way of seeing this important additional information into print. Many properties have key source material such as the Lorimers' own manuscript account of their restoration of Kellie. If reproduced, it would greatly enhance visitor appreciation of the property.

I am particularly envious of the National Trust's annual annexing of a monthly issue of the art magazine, *Apollo*, to broadcast recent research into aspects of their collections. In the short term, we can facilitate access to the collections and encourage others to publish their research. For example, we hope Annette Carruthers will write up the Barnsley sideboard that was especially made in 1971 for the sideboard recess at Bute House in Charlotte Square. Sadly this elegant piece is now regarded as unfashionable and has been removed from the house, but listening to its merits as described by an expert one can fondly hope that it will at some point be returned to its intended recess in the house. The Trust's own membership magazine, *Heritage Scotland,* is increasingly tackling more ambitious curatorial topics such as bulletins about new work like the recent dramatic return of the very large decorative paintings by Malleyn to the dining room at Pollok House after 30 years in storage.

The Scottish Cultural Resources Access Network (SCRAN) presents great opportunities to disseminate images of our collections and information about them, and I am glad to say that our input to this exiting partnership initiative is being made by my Trust colleagues in the Education Department. An initiative I very much hope to bring to fruition is the revival of the Trust's Summer School along the lines of Attingham and Royal Collection Studies. The obvious place to pursue this is in the Grampian Region where we have built up an extraordinary concentration of houses to which Brodie and House of Dun are also readily accessible.

The Author

Ian Gow was appointed Curator of the National Trust for Scotland in February 1998. He was previously Curator of Architectural Collections in the National Monuments Record of Scotland, and before that worked in London with the Ancient Monuments Division of what is now English Heritage. A respected scholar and prolific writer much in demand as a lecturer, he is the author of many articles on the decorative arts and architecture of Scotland, as well as several guidebooks including Duff House, the Palace of Holyroodhouse and Floors Castle. His book *The Scottish Interior* was published by Edinburgh University Press in 1992.

References

Borley, L., 'Managing Strategies and Financial Considerations: Historic Properties', in Harrison, R. (ed), *Manual of Heritage Management*, Butterworth Heinemann & Association of Independent Museums, 1994.

Croft, T., 'What Price Access? Visitor Impact on Heritage in Trust', in Fladmark, J.M. (ed), *Cultural Tourism*, Donhead, 1994.

Learmont, D., 'The National Trust for Scotland: Presenting Scotland's Historic Houses', in Ambrose, T. (ed), *Presenting Scotland's Story*, HMSO & Scottish Museums Council, 1989.

Morris, A., McCrone, D. & Kiely, R., 'The Heritage Consumers: Identity and Affiliation in Scotland', in Fladmark, J.M. (ed), *Sharing the Earth:: Local Identity in Global Culture*, Donhead, 1995, pp. 73–87.

Tait, A.A. (ed), *Treasures in Trust*, HMSO & NTS, 1981.

Thompson, J.M.A. (ed), *Manual of Curatorship*, Butterworth Heinemann & Museums Association, 1992.

The Culloden Sampler

17

SCOTS IMAGE MAKERS
Past Lessons from Tourism

Gordon Adams

Against a background where both cultural institutions and commercial providers are united behind a choice for expansion in visitor numbers, this chapter examines what we can learn from the original period of rapid growth of Scottish tourism in the 19th century. It draws some lessons from this historical analysis with relevance for practice today, and goes on to explore some implications for future policy.

In the last decade, there has been steady growth in the total expenditure by tourists in Scotland. There seems to have been a slight decline in 1998, which was probably associated with the strength of the pound. However, there has been very steady long-term growth from European and North American markets, and, even if the expenditure by English and Scottish visitors has been more volatile, there is little reason to believe that Scottish tourism will suddenly decline drastically.

There has also been an assumption in Scotland in recent years that it would be satisfactory if Scottish tourism continued to expand indefinitely. This is probably associated with fears that employment in other sectors of the economy, particularly agriculture, will decline, and may also be associated with a deep-seated assumption that there is no limit to the benefits of economic expansion. At present, however, it is likely that employment in the industry is stable (increases in expenditure may not lead to increases in direct employment because of the scope for productivity improvements) and that tourism activity is sustainable in both economic and ecological terms. Further expansion at the height of the season (August) would require substantial infrastructure expenditure to supply extra hotel beds, and better roads, and more ferries.

In ecological terms, our mountains and cities can cope with the numbers of tourists in August, but with some difficulty. Mountains are still being degraded, although path repairs are now removing some of the worst damage. Litter in the countryside, particularly on beaches, seems to be getting worse, and improvements in, for example, beach litter collection seems unlikely within the current local government expenditure plans.

Government policy is to concentrate on attracting additional visitors in the shoulder months, but that may not be possible. The likely main growth markets are overseas, and foreign visitors are much more concentrated in the summer season than are Scottish and English visitors. It is the author's belief is that there is still plenty of room for further growth in Scottish tourism, if additional expenditure is channelled to repairing the damage caused by tourism. Indeed, if we are serious about tourism in sustainable terms, we should begin to consider the difference between the maximum and optimum levels of tourism. Scottish tourism is not growing as fast as world tourism, so we are losing market share, but we should not necessarily worry about that. Tourism has been a very mixed blessing in many countries, and Scotland does not have the ecological and cultural disasters that tourism has brought to, for example, many Mediterranean resorts.

TOURISM IN THE NINETEENTH CENTURY

It is well known that developments in Scotland had a crucial role in the Industrial Revolution in the late 18th and early 19th century. Technological and commercial changes were allied to an expansion of markets and to political stability, and many Scottish firms became eminent in industries related to steam power and iron and steel production. It is less well recognised that many of the current aspects of world tourism similarly occurred first in Scotland.[1,2]

The concept of the attractiveness of a visit to Scotland came largely from literary sources, and primarily from Sir Walter Scott, but the marketing of Scotland by Scott was allied to transport improvements so that travel to Scotland became feasible as well as attractive. The changes that the railways brought to Scottish tourism are comparable to the changes that jumbo jets and computer reservation systems have recently brought to world tourism. Technological changes have now made countries all over the world into potential tourist destinations for a very large market. That market is at present largely in Western Europe and North America, but is rapidly spreading to, for example, India and South America.

Is it feasible for Scotland to learn from its 19th century success in tourism and repeat the trick in the 21st century? What was the process by which the idea of a holiday in Scotland was communicated to what was then, and still is, our largest market: the English middle class?

The importance of Sir Walter Scott can hardly be over-emphasised. He did not invent a romantic Scotland (and, strictly speaking, perhaps should not even be classified as a Romantic) but his popularity was quite extraordinary, and his role as a promoter of Scotland was recognised at the time. The English Victorians loved Scott.

However, Scotland had burst on to the world's intellectual scene in the late 18th and early 19th century in a way that amazed both participants and observers. The reasons for the sudden intellectual advance are still not completely understood, in the sense that the Scottish model could be repeated elsewhere, but Scottish development can be associated with political, commercial, economic, and technological changes. Scotland was at the forefront of technological development in a way perhaps comparable to California today. Sir Walter Scott was the George Lucas of his day and we can imagine the effects on Scottish tourism if Star Wars had been located in the Trossachs.

But Scott was selling poems and stories to a public that was already enamoured of romantic Scotland. The influence of Macpherson's Ossian (published 1760) is also well known with his influence, for example, on Napoleon and the painter Ingres. Macpherson was denigrated at the time and also much later, and the latest conclusion seems to be that there was much more to Macpherson's work than was admitted by many critics.[3] But, in the present context, it is not really relevant whether or not Macpherson was a fraud. His publications had immense influence in persuading the world that Scotland was a fascinating place to visit. In 1785, Boswell (1740–1795) published 'The Journal of a Tour to the Hebrides with Samuel Johnson'. The influence of Burns, great as he was, would probably not have been as great in England, had Macpherson and Boswell not opened the door on Scottish (and particularly Highland) heritage.

Scotland had played a crucial role in the wider European Enlightenment of the 18th century: defined by Schama as a 'time when scientific inquiry and poetical sensibility seemed effortlessly and wittily married.'[4] But, Scotland was also to have a crucial role in the Romantic movement, and this role was the key to the original development of Scottish tourism. Of this movement the Oxford Companion to English literature explains: 'In literature and art the classical, intellectual attitude gave way to a wider outlook, which recognised the claims of passion and emotion, and in which the critical was replaced by the imaginative spirit, and wit by humour and pathos'. Scotland, therefore, was interesting to the outside world in both the Enlightenment and in the Romantic period. But the disparaging remarks of Johnson had changed dramatically to the admiration of the English poets. Scotland became a beautiful country and it was as a beautiful country that it became a tourist destination.

Wordsworth (1770–1830) toured Scotland in 1801 and 1822. In 1802 Wordsworth with Coleridge, published the influential 'Preface to Lyrical Ballads, with Pastoral and Other Poems'. Wordsworth wrote 'Yarrow Unvisited' in 1803 and 'Yarrow Visited' in 1814. Keats (1795–1821) toured Scotland in 1818. Turner (1775–1851) was painting in Edinburgh when George IV (who counted Scott as a personal friend) visited Scotland in 1822. Scotland had also received great publicity in London through a series of brilliant Scottish painters: Ramsay (1713–1784), Raeburn (1756–1823), Geddes (1783–1844), and Wilkie (1785–1823). Scott (1771–1832) published 'The Lay of the Last Minstrel' in 1805 and 'The Lady of the Lake' in 1810. And Burns (1759–1796) was the authentic Scottish version of the 'hero as man of letters' as described by Carlyle (1795–1881). Byron (1788–1824) was half-Scottish and wrote of 'Dark Lochnagar'.

Scott 'ingeniously combined the patriotic and feudal nostalgias', and was astonishingly popular.[5] However, Scotland as a tourism destination was taking off before Scott. Durie gives the starting date for Scottish tourism as 1810 and associates the start with 'The Lady of the Lake', but also notes that 'The Traveller's Guide through Scotland and its Islands' was in its third edition by 1806. Mitchell notes that an early tourist guide of 1797 mentions frequent foreign visitors to Ben Lomond.[6]

Paul Scott has provided examples of Scott's influence on, for example, Pushkin, Hugo, and Balzac, and provides a wonderful quotation from Mark Twain on Scott and the American Civil War: 'Sir Walter had so large a hand in making Southern character, as it existed before the war, that he is in great measure responsible for the war.'[7] The influence of a romantic Scotland on 19th century music is also remarkable with composers such as Haydn (1732–1809), Beethoven (1770–1827), Schubert (1797–1828), Mendelssohn (1809–1847), Berlioz (1803–1869), Chopin (1809–1849), and Debussy (1862–1918) all producing works with Scottish themes.[8]

At a time when the Industrial Revolution was in full swing in Central Scotland, the country had become a romantic destination. And tourism was spreading to the Highlands in mid-century when famine was still prevalent. The smoke from Glasgow could be seen from forty miles away in the mid-19th century, and the conditions were atrocious for workers who flooded in from rural Scotland, and later from Ireland, but Scotland (and in particular the Highlands) had secured a reputation as a romantic destination to add to the reputation of Edinburgh as an intellectual capital.

Later, even industrial Glasgow became romantic in for example Kipling's 'MacAndrew's Hymn' in 1893: 'Lord, send a man like Robbie Burns to sing the song of steam'. And Checkland pointed out that it is not by chance that the engineer on the Starship 'Enterprise' is called Scottie, even if to Scottish ears he seems to have a Belfast accent.[9]

In the second half of the 19th century, just in case Scott had not done enough on his own to publicise Scotland, Prince Albert announced that Deeside reminded him of parts of Germany and Switzerland, and Queen Victoria herself gave Scotland her approval through publication in 1868 and 1883 of parts of her diary. It is difficult to conceive of a more effective way of promoting Scottish tourism. A huge market was becoming available in England as wealth increased throughout the 19th century. The safe Jacobitism of Scott, and the praise of the royal family, were particularly attractive to wealthy Christians of Tory leanings. (Newman was a great admirer of Scott.) Scott and Victoria managed to dampen any latent Scottish–English antipathy. If the Queen holidayed in Scotland, English patriotism could include Scotland, and royal approval of Scotland could convince Scots that North Britain had come in from the cold.

Towards the end of the century, Andrew Carnegie in the United States and his equivalent in Canada, Donald Smith (later Lord Strathcona) acquired holiday homes in Scotland (at Skibo near Dornoch and in Glencoe) to celebrate the land of their birth. Again, in case that was not enough, golf exploded in popularity in the 1880s, and again the wealthy English market was attracted.

The development of Scotland as a tourism destination, however, could not have been realised without technological improvements in transport, first with regard to travel by boat, and then, crucially, with regard to travel by railway, which connected all the main towns of Scotland and England in the 19th century. The image of Scotland created by literary figures from Macpherson and Burns to Scott and Queen Victoria would have been attractive without transport improvements, and after the railways, the tour operator, Thomas Cook arrived to tap the English market. But without transport improvements the tourists would not have been able to arrive. It was the railways that could unlock the market created by the authors and artists.

Cook's first tour to Scotland was in 1846 and occurred before the railway network connecting England and Scotland was completed.[10] Cook's tourists travelled from Leicester to Fleetwood by train, from Fleetwood to Ardrossan by boat, and from Ardrossan to Glasgow and Edinburgh by train. Moreover the first trip seems to have had shades of Fawlty Towers with no lavatories on trains, meals failing to materialise and seasickness on the voyage. However, formal welcomes from the cities of Glasgow and Edinburgh seem eventually to have created general bonhomie, and by the 1850s Skye and Iona were on the tourist route for Cook's tours. It is amusing that the Local Authorities had seen the need to welcome tourists some 150 years ago, but it is also astonishing that Skye had become a tourist destination at the very time that the authorities 'decided, to put the matter bluntly, to starve crofters into emigrating'.[11]

Nevertheless, the development in Scotland of what we now call the package tour was quickly blocked. Cook fell out with the railway companies in Scotland and in 1862 lost his ability to obtain cheap rail tickets. Cook, therefore, with some difficulty at first, was forced to turn his attention to continental Europe. This is an extraordinary outcome, which deserves more investigation. There seems to have been some snobbery in Scotland that the tourists were not of satisfactory social class, although of course Cook was inevitably dealing with the English middle class. At any rate the rail package tour was stifled in its infancy and never recovered. And, with the recommendations that followed from Queen Victoria in 1868, 19th century Scotland became a decidedly up-market destination.

To summarise so far: Scottish tourism developed quickly and spectacularly in the 19th century. The main external market was in England but there were important ramifications in continental Europe. The tourists usually had been influenced directly or indirectly by Sir Walter Scott. Technological advances made the desire to travel feasible.

So far, however, I have discussed Scott and the romantic authors as if they were simply superior advertising agencies. In reality, of course, Scotland is an astonishingly beautiful country and it is an insult to the Trossachs to imply that tourists then and now only came because of Scott's publicity. This is why we can understand why the decline in popularity of Scott as an author did not lead to the death of Scottish tourism. Even Paul Scott, one of Sir Walter's most valiant apologists, admits that: 'Sometime during the 1920s and 1930s, Scott became very unfashionable and was assumed to be unreadable.'[12]

LESSONS FOR TODAY

What lessons from this 19th century development could be relevant today? First, that Scott alone was not responsible. Scotland would have been a romantic destination as tourism developed even if Scott had not existed. Macpherson and Burns pre-dated Scott. The Scottish Enlightenment had already made Scotland an interesting place to read about and visit. Edinburgh was an interesting place to visit before 'The Heart of Midlothian' was published. Queen Victoria's husband might not have liked Deeside, and Queen Victoria might not have liked Scotland.

The necessary conditions of an attractive destination, good publicity, and technological advances in transport needed the response which was provided by Cook, the tour operator, by hoteliers all over the country, and by guide book publishers like John Murray. Perhaps one of the most important factors was that the newly industrialised population of Britain still had active memories of rural life, often at first hand, and so romantic tales of woods and lochs were easy to comprehend in a way not applicable nowadays when the British population has been urbanised for more than 150 years. Fashions as set by the royal family were extremely important but fashion is fickle. Hamilton has recently shown that golf in Scotland experienced important fluctuations in popularity before it took off to conquer the world.[13]

The second lesson from the 19th century is that the original development of Scottish tourism occurred without any of the state involvement that we now almost take for granted. This was not inevitable. The state in Scotland in the 18th and 19th centuries was perfectly capable of undertaking planned economic development, particularly in the Highlands (for example in the activities of the British Fisheries Society in the 18th century and the activities of the Congested Districts Board in the late 19th century) and in many programmes to assist emigration to, for example, Canada. Nevertheless the general spirit of the age was that economic development should be left to the private sector. Nowadays, a vast array of state and state related bodies are involved in tourism development in Scotland, and it is sobering to realise that the most spectacular development of Scottish tourism occurred without state involvement.

The stakes are high in tourism. We do not know whether the overall intervention by the state is cost effective, but the industry is now so substantial that it might be reckless simply to remove all subsidies on the grounds that development occurred without state involvement 150 years ago. Tourism in Scotland is now relatively more important than in most countries. In terms of external receipts per head of population, Scotland is well up in the international league table.

Tourism Receipts per Head of Population ($US 1995)
Policy & Financial Management Review of STB, Scottish Office, 1998, p. 18.

Austria	1582
Switzerland	1036
Spain	639
Wales	598
Ireland	581
Scotland	539
Belgium	520
Italy	476
France	473
England	358

Of course the conclusions to be drawn from this table depend on national boundaries. Parts of France and England (e.g. the Lake District) have higher receipts per head than Scotland as a whole. But parts of Scotland (e.g. the Highlands) also have higher receipts than Scotland as a whole, and, with these caveats, the table does provide a satisfactory single indicator of the relative importance of tourism in parts of Europe.

The state is heavily involved in promoting Scottish tourism but through a remarkably complicated system. The lead government agency for tourism is the Scottish Tourist Board with government funds of about £20 million. Most of the government's money for tourism promotion and development is outwith the jurisdiction of the Scottish Tourist Board. The total state budget for tourism promotion in various forms is about £85 million to £110 million when the contributions of the Local Enterprise Companies (LECs), Local Authorities, and a variety of Non-Departmental Public Bodies (NDPBs) are included. Tourism is a devolved matter and this budget is now the concern of the Scottish Parliament. The main public sector bodies are:

14 Area Tourist Boards (ATBs)
22 LECs (nine in the Highlands and Islands)
30 Local Authorities
8 Scottish NDPBs
1 British NDPB

The Scottish NDPBs are the Scottish Tourist Board, Scottish Enterprise, Highlands and Islands Enterprise, Historic Scotland, Scottish Arts Council, Scottish Museums Council, Scottish Natural Heritage, Scottish Sports Council. The British NDPB is the British Tourist Authority. Co-ordination of all these bodies is clearly very difficult and much overlapping of activity exists, although strictly speaking all these bodies have different objectives. Nevertheless £100 million is a substantial budget if it was concentrated on a few objectives. At present the main tourism budgets (from the Scottish Tourist Board, British Tourist Authority, Scottish Enterprise, and Highlands and Islands Enterprise) have to cover:

Advertising electronically, in print and on TV
Training, mainly through LECs
Financial assistance for visitor attractions, mainly by LECs
Provision of Tourist Information Centres through 14 ATBs
Accommodation grading and classification programmes

There is no end to the possible permutations for improving the administrative system for supporting Scottish tourism. However, one simple way would be to transfer (often restore) the Local Enterprise

Company powers to the local authorities. Similarly the Area Tourist Board functions could be transferred (or restored) to local authorities or could just be handed over to the private sector as in France (with the Chambers of Commerce), and in Canada, and in the United States.

If we assume for present purposes that state promotion of an industry is a sensible way to proceed what can we learn from the 19th century development of tourism that would be relevant for spending the current budget? Are there reasons to believe that concentration of the tourism budget on fewer objectives would be more productive?

One lesson from the 19th century was that the Enlightenment and the Romantic movement were both intellectual attractions. People came to Scotland because it was a beautiful and interesting country, and these are still the reasons why people come to Scotland.[14]

FESTIVALS AND FILMS

By far the most successful tourism development in Scotland this century has been the growth of the Edinburgh Festivals in August each year. The main components of the Festivals are the International Festival (concentrating on music and drama), the Military Tattoo, and the Festival Fringe. They are astoundingly successful and are estimated to create for three weeks the equivalent of over 4,000 full-time jobs.[15]

Most government estimates of tourism related jobs include part-time and seasonal jobs and the 4,000 full-time equivalent jobs that result from only three weeks activity may well account for more than 5 per cent of all jobs in tourism in Scotland. Formal marketing also seems to be relatively unimportant for a 1992 study concluded that word of mouth was the most important method of hearing about the festivals.[16] About one-half of visitors to the Festivals are from Scotland, one-third are from England, and one-sixth are from overseas.

The Edinburgh Festivals are the most successful arts events in the world and, although they do receive some financial assistance directly and indirectly from both local authorities and central government, the Festivals could not in any way be said to be state sponsored events. The Festivals have grown and grown because of the enthusiasm of the promoters and audiences since the founders decided in the late 1940s that Europe needed a break from the seriousness of fighting Hitler. Moreover, through the leadership of the Fringe in particular, the Edinburgh Festivals are often extremely innovative in artistic terms.

The comparison between the Festivals in the city of Scott, and the activities of Scott himself, is revealing. It was intellectual inspiration that brought the original tourists, and it is intellectual activity that inspires the Edinburgh Festivals.

However, The Edinburgh Festivals cannot easily be copied, and indeed many delegations from around the world have examined the Festivals to see if the design can work elsewhere. In particular, the Festivals have the great advantage for the organisers of taking place at the height of the international tourist season in August. Attempts in Scotland to emulate the Edinburgh Festivals have not yet been fully successful but should be continued.

Glasgow has experimented with Mayfest (labelled in some quarters as a Scottish version of the Edinburgh Festival) and the Highlands are currently experimenting with a Highland Festival spread throughout the Highlands in early summer. Attempts have also been made to spread Edinburgh events to, for example, Dundee. Inevitably, other Scottish events suffer from not being able to take the ideal dates in August. Nevertheless, artistic events do seem to be an ideal method of attracting visitors to Scotland, given that they are mainly indoor activities (and, therefore, comparatively seldom affected by the weather), and given Scotland's reputation (which stems from the Enlightenment and from Scott) as a destination for people who think.

However, it may be that the promotional activities of Scott are in fact being repeated at present, without any overall plan, and without state involvement, through the recent increase of films about Scotland. The blockbuster movies like Braveheart and Rob Roy have been accompanied by a series of other Scottish related films. Recent examples include Local Hero, Breaking the Waves, Trainspotting, Shallow Grave, Carla's Song, Mrs Brown, My Name is Joe, and Orphans. There is no common theme to these films. Local Hero and Trainspotting are hardly clones. But they all present aspects of Scotland to the world, and some of these films have marketing budgets far in excess of anything that can be contemplated by a government body in Scotland.

CULTURE AND THE ENVIRONMENT

The second tourism related development in Scotland that has been astonishingly successful has been the growth of outdoor activities, particularly walking, and particularly in the Highlands. For example, the number of people completing the ascent of all the hills over 3,000ft is still growing exponentially. This growth is certainly a worldwide phenomenon presumably largely associated with rising incomes. However, it is easy also to associate the growth in visitors coming from England to walk in Scotland with the romantic images of Scotland promoted by Scott and

Queen Victoria, and with the concept of Scotland in the late 19th century as the home of golf.

The arts and the natural environment are the strongest tourism attractions of Scotland and they have been successful as tourism attractions for more than 150 years. If the current state budgets currently allocated to tourism were concentrated more on the arts and on the environment, the overall effect in promotional and development terms might well be greater. In terms of adequate provision of our most valued landscapes, the prospect of National Park status for areas like Loch Lomond and the Cairngorms is to be welcomed.

However, assistance for the arts and for the environment is provided primarily by the Scottish Arts Council and by Scottish Natural Heritage, and is not really the direct concern of the main tourism agencies. In business terms, production and marketing have been divorced. And, just to complicate matters, economic development is categorised as the responsibility of the Enterprise networks. Worse still, the cultural institutions of museums, galleries and libraries are inadequately engaged. A top priority should be to enhance existing mechanisms for harmonising policy and collaboration across all relevant sectors for both product delivery and marketing.[17]

The key lesson from 19th century experience is that concentration on artistic and environmental matters can produce its own publicity. When allocating the overall budget for tourism, we should concentrate on developing cultural products and preserving the environment, if necessary at the expense of other tourism topics.

The Author

Dr Gordon Adams is now attached to the Business School at Napier University. He was Director of Planning and Development at the Scottish Tourist Board for fifteen years. Before that he was an economist with the Highlands and Islands Development Board and a lecturer in Town and Regional Planning at Glasgow University. After obtaining his PhD at McGill University, he worked as a civil servant with the Canadian Federal Government, being mainly concerned with economic development strategies for Newfoundland and the Maritime Provinces. He has been a visiting lecturer at universities in Poland and India, and an adviser for the United Nations in Saudi Arabia.

References

1. Seaton, A.V., 'The History of Tourism in Scotland: approaches, sources, and issues', in MacLellan, R. and Smith, R. (eds), *Tourism in Scotland*, Industrial Thomson Business Press, 1998.
2. Durie, A.J., 'The development of Scotland as a tourism destination', in Seaton, A.V. et al. (eds), *Tourism: The State of the Art*, John Wiley, 1994.
3. Ferguson, W., *The Identity of the Scottish Nation: An Historical Quest*, Edinburgh University Press, 1998, pp. 227–249.
4. Schama, S., *Landscape and Memory*, Fontana Press, 1995, p. 19.
5. Schenk, H.G., *The Mind of the European Romantics*, Anchor Books, 1969, p. 35.
6. Mitchell, I., *Scotland's Mountains before the Mountaineers*, Luath Press, 1988, p. 24.
7. Scott, P.H., *Walter Scott and Scotland*, Saltire Society, 1994, p. 2.
    See also by the same author: 'The Image of Scotland in Literature', in Fladmark, J.M. (ed), *Cultural Tourism*, Donhead, 1994, pp. 363–373.
8. Fiske, R., *Scotland and Music*, Cambridge, 1983.
9. Checkland, S.G., *The Upas Tree: Glasgow, 1895–1975*, Glasgow University Press., 1977.
10. Brendan, P., *Thomas Cook: 150 years of Popular Tourism*, Secker and Warburg, pp. 38–56.
11. Hunter, J., *The Making of the Crofting Community*, John Donald, 1976, p. 76.
12. Scott, op. cit., p. 3.
13. Hamilton, D., *Golf: Scotland's Game*, Partick Press, 1998.
14. Adams, G., 'Access to a Nation's Assets: Challenges for Scottish Tourism Policy', in Fladmark, J.M. (ed), *Sharing the Earth: Local Identity in Global Culture*, Donhead, 1995, pp. 191–200.
    See also by the same author: 'The Pull of Cultural Assets', in Fladmark, J.M. (ed), *Cultural Tourism*, Donhead, 1994, pp. 113–122.
15. City of Edinburgh Council, *Edinburgh Festivals Economic Impact Study*, 1996.
16. Scottish Tourist Board, *Edinburgh Festivals Study 1990–1991*, 1992.
17. Kotler, P. et al, *Marketing Places: Attracting Investment, Industry and Tourism to Cities, States and Nations*, The Free Press, 1993.

18

MUSEUMS WORKING TOGETHER
A National Strategy for Scotland

Jane Ryder

Once in a lifetime we may be offered the opportunity to remake the political and cultural landscape of our society. That is the opportunity and the challenge we are now offered in Scotland, and this volume adds much of substance to what has already been written, both about the implications of now having a Scottish Parliament and a new Museum of Scotland. The latter stands as a cultural icon in its own right, and as a medium for representing and reinterpreting the nation's history.

The excellence of the architecture and the wealth of the collections at the Museum and at the Dean Centre of the National Galleries would in any case have attracted international interest, but both projects form part of a much wider cultural and political continuum which embraces the devolution referendum of 1997, the elections of 6 May 1999, and the terms of the coalition agreement between Labour and the Liberal Democrats. If the Museum of Scotland is, in Duncan Macmillan's words 'a focus for the kind of cultural energy that has given Scotland back its Parliament',[1] the prospect of constitutional change has itself been a stimulus to a debate about the nature of the cultural landscape and how this might develop in the future.

As the membership organisation of the 322 non-national museums, the Scottish Museums Council has worked with the other national agencies (Scottish Arts Council, Scottish Screen, Scottish Library and Information Council and the Convention of Scottish Local Authorities), to argue the case for a comprehensive national strategy which recognises the contribution arts and culture could make to a newly invigorated civic society. Publication of our advocacy document, *Creative Scotland: A Case for a National Cultural Strategy*, this year was intended to highlight the value of arts and culture and their role as agents for social as well as economic development.[2]

We therefore welcome the principles set out in the coalition agreement for two main reasons. First, we believe that arts and culture have a central role in shaping a sense of community and civic price in the new Scotland. Second, we will invest in Scotland's diverse cultural life and heritage. We were also delighted that the coalition partners accepted the case for a national cultural strategy and have already launched an extended consultation process intended as a first step towards developing that strategy.

At the same time, the Scottish Museums Council had recognised that the creation of the Scottish Parliament provided a unique opportunity to take a fresh look at museum provision across Scotland. To understand the route we adopted and the conclusions we reached, an understanding of current museum policy and structures in Scotland may be useful. Essentially, central government has three direct revenue clients: the National Museums of Scotland (NMS), the National Galleries of Scotland (NGS) and the Scottish Museums Council (SMC). Having started as an organisation which provided practical advice to its member museums, the Council has been increasingly developing as a more strategic organisation. However, we do not have responsibility for NMS and NGS and (in contrast to the arts or libraries sectors) there is no single organisation or forum which has a strategic remit for all museums in Scotland.

In January 1998, we decided the view that devolution would inevitably mean a much higher profile for culture, and that this was an opportunity to argue for a review of government thinking and the development of specifically Scottish policies, including a new inclusive policy for museums. We therefore took the decision to consult and develop a 'national strategy' in collaboration with NMS and NGS. The Directors of NMS and NGS were members of the distinguished steering group, headed by our Chair, Professor Malcolm McLeod, and including museum and non-museum professionals. The author spent much of last year consulting widely with members and non-members and writing the *National Strategy for Scotland's Museums*, which was finally endorsed in December 1998, not only by the Council, but also by the National Museums of Scotland and the National Galleries of Scotland.[3]

THE CASE FOR AN INCLUSIVE STRATEGY

Perhaps the most important and most radical recommendations of the Strategy was the proposition that there is a need for a national strategy in the first place. Equally important is the proposition that such a strategy should not be restricted to ad hoc funding decisions, but includes responsibility for developing a coherent policy framework within which museums throughout Scotland can be developed for the public benefit. In acknowledging that there is a case for a 'National Cultural Strategy', it does seem that the new Scottish Executive has accepted that there is a need for a national overview of culture, including museums within that framework. It also seems that government now accepts that cultural organisations such as museums can deliver a complex range of socio-economic benefits. In museum terms, this government approach, allied with the recommendations of the *National Strategy for Scotland's Museums*, should have potentially significant planning considerations, not only for the Minister, Committee and Civil Servants with designated responsibility for museums, but also for their colleagues with responsibility for school education, lifelong learning, tourism and information technology in particular.

Historic funding patterns have meant that museums in Scotland have been under-valued and underfunded by central government over the last decade. Support for NMS and NGS is certainly not over generous compared to similar national museums in England, while support for non-national museums is even more limited. The only direct central government funding for museums has been via the Council, and an annual National Acquisitions Fund of about £200,000 administered by it. The 322 local museums are funded through a decreasing amount of local authority funding, through limited commercial operations and through capital project funding from the Heritage Lottery Fund. In an era of increasing pressure on local government finances, this has meant that local museum services (as other services) have suffered, not only in terms of reduced funding, but also by being neglected in forward planning and policy debates. Support from local authorities for independent museums is reduced and although the total figure has never been substantial in terms of local authority budgets, this support has been critical to the survival of the independent museums, whether for the group of large industrial museums or for smaller rural museums.

Potentially, all of this will have disastrous long-term effects upon museum services and the future of collections. We have therefore argued that it is critical for the new government and local authorities to acknowledge the dangers facing the museum inheritance, and to act to reverse the downward spiral of funding, reinstating and where appropriate increasing support. Indeed, there was overwhelming recognition from the consultees that the very lack of a coherent policy had meant that previous funding decisions had in many cases been arbitrary, poorly considered and did not necessarily deliver long term benefits for museums or their users. Bearing in mind that the museum community developed its own national strategy, it would seem reasonable to suggest that the next two recommendations are also radical in their potential impact.

In the first place, we recommended that there should be a more strategic approach to museum provision which would aim to resolve the clear anomalies in the pattern of museum provision throughout Scotland, particularly anomalies in the pattern of funding and would embrace the principle of sustainability. We also recognised that given the anomalies and changing patterns of use and expectation, it is inevitable and in many ways desirable that there should be a restructuring within the museums sector. There is no doubt that this will mean a reduction in the number of existing museums: the question is whether the restructuring will be achieved as a result of market forces, the failure of independent museums, the continuing attrition of local authority services, or whether this should be a managed process with some strategic coherence.

The Council and its members, NMS and NGS were all clear that the managed process with some strategic coherence was necessary, and we formulated long term objectives of a managed restructuring: first, to secure the future of nationally important collections which are not currently the responsibility of the NMS and NGS, and second, to ensure stable revenue funding base for a network of museums, including non-national museums as well as the national institutions.

As will be appreciated, the principle of an inclusive policy developed along these lines would be a radical innovation for the new Scottish Executive. If government now accepts that principle, clearly we need to develop acceptable criteria to ensure that the restructuring actually achieves those objectives. At the same time, in arguing the case for a new approach to planning and funding, we recognised the need for greater accountability at every level, as part of the new political dynamic which rightly insists that those in receipt of public funding must demonstrate value for money, not only in terms of efficient administration, but also in meeting key objectives. Whilst this combination may sound unattractively bureaucratic, there can be little doubt that in an arena where there has been no debate about key objectives and few criteria for judging the quality of museums services, the development of objective criteria, appropriate standards and greater accountability would have enormous benefits in raising the profile of museums and in establishing credibility with key funders. However, it is seen as essential that the museum community continues to take the initiative, and is proactive in developing the standards framework within which museum services can be adjudged. In the months since publication of the National Strategy, the Council has therefore devoted considerable time to developing an integrated standards framework, as set out in *How Good is your Museum Service,* which marries good professional theory and practice, with current political imperatives and statutory requirements.

Whatever the political imperatives or requirements, a museum service is only a hollow shell without collections at its heart. A crucial section of the National Strategy therefore developed a series of recommendations for management of the collections that aim at more effective use of limited resources, with an emphasis on encouraging co-operation and joint initiatives. The first priority should be a National Audit of existing collections and associated services. We recognise that this would be a long term project, extending over perhaps three to five years, but without better information about the collections and services there is little prospect of making informed choices about restructuring or ensuring access to those collections.

There are a number of existing schemes which might serve as models including the Netherlands Delta Plan and Register of Historic Ships currently being compiled by the National Historic Ships Committee of the United Kingdom.[5] We see external validation rather than self-assessment as essential to the credibility of such a project. However, if an audit is to review our premises as well as collections, there also needs to be a related programme of research into potential usage patterns, visitor expectations and access requirements to underpin the possibility of a strategic approach to museum provision throughout Scotland.

A clear theme which runs throughout the National Strategy is an emphasis on national support and practical advice being delivered on a group basis. This principle is well recognised in other service areas and, in our consultation, respondents indicated that, not only would this help management, but it would also help to address the increasing sense of professional isolation where there are fewer and fewer specialist staff in any discipline. This has clear resource and management implications for strategic and support agencies such as SMC and the Heritage Lottery Fund, but we have already found that implementing this approach is having an immediate and beneficial impact in our own work. An outstanding example is the creation of our first regional post in Inverness, jointly funded by Highlands & Islands Enterprise. We are also helping to develop specialist networks, and further developing national policy via working parties which draw on the expertise of non-SMC staff, including staff of NMS and NGS as well as non museum organisations.

If preservation of the collections has always been the key issue for museum professionals, there is no doubt that the principle of public access, both physical and intellectual, is integral to the modern concept of a museum. We therefore devoted time to developing principles of access, and a series of recommendations which attempted to balance the area of conservation for future public benefit with requirements of current users.

Physical access is obviously a priority, and we included proposals, not only for physical access to local collections, but also an extended loan scheme known as the National Loans Scheme. This Scheme has been jointly developed by SMC, NMS and NGS, and it would provide extensive access on a national and reciprocal basis on collections while at the same time providing long term benefits in the form of improvements to museum premises and skilling of staff, particularly in security and environmental areas, where we might draw on the expertise of NMS and NGS. However, we also emphasise that remote access is particularly important in Scotland where geography means it is impossible to ensure physical access for many potential visitors.

The Scottish Cultural Resources Access Network (SCRAN) provides multimedia access to a selection of images from museum collections. Even in the short time since this partnership was established, information and computer technology (ICT) has continued to open up significant new possibilities and expectations. Indeed, the whole area of ICT is critical to the development of museums. In the months since the publication of the National Strategy, the Council has set up an Information Working Party which includes representatives of NMS, NGS, SCRAN and Scottish Libraries Information Council. This has been considering in greater depth, a range of ICT issues already touched on in the National Strategy, including the question of infrastructure, intellectual property rights, education and technical standards, and the promotion and resourcing of training.

Since we embarked on development of the National Strategy, we have made significant progress. But there are two critically important areas where we did not produce definitive recommendations, recognising that these are choices for the Scottish Executive. Firstly, we did not seek to define the role of the National Museums and the National Galleries within the policy framework. The present position is that the primary responsibility of NMS and NGS is to their own collections. The staff of both certainly play an active part in the museum community, providing specialist curatorial advice and in some cases even acting as Trustees of independent trusts.

Over recent years, NMS and NGS as organisations have also developed important joint initiatives with individual museums, such as the National Galleries of Scotland projects at Duff House and Paxton House, or the National Museums ticketing scheme with a group of independent museums. They have also developed important joint programmes with SMC and others, such as SCRAN and the National Loans Scheme. But neither NMS nor NGS would claim to have fully comprehensive collections. For example, NMS has deliberately not collected in certain industrial areas, such as mining and maritime, leaving this to the relevant independent museums. Nor, because of their legal status and because of historic funding patterns, are NMS or NGS resourced to deliver a fully comprehensive national service or strategic overview.

As far as non-national museums and organisation are concerned, the development of joint initiatives and joint programmes is therefore very much at the discretion of the Trustees and management of NMS and NGS within their available resources. It is significant that one of the questions posed by the Scottish Executive in the National Cultural Strategy consultation is: 'what should be the relationship of the national institutions to local authorities?'. At this early stage of the consultation process it is too early to say how detailed a response we can give or what changes government might introduce, but I can confidently say that the issue is not only the national institutions relationship with the 32 local authorities, but also with the range of independent museums who make up more than half of the number of museum organisations in Scotland.

The second area which we discussed but where we deliberately refrained from definitive recommendations was the question of appropriate structures. We recognised that one of the greatest challenges we set for government was to align funding and strategic planning for the sector overall, and to manage the necessary redefining of relationships to achieve this.

THE STRATEGIC OPTIONS

Among the options we explored and set out, the first was the proposition of a national museums service, where the relevant government department would provide strategic leadership with no arms length intermediaries interposed between it and those in receipt of public funds. Democratic accountability is through the Minister to Parliament. The advantage of the national museums service funded directly by central government would be strategic coherence, clear commitment to the future of collections and a comprehensive network of nationally supported museums and galleries with specialist services possibly delivered on a regional basis. While this certainly has some attractions in purely professional terms, it completely cuts across moves to subsidiarity and community based planning, and it would represent a seismic shift in the landscape of museum provision in Scotland. Politically it seems unlikely this would be an acceptable option, although it has been suggested, and indeed adopted in other sectors, such as education.

The second option is the creation of an arms length intermediary, which has a remit for museums as a whole, including both national and non-national museums. All funding from central government would be directed through this intermediary, which would have a strategic remit irrespective of the source of funding. This would be a fundamental change for the sector and would radically affect all museums: NMS and NGS would no longer have a direct relationship with central government and the Council if it continued to exist would no longer be responsible for strategic direction for the non-national sector. The governance of the new body should recognise the interests of all stakeholders, including the local authorities whatever their developing role, and practitioners and users. With a new form of governance, a new body would have an authority and credibility with central and local government, and the independent sector and with users, and this offers the best opportunity to develop the coherent policy framework and targeted resources so badly needed by museums.

This option would be consistent with any restructuring of the sector which looked to secure the future of non-national museums as well as the National Museums and National Galleries. Funding via this arm's length intermediary should include not only funding for the National Museums and National Galleries but increased funding from government. This might include new partnership funding arrangements and should also include a challenge fund targeted at the non-national museums. A 'spend to save' challenge fund should be used to encourage restructuring of both independent and local authority museums, delivering programmes which allowed interim stabilisation linked to careful rationalisation, the type of scheme already available to arts organisation and in other sectors such as health and education. It would be essential to ensure that the intermediary continued to provide or enable the specialist advice and support currently provided by SMC to its members. My own view is that there are considerable merits in an integrated organisation where a strategic view is informed by first hand knowledge, and practical advice is in turn informed by strategic understanding.

A third option would be a structure in which strategic advice to government and to museums is provided by a single agency which is not responsible for funding, in particular not responsible for funding NMS and NGS. This is the model historically operated in England via the Museum and Galleries Commission (MGC) and proposals for the new Museum, Library and Archives Council suggests that the new body will have an even more strategic, less executive role than the current MGC. In Scotland, SMC already fulfils this strategic role for the non-national museums and extending SMC's remit would seem to achieve a sensible continuity of policies and expertise. However, if SMC's remit were to be extended, we suggested the present membership structure should be amended to allow NMS and NGS to participate formally in SMC membership and governance. An alternative which in my view may be preferable is a new organisation.

As with the preceding scenario, option three is consistent with any restructuring of the sector which looked to secure the future of non-national museums and, in theory, a single strategic body should be well placed to provide strategic leadership. However, if the arm's length intermediary has little or no financial input into the sector, experience has shown that there are difficulties in providing strategic leadership where profound sectoral change is necessary. If this route is adopted, then at the very least, the arm's length intermediary should be the vehicle for a 'spend to save' challenge fund used to encourage restructuring of both independent and local authority museums.

Option four develops a partnership approach in which the status quo is retained, but the relevant organisations (NMS, NGS and SMC) build on improving relationships and develop stronger functional networking and joint delivery of programmes in a more structured way. The National Strategy already identifies areas which can be developed using this approach, and the option will be the more realistic if there is an opportunity for all parties to have a greater dialogue with the Minister, Scottish Executive and parliamentary committees.

The option has its attractions, as it allows NMS and NGS to retain their current status and the Council to preserve its present membership structure and accountability to those whose interests it represents, but it may not deliver strategic coherence. This is particularly true if central government were to provide additional funding intended to meet a range of more complex cross sectoral objectives or if central government were to create one or more new revenue clients e.g. a new 'National Museums & Galleries in Glasgow'. If this option is adopted, SMC as the intermediary should be the vehicle for 'challenge funding' to encourage restructuring of both independent and local authority museums.

The choice of structure therefore depends to some extent on how government views the role of the National Museums and National Galleries but more importantly whether government is persuaded by the arguments of the National Strategy that a more integrated approach to policy development and an aligning of funding and strategic planning will deliver the national benefits which we claim. Above all, it depends on the future relationship between central and local government in Scotland. This is a much wider political issue, by no means confined to museums. Bearing in mind that 83 per cent of local government funding is remitted from central government, the balance between central government direction and local government autonomy is an extraordinarily sensitive political issue which has to be taken into account in further developing any strategic approach or any reallocation of funding. It is not an issue which can be resolved without a great deal of further debate and although the National Cultural Strategy consultation, ongoing at the time of writing, is an opportunity to engage in that debate, the rebalancing and resolution of central and local government relationships within the new constitutional framework is a much longer term issue.

The sub-title of this volume is 'Shaping National Identity'. As should be clear from the above, the author believes passionately that the image of Scotland is shaped, sustained and reflected in the collections and activities of museums and local communities throughout the country, not only in the magnificent buildings and collections of the National Museums of Scotland and the National Galleries of Scotland. With the establishment of the new parliament, we have a unique opportunity to develop an imaginative and innovative national strategy for museums to address the aspirations the opportunities and the challenges which face modern Scotland. Indeed, it is not just an opportunity, it is also our responsibility, and one which all those interested in the future of Scotland, as well as its past, should embrace with commitment and enthusiasm.

The Author

Jane Ryder has been Director of the Scottish Museums Council since 1995. She developed and wrote the *National Strategy for Scotland's Museums* in anticipation of devolution, and has given much time to developing a framework for standards, including writing 'best value' guidelines for local authorities. She is a Director of SCRAN and SCRAN IT and was one of the team responsible for developing its IP licensing framework. She is a member of the UKOLN Interoperability focus and convenes the Scottish working party which is developing a national information strategy for Scotland's museums. After reading medieval history at St Andrews University she qualified as a solicitor in England and then Scotland. As a partner in an Edinburgh firm, she specialised in maritime law and is author of the standard textbook on professional practice for Scottish solicitors. She has served on the Council of the Law Society of Scotland, being Convenor of the Insurance Committee, as well as on the Expert Panel which drew up the Code of Conduct for Members of the new Scottish Parliament. She is a member of the Board of Management of Stevenson College of Further Education and is the Company Secretary of the Scottish Refugee Council. She has an interest in music, is a Director of the Dunedin Consort, and is currently learning to play the cello.

References

1. Macmillan, D., in *Scotland on Sunday*, 1 August, 1999.
2. Scottish Museums Council et al, *Creative Scotland: A Case for a National Cultural Strategy*, Scottish Museums Council et al, 1999.
3. National Museums Council, *A National Strategy for Scotland's Museums*, Scottish Museums Council, 1999.
4. Scottish Museums Council et al, *How Good is your Museum Service*, Scottish Museums Council, 1999.
5. www.st-andrews.ac.uk/institutes/sims/nhsp
6. www.scran.ac.uk

Further Reading

Ambrose, T. (ed), *Presenting Scotland's Story*, HMSO, 1989.

Brankin, R., *Celebrating Scotland: A National Cultural Strategy*, Scottish Executive, 1900.

Scottish Museums Profile

- 313 non-national sites:

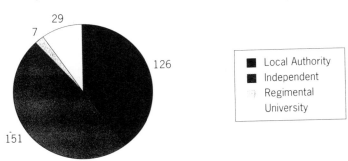

- national sites:

NMS: Royal Museum of Scotland, Edinburgh

Scottish United Services Museum, Edinburgh Castle (reopens 2000)

Museum of Flight, East Fortune

Shambellie House Museum of Costume, New Abbey

Museum of Piping, Glasgow

Scottish Agricultural Museum, Ingliston (closes 2001)

Museum of Scotland, Edinburgh (opens November 1998)

Museum of Scottish Rural Life, Kittochside (opens 2001, replaces Ingliston)

NGS: National Gallery of Scotland, Edinburgh

Scottish National Portrait Gallery, Edinburgh

Scottish National Gallery of Modern Art, Edinburgh

Duff House, Aberdeenshire

RSA, Edinburgh (tenants)

Dean Centre, Edinburgh (opens March 1999)

19

SCOTLAND IN A NEW LIGHT
Towards a Collective National Image

Russel Griggs

In 1994, a group of leading members from the business community met at Hopetoun House under the chairmanship of Lord MacFarlane of Bearsden to discuss how Scotland could shapen its national image. Special regard was to be paid to developing a collective and united way of presenting ourselves to the rest of the world. Their concern was that Scotland is a small country, and as such must focus on external markets to exploit her commercial potential in the modern world. The meeting concluded that Scotland had strong latent brand equity, but this was not being used to fully maximise its commercial value.

The meeting resolved that urgent action was required to promote a programme to 'exploit the Scottish equity to maximum effect'. There was agreement that a more cohesive attitude and approach would benefit all, and it was decided to start a collaborative initiative to be known as 'Scotland the Brand'. It would first create a 'country of origin' device or national logo which companies and organisations could use throughout the world to establish a more coherent national image. It would then go on to develop an agreed Scottish branding 'proposition' so that Scotland's identity could be more clearly perceived by the international community. To take this forward, it was later decided to initiate research under 'Project Galore' to discover how Scotland is perceived both at home and abroad, as explained below.

Scotland the Brand was formally launched in 1997, and is part of the main public economic development agency, Scottish Enterprise. It operates from an office in Glasgow, and its funding comes primarily from the public purse for core functions, although it enjoys substantial support from the private sector for specific initiatives. Its corporate mission is to facilitate cohesion in the image and marketing of Scotland to deliver real commercial benefits and contribute towards raising Scotland's profile globally.

Good progress has been made in a number of areas. We have created a distinctive country of origin device, which companies can license to show their product and demonstrate that it comes from Scotland. By the end of the millennium, 200 companies will have been authorised to use the device and Scotland the Brand has undertaken an active programme of integrated marketing events throughout the world.

What follows focuses mainly on Project Galore: its process, results and outcome, as well as on some of the challenges yet to be met. It is about more than the Scotland Device, as its research output explores the 'Hopetoun House hypothesis' that Scotland has a strong brand equity. To those of us directly involved, it has been a source of satisfaction that the essence of the Galore findings has been corroborated by research carried out by others, such as Locate in Scotland, Scottish Power, the Royal Bank of Scotland and the Bank of Scotland.

THE FATHER OF NATIONAL BRANDING

Before looking at where we are today in terms of image, it is worth reflecting on when it all started. This takes us back over 150 years to the time of Sir Walter Scott, and particularly to the time of the visit by George IV to Edinburgh in 1822 (see Cannizzo in Chapter 14). What transpired before and after this event could be described as a highly effective and successful branding exercise, supported by 'government' and masterminded by Scott. Reading the findings of the new research outlined below, one can imagine the current image as the outcome section of a consultant's report written by Scott for George IV.

The crucial role played by Sir Walter Scott is that it was he who first defined the product and its provenance, which lie at the heart of Scotland's present image, identity and brand profile. Most importantly, Scott set in place a clear agenda which those involved in promoting Scotland and marketing its products have earnestly and unswervingly followed for over a century and a half.

This was recognised by *The Glasgow Herald* when it declared only ten years later: 'Thousands from foreign lands are yearly visiting our shores to tread the localities which he has given to fame.'[1] Almost half a century later, in 1871, The Cornhill Magazine confirmed: 'Scott invented the modern Highlander.'

Despite his approach being historically based, Scott certainly did not limit himself to providing an accurate reflection of the realities of Scottish history and life. He knew perceptions had to be changed and if this meant donning rose-coloured spectacles and reinventing history, this would not present an insurmountable problem. It is fair to assume that Scott believed that, if it was for the greater good of his fellow countrymen, his King, and no doubt himself, the ends would more than adequately justify the means. Indeed, the challenges which he faced in establishing the new identity for Scotland must have been daunting given the range of deep seated negative perceptions held about Scotland and its people in the years immediately following the Jacobite rising of 1745.

The Scots were at that time widely considered by those south of the border to be erratic, dangerous and unreliable. In the literature of the time, the Scots were described as rebellious, violent, immoral, drunken, braggish and boastful, disloyal and dishonest to a man, and totally devoid of industry. Within less than half a century, the 'make-over' by Scott had successfully established a new brand image for Scotland, supported by a range of positive perceptions concerning the Scots. As a direct result of his work, Scots have since been generally perceived as loyal, honest, god-fearing, humble, and industrious.

The market response to the perceptions created by Scott has proved so strong, appealing and enduring, and the identity he provided for Scotland and its people so clearly defined, that any subsequent view of the country which did not conform to his vision has had little impact on the way in which Scotland is perceived. An attempt will be made below to show that as a direct consequence of Scott, not only is Scotland's image now caught in a time warp, but it may also be that many important and valuable aspects of Scotland have either been ignored or positively rejected since.

DOES NATIONAL IDENTITY MATTER TODAY?

There has been much recent debate about whether national identity matters much in today's global village, but there is strong evidence to suggest that it is still a key factor in decision-making at all levels, both by governments and by the business community. Michael Porter asserts that: 'The role of the home nation seems to be strong, or stronger, than ever. While globalisation might appear to make the nations less important, instead it seems to make them more so.'[2] Drawing on recent research, Wally Olins shows that '72 per cent of 200 of the world's leading companies cited the nation's image as important when they make purchasing decisions', and Simon Anholt claims that: 'Throughout the twentieth century, most of the really successful brands have come from countries that are successful brands in their own right, and substantial transfer of imagery and brand equity can often be seen to occur between the two.'[3]

In 1997, the Scottish people voted in a referendum to create their own devolved Parliament for the first time in 300 years, and the significance of this constitutional event has raised Scotland's visibility in the world, especially amongst its huge expatriate community. As Donald Dewar, then Secretary of State for Scotland, now First Minister of the new Scottish Executive, proclaimed: 'The international publicity and higher public profile that devolution will provide for Scotland can be capitalised on and used to help us to create or reinforce favourable images of Scottish products and of Scotland as a desirable place to invest.'

The civic and commercial momentum created by devolution offers a unique opportunity to reinforce and enhance the perception of national identity, both from a domestic and international point of view. In regard to the former, one of our recent surveys of all sectors of the Scottish business community revealed that 75 per cent of respondents felt their business contained Scottish values, 77 per cent felt that having a Scottish identity was important, 67 per cent considered that their Scottishness gave them a distinct advantage in the marketplace, and 77 per cent supported the creation of a Scottish proposition, as elaborated at the end of this chapter.

THE GALORE RESEARCH

Early output from Project Galore helped to confirm our focus on two basic objectives: First, to create a personality or proposition for Scotland that will carry us into the new millennium, enabling us to articulate in simple terms how we want to talk about ourselves and how we want others to see us. Second, to get all, from the largest organisation to the person in the street, including those of Scottish descent living abroad, to agree with it and use it.

These objectives have implications extending beyond the business community, especially at a time in the nation's history when all sectors need to stand together in solid coalition by saying the same thing about Scotland and the Scots. The results of our latest research strongly supports this notion. It took almost two years and was conducted in a number of stages by CLK, an internationally renowned specialist firm in brand research and development. Core funding was provided by Scottish Enterprise, with significant financial support from Marks & Spencer, United Distillers & Vintners, Stagecoach, and British Airways, all of whom feel that Scottishness and the image of Scotland is important to them.

The research fell into four stages: First, relevant information that had been written in the last twenty years and beyond was read and sifted to discover what it said and what the congruence was. Second, a hypothesis was formed to the effect that four core values were associated with Scotland: integrity, tenacity, inventiveness and spirit. These values would serve as 'characteristics' around which Scotland could be discussed and assessed. Third, these values were turned into concepts which 'consumers' around the world would understand.

The fourth and final stage was comprised of focus studies in England, France, Germany, Spain, USA and Japan, as well as at home in Scotland. In each of these countries, we had eight focus discussion groups of two hours duration, and the same number of one hour in depth interviews. In Scotland, we held 20 in-depth interviews. The people interviewed, both for the groups and individually, were selected randomly from groupings known as 'successful idealist' or 'comfortable belongers' (ABC1). To ensure a representative outcome for Scotland, we used four extra focus groups of C2DEs. In total, over 650 people took part internationally.

SCOTS ON SCOTLAND

Work with the Scottish groups conveyed a sense of identity based on the notion that 'we are recognisable in a way other countries would give their eye teeth for'. This recognition manifests itself in tartan (which we have a huge attachment to and pride in when it is used properly, but a huge distaste for when it is not), our names, the landscape, our music, our voices, our distinctive culture, our history, our democracy which is rooted in our communities and folk tradition.

'We know who we are' say the people of Scotland, and then they reflect momentarily and wonder whether all this matters in today's world. Throughout the work with the groups, there was a constant look at what we would like to be, and then a wonder about whether we are still like this, or do we need a new definition for ourselves in the modern world? We also believe that we are a country which matters both to ourselves and to others, based on the notions that we are:

1. A civilised, educated, skills-rich, astute, and responsible nation.
2. A country with a small population and accordingly not an industrial giant.
3. An urban economy where the cities now play a much more important part than the rural community (this perception being true of rural and town dwellers alike).
4. A country with a large global population descended from Scots which greatly outnumbers our home population.

Although the groups met only a few months before the first Scottish parliamentary elections, there was little discussion about the outcome of these, but there was a constant and recurring struggle to resolve issues associated with our identity in the shadow of England. In other words, there was less concern about the workings of the new Parliament, than there was about our relationship to our southern neighbour. Indeed, it could be hypothesised that Scottish preoccupation with the new parliamentary status is focused on recapturing our values in relationship to the United Kingdom.

Scots also believe that we are a country with strong virtues and there is considerable quiet pride taken in the Scottish attitude to work, way of life, and moral philosophy. The counterpoint to this is the distaste for the Hollywood hype that films like *Braveheart* bring: 'we liked the movie, but did not like its inaccuracies or the picture it paints.' Many were also concerned about the aggressiveness that some forms of nationalism might bring against others.

Surrounding all the above is our great propensity not to boast, so we dislike any claims which could be considered as us showing off. In contrast to this is our acknowledgement that our restraint and silence have been strongly in-bred into us with the result that 'the English get the credit for Scottish inventions by telling the world they are 'British'. Indeed, the failure to blow our own trumpet has been and still is a major handicap. Accordingly, we have this unhappy and uncomfortable conflict between dignity and pride.

Loss of dignity also manifests itself in our dislike or an even stronger deep-seated loathing of dependency on others, and especially on others outside of Scotland. Currently, this dependency is perceived as manifesting itself in a disproportionately high allocation from Westminster on a per capita basis, an ailing industrial base, and as a tourism-dominated economy.

Another deep concern is our focus on jobs and not on indigenous business growth. The Scottish people appear to have clearly defined intellectually their views in this area, which commend and understand that inward investment can provide jobs, but they see prosperity for Scotland coming only from the growth of indigenous industry. Scotland as a country has gone through an astonishing industrial and economic revolution in the last 20–30 years, and much of the industry that was Scotland in the pre-World War II era has gone and been replaced by others which are not as large or visible as those that were there before. Like any industrial revolution in such a short period of time, it leaves its scars on the people and the country, which it has taken long to come to terms with. Resulting from this Scotland sees itself as dependent on England, and therefore does not see England as a preferred partner.

Interestingly, the research revealed that the English see the moving of the Scots and the Welsh to their new parliamentary status as being a threat to their own identity. The English hold the Scots on a pedestal in terms of their strong identity, belief in themselves, tradition of democracy, and they are considered less class oriented. The research confirmed the four values of our hypothesis by assigning them high scores, representing the key characteristics of who we are and where we want to be:

> *Integrity*, we are strongly attached to this virtue, and believe ourselves to be more ethical than most.
> *Tenacity*, we believe we are very tenacious and that we deliver
> *Inventiveness*, a source of national pride in need of rediscovery, as we believe that we were inventive but are no longer so, and we are proud of our historic track record, but feel bypassed by 'the big ideas'. We are subsumed into Britishness and we are really better at innovation, or 'being Japanese' in harnessing the ideas of others.
> *Spirit*, we value our positive spirituality, but see ourselves as 'flegmatic' poets rather than 'visionary' artists.

Another impression to emerge is that there is a strong feeling that we are not sure what these virtues add up to for Scotland today, and whether they matter to the world. It also appears that Scots are tired, or indeed fed up with what they see as 'rhetoric' or ' wide statements' about issues which do not give concrete examples or demonstrate reality. If the Scots are to regain their belief in inventiveness and the strength of ingenuity, then they will need key institutions and individuals to lead by example as role models in their own community. This will allow the Scottish people to regain any lost faith they have in their own skills and ability. This is crucial to any change.

HOW WE THINK OTHERS SEE US

We found that the Scots at home believe that the world has a fairly limited view of them, an impression gained from tourism, premium products, our Diaspora, a little from inward investment, and from myth. We are very buoyant and confident about the admiration for Scotland from the former British colonies to which many Scots emigrated over the centuries, but we are much less certain about the rest of the world.

It is widely believed that 'we are British and not Scottish as far as the modern world is concerned.' In regard to the expatriate community overseas, we believe that 'they all want to trace their roots back to Scotland.' Whilst this is seen as a strong and confident attribute by the

Scots at home, it is also a key reason why the expatriate community overseas is not as attached to its original homeland, as say Irish counterparts. Scots abroad, especially those beyond the first generation, may wish to know where they came from, but they do not seem to be as interested in what their mother country looks like and stand for today.

Expatriates of Ireland, on the other hand, are as interested in helping their country as they are in investigating their ancestry. This is why they currently add huge commercial and political clout to their mother country by actively seeking to enhance its competitive position. The role that such overseas communities play in the wider world represents a considerable asset, an advantage not enjoyed to the same extent by Scotland, since the loyalties of our expatriates are not sufficiently roused to provide active support. This is not intended as criticism, but an observation of fact, which may be or could be changed. Devolution for Scotland may indeed provide the necessary impetus for change in attitudes, and there are signs that the desire to engage with and learn more about contemporary Scotland is there, but it will require desire and commitment on both sides to make progress on this front.

Seen from Scotland, it is hoped that we are regarded as civilised, richly varied, lively, urban, friendly, highly educated, dynamic, inventive, modern, and entrepreneurial. We fear, as largely confirmed below, that the world sees us as dominated by the tourist picture, beautiful but empty, a small country happy to live off exporting whisky, salmon, shortbread, golf and Fair Isle jerseys, locked in the past, and quaint. We also fear it is widely believed that we export more people than products.

We have much more confidence in the exported people of Scotland than the products and in how we do things than in what we produce. This feeling links strongly to the inability of the Scottish people to associate with who our indigenous companies are, and what they do and probably demonstrates the deeply 'iconic' nature of the Scottish people.

When the author was growing up in Scotland in the 1960s, the Hillman Imp was rolling off the assembly line at Linwood, the QE2 and other great ships were built on the Clyde, and we could see, feel and touch what we produced. Today, our indigenous industries, and indeed our inward invested ones, are in products and markets which have much less visible and distinctive products. We therefore have greater difficulty in seeing and defining 'what is ours'. In a country like Scotland, where identity is so important to the people in a wide variety of ways, it is easy to see how these new industries have not yet had time to embed themselves in our national psyche.

Scotland is clearly seen and identified as a 'country' by the world.
Indeed, if you gave the world a pad and asked them to draw a
picture of Scotland, most people could do it and the visuals would
probably be much the same.

As a nation, we are positively viewed by the world, and in a sense
enjoy 'pedestal' status. Therefore, whilst there are some challenges
to address, Scotland has many more positives than negatives, and
we should start from these positives rather than trying to 'reinvent'
ourselves.

The above summarises the findings from the external focus groups. The
main positive perceptions that others have of Scotland are that it is a
serious holiday destination, with attractive landscapes and cultural
heritage, and with strong traditions still intact. We are seen very much as
a rural economy, with a clean, spacious and unspoilt environment. There
is less awareness of our urban lifestyle and economy, as experienced by
Scots today. Popular films with a rural setting, such as *Braveheart, Rob Roy,
The Bruce* and *Loch Ness*,[4] may be part responsible. Another reason may be
the recent focus by the media on places like Dunblane and Lockerbie
which has again reinforced the impression of an entirely rural Scotland.

Although we are seen as having a cool, dull and rainy climate, we should
not assume that our climate is a disincentive to all, the Irish having made a
marketing virtue of the mystic quality of their misty landscapes. We are
also seen as having a good quality of life with a slow pace, and we are
regarded as honest, self assured and warm people.

On the negative side, Scots are seen as inward looking and not
motivated to make progress. We are perceived as being unsophisticated
compared to the rest of the modern world. From a commercial and
business standpoint, we are seen as having little modern technology and
related expertise, and possessing little commercial or logistical
infrastructure. For example, the Germans were surprised to find that we
had dual carriageways, and the Americans that we had international
airports. Most of the world does not seem to be aware of Scotland's recent
industrial development, which poses opportunities as well as a challenges.

However, the world has a large amount of latent respect for Scotland
based on a general dissatisfaction with aspects of modern life and its lack
of integrity and loss of traditional values. This was a common thread,
especially strong in the US and Japan, where they feel that a headlong rush
to new technology and wealth has been at the expense of many core
values. In many ways, Scotland is idealised as an 'island in the past'
whose traditions and heritage is maintained, and where integrity still

exists and a strong sense of self still predominates. Many parents in the groups saw Scotland as the place they would like to bring up their children away from lawlessness, drugs, abuse and the disintegration of urban society.

It can not be stressed strongly enough how important these values are to Scotland's place in the world, and we should do nothing to harm them or to reduce their positive impact. This would be a retrograde step, as many other countries, governments and companies would give their eye teeth for the value this adds to the national identity of Scotland. With reference to the set of values in the original Galore hypothesis, our conclusions can be summarised as follows:

> *Tenacity*, was seen as totally credible and highly valued. However, on its own it does not provide the basis for any reassessment of the image of Scotland, being a value which has strong historical links, so that it could take us backwards as easily as forward.
>
> *Integrity*, this the strongest of all Scotland's values and provides a strong motivating bond to the world as it shows the personification of 'a country that believes in itself', and Scots being seen as people who 'do not tell lies'. What we say is believed, which is both a great strength and a great responsibility.
>
> *Inventiveness*, the world (excluding England) knows little of Scotland's historic inventiveness, let alone its modern contributions, this being a crucial gap in the image of Scotland. Creativity is seen as central to the success of modern and prosperous nations, and here is a big challenge, if Scotland is to assume its rightful place in the new global village. In doing so, we must not let it overshadow the other traditional values for which Scotland is admired.
>
> *Spirit*, was clearly recognised, but again like the Scots themselves, the artistic or more expressive side was seen as surprising but desirable. It adds a dynamic, welcoming, progressive and communicative side to the world's perception of Scotland.

THE CHALLENGES

The research has confirmed that others have a strong desire to see Scotland take its place on the world stage, but there are worries that in doing so it could lose its traditional strengths and values. This dilemma is caused by the recognition by other countries that their rush into the 'modern world' has been at the expense of some of their native traditions. For Scotland to do the same, would be regarded as a backward step. Therefore, whatever we do, must not be seen as 'new' or 'as a change' but as something building on values that have always been there, but may not have been fully recognised before.

The view held by the rest of the world that they have heard 'no real new news of Scotland' may come as a surprise to many Scots, given the amount of resource that is focused by government agencies, companies on marketing and selling our products. At the heart of this apparent dichotomy may well be the arrival and prevalence of niche marketing for much of our selling.

Niche marketing as a concept is to target a product at the customers who desire it and nobody else. Niche marketing can limit or preclude the general leverage or image building that non-customers pick up from mass marketing methods. Accordingly, it may not be so surprising that, in a country using sophisticated niche marketing, the general perception of the nation remains unaltered. Niche marketing could be argued to act at odds with, or not to be benefit, our overall national identity.

From what the world thinks and perceives of our nation, the following can be concluded: 'Scotland represents an ideal and likeable, but remote country, which in theory is capable of joining the 21st century, but has not yet demonstrated this capacity in practice.' Therefore, the task both for the world at large and Scots at home is to: 'retain the truth of Scotland's values, yet surprise the world into a radical reassessment of what it offers today.'

The key finding of the Galore research is that Scots and others largely agree on how they see Scotland. It generates admiration and affection throughout the world, and 'Provenance Scotland' is highly motivating. However, Scots appear to be silent about what they can offer, so the key question to emerge from the world is: does Scotland want to engage with the rest of the world and move forward?

Timeless tradition is at the heart of Scotland's equity, so whilst we need to move forward, it must not done in such a way that it would destroy the cultural integrity on which the perception is based. Others envy Scotland its historic landscape, and what is perceived as its enduring traditions. Scots at home agree with this view, but feel that, whilst their values have not changed, their lifestyles have, and Scotland is a modern country. However, the world thinks, and Scotland fears, that it is in a time warp which stops this recognition.

The romantic perceptions created by Sir Walter Scott were sometimes rooted in a rather free interpretation of history, and the research shows that their value can be a constraining factor on presenting a future image of Scotland in tune with today's global marketplace. In doing so, we must make certain that we are not seduced into throwing the baby out with the bath-water in an attempt to be up to date and 'modern'. People who have never encountered the Scots, feel they know and admire them and see them as the living product of an admirable past. The challenge facing us is to build a bridge between then and now.

It follows, that the way forward for Scotland, is not to 'reinvent' or 'recreate' our identity but to develop, refine, and re-focus what we have with new images that exemplify what we stand for today. In this we have to cleverly weave together old and new images of inventiveness so that the whole remains as one seamless identity. We must not be perceived to have added bits and pieces for effect rather than substance. If this can be achieved, and all Scots collectively agree to talk and present Scotland in this way, then Scotland will have achieved its task to: 'retain the truth of Scotland's values, yet surprise the world into a radical reassessment of what Scotland offers today.'

Projection of a collective image does not necessarily mean us all using the same 'logo' or the same 'strap line', or using the same generic images for international advertising to 'show Scotland as it is today'. However, it does mean all of us talking in the same way about Scotland, both in terms of culture and enterprise, and in order to do that we will need to work in close unison across the sectors. In all this we must not ignore the influence of the media in shaping public perceptions. As Marshall McLuhan asserted in 1962: 'by the end of this century, our perception of reality as dictated by advertising, public relations and the media could, in many ways, become more relevant to our decision making process than reality itself.'

To make progress on this front, there is an urgent need for a wide partnership to initiate action on the production of a 'brand book' for corporate use by all of us who represent the nation in one way or another. It would set out how to refer to and project Scotland to others, structured around a multidisciplinary storyline, providing the generic framework within which each sector can slot its specific requirements. This would give the strength and cohesion to the image of Scotland that it appears we all desire but have not yet succeed in formulating. Scotland the Brand stands ready to provide input and support on behalf of the enterprise network, but it will require joint working and active participation by all sectors to produce a reference book and associated material for different media, if we are to do justice to Scotland's diverse wealth of heritage assets.

The Author and Acknowledgements

Professor Russel Griggs is Executive Director of Scotland the Brand and was born in Edinburgh. He holds a BA in Commerce from Heriot Watt University, and is a visiting Professor of Entrepreneurship at Glasgow Caledonian University and an Honorary Professor of Marketing at Glasgow University. He is also associated with Boston University and Georgia Southern University in the US. Following a career in marketing and selling in areas as diverse as health care and consumer flooring, including service as CEO of a company involved in advanced materials, he joined Scottish Enterprise in 1990, where he has held various senior posts with a business development focus in Scotland and the US. He sits on the Board of several private companies as well as being the Chair of the new Advisory Board for the Crichton University Campus in Dumfries.

The author is grateful to the Editor for his help and encouragement, as well as his hours of work on the above text, which made the contribution to this volume possible.

References

1. *The Glasgow Herald*, 27 September 1832.
2. Porter, M., *The Competitive Advantage of Nations*, Collier, 1989.
3. Anholt, S., 'Nation-brands of the twenty-first century', in *Journal of Brand Management*, Vol 5, No 6 (July), 1998.
4. Seaton, A.V. & Hay, B., 'The Marketing of Scotland as a Tourist Destination 1985–96', in MacLelland, R. & Smith, R. (eds), *Tourism in Scotland*, International Thomson Business Press, 1998.

Further Reading

British Tourist Authority, *Branding Britain*, BTA, 1997.

de Chernatony, L. & McDonald, M.H.B., *Creating Powerful Brands: The strategic route to success in consumer, industrial and service markets*, Butterworth Heinemann, 1994.

CLK, *Galore Project Research Report*, Scotland the Brand, 1998.

Fladmark, J.M., 'Cultural Capital and Identity: Scotland's Democratic Intellect', in Fladmark, J.M. (ed), *In Search of Heritage:– As Pilgrim or Tourist?*, Donhead, 1998.

Fraser, M. (ed), *Essential Scotland: 70 perspectives on the New Scotland from leaders in their fields*, Agenda Publishing & Scotland the Brand, 1998.

Interbrand, *Brands: An International Review*, Mercury Business Books & Golden Arrow Publications, 1990.

Kotler, P. et al, *Marketing Places: Attracting Investment, Industry and Tourism to Cities, States and Nations*, The Free Press, 1993.

McCrone, D. et al, *Scotland – the Brand: The Making of Scottish Heritage*, Edinburgh University Press, 1995.

McLuhan, M., *The Medium is the Message*, HardWired, 1997.

Russell, G., 'Scotland the Brand', in Fraser, M. (ed), *Essential Scotland: 70 perspectives on the New Scotland from leaders in their fields*, Agenda Publishing & Scotland the Brand, 1998.

Scottish Tourism Research Unit, *Newhorizons: International Benchmarking and Best Practice for Visitor Attractions*, Scottish Enterprise, 1998.

PRODUCT OF

242

20

HERITAGE INTERPRETATION
From Equity Audits to Branding

Magnus Fladmark

Heritage interpretation can be defined as the art of using tangible assets selectively to tell the story of places or artefacts so that it has a memorable impact. As a planning and management tool for making heritage assets accessible to the visiting public, its main purpose is to stimulate interest and give meaning to what is being presented. The concept is now applied in fields as diverse as education, museums, galleries, parks, heritage centres and tourism.

Until recently, it has been regarded as a specialised activity assigned relatively low priority by senior management. This is now beginning to change, due to a realisation that the resource audits at the centre of interpretation are performing much the same function as audits in marketing and brand development. These are collectively referred to below as 'equity audits', their purpose being to identify the most valuable assets of a place, an organisation or a product in relation to the customer base and competitors. The assets which scores the highest 'uniqueness' ranking represent the prime equity of an operation.

This chapter provides a summary of research undertaken at The Robert Gordon University throughout the 1990s to examine how equity audits are deployed in decision making across the board of interpretation, marketing and brand development. The focus was on enabling agencies and custodians of heritage assets in Scotland, mainly in the public sector. For comparison, leading to some interesting findings, the work also included study of how corporate heritage assets are used by three major private sector companies.

In the knowledge that individual organisations plan for different purposes and assign priorities accordingly, the main aim of the work was to discover patterns of convergence and divergence in practice, focusing on the synergy between related areas of activity. An attempt was made to identify cross-sectoral opportunities for collaboration, with a view to formulating briefs for later case studies. The conceptual framework developed by the author for strategic audits is illustrated in Figure 1, and for work at site or institutional level in Figure 2. In the case of museums and galleries, the resource base would be represented by their collections. The main stages in the process of decision-making are:

1. equity audit and theme selection
2. matching themes and markets
3. brand and marketing strategy
4. product development and testing
5. storyline and presentation
6. customer feedback and review.

HISTORY AND LITERATURE

Although interpretation as practised today owes much to the US National Park Service, it is generally accepted that the concept originated in Scandinavia in the late-19th century. The Norwegian collector, Anders Sandvig opened one of the world's first open air museums at Lillehammer in 1887. However, the most influential pioneers to develop the philosophy behind rural country life museums was the Artur Hazelius. His creation of Skansen in Stockholm in 1891, was seen as an initiative very much concerned with the shaping of Swedish national identity (see Chapter 22).

There is a clear evolutionary distinction between Europe and the US. In Europe, interpretation had an ethnological bias, while in the US it tended to be more concerned with the natural environment. After returning from Europe in the 1930s, highly enthusiastic about the Scandinavian folk museums, John D. Rockefeller Jnr played a significant role in bringing the European philosophy to North America. A direct result of his visit was the creation of Colonial Williamsburg, which served as a model for later replicated historic villages.

Through this exchange across the Atlantic, began a metamorphosis in the development of interpretive philosophy: the blending of the ethnological with the ecological. Freeman Tilden was the first writer to embrace both in *Interpreting Our Heritage*, drawing on work experience with the US National Park Service.[1] Perhaps not surprisingly, his book had a strong influence on work by the first English national parks. As part of their remit to enhance the enjoyment and understanding of the countryside for the public, interpretation became a means by which this could be further achieved. Under the leadership of Foster and Aldridge, the Peak District National Park pioneered many initiatives in the 1950s. They later moved to Scotland, and the author has written a full account of development and application of their methodology within a Scottish context.[2]

It was the establishment of the two Countryside Commissions in 1968 which created a national focus for embracing the subject. They had the mandate and resources to encourage a large number of bodies to introduce interpretation as part of their operational strategies. Their pioneering work was enhanced by enabling legislation which empowered local authorities and others to create regional and country parks as places in the countryside to which large numbers of day visitors could be attracted.

Aldridge's book, *Principles of Countryside Interpretation*,[3] along with Ross Noble's *Country Heritage: An Interpretive Plan for Biggar and District*,[4] adapted the Tilden philosophy to Scottish circumstances, but both these are now more than twenty years old. The proceedings from the 1988 World Congress on Heritage Presentation and Interpretation provided a series of helpful texts edited by Uzzell, while more recent contributions to the subject can be found in the *Manual of Heritage Management*, edited by Harrison,[5] and in Aldridge's guide on *Site Interpretation* for the Scottish Tourist Board.[6] Recent US texts have been produced by Ham and Veverka, and a major new publication has been issued by the Tourism and Environment Initiative, entitled *A Sense of Place: An Interpretive Planning Handbook*.[7,8,9] Guidance manuals have also been issued by Historic Scotland and the Association of Scottish Visitor Attractions.[10,11]

Although the main body of literature is beginning to extend beyond methodologies used in the environmental sector, there are still few texts treating the subject adequately in relation to museums, galleries and libraries. A strong attachment to separate functions remains, such as exhibitions, education and publications, without interpretive audits providing a unifying process of working. Although the code of conduct for museum professionals states that 'interpretation in its broadest sense is one of the core activities of museums', the word interpretation is absent from any of the chapter headings in the 1992 *Manual of Curatorship*.[12]

However, recent years have seen a new synergy beginning to appear between culture and enterprise, demonstrated in an increasing awareness of the tenets of interpretation by those concerned with product development, as well as by those charged with marketing and corporate branding. Evidence of this includes the multi-agency initiative known as Scotland the Brand (see Chapter 19), transferred to the Local Enterprise Network of the tourism development function, and the 1998 study report from the Scottish Tourism Research Unit, *Newhorizons: international benchmarking and best practice for visitor attractions*,[13] which is focused on the cultural sector and was commissioned by Scottish Enterprise. The most recent contribution touching on the reciprocity of culture and enterprise was McKiernan's *Scenarios for Scotland*.[14]

On the subject of marketing and branding tourist destinations, we now have Glen's work on *Interpreting St Andrews*,[15] following Aldridge's earlier success with *Dundee's Heritage*.[16] Evans has dealt with *Expos and Garden Festivals*,[17] and the European 'City of Culture' programme represents a strategic manifestation of the more integrated approach during the 1990s. The international nature of the trend has been reinforced by several books, including *Marketing Places* by Kotler et al and Porter's *The Competitive Advantage of Nations*.[18] Although *Branding Britain* was a welcome initiative by the British Tourist Authority,[19] *The Makers of Wales Campaign* stands to date as the best UK exercise in linking equity audits to the shaping of national branding. Scotland the Brand's publication of *Essential Scotland* was also a welcome first step towards integrated identity-building.[20]

Other recent works relevant to equity audits worth mentioning are *Scotland: A Concise Cultural History*,[21] *Scottish Sport in the Making of the Nation: Ninety Minute Patriots?*,[22] *Encyclopaedia of Scotland*,[23] *Scotland – the Brand: The Making of Scottish Heritage*,[24] *The Identity of the Scottish Nation: An Historic Quest*,[25] and *The Scottish Nation 1700–2000*.[26] However, the initiative to hold the greatest potential for introducing new thinking into public policy is a recent consultative document issued by the Scottish Executive, entitled *Celebrating Scotland: A National Cultural Strategy*.[27]

The following sections provide brief profiles of reviewed organisations, arranged into five groups: tourism, national library and archives, material culture and the arts, built and natural environment, and private enterprise.

TOURISM

The Scottish Tourist Board is responsible for strategic marketing at national level, promoting Scotland as a whole rather than its constituent parts, the latter being the responsibility of Area Tourist Boards (see Chapter 17). The training and quality assurance functions are shared with the Local Enterprise Network. The Board's main focus is on market research, promotional publications, conferences and publicity campaigns. Its advisory publications include *Site Interpretation: A practical Guide* and *Visitor Attractions: The Key to Success – a development guide*.

As will be gathered from Adams,[28,29] the Board operates in part through standing partnerships, the Scottish Tourism Co-ordinating Group being the principal vehicle for formulating strategic policy. Chaired at ministerial level, it produced *Scottish Tourism: Strategic Plan* in 1994, which set out how the twelve participating agencies would contribute within a joint framework of action. At the time of writing, consultations were in progress to update the plan in the year 2000. In terms of customer access, an important new initiative has been introduction of an on-line database called 'Ossian', which holds information on where to stay, how to travel and what to see in Scotland.

The Board was party to establishing the Association of Scottish Visitor Attractions, created to represent providers. It encourages members to pursue high standards of interpretive planning and organises seminars and workshops to raise interest and competence in the subject. It has produced a members-only guidance document, alongside a sister-publication on marketing. Among the subject specific partnerships sponsored by the Board is the Tourism and the Environment Initiative, operating under the auspices of the Tourism and Environment Task Force, which concentrates on strategic issues relating to sustainable tourism. The initiative has identified interpretation as a priority area, and it was responsible for publishing *A Sense of Place: An Interpretive Planning Handbook*.[30]

The Board has supported a series of tourist trail initiatives,[31] and there is a Tourism and the Arts Task Force to promote closer links between the tourism industry and arts organisations, but there does not appear to be an overall framework for undertaking national equity audit to inform strategic policy in a coherent manner. There has been no equivalent to the British Tourist Authority's *Branding Britain*,[32] and a challenge for Scotland is the question of how to promote tourism gateway locations, such as Edinburgh, Glasgow, Dundee, Aberdeen and Inverness, within a national framework of equity audits and branding. For this there are valuable lessons to be drawn from past work, such as Aldridge's interesting studies of the heritage assets of Dundee and its hinterland, which led to Discovery Point and Verdant Works.

NATIONAL LIBRARY AND ARCHIVES

The National Library of Scotland has the statutory status of legal deposit library with the obligation to acquire all books published in the UK. The central aim of its corporate plan is: 'to promote the use and interpretation of the Library's collections and awareness of its services'. Interpretive activity is the responsibility of the exhibitions and publications division in the Public Services Department., the latter also embracing media affairs, sponsorship, advertising, and management of retailing and special events. As might be expected from an organisation concerned with literature, interpretation plays a significant role across many functional areas.

247

Alongside its own exhibitions and publications, the Library offers advice and guidance, and is involved in research and conference activity. At site level, the focus is on the interpretation of its collections and the display of artefacts, and externally it makes frequent inputs to local or regional interpretive planning initiatives. Large scale initiatives take the form of major exhibitions, often in collaboration with other organisations. These are promoted throughout Scotland and some are taken to other venues after their initial showing in Edinburgh. Many have a commemorative content celebrating the work of notable figures or major institutions, recent examples being: Robert Louis Stevenson in 1994, the Bank of Scotland and the 250-year anniversary of the Jacobite Rebellion in 1995, and Robert Burns in 1996. Interpretation is used in this way as a marketing tool to raise awareness and to make its collections more accessible to the public.

The National Archives of Scotland serve as a repository and custodian for public and legal records, as well as for many local and private archival collections. It does not have a specific policy statement on interpretation, but the activity is central to its publication, exhibition and education programmes. It collaborates widely with a multitude of organisations and contributes to local interpretive initiatives through providing information and advice. In collaboration with other agencies, it is currently developing an information system to provide on-line access to more than forty archives across Scotland through the Scottish Archive Network (SCAN).

The Royal Commission on the Ancient and Historical Monuments of Scotland has responsibility for surveying and recording the built environment, for promoting awareness and understanding of surviving assets, and for holding the National Monuments Record of Scotland. Its extensive library is open to the public and access is positively encouraged to its immense holdings. Furthermore, their publication programme is designed to disseminate knowledge of the processes governing the survival of archaeological monuments, built heritage and cultural landscapes.

In its advisory role, the Commission serves as a key source of information and data, which is of great value to those seeking to interpret Scotland's built heritage. Although the word interpretation does not appear in corporate documents, many of its activities certainly come within the accepted definition, especially its collaborative input to interpretive planning by others. The three organisations referred to in this section have all acknowledged the potential value of a national framework for collaborative audits for interpretation, marketing and brand development.

The National Museums of Scotland came into being in its present configuration in 1985, with the Royal Museum being its central facility in Edinburgh. The dispersed units are the Scottish United Services Museum, the Museum of Flight, Shambellie House Museum of Costume and the Scottish Agricultural Museum. Sitting alongside the Royal Museum in Chamber Street, The Museum of Scotland was added in 1998 as the showcase of Scottish identity (see Chapters 1–12). The existing Scottish Agricultural Museum is to be moved to Wester Kittochside near East Kilbride, opening there in 2001 as the Museum of Scottish Country Life. It is being developed in partnership with the National Trust for Scotland, and will show rural life and work from before the Industrial Revolution to the mid-19th century when horse power gave way to the tractor.

Staff are actively involved in supporting the wider museum community in Scotland and advise others on best practice, based on internal guidance for interpretive planning of exhibitions. Although progress is being made, the institution as a whole is still finding its way towards an integrated strategy embracing interpretation, marketing and corporate branding. Encouraging signs are use of volunteer guides, outreach activity and a more open lending policy. However, there still appeared to be a propensity for each part of the National Museums to work in isolation. The situation is made difficult by the fragmented nature of organisational responsibilities, the function for wider national and regional strategic guidance falling to the Scottish Museums Council (see Chapter 18).

The research identified a desire on the part of both organisations for a national museum strategy, including rules of engagement for their working relationship with other sectors. An issue frequently mentioned was the need for a clearer collective image of museums as interpreters of cultural identity, and the danger of over-provision of visitor attractions with a resultant lack of viability. A number of multimedia projects have been started, the main initiative being The Scottish Cultural Resources Access Network (SCRAN), supported by several cultural and environmental organisations, with funding from the Millennium Commission. The initiative is designed to create interactive educational programmes and a national database of text, pictures and sound from public collections across Scotland. Long term, it will provide a state-of-the-art educational resource via the Internet and on CD-ROM, representing a powerful interpretive tool and a mechanism for marketing the organisations involved.

The National Galleries of Scotland, like the National Museums, has a dispersed organisational configuration with the principal units in Edinburgh and outposts at Duff House in Banffshire and Paxton House in

Berwickshire (see Chapters 13 & 14). In common with the Museums, each operational unit would however appear to function independently of the others. Although joint promotional leaflets are published for their exhibition programmes, there does not appear to be a shared framework for equity audits embracing all collections.

The concept of interpretation, as applied in the environmental sector, is not widely subscribed to by staff, but some activities come within the accepted definition, especially for education, outreach and publications. On-site interpretation within the galleries is purposefully low key, with paintings and other objects being supported by simple plaques providing minimal information such as the name of the artist, the date of the object and a limited description. In addition, various multi-media techniques and audio-guides are used, and there are themed exhibitions and lectures.

The research project also included three important university collections: The Hunterian Museum and Art Gallery in Glasgow, The Marischal Museum in Aberdeen and The Talbot Rice Gallery in Edinburgh. The collections clearly play a key role in promoting awareness of the universities both at home and abroad, implying a strong synergy between interpretation and marketing. Student recruitment is central to their marketing, mainly targeted at schools, and museum staff work closely with colleagues responsible for such outreach activity. Lectures are held and educational packs are produced to complement exhibitions. All three are keen to be part of collaborative initiatives and to participate in a wider interpretive network, an Aberdeen example being inclusion of the Marischal Museum in *Grampian's Treasures: Once Discovered Never Forgotten*, highlighting twelve of the area's top visitor attractions.

The Scottish Arts Council is the agency responsible for implementing public policy to support the full spectrum of arts. Its objectives are achieved through a combination of giving grants others and by pursuing joint initiatives. Although the Council does not identify interpretation as a distinct activity, it is implicit in several operational objectives. As an enabler, it encourages the production of interpretive publications designed to promote supported initiatives. Furthermore, it has funded research on interpretive exhibitions by the Centre for Contemporary Arts in Glasgow and the Fruitmarket gallery in Edinburgh, as well as a study investigating the use of CD-ROM for interpretation of the arts.

The Council also supports touring exhibitions and major events such as the Book Festival in Edinburgh, the St Magnus Festival in Orkney, and the National Gaelic Arts Project. In other words, it is a major player in raising cultural awareness at home, and in fostering a progressive image of Scotland abroad. In the field of strategic policy, it is active in cross-sectoral initiatives, such as the Tourism and the Arts Task Force, and it led the partnership which produced the 1994 *Charter for the Arts in Scotland*.

It would seem that the older the organisation is, the more difficult it is to break out of compartmentalised boxes based on conventional disciplines, such as curatorship, education and exhibition design. Indeed, each discipline is further subdivided into areas of expertise (see the author's contribution to the 1998 volume in this series). Although staff in each department still tend to be preoccupied with their individual specialism, some senior managers are now making serious efforts to introduce working practices which seek to harmonise the functions of technical interpretation, marketing and branding within a shared framework of equity audits. There are also encouraging signs that a collective policy is being developed to govern procedures for loans and exchange of artefacts among the institutions discussed in this section.

BUILT AND NATURAL ENVIRONMENT

Historic Scotland is the arm of government responsible for identifying and protecting ancient monuments and historic buildings, and for assisting owners with maintenance and repair. As well as managing the 330 properties in its care, it ensures that archaeological surveys and excavations are carried out at threatened sites. It is also concerned with raising standards of conservation practice, and has an obligation to present its properties to the public (see Chapter 15).

The presentation function means that the principles of interpretation are enshrined in its aims and objectives. Increased recognition of its importance arose from visitor surveys in 1986 which highlighted the need for more interpretation at individual sites. Since then, an interpretive board with artist's impression has been placed at all but a few sites. In 1998, an operational policy paper and technical manual for site interpretation were produced for the guidance of their own staff.

Alongside its current TV advertising campaign, other evidence of an interpretive approach is found in its many books and leaflets. Other interpretation related activities are education programmes, exhibitions, trails, demonstrations, re-enactments and the display of artefacts. The aim is to achieve a coherent set of thematic identities for individual properties within the framework of a national strategy. Collaboration with others is extensive, including contribution to and involvement in local interpretive planning, such as that at Kilmartin Glen in Argyll.[33]

The National Trust for Scotland is the largest voluntary conservation body in Scotland, with 228,000 members and over 100 properties in its care (see Chapter 16). Its corporate policy recognises the role of interpretation in the presentation of its properties, and it has been a major player in the development of interpretive methodology in Scotland, having been an active partner in various early initiatives in the 1970s.

Its education policy states that 'the Trust aims to provide relevant and informative interpretation at its properties, presented in ways which will enhance and enrich the experience of visitors'. Property management plans specify interpretive requirements, a diverse range of interpretive media are deployed, and each property is individually assessed and regularly reviewed when deciding on the most appropriate form of presentation.

Training programmes, both internal and jointly run with others, include interpretive skills, the training of countryside rangers and property guides being of prime importance due to the Trust's preference for person-to-person interpretation. Interpretation policy is also reflected in its publications, as well as across the board of activities such as shaping of corporate identity, marketing and fundraising.

The Royal Incorporation of Architects in Scotland is the professional body for 'chartered architects' in Scotland. Although its prime purpose is to promote the interests of the profession, it was included in the research because of its stated objective 'to foster the study of the national architecture of Scotland...' Indeed, it is the only professional body in Scotland to have made a significant contribution to heritage interpretation. Under Charles McKean's Secretaryship, it launched a series of illustrated architectural guides. The first was published in 1982, and 22 out of 34 planned volumes have been completed, along with several other books on heritage themes.[34,35,36,37]

The Incorporation also makes Scottish architecture, old and new, accessible to the general public through its programme of exhibitions. An example of this was their jubilee travelling exhibition, *For a Wee Country*, accompanied by McKean's essay, *Architectural Contributions to Scottish Society Since 1840*.[38] The interpretive approach to their exhibition strategy is based on themes governed by geography, period styles or the work of prominent architects. In terms of promoting awareness and marketing the virtues of Scotland's built environment, its annual conference conventions are also important. Held at different venues, these attract participation from overseas and are frequently organised in partnership with counterpart institutions in other countries.

Scottish Natural Heritage was established in 1992 when the Countryside Commission for Scotland and the Nature Conservancy Council for Scotland were combined into a single organisation. Its principal aims are to conserve and enhance the natural heritage of Scotland, to further its understanding, and to facilitate its enjoyment. Interpretation is a key element in securing these aims and considered to be an effective way of influencing attitudes and behaviour. Operationally, it is part the education function, and is seen as a vehicle for the dissemination of public environmental policy. Basic principles are set out in two key documents: *Learning to Live With Our Natural Heritage – SNH's Environmental Education Initiative*, and *Provoke, Relate, Reveal – SNH's Policy Framework for Interpretation*.

Integrated planning, whether at site or area wide level, is considered essential for the success of interpretive projects, and a staff guidance folder has been introduced. This is followed at its own sites, and application of its principles is a prerequisite where grant aid is provided to others. At a strategic level, it is active in the promotion and support of area-wide initiatives, and they are a leading partner in several inter-agency initiatives. It is also active in advisory and training provision, believing that training can significantly help improve the quality of visitor provision.

The Scottish Wildlife Trust is a voluntary organisation with a membership of 15,000 and over 50 local volunteer groups. Its mission is to protect wildlife, achieved through an extensive network of nature reserves and by working to raise awareness. Interpretation plays a key role in the management of reserves, receiving equal consideration to other functions, and in the maintenance of corporate presentational style.

In 1994, a policy paper was published, supported by two documents: *Guidelines for Producing Reserve Leaflets* and *Guidelines for Producing Reserve Interpretive Panels*. A third paper provided guidance on how the interpretation policy was to be applied at individual reserves: *A Strategic Overview of Interpretation on Scottish Wildlife Trust Reserves*.

The Trust's system for monitoring the effectiveness of interpretive provision is worthy of emulation by others, as is their stringent procedures for quality control. Interpretation policy forms part of its educational programmes, and both activities are seen as an integral part of a wider decision-making process, including marketing and promotion. A range of media types are utilised: from high profile visitor centres to self-guided trails, guide books, interpretive boards and on-site rangers.

Although there is extensive collaboration with agencies in the cultural sector by the above organisations, it was felt that an integrated national framework would be helpful to provide a context for individual equity audits. For those concerned with the natural environment, access to a national database would be valuable for regional correlation of wildlife habitats and visitor provision. This was considered important, as the location of many visitor centres makes access by public transport difficult, thus favouring the private car and undermining the principle of sustainability. However, it was felt that such arrangements would only work if made mandatory through collective agreement across the sectors.

The Bank of Scotland was founded by Act of Parliament in 1695, and moved to its present headquarters on The Mound in Edinburgh in 1806. In recognition of its long and distinguished history as a national institution, it has committed itself to creating an archive for its collection of historical records, as well as their interpretation and presentation to the public. The motive for this is to use the equity of the Bank's heritage assets for corporate branding to underpin its commercial activities.

The research revealed that there are three quite specific purposes for the archive department. First, to help differentiate the Bank from its competitors in an industry in which all offer virtually identical products and services. Second, to help build legitimate self-confidence in the Bank's staff as part of an organisation with a long track record of success. Third, to promote those activities which will support the Bank's public image, and to this end a museum was opened on The Mound in 1987 to provide a focus for a range of activities, including lectures and tours.

In addition to the museum, an educational programme has been developed which encourages school and other group visits to the museum, as well as a range of other activities supporting the core archival function, such as staging conferences. For example, it organised the European Association for Banking History Conference in 1995, and a commemorative book was published the same year, entitled *Bank of Scotland 1695–1995: A Very Singular Institution,* written by the Bank's Archivist, Alan Cameron.[39]

The Bank also makes a significant contribution to what might be called subliminal heritage interpretation. Like many other national banks, it promotes heritage awareness among the public by showing the portraits of national heroes on bank notes, as well as picturing other aspects of Scottish life. Compared to the number of people exposed to overt interpretation in museums, galleries and publications, the subliminal impact of every citizen handling bank notes with such images on a daily basis is bound to have a profound effect on heritage awareness and national pride.

The Royal Bank of Scotland was established in 1727 and moved its present HQ to Dundas House at St Andrew Square in Edinburgh in 1828. The archive department is housed there, with responsibility for interpretation of the Bank's historical collections associated with all operations in UK and beyond. A variety of interpretive methods are employed, and its educational programme is currently focused towards school groups who are able to visit the archives for a guided tour. The supply of information is a core activity for both external and internal enquiries., normally on the history of the Bank, and the department has developed a range of information sheets covering popular subjects.

An important feature is the production of small scale exhibitions on behalf of branches celebrating a particular anniversary. The department also maintains changing displays at the City of London office and a small museum at Child & Co in Bolton, which has a five year theme cycle. It also designs and produces interpretive literature, which is normally in the form of small leaflets on the history of particular banks or branches. Examples are *36 St Andrew Square: A Short History*, incorporating an Edinburgh map and guide, and *Short History of the Royal Bank of Scotland*, both available free of charge.

A database is maintained of branch and bank histories, with the capability of highlighting anniversaries in advance so as to allow sufficient time for production of exhibitions and publications. Interpretation is regarded as a supporting function to enhance prime company objectives, in line with the philosophy adopted by the Bank of Scotland, and it is part of Corporate Affairs alongside sponsorship and marketing.

United Distillers & Vintners is part of the Diageo Group, and is engaged in production, marketing and sales world-wide. As the name implies, a large number of private distillers and vintners have been brought together through acquisition under a united umbrella. Many of these were family concerns with long traditions and well established brand names, and one of the present company's greatest assets is its brand portfolio.

For the purpose of safe storage and ease of access to the large volume of historical documents and artefacts inherited from the original companies, the material has been assembled in a central archive. In a corporate sense, it functions like a museum or a gallery, although access is by appointment only. Its declared purpose is to be 'used as a marketing resource, for educational research, and as a source of inspiration for new brand development'. The following statement from the corporate brochure is indicative of the archive's content, and the company's approach to identifying brand equity:

> Many of the advertising and promotional activities of our past have become contemporary classics in their own right. The famous Johnnie Walker striding man, for example, in all his various guises, from porcelain to bronze, has become a collector's item the world over. And when animal-lover James Buchanan first used the black and white terrier dog in his advertising in the 1890s, he inadvertently created one of the world's most famous and enduring Scotch whisky trademarks.

The archive function is given high priority by senior management, and work directly concerned with interpretation includes undertaking audits of the archive collections, the giving of advice and supply of information. Requests for help are mainly associated with brand development, commemorative events, promotions, publications and exhibitions.

The company makes a major contribution to the tourism infrastructure in Scotland through visitor facilities at 16 distillery sites. These vary, but include retail facilities, interpretive exhibitions and guided tours of the production process. The main interpretive theme in each case is normally built around local features of the distilling industry and personalities from the founding families. There is a policy of working closely with local councils and voluntary groups. In addition to the guides used for conducted distillery tours, the company also has interpreters associated with the collection of brands. The designation used is 'Brand Ambassador', and the concept is of wider interest from the point of view of both heritage interpretation and the promotion of corporate identity:

> A network of roving Brand Ambassadors, chosen for their in-depth knowledge of our brands and their ability to communicate their enthusiasm to others, are used for presentations, promotions and ceremonial occasions all over the world. Each Ambassador's understanding has developed over many years, and they have a unique stock of personal insights and anecdotes to share with their audience. This approach has proved, time and time again, that as the mysteries of our brands are unravelled to a whole new audience of contemporary customers, there is nothing like the personal touch to bring the past alive.

An important form of collaboration across the sectors is through corporate sponsorship, a notable example of creative partnership being the Deskford Carnyx project. This visionary initiative in creative heritage interpretation, led by Dr John Purser, was concerned with making a replica of an ancient musical instrument.[40] Its production was funded by another distiller and a Glenfiddich Living Scotland Award, and its subsequent promotion and use was made possible with support from United Distillers & Vintners. Thanks to this partnership, we now have a major national treasure in the form of a playable carnyx, housed at the National Museums. Another example is the painting, known as *The Monarch of the Glen* by Sir Edwin Landseer, which has been lent by the company to hang in the Scotland and the World Gallery of the Museum of Scotland.

Although the company does not run a regular programme specifically for monitoring customer response to interpretive provision at visitor facilities, their strategic marketing is informed by a wider programme of market research. The corporate ethos on this front is 'listening and learning', where the voice of the customer takes precedent over marketing theory and perceptions of staff.

The principal lesson to be drawn by those working in other sectors is how a major commercial company has shaped its corporate image and developed competitive edge by maximising the heritage of its products. A second lesson is that interpretation must be robustly articulated at the heart of decision making if the full potential of corporate heritage assets is to be realised. The third lesson is the capacity for surfeited action by staff when corporate strategy provides a framework for seamless integration of internal operations and collaborative ventures in partnership with others.

CONCLUSIONS

The study findings confirmed that making heritage assets accessible through interpretation, whether it be for education or wealth creation, has now become an activity of central concern to many organisations across all sectors. However, organisations differ a great deal on how they define the activity, where they place it in line management structures, and the priority given to it in the process of corporate policy formulation.

A sharp contrast in approach exists between environmental organisations and museums and galleries. The latter tend to have an introverted focus on their collections, the former work within a broader context embracing both built and natural resources. In terms of the process defined at the beginning of this chapter, it seems to be common practice to select themes without first undertaking a substantive equity audit, and market analysis is often rather cursory. These factors combine to produce poor strategic vision and a tenuous relationship between provider and customer.

It was also found that assessment of visitor opinion to inform marketing strategies is mostly of an ad hoc nature, and the research indicated that there is an urgent need for attitudinal change amongst both enablers and providers. Many at the centre of interpretive work follow a supply dominated philosophy, still listening to their own voice rather than asking the question: 'who are our visitors and what is their motivation for coming?' A proper balance between supply and demand can only be achieved through more focused research on the voice of the visitor, and a collaborative programme of visitor surveys should be a top priority.

Interpretation has in some quarters assumed the status of a separate professional discipline, especially in some environmental agencies, and in the public sector it is most frequently associated with educational programmes and the planning of exhibition displays. This has tended to marginalise the activity and assign it to a subservient position in policy making. The seamless integration of equity audits and marketing as practised by the private sector should be adopted by public agencies to establish the necessary synergy.

Some of the voluntary organisations and the universities have already achieved a remarkable degree of success in this regard by integrating related activities. They have given heritage interpretation a firm footing within a unified process of corporate planning, where it is fully integrated with resource management, educational programmes, corporate identity and marketing. The same can be said for the custodians of records and literature which provide an often undervalued service to others and they have at times also given leadership in partnership ventures, such as the Burns and Stevenson touring exhibitions. More attention should be given to benchmarking of best practice as a means of improving quality and competitiveness.

The study identified 'subliminal access' as an important area for further work. This stands in contrast to the overt mode of providing access through interpretation as practised in museums and galleries. The idea emerged from studying the commercial sector, especially the practice of the banks which engender public heritage awareness by showing pictures of national heroes and cultural assets on bank notes. Compared to the number of people exposed to overt interpretation, the subliminal impact of every citizen handling bank notes with such images on a daily basis is certain to have a profound effect on heritage awareness and national pride. The same principle applies to commemorative stamps and the subject is an obvious candidate for future research.

Inter-agency collaboration on public access to heritage assets is at present mainly confined to exchange of promotional literature. More needs to be done, and the impact of mainline programmes of interpretation by the cultural agencies would be greatly enhanced by products being developed in institutional unison so that there is strategic coherence in what can be seen in museums, galleries and libraries at any one time. There is also an evident need to develop and promote a better understanding of the relationship between conservation of heritage assets and the use of such assets to generate income and employment, and the focus of new research should be on the reciprocity of culture and enterprise.

Institutional fragmentation and reductionism within the cultural sector represent one of the major issues identified by the research. Partnership initiatives are mostly pursued on an ad hoc basis, and individual agencies are at present developing their programmes in a strategic vacuum. It is suggested that a standing partnership mechanism be established to facilitate development of a comprehensive set of cultural profiles based on shared equity which together would represent the essence of national iconography. This would provide a broadly based equity as the shared context for a variety of branding purposes.

The Museum of Scotland stands out as an obvious focus for such an exercise, aiming as it does to construct and make accessible to the public a comprehensive story of the nation's material culture. It serves as a model in this context, representing the nearest Scotland has come to convey a holistic image of herself. A set of national profiles constructed on such a foundation would in turn provide the framework within which regional and local heritage profiles are formulated for the purpose of interpretive planning.

The organisations which have adopted internal guidelines for interpretive planning expressed a positive attitude to collaborative partnerships, and there appeared to be broad support for a cross-sectoral initiative to establish common ground for definitions, procedures and quality assurance. Most importantly, clarification is needed on the rules of engagement for area-wide projects, such as initiatives to identify the equity of tourism gateway destinations.

The concluding proposal is to recommend that a standing committee be established in the form of a 'heritage forum' with broad representation across the sectors. It is essential that the Enterprise Network and Scotland the Brand participate, and it would be desirable to have input from the commercial sector, such as from one of the banks or a company like United Distiller & Vintners. The forum should be initiated by The Scottish Executive and chaired by the appropriate Minister. The proposal is made in response to the Executive's recent consultation document, *Celebrating Scotland: A National Cultural Strategy*. For this strategic initiative to be effective, it has to go beyond being concerned solely with 'cultural enterprise'. It should also embrace the 'culture of enterprise'. A creative synergy between those two was the hallmark of the Enlightenment in the 18th century, and the strategy planned by the Executive represents an opportunity to recapture this spirit in a New Enlightenment of the 21st century. If done well, it will reaffirm the equity on which both the substance and the image of our nation is built.

The Author and Acknowledgments

Professor Magnus Fladmark started the Aberdeen heritage programme in 1992, embracing a new MSc focusing on the reciprocity of culture and enterprise. After studying horticulture, architecture and town planning, he worked in The Scottish Office and then led an ODA programme at Edinburgh University. While Assistant Director of the Countryside Commission for Scotland, he also served as Chairman of the RTPI in Scotland and established the Sir Patrick Geddes Saltire Planning Award. A prolific author and contributor to many government policy documents, his advice is widely sought both at home and abroad, and his MSc is now taught in Russia and he is helping to establish The Heyerdahl Institute in Norway. He was recently made an Honorary Fellow by the RIAS for service to Scottish heritage affairs.

The author is grateful to Professors Eric Spiller and Seaton Baxter and Dr Alan Marchbank at the National Library of Scotland for helping to secure the necessary research funding, and to Stephen Emerson who undertook part of the field work. He is much indebted to Dr David Silbergh for assistance throughout the research and for helpful guidance with the above text, and thanks go to Ian Douglas and Rodney Strachan for constructive editorial input.

References

1. Tilden, F., *Interpreting our Heritage*, The University of North Carolina Press, 1957.
2. Fladmark, J.M., 'Discovering the Personality of a Region: Strategic Interpretation in Scotland', in Fladmark J.M. (ed), *Heritage: Conservation, Interpretation and Enterprise*, Donhead, 1993.
3. Aldridge, D., *Principles of Countryside Interpretation and Interpretive Planning*, HMSO, 1975.
4. Noble, R.R., *Country Heritage: An Interpretive Plan for Biggar and District*, Biggar Museum Trust, 1976.
5. Harrison, R. (ed), *Manual of Heritage Management*, Butterworth Cambridge University Press, 1993.
6. Aldridge, D., *Site Interpretation: A Practical Guide*, Scottish Tourist Board, 1993.
7. Ham, S.H., *Environmental Interpretation: a practical guide for people with big ideas and small budgets*, North American Press, 1992.
8. Veverka, J., *Interpretive Master Planning*, Fakcon Press, 1994.
9. Carter, J. (ed), *A Sense of Place: An Interpretive Planning Handbook*, Tourism & Environment Initiative, 1997.
10. Historic Scotland, *Operational Policy Paper No 6: Site Interpretation at Properties in Care,* 1998.
11. Historic Scotland, *A Manual for Site Interpretation at Properties in Care,* 1998.
12. Thompson, J. M.A. (ed), *Manual of Curatorship*, Butterworth Heinemann & Museums Association, 1992.
13. Scottish Tourism Research Unit, *Newhorisons: international benchmarking and best practice for visitor attractions*, Scottish Enterprise, 1998.
14. McKiernan, P., *Scenarios for Scotland*, University of St Andrews, 1999.

15. Glen, H.G., 'Interpreting St Andrews', in Fladmark, J.M. (ed), *Cultural Tourism*, Donhead, 1994, pp. 260–273.
16. Aldridge, D., *Dundee's Heritage: A Strategy for Interpretation*, Scottish Development Agency (The Dundee Project), 1984.
17. Evans, B., 'Celebration of Enterprise: Expos and Garden Festivals', in Fladmark, J.M. (ed), *Cultural Tourism*, Donhead, 1994, pp. 45–66.
18. Kotler, P. et al, *Marketing Places: Attracting Investment, Industry and Tourism to Cities, States and Nations*, The Free Press, 1993.
19. British Tourist Authority, *Branding Britain*, BTA, 1997.
20. Fraser, M. (ed), *Essential Scotland: 70 perspectives on the New Scotland from leaders in their fields*, Agenda Publishing & Scotland the Brand, 1998.
21. Scott, P.H. (ed), *Scotland: A Concise Cultural History*, Mainstream, 1993.
22. Jarvie, G. & Walker, G. (eds), *Scottish Sport in the Making of the Nation: Ninety Minute Patriots?*, Leicester University Press, 1994.
23. Keay, J. & Keay, J. (eds), *Encyclopaedia of Scotland*, Harper Collins, 1994.
24. McCrone, D. et al, *Scotland – the Brand: The Making of Scottish Heritage*, Edinburgh University Press, 1995.
25. Ferguson, W., *The Identity of the Scottish Nation: An Historic Quest*, Edinburgh University Press, 1998.
26. Devine, T.M., *The Scottish Nation 1700–2000*, Penguin, 1999.
27. Scottish Executive, *Celebrating Scotland: A National Cultural Strategy*, Scottish Executive, 1999.
28. Adams, G., 'The Pull of Cultural Assets', in Fladmark, J.M. (ed), *Cultural Tourism*, Donhead, 1994.
29. Adams, G., 'Access to a Nation's Assets: Challenges for Scottish Tourism Policy', in Fladmark, J.M. (ed), *Sharing the Earth: Local Identity in Global Culture*, Donhead, 1995.
30. Carter, J. (ed), *A Sense of Place: An Interpretive Planning Handbook*, Tourism & Environment Initiative, 1997.
31. Silbergh, D. et al, 'A Strategy for Theme Trails', in Fladmark, J.M. (ed), *Cultural Tourism*, Donhead, 1994, pp. 123–146.
32. British Tourist Authority, *Branding Britain*, BTA, 1997.
33. Macinnes, L., 'Towards a Common Language: The Unifying Perceptions of an Integrated Approach', in Fladmark J.M. (ed), *Heritage: Conservation, Interpretation and Enterprise*, Donhead, 1993, pp. 101–111.
34. Sinclair, F., *Scotstyle: 150 Years of Scottish Architecture*, RIAS, 1984.
35. McKean, C., *The Scottish Thirties*, RIAS, 1987.
36. Campbell, S. (ed), *Scottish Architecture in the Nineteen Eighties*, RIAS, 1990.
37. Howard, D. (ed), *The Architecture of the Scottish Renaissance*, RIAS, 1990.
38. McKean, C., *Architectural Contributions to Scottish Society since 1840*, RIAS, 1990.
39. Cameron, A., *Bank of Scotland 1695–1995: A Very Singular Institution*, Mainstream, 1995.

40. Purser, J., 'Homecoming of the Deskford Carnyx: After 2000 Years of Silence', in Fladmark, J.M. (ed), *Cultural Tourism*, Donhead, 1994, pp. 375–384.

Further Reading

Aldridge, D., *Discovery Centre: Outline Interpretive Prospectus*, The Dundee Project, 1987.

Banks, I., 'Archaeology, Nationalism and Ethnicity', in Atkinson, J.A. et al (eds), *Nationalism and Archaeology*, Cruithne Press, 1996.

Chernatony, L de & McDonald, M.H.B, *Creating Powerful Brands: The strategic route to success in consumer, industrial and service markets*, Butterworth Heinemann, 1994.

Fladmark, J.M., *The Wealth of a Nation: Heritage as a Cultural and Competitive Asset*, The Robert Gordon University, 1994

Fladmark, J.M., 'Cultural Capital and Identity: Scotland's Democratic Intellect', in Fladmark, J.M. (ed), *In Search of Heritage as Pilgrim or Tourist?*, Donhead, 1998.

Gold, J.R. & Gold, M.M., *Imaging Scotland: Tradition, Representation and Promotion in Scottish Tourism since 1750*, Scolar Press, 1995.

Interbrand, *Brands: An International Review*, Mercury Business Books & Golden Arrow Publications, 1990.

Seaton, A.V. & Hay, B., 'The Marketing of Scotland as a Tourist Destination 1985–1996', in MacLellan, R. & Smith, R. (eds), *Tourism in Scotland*, International Thomson Business Press, 1998.

Uzzell, D., *Heritage Interpretation: The Natural and Built Environment* (Vol 1), *The Visitor Experience* (Vol 2), Belhaven Press, 1992.

THE RESOURCE BASE

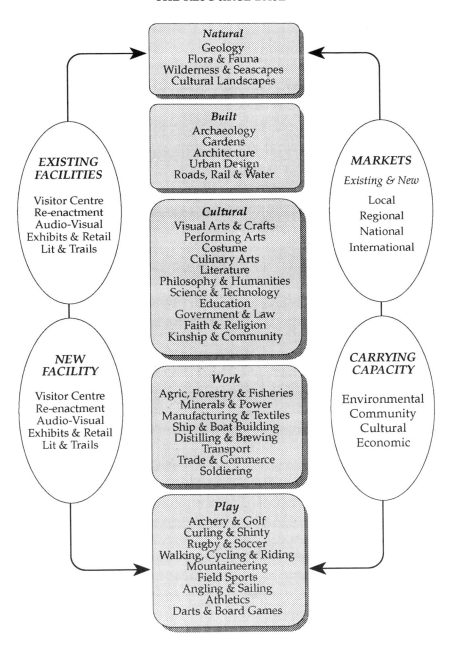

Natural
Geology
Flora & Fauna
Wilderness & Seascapes
Cultural Landscapes

Built
Archaeology
Gardens
Architecture
Urban Design
Roads, Rail & Water

Cultural
Visual Arts & Crafts
Performing Arts
Costume
Culinary Arts
Literature
Philosophy & Humanities
Science & Technology
Education
Government & Law
Faith & Religion
Kinship & Community

Work
Agric, Forestry & Fisheries
Minerals & Power
Manufacturing & Textiles
Ship & Boat Building
Distilling & Brewing
Transport
Trade & Commerce
Soldiering

Play
Archery & Golf
Curling & Shinty
Rugby & Soccer
Walking, Cycling & Riding
Mountaineering
Field Sports
Angling & Sailing
Athletics
Darts & Board Games

EXISTING FACILITIES
Visitor Centre
Re-enactment
Audio-Visual
Exhibits & Retail
Lit & Trails

NEW FACILITY
Visitor Centre
Re-enactment
Audio-Visual
Exhibits & Retail
Lit & Trails

MARKETS
Existing & New
Local
Regional
National
International

CARRYING CAPACITY
Environmental
Community
Cultural
Economic

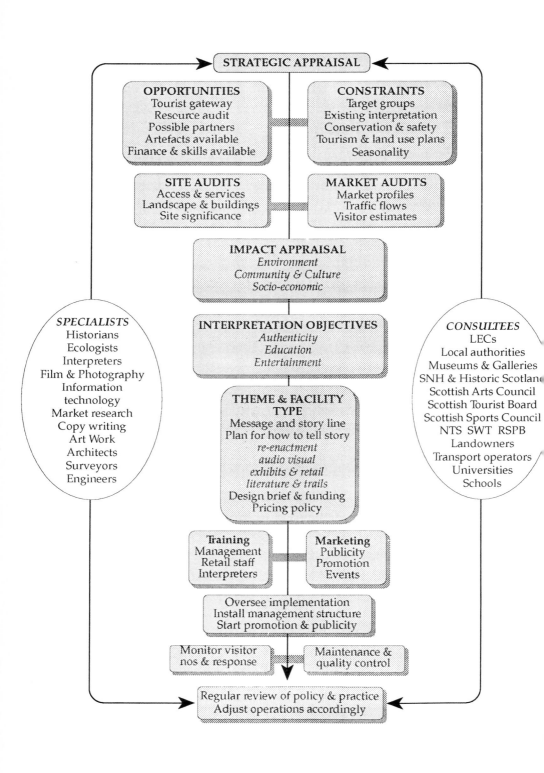

STRATEGIC APPRAISAL

OPPORTUNITIES
Tourist gateway
Resource audit
Possible partners
Artefacts available
Finance & skills available

CONSTRAINTS
Target groups
Existing interpretation
Conservation & safety
Tourism & land use plans
Seasonality

SITE AUDITS
Access & services
Landscape & buildings
Site significance

MARKET AUDITS
Market profiles
Traffic flows
Visitor estimates

IMPACT APPRAISAL
Environment
Community & Culture
Socio-economic

INTERPRETATION OBJECTIVES
Authenticity
Education
Entertainment

SPECIALISTS
Historians
Ecologists
Interpreters
Film & Photography
Information
technology
Market research
Copy writing
Art Work
Architects
Surveyors
Engineers

**THEME & FACILITY
TYPE**
Message and story line
Plan for how to tell story
re-enactment
audio visual
exhibits & retail
literature & trails
Design brief & funding
Pricing policy

CONSULTEES
LECs
Local authorities
Museums & Galleries
SNH & Historic Scotland
Scottish Arts Council
Scottish Tourist Board
Scottish Sports Council
NTS SWT RSPB
Landowners
Transport operators
Universities
Schools

Training
Management
Retail staff
Interpreters

Marketing
Publicity
Promotion
Events

Oversee implementation
Install management structure
Start promotion & publicity

Monitor visitor
nos & response

Maintenance &
quality control

Regular review of policy & practice
Adjust operations accordingly

21

ANCESTRAL VOICES
Makars of Music and Identity

John Purser

Now and again an artist is asked to do something vaguely practical, and when Richard Murphy architects, via John Creed, asked me to write a text for a new block of flats in the Canongate on Edinburgh's High Street, I was naturally excited by the challenge. Of the many great streets in European cities, Edinburgh's High Street is one of the finest, and even in its rare moments of quiet is filled with the voices of our ancestors.

John Creed has made the replicas of two carnyxes, one Trompa Creda and two early Christian bells, so he and I are becoming a bit ancestral ourselves, but hitherto it has been myself who has been the proposer, John the maker. This time we were both to be makers, John hand-forging my text in steel letters mounted on an exposed steel beam above the shop-front on the ground floor, but going round the corner into the close that leads to the new Scottish Poetry Library. The text reads: 'a nation is forged in the hearth of poetry'. The 'of poetry' bit is round the corner in the close, so that the poets are duly honoured. However, the main part of the text makes sense on its own because, if you are walking up (rather than down) the street, you will not see that bit unless you turn and look back. John has dropped the position of the final 'h' in hearth so one can also read the word 'heart'.

What has this got to do with 'Heritage and Museums: Shaping National Identity'? A great deal: for Heritage, read Poetry; for Museums, read the High Street of Edinburgh; and for National Identity, read Scotland. Shaping and Forging belong together, and the image is that of the hearth.

The basic image of forging something in a hearth is appropriate to the material, steel, which is itself forged in a hearth; and to the fact that the architect had made a point of exposing it. The concept of a hearth, however, refers fundamentally to the concept of a home, and in declaring on the facade of the building that a nation is forged in the hearth, the vital role in society of the individual citizen and, in particular, householder is duly honoured. Whoever rents or purchases a flat in the property has a fundamental connection with that which is written upon it. In fact there are no hearths in these new flats: but the image will never leave us, remaining almost as potent today as in the hearths and homes at Skara Brae from 5000 years ago with a little bone flute and bone whistle buried nearby.

Those ancient buildings can not be called Scottish, but they are a part of Scotland now and a part of our national identity. Nationhood is fundamentally relevant to the site and time of the new building: in the year in which the Scottish Parliament reopened and close to the site of the new parliament buildings.

The short section 'of poetry', can not be read in isolation, but this somewhat cryptic aspect of it has a certain poetic value. To discover its relevance, the poets must go out into the street and take their part in the world at large, and yet the statement they encounter in that world is that their worth is related to the interior source of society: the hearth and home. But for those in the street who are content with what they read on the facade, there remains the potential of surprise should they discover that what they thought was a complete sentence is not necessarily so. The hearth alone may suffice, but if poetry is honoured in the household, then a society, a nation, has truly enduring strength.

The Scots word for a poet is 'makkar' – a person who makes things, and the concept of the nation as a poem or song was the subject of the last statement of the last speaker of the last Scottish Parliament in 1707. As he descended from his chair, he said 'Thus endeth an auld sang'. The text therefore carries within it an echo of our national and parliamentary past, and honours those who have sustained their validity through the intervening centuries. So the text is intended both as an individual and a national homecoming.

But in forging our identity we must distinguish between the true art of the smith and the cheating art of the forger, and it is here that the dangers lie for museums and for archaeo-musicologists such as myself. The dangers are legion enough within the historical period; but with pre-history we are dealing with material evidence only. The voices we add, the explanatory texts, the attitudes we assume on our own and on our ancestors' behalfs, are not ancestral but modern. What is more, the nation of Scotland cannot be said to have had any existence as such until early mediaeval times. How then can I hope to refer to 'ancestral voices' with any degree of authenticity?

The ancestral side is not so difficult. No doubt our gene pool is much enriched by the comings and goings of genes: but that much of the blood of our ancestors was pulsing on this part of the world's geography thousands of years ago is highly likely; and that the environment (notwithstanding changes in climate and culture) has acted upon our genetic inheritance in ways peculiar to this part of the world is a reasonable assumption. But when we come to the sounds our ancestors made, what more can we do except stick to the Darwinian basics and cry like a baby or scream with terror or laugh with joy?

The answer lies in the fact that we do have original material evidence capable of making sound: material evidence that has its own voice.[1] In previous papers I have outlined the approach to discovering what two of those voices could, indeed must have sounded like: the carnyx[2] and the triple pipes.[3] Wonderful work has been done in Ireland by Simon O'Dwyer in collaboration with the National Museum of Ireland, establishing the sound world of the bronze age horns and crotals and, recently, in the reconstruction of the 2,000-year-old Loughnashade Trumpet, the Trompa Creda which comes from one of the most important sites in the history of the Celtic-speaking peoples – Emain Macha near Armagh in Northern Ireland.

Since then we have reconstructed bone whistles from Skara Brae and have played an original two metre long bronze trumpet in the National Museum in Dublin, some 2,000 years old and still in perfect condition. We are in the process of reconstructing the short trumpets which appear on Pictish stones and, famously, in the 8th century Hiberno-Saxon Canterbury Psalter; and we are also reconstructing a two metre long reed instrument made of willow, found several feet down in a peat bog in Ireland, yet to be carbon-dated but certainly BC.

All these reconstructions bring together an increasing body of evidence from parts of the world which have had, and continue to have, close cultural ties. For instance, bronze smiths trained in an Irish style were working in Orkney and at Jarlshof in Shetland around 800 BC, which is towards the close of the period of the bronze age horns. Quite literally, our identity was already being forged in the hearth nearly 3,000 years ago, and that identity points to a particularly close relationship with Ireland.

More recently, the Irish Trompa Creda and the Carnyx found in Scotland are near contemporaries from the late iron age. They have many similarities in their manufacture and come from cultures which we know to have been in contact with each other. The same applies to the triple pipes. We can therefore legitimately bring together a lot of this evidence and what we discover is a world of musical instruments rich in variety and whose enormous musical potential we are only now beginning to realise.

One of the ways in which we continue to explore this potential is by relating the instruments to structures where they might have been used. Naturally, matching the structure and the instruments in terms of their dating is a matter for debate, but the length of time over which structures, such as the megalithic tomb of Maes Howe, were potentially in use is now much more generous than was hitherto accepted. Viking inscriptions on the tomb walls declare that 'it is long ago that a great treasure lay hidden here', and by treasure they meant metals unknown to the builders of Maes Howe. Were they referring to earlier Viking burials, or had the tomb been in use for ritual purposes in the bronze and iron ages, and for access to the bones of our ancestors?

The last burial within a structure does not mean that its significance as such is ended. In most of our cathedrals, burials have come to an end through lack of space; but we still visit them partly because they are burial chambers for important saints or poets or aristocrats, many of them dead for at least 1000 years. Evidence in support of such a continuity of significance from the neolithic into the iron age has emerged at Howe,[4] and of course the stone circles have been available to all for millenia.

This continuity is more than something we sense in our wishful thinking. It is tangible, observable, and demonstrable. In my contribution to the 1998 volume in this series of books, I explored the relationship of the Scots origin myth to musical expressions of a longing to be reunited with the music of the spheres, the heavenly harmony, the voices of the Cherubim. One of those expressions (the Hamilton Mausoleum) was fantastical: another (Clerk's cantata relating to the Darien Scheme) was rooted in an extraordinary combination of commercial instinct and missionary vision. In all of them a deep sense of the enduring mystery of human existence and of spiritual longing is present.

But it is not exclusively a Christian longing. To the composers of all the music I referred to, and to the builders of the structures with which the music can be associated, the relics of older religions were there to be seen and commented upon. The Duke of Hamilton's Mausoleum harked back to the Nile: a Roman temple dismantled by a neighbour was rebuilt by Clerk in his own grounds: and the great cathedrals of St Andrews and Glasgow were aligned with the rising sun just as were the temples of prehistory aligned with a variety of heavenly bodies. These were, of course, internationally accepted conventions, but in Scotland we had and have a peculiarly rich heritage of megalithic structures – rich enough to be commented upon even by Diodorus Siculus in the 1st century BC. In 1995, Aubrey Burl writes of Diodorus' observations as follows:[5]

> Mentioning a 'spherical temple', thought to be his vague idea of a stone circle, he wrote that in it '(The Moon) dances continuously

the night through from the vernal equinox until the rising of the Pleiades...'. This temple has often been interpreted as Stonehenge but that is an astronomical impossibility. The Wiltshire ring is 500 miles too far south of the correct lunar latitude.

If the 'spherical temple' was not Callanish it is a remarkable coincidence that it was only the moon, the equinox and the Pleiades that Diodorus mentioned. Callanish seems associated with all of them. The avenue was directed towards the southern moonset: the western row was oriented on the equinoctial sunset. Although other stars are feasible targets the eastern row could have been aligned on the Pleiades around 1550 BC, the third of the heavenly bodies named by Diodorus.

Callanish, Maes Howe, the Stones of Stenness: these are places which are part of our spiritual repertoire. They may lie dormant and unattended for centuries, but they are there and, when we are ready for them, they take on a new significance as we once more explore their meanings.

Places, whether natural or man-made have their own voices too, and I touched briefly on this in *In Search of Heritage*.[6] Since then, under the auspices of Sabhal Mor Ostaig (the Gaelic College on Skye) and SCRAN (Scottish Cultural Resources Access Network), a group of us travelled to record instruments and voices in Maes Howe, Skara Brae, at the Stones of Stenness, the Ring of Brodgar, and the Dwarfie Stane in Orkney, and at Clickhimmin in Shetland (weather prevented a visit to Mousa Broch).

What these recordings revealed was that the potential of the instruments was often enhanced by the acoustic of the structure, and in this we found ourselves endorsing the ground-breaking work of Aaron Watson and David Keating.[7] Maes Howe, though by nature a dry acoustic, being an enclosed and relatively small chamber, enormously enhanced the natural harmonics, both of the human voice and of the bronze age horns.

The Stones of Stenness, though now only a fraction of the original structure, quite clearly reflected and transformed any sound directed straight at them, especially from any loud instrument such as a horn or trumpet played from the opposite side of the circle. There is no doubt whatever that the complete circle must have created a very noticeable and potentially exciting acoustic environment. The huge flat surfaces of the stones reflect the sound back across the circle, and the gaps between allow for sound to pass through, though with less power, to reach at least as far as the exterior encircling dyke, which might have acted as a position for an audience or other participants in whatever rituals took place. These effects would be noticeable even with the human voice alone, or with stones, drums or bone flutes and whistles, all available at the time of construction, at which period they may very well have been using wooden or natural horn trumpets. Moreover the chevron shaped stone is itself a ringing rock, though not as clearly so as the great recumbent stone at Arn Hill in Aberdeenshire.

With respect to the speculation that wooden or natural horn instruments might have been available during the neolithic period, we are of course dealing with inference only. To our knowledge no such artefacts have survived from the neolithic in Scotland and Ireland; but whether this is because they did not use them, or because wood and horn are less likely to survive, we do not know. It is certainly hard to imagine that the bronze age horns, shaped as they are like animal horns, were not derived from earlier types using pre-metal age materials.

This is research in its earliest stages. The effect of some of these instruments in the great stone forts in Ireland, such as the Grianan of Aileach, has yet to be gauged, and there are many more chambered tombs and stone circles and henges to be investigated in Scotland. Ultimately, the value in modern cultural terms of all this research is not so much in the words that are written as in the sounds and sights that are brought into being by the conjunction of the instruments themselves and the sites with which they may reasonably be connected, and these I cannot reproduce in a paper as I have done in my lecture.

The thrill of seeing and hearing an instrument in an appropriate environment is no forgery: it is a real and powerful experience. Of course we can never truly reproduce the voices of our ancestors, any more than we could do so for any dead forebear until recording techniques were developed. But we can at least make a reasonable and reasoned attempt to evoke something of the sound world that was available to them. When, with our own living breath, we set in vibration an instrument we know was used three thousand years ago (and we can check some of our reconstructions against the sounds of playable originals) then surely we can believe that we we are indeed hearing the sound if not the speech of the ancestral voices of those instruments.

In such reconstructions, the makkar is still at work, and for me, and for those with whom I am privileged to work – in particular John Kenny, master of the carnyx and Simon O'Dwyer, master of the bronze age horns – the hearth of John Creed, the master smith, is a hearth of enduring poetry.

The Author

Dr John Purser is a graduate of Glasgow University and the Royal Scottish Academy of Music and Drama. A great polymath of Renaissance stature, his distinguished career has embraced work as a composer, musician, poet, dramatist, broadcaster, writer and university lecturer. He is known for his energetic campaigning for Scottish culture, which has included a major BBC Radio Scotland programme on the history of Scottish music, and he wrote the seminal work *Scotland's Music* (Mainstream, 1991). He has been at the forefront of work to recreate several ancient musical instruments based on archaeological evidence, as well as initiatives to restore their use in musical performance.

References

1. Purser, J., 'The Timeless Heritage of Music', in Fladmark, J.M. (ed), *Heritage: Conservation, Interpretation and Enterprise*, Donhead, 1993, pp. 301–310.
2. Purser, J., 'Homecoming of the Deskford Carnyx after 2000 Years of Silence', in Fladmark, J.M. (ed), *Cultural Tourism*, Donhead, 1994, pp. 375–384.
3. Purser, J., 'On the Trail of Music: Origins of the Scottish Triple Pipes', in Fladmark, J.M. (ed), *Sharing the Earth:: Local Identity in Global Culture*, Donhead, 1995, pp. 149–162.
4 .MacKee, E.W., 'Continuity Over Three Thousand Years of Northern Prehistory: The 'Tel' at Howe, Orkney', in *The Antiquaries Journal*, Vol 78, 1998.
5. Burl, A., *A Guide to the Stone Circles of Britain, Ireland and Brittany*, Yale University Press, 1995, p. 150.
6. Purser, J., 'Voices of the Cherubim: a Musical Odyssey to Scotland', in Fladmark, J.M. (ed), *In Search of Heritage as Pilgrim or Tourist?*, Donhead, 1998, pp. 55–75.
7. Watson, A. and Keating, D., 'Architecture and sound: an acoustic analysis of megalithic monuments in prehistoric Britain', in *Antiquity*, Vol 73, No 280, June 1999, pp. 325–336.

Playing the Carnyx at the Ring of Brodgar in Orkney.

INTERNATIONAL EXCHANGE

Learning from Others

22

NATIONALISM AND MUSEOLOGY
Reflections on Swedish Experience

Stefan Bohman

With a few exceptions, national identity in Sweden has been automatically linked to the joint polity and territory of the nation. It is true that Swedes who live close to the borders with Norway, Finland and Denmark may feel some affinity with their neighbours across the border. In regional terms, you are most certainly likely to feel like a 'jamte' in the region of 'Jamtland', but the vast majority of Swedes who live in the southern parts of the country do not question the fact that they are Swedish, and they have no desire for their region to become an independent State.

Despite the fact that it is a long time since the Swedish people had to struggle for independence and nationhood, the question of national identity has been an important matter from the beginning of the 19th century to the present day. Many groups in society considered it important to strengthen the feeling of Swedish nationalism. In particular, both the nobility and the bourgeoisie endeavoured to define the significance of being Swedish in such a way that it made good sense to all Swedes.

A manifestation of this sentiment was found in the philosophy of Artur Hazelius and the establishment of the Nordic Museum. He emphasised the history of our kings, the great artists, and above all, the peasant culture, which served as a model for a desirable Swedish national identity, in contrast to what was perceived as the treadmill of urban industries. It was by no means a coincidence that Viktor Rydberg and his criticism of industrialisation became popular even within the labour movement. There was general agreement that Swedes should gain knowledge about themselves primarily through the pure and unsophisticated nature of the rural communities. In consequence, the cultural heritage to be collected and displayed would consist of various items related to the simple life of the countryside.

According to Hazelius, these collections should be interpreted in such a way that everyone would understand how significant this cultural heritage was to the nation. He intended that the building designed for the National Museum should 'imbue the people with a strong and mighty sentiment and thus act in the direction of patriotic arousal', a notion which the establishment understood and endorsed. Baron O. Hermelin wrote: 'the treasures we hide in these halls should in many ways give us strong revivals. First and last the revival of patriotism.'

The nationalistic purpose of museum activities was further strengthened in 1893, when Hazelius instituted the Swedish National Day, to be celebrated at Skansen. However, there were those who criticised the focus on nationalism and the thematic emphasis on peasant culture. August Strindberg, who earlier had been very positive towards the Nordic Museum and Skansen, made one of his literary characters assert the following in 1904:

> You do know that all nations die, from education, from pampering, from prevention of cruelty to animals and from ethnographic museums. Those who now turn back to look at their excrement will face death. That's what the nation is facing when it looks back on the battles of Lutzen and Narva, on Gustavus III and The Swedish Academy, on bell towers and ramshackle cottages filled with lice and peasant drinking vessels. They just turn around, point to their excrement and say: look, this is what we have done! Well, if they don't get theirs done soon, we'll never get the chance to do ours!

Strindberg raised questions that are still crucial to museum activities today. Which aspects of our cultural heritage should be selected and preserved? Whose history is emphasised in order to be defined as our collective national history? How is it displayed, and for whom? The labour movement and the bourgeoisie who financed Hazelius had different answers to these questions, which reflected divergent views on how to strengthen Swedish nationalism.

THE NATION AS A CONSTRUCTION

Raymond Williams made the point that the importance of the concept of the nation state and nationalism increased in Europe during the 19th century. According to him, a sense of national belonging derived from something other than the 'political nation', or the state. The Swedish ethnologist, Orvar Lofgren, has written about the development of Swedish nationalism during the 19th century. Both Lofgren and Williams stress that the 'nation' is something that is created. Although, for those who promote nationalism, the nation is generally seen as something existing in an objective sense, which you have to understand and accept. For nationalists, the nation, with all its distinctive peculiarities, is something that has existed since the very beginning of time and is recognised by those who are sufficiently wise and culturally sensitive.

The underlying issue here is the question of what factors contribute to the manifestation of nationhood. There are many to choose from, and different groups have used different combinations in nation building. Williams writes that during the 19th century, language and racial affiliation were common reasons for the feeling of belonging to a certain nation. Other factors governing the construction of nations are a shared religion, common customs, a unique landscape, a shared history and a shared mentality.

In this context, it is interesting to refer to the United States where neither language, history, custom nor religion were regarded as suitable foundations for the construction of the nation and its national identity. Instead, the US constitution became the focal point of North America's national identity, which was enough to maintain a strong sense of nationalism. Jurgen Habermas has suggested that such a constitutionally based nationalism could be created within the European Union.

Thus it can be argued that a nation is defined by that which people choose to regard as their concept of a nation. From the beginning of the 19th century onwards, people, often unconsciously, agreed on certain constituent parts that manifested their own nationhood. In Sweden, it was decided that the nation was characterised by a special kind of mentality that was based, among other things, on its history and unique landscape.

Although seldom consciously decided, these agreements can become universal truths. For example, it was generally believed that the Swedes have always, or for a long period of time, possessed certain qualities that make them unique. The quest for the Swedish mentality and Swedish history is still ongoing. In 1993, an exhibition with the title 'The Swedish History' was held by the Nordic Museum in Stockholm. Accordingly, this form of objectification of nations and national characteristics is still a central part of the nationalism that began to develop during the 19th century.

According to Ehn and Frykman, Swedish everyday life and cultural patterns will be produced as long as a Swedish society exists. The fact that the State exists implies that national characteristics and national peculiarities are produced. The very assertion that national peculiarities exist is in itself a self-fulfilling prediction. Certain peculiarities and habits are established simply because people live up to the assertion. Then, when this has become a reality, Swedish mentality and culture truly exist.

An essential element in the creation of a strong regional identity is that people ignore the fact that the region is a concept of the human mind. It is assumed that the region becomes an objective phenomenon, or a 'natural' region that exists irrespective of what people think and believe. Eva Ostberg goes as far as to claim that if you do not succeed in making the region 'appear as the 'natural' identification...the whole project will collapse.' However, this analysis does not set out to reach the conclusion that nations and regions do not exist, but it does demonstrate that they are only perceived entities as long as a fairly large proportion of people assert their existence. They are therefore essentially self-fulfilling predictions.

Cultural histories in general, and museums in particular, have always played an important role in this process. Among other things, museums participate in stipulating which phenomena are to be emphasised as typical of the region, and therefore worth building a regional identity upon. What is considered 'fine and worthy enough' to exhibit in a museum will often also be perceived as the most typical characteristics of the region.

THE USAGE OF HISTORY

Key words in this brief analysis are the purpose behind objectives, themes, stereotypes, oral folk tradition and interpretation. These are adopted as a basis for analysing how the usage of history operates.

Formation of the nation as a purpose and objective for the usage of history is still more or less socially given. An essential part of this is the focus on national identity, which is again socially given. Ehn and Frykman claim that national identity has a unique ability to override other allegiances, such as ethnicity, class, gender, religion or age group.

The selection of subject theme has been partly dependent on the nature of the museums. The Royal Armoury, The National Museum and the Nordic Museum have in part different main themes. Mette Skaugaard writes about how the selection of farmhouses displayed at the Frilandsmuseet in Copenhagen played a decisive role in the creation of national symbols: 'In other words, the musealisation of folk culture can be regarded as an important factor in making folk culture an integrated part of the national identity established at the time.'

As a result, folk culture was translated into stereotypes that reflected a spontaneous part of everyday life, a representative symbol of 'all things national'. It was a question of finding the most suitable setting for the most typical farmer: *rotnorsk och purfinne*. In Sweden, the Dalecarlian region and its culture became a place of pilgrimage, and this culture was documented, displayed and idealised.

The concept of interpretation is about the necessity of understanding one's peasant origin in order to become a decent man. 'Know yourself' as Hazelius put it, which was his motto when creating museums. It was also about Swedes not having the ability to fully appreciate their landscape, as in a 1909 art review by Carl G Laurin: 'Many a shepherd boy has no eyes for the smooth movements of the blazing sun reflecting in the sea, nor for the beauty offered by the swans flying over dark blue waters.'

This paternalistic attitude reflected the view held by the bourgeoisie in the Scandinavian capitals of Stockholm, Copenhagen and Oslo. They believed that they themselves possessed the objective truth. They knew that the shepherd boy was wrong and that they were right concerning the appreciation of landscapes, the peasant culture and the role of the nation. They had decided how vital this knowledge was, and considered the values behind it as self-evident and natural. Acceptance of these objective values was regarded as a pre-condition for interpretation to be successfully realised.

The emergence of the social sciences also played a part. By establishing academic disciplines based on the study of social structures and values, this perception of identity was strengthened, as it was made to appear even more natural and self-evident. Ethnology became an academic discipline at the beginning of the 20th century, and even oral folk tradition became a subject for scientific study, as illustrated by the foundation of Upsala Landsmålarkiv (an archive of papers in the Upsala dialect). The integration of museums into the process of academic study is reflected in the fact that the Professorship in Ethnology at the University of Stockholm is shared with the Nordic Museum.

The so-called 'Military Festival' held at Skansen in 1914 serves as an example of Swedish usage of history in practice. As part of the programme, soldiers and commanders dressed in contemporary costume, and enacted different famous scenes from Swedish military history. Among incidents dramatised were the Tumult at Bender with Charles XII, and Sven Dufva's Last Battle at Virta Bridge from the famous epic by Runeberg. For the occasion, a small bridge was built over a pond. On the bridge, a tall and muscular man stood and pushed Russians into the water 'accompanied by the unrestrained enthusiasm of the audience.' Finally, there was a glorious procession where the dead hero was carried on a bier with the blue-and-yellow Swedish flag flying. The audience was also shown 'genuine bivouacking performed by the infantry and the cavalry.'

Fact and fiction were mingled indiscriminately, and oral folk tradition was given free rein. The Tumult at Bender, which took place on 1 February 1713, and Runeberg's epic poem about Sven Dufva were considered of equal historical merit. One newspaper, Stockholm's *Dagblad*, referred to the events as 'two of the most famous ones in our military history'. The epic poem about Sven Dufva was absorbed into national rhetoric to such an extent that the episodes of the poem were thereafter accepted as real events of Swedish military history. One reason for placing the events in an equal historical position was probably the fact that they were both examples of 'a fine old male Swedish tradition where one man fights the dozen', as reported by a journalist in the *Dagblad*.

As a symbol for a desirable Swedish ideal, Sven Dufva could be perceived as a person to have existed in the real world, as real as Charles XII. But the most important thing was not really whether Sven Dufva had existed or not, but whether he could have existed, or rather that he ought to have existed. This is an example of how sheer fiction, with historic interpretation as an end, is used to illustrate one form of national stereotype, and how this stereotype was made to appear factual through being placed in an equal position to a real historical occurrence.

NATIONALITY AND MUSEUMS TODAY

A report published by the Swedish government in 1995 states that: 'One aim designed for the museums is that they should encourage national, regional and local identity.' It is a clear directive, urging museums to focus their activities on, among other things, the formation of a national identity. What is the significance of this aim, and why is it considered relevant in Sweden today?

No answers are given to these questions in the report. It only calls attention to the symbolic value of the cultural identity of a city, a region or a nation in the interplay with other countries. It also says that people lacking in historical awareness and knowledge about their 'own native roots' are easily manipulated and may fall victim to 'false descriptions of reality.'

Does the report represent something new in relation to previous government reports? In a public debate held at The Nordic Museum in May 1996, the newly appointed Minister of Culture, Marita Ulvskog, was of the opinion that Swedes lack knowledge and pride in their national and regional cultural heritage, when compared to many immigrants. According to her, one task would be to increase the Swedes' knowledge and pride in such a way that would allow them to meet the immigrants in a more constructive way and also enable us to better understand their cultures. However, she also pointed to the risk that excessive national pride might degenerate into a weapon for aggressive nationalism. In other words, good nationalism can become evil nationalism.

Why is this picture of the Swedes, as being a people who lack a sense of historical awareness, painted so frequently today? No one has carried out surveys and produced evidence to show that Swedes are less knowledgeable about and proud of their national history, but the 1993 museum exhibition entitled *The Swedish History*, is relevant here. Its focus was on the formation of the nation, more so than in any other large museum project carried out during the last few decades. The project manager, Sten Rentzhog, wrote in the official exhibition catalogue that:

> The aim is that we will rediscover our history, that history once again will be alive in our society and in our hearts. Our sense of national belonging consists of the language and the history we have in common. All too long we have believed language was enough...A great part of the feeling of being lost, which exists in the Swedish society of today, is due to the fact that we have lost contact with our past.

Several commentators questioned the exhibition manifesto. In terms of historiography, the focus on the formation of the nation was not obvious. Anders Bjornsson wrote in *Aftonbladet* and *Sydsvenska Dagbladet* that it is useless to search for the pure Swedish national history before the 19th century:

> Then we were a part of a common European history where the borders between the states were continuously moved back and forth...It was easier to move from one state to another than to move to another parish in the very same part of the country. Neither national identity nor national governments existed, only dynastic vicissitudes and cabinet politics did exist.

One of the editorial writers in *Sydsvenska Dagbladet* claimed that the exhibition showed that Sweden has a touch of the European nationalistic flu and he draws upon Einstein, who said 'that nationalism is the chicken pox of mankind, a children's disease which reveals the immaturity of mankind.' In a polemic between *Blekinge Lans Tidning* and *Sydsvenska Dagbladet* it was stated that: 'with a clear conscience you can take an interest in the history of Latvia and Tanzania, the US and Uganda but when it comes to The Swedish History...just by saying it, you can hear the sound of jackboots marching.'

European integration has become a new external factor to influence the way we interpret and use our history. In the book, *The Process of Making Sweden Swedish*, both Frykman and Orvar Lofgren draw parallels with the 1890s, when the then growing nationalism stood out in clear relief against strong contemporary internationalism. In the programme for *The Swedish*

History exhibition, Rentzhog wrote about what he meant to be the Swedes' lack of historic perspective: 'This is extremely serious now when we are discussing the possibility of Sweden entering the European Union, and when we are in a period of economic crisis including a prevalent pessimistic view of the future.' Svante Beckman claims that the strong pressure of internationalism experienced during the 19th century today leads to the fact that, paradoxically, we stress parts of the cultural heritage which separate us from, rather than those which unite us to, other European countries.

ARE SWEDES BAD AT HISTORY?

Many Swedes share the stereotype saying that they are generally bad at history. A common feature of both the answers to questionnaires and exhibition propaganda is that the stereotype concerns some Swedes, but this author has neither read nor heard any convincing arguments that presupposes a harmful lack of historic knowledge of one's own nation.

How can this alleged lack of a sense of history be explained? One of the respondents to the Nordic Museum survey wrote: 'I think they are more aware of history in other countries where they have had conflicts and revolutions. It has always been so safe and secure to live in our country that we have never reflected upon taking care of our history.' According to this point of view, the reason for a lack of national feeling is that the existence of the Swedish State has not been threatened for a long period of time. As already mentioned, this line of reasoning was also followed in the early part of the 20th century.

One prominent characteristic of stereotypes is that they live a life of their own. Like legends, they are often told in the belief that they are true, but without supportable empirical knowledge. None of those who have stressed today's lack of historical awareness and sense of identity have referred to any study supporting the assertion. In 1980, Jan Thavenius wrote in similar terms, and argued that the 'thoughts of restoration' are unsupportable because they are not based on historical evidence. Indeed, the reasoning has not only been about how much Swedes of today know about history, it has been equally much about which version of history they know.

The notion that the Swedes are a people whose identity is particularly weak, and who lack pride and knowledge about their own history, is part of an old national stereotype, referred to by Heidenstam in the 19th century. In an article written in 1933, on *National self-searching*, Herbert Tingsten asserts that this stereotype exists as a self-reflecting notion among almost all European nationalities and peoples. He quotes Heinrich von Treitschke, who wrote that the Germans 'suffer from a weak feeling for their nation, and from an exaggerated respect for others.' Tingsten also quotes French cultural commentators, writing that: 'We have lost our national feeling for the benefit of the Nordic people...the deplorable, unfortunate state of mind of the French who derive a gloomy pleasure from disparaging and underrating themselves.'

GOOD OR EVIL NATIONALISM

It is important to understand the purpose and objectives behind the usage of history and the focus it is given, and how themes and stereotypes are selected for ideological and political reasons. In this context, it is not inferred that the skinheads' usage of history will necessarily be the dominant way in which history is used in Swedish society. However, their activities are an example of values nourished by the public, and they strengthen the focus on national history and identity, but they also help to stress regrets as an important factor in historiography.

The ethnologist, Anna Lundstrom, has undertaken a study on the skinheads paying homage to Charles XII in Stockholm on 30 November 1991. According to her, the stress on national matters is fundamental to their identity as skinheads. This thematic focus gives the group an identity, which, according to them, is irreproachable or, at the very least, defensible. The emphasis on national identity is regarded by them as a token of social responsibility, which they take seriously and expect the establishment to respect.

Since history and cultural history are so important to skinheads, they generally regard local folklore societies and museums as important institutions. For example, Hazelius is regarded as the defender of what is considered genuinely Swedish and his name is used in their rhetoric of racial supremacy and preservation of national values. Skansen, founded by Hazelius, is depicted as a sanctuary of Swedish culture on the verge of extinction. For that reason, many skinheads dedicate themselves to the activities of Skansen, as put by one commentator:

> Just wait and you will see, now it's going to be a row about Skansen too. Well, that's since Hasse Alfredsson took over and wanted Skansen to be so very international. There are already a lot of people who have said: see, now that's gone down the drain too. It was so Swedish and typical! So, there are a lot of people who feel very aggressive about it and they will definitely increase in number. Instead, someone ought to improve Skansen with some truly Swedish stuff.

The boundary between what is perceived as good or evil nationalism is of course not fixed: it is perceived differently by skinheads, museum employees and those responsible for cultural policy. From the respondents to the Nordic Museum survey, I believe the following statement to be the most representative: 'It is a shame that neo-nazis have made the anniversary of the death of Charles XII their business, that makes it impossible for honourable and peaceful people like me to continue such traditions.' The majority of Swedes share a longing to find a relevant and socially accepted way to express a 'healthy feeling for their native country.'

Most people condemn the skinheads' usage of history. However, if public discussion constantly distinguishes between good and evil nationalism, the boundaries are not always obvious. The usage of symbols such as the Swedish flag and the national anthem are clear examples of the difficulty of agreeing where the line is to be drawn. One current example is the heated debate about whether the singing of the national anthem in schools stands for good or evil. In wider society, there is an ongoing ideological fight about where the boundary should be drawn, to define what is acceptable.

In this it is important to distinguish between cause and effect, and more attention should be given to reaching a better understanding of the causes which motivate nationalism. These can be internal or external to the nation, an example of the latter being the European Union, which is considered a benign factor in current public debate. For example, it was referred to in the promotional material for *The Swedish History* exhibition.

THE QUESTION OF IDENTITY

At the 1993 European Museum Conference in Paris, there was heated discussion concerning the national and political role of museums. Representatives from Eastern Europe, not least from former Yugoslavia, considered the issue very important. The Basque representative regarded her museum as an institution that safeguarded Basque nationalism within the Spanish state. She felt that the museum should exhibit and point to Basque identity and national peculiarities with regard to language, culture and race. Her boundary between what was considered good or evil nationalism was drawn differently to that considered acceptable to most of the Swedish museum employees.

Another dimension is today's search for the lowest common denominator representing the essence of our national identity: what we have in common that could be called genuinely Swedish. Most people would say that it exists and that it is possible to articulate it. This view is a close cousin of the axiom that the strengthening of one's own identity is a good thing, whether it is considered in local, regional or national terms. Indeed, all groups seem to agree on this.

On one hand, it is claimed that with a strong identity of our own it will be easier for us to meet other cultures in an open-minded way. On the other, it is claimed that we need a strong identity of our own in order to protect ourselves more effectively against other cultures. Where the boundary between these two notions is drawn remains very unclear.

To some, identity is a collective concept of why we need history and museums. The social anthropologist, Thomas Hylland Eriksen, writes in the book, *History, myth and identity,* that the usual answer to the question of why the past is so important, is that 'it gives us an identity'. But he goes on to say that 'this is a hollow and empty answer to a complicated question.' The issue that there are different kinds of identities is seldom addressed in museums. Many of the identities are, in the eyes of this author, harmful. If we, as museum employees, propagate the notion that a strong identity based on knowledge of Swedish history is a good thing, then we also have to decide which history and identity we consider to be good.

The Author

Dr Stefan Bohman obtained his doctorate in Ethnology at University of Stockholm. He is Head of the Research and Education Department at the Nordic Museum in Stockholm, and teaches museology at the University of Umeå. He is also Vice Chairman of the National Board for Museological Research. A prolific writer and popular lecturer, his latest book, *History, Museums and Nationalism,* was published in 1997.

References

Alexander, E., *Museum Masters*, Nashville, 1983.

Azoulay, A., 'With Open Doors: Museums and Historical Narratives in Israel's Public Space,' in Sherman and Rogoff (eds), *Museum Culture*, Minneapolis, 1994.

Beckman, S., 'Om kulturarvets väsen och värde', in *Modernisering och kulturarv*, Stockholm, 1993.

Bohman, S., *Historia, Museer och Nationalism (History, Museums and Nationalism)*, Stockholm, 1997.

Eriksen, A., 'Å Lytte til Historiens Sus', in *Kulturella perspektiv*, No. 4, Umeå, 1995.

Gellner, E., *Culture, Identity and Politics*, Cambridge, 1988.

Hylland Eriksen, T., *Ethnicity and Nationalism*, London, 1993.

Kavanagh, G., *Museums and the First World War: A Social History*, Leicester, 1994.

Lindqvist, H., *En Vandring genom Den Svenska Historien*, Stockholm, 1993.

Lundström, A., *Vi äger gatorna i kväll. Om hyllandet av Karl XII i Stockholm den November 1991*, (Gatan är vår. Ritualer på offentliga platser), Stockholm, 1995.

Skaugaard, M., 'The Ostenfeld Farm at the Open-air Museum: Aspects of the Role of Folk Museum in Conflicts of National Heritage', in *Nordisk Museologi 2*, Umeå, 1995.

Sundin, B., 'Upptäkten av hembygden: Om Konstruktionen av Ragional Identitet', in *Den Regionala Särarten*, Lund.

Tingsten, H., 'Nationell Självprövning',in *Svenska Krusbar*, Stockholm, 1995.

Tunbridge, J.E. & Ashworth, G.J., *Dissonant Heritage: The Management of the Past as a Resource in Conflict*, John Wiley, 1996.

Urry, J., 'How Societies Remember the Past,' in Macdonald and Fyfe (eds), *Theorizing Museums*, Oxford, 1996.

Walsh, R., *The Representation of the Past*, London, 1992.

23

THE IMAGE OF DENMARK
Museums as Sanctuaries of Identity

Mette Bligaard

The prominent archaeologist and director of Denmark's National Museum, J.J.A. Worsaae, wrote a review article in 1884 on the archaeological and historical museums in Scandinavia and beyond, in which he reviewed the development of Danish museums in the 19th century. He emphasised that the point of departure in Danish museology was the splitting up, at the beginning of the 19th century, of the Royal Collections (the *Kunstkammer*) and the creation of a number of special museums arranged in accordance with new scientific methods. After having acknowledged the impetus received from France, in particular from Alexandre Lenoir's *Musée des Monuments Français*, Worsaae asserted:

> The new museum idea immediately caught on in smaller countries, especially in countries where the national independence of the people was repressed or in danger, and where the hardships of the present were eclipsed by a past, which with regard to nationality was seen as more pure and happy. Thus there is no doubt that, first and foremost, it is the strong national movements which have given museums a new and hitherto unknown cultural, historical, and popular importance. In this respect it is significant that the zeal to create national collections of antiquities and to preserve national monuments first appeared, and was most ardently pursued in smaller countries, where the nationality and independence of the people appeared to be particularly threatened, e.g. in Denmark, Hungary, Bohemia, Ireland, Scotland and Holland.[1]

In Denmark, a national consciousness was slowly developing by the middle of the 18th century when people of the middle class began to identify themselves with the nation, its language and its history as a reaction against the predominance of foreign aristocracy at the royal court. In 1776, a law governing the right of citizenship made it impossible for anyone but Danish citizens to hold a government post. Thus the concept of nationality was accepted by the multicultural Danish monarchy, and the images of national identification were found in a shared Nordic culture. These circumstances sparked a romantic revival based on renewed interest in the Nordic past and prehistoric monuments, as well as in Norse literature and the Icelandic sagas. This revival later grew into a populist movement, which perceived folk culture as the very core of the nation, and the heritage associated with the folk life of peasant culture became a vital factor in the boosting of national consciousness. The advent of the modern public museum is closely linked with the emergence of 'Nordic Antiquity' and 'Folk Life' as national identification models.

Museums took on a new role: they established themselves as the sanctuaries of the nation. From being cabinets of curiosities for the prince to enjoy, or scientific collections for the learned to contemplate, they became instruments for national education and propaganda. The role of museums in the shaping of national identity was, according to Worsaae, *the* important characteristic of the 19th century museum movement, and the necessity to preserve the national heritage, ancient monuments in the countryside, as well as tools and artefacts dug out of the earth, became the focus of attention. The exhibition of these objects of the past in public museums, at first arranged systematically in chronological order in showcases, later displayed in their 'natural' settings in an attempt to convey context, were intended to inspire the visitor with national sentiment and pride.

The prefix 'national' was used for the first time in connection with a museum in Denmark in 1806. In that year Rasmus Nyerup, antiquarian and university librarian in Copenhagen, visualised a national museum as 'an asylum for the slowly disappearing ancient national monuments,' and 'a temple for the remains of the spirit, language, art and power of our past, where every patriot can study the successive advance of the nation's culture and customs'.[2]

In other words, the setting up of a national museum was a rescue operation as well as an educational project. A year later, in 1807, a Royal Commission for the Preservation of Antiquities was appointed by the King. It had a dual purpose: partly to take responsibility for the protection of ancient monuments throughout the country, partly to found a national museum of Danish history. A systematic survey and collection of prehistoric antiquities commenced, and from then on the preservation of this part of the national heritage was a state concern.

Indeed, at this time, Denmark felt threatened in its identity. In 1801, as a consequence of the Battle of Copenhagen, the seafaring nation had been deprived of its fleet. The Royal Commission was established only a few months after the British bombardment of the Danish capital. As a disastrous outcome of the Napoleonic War, Denmark had to cede Norway to Sweden in 1814. The breaking up of the union between Denmark and Norway was preceded by economic disaster. In 1813 the state went bankrupt.

The need to reassert Denmark's identity resulted in a spiritual and national awakening touching all layers of society, in which museums played an important part. As Worsaae rightly pointed out, the splitting up of the *Kunstkammer*, dating back to the 17th century, was the beginning of modern museology in Denmark. This collection, like its European counterparts, was a collection of rarities arranged as a mirror of the universe.

During the years following the disasters at the beginning of the 19th century, the *Kunstkammer* collections began to be successively broken up, and were rearranged according to new scientific methods in a series of special collections with chronology as the governing system and, most importantly, they were made accessible to the general public.

The Museum of Nordic Antiquities was opened to the public in 1819. During the next three decades it was followed by a Royal Museum of Fine Arts, where the works were displayed chronologically and according to national schools, a Royal Arsenal Museum, a Collection of Classical Antiquities, and a Collection of Coins and Medals. An Ethnographical Museum, the first in the world, was opened in 1841 while the natural science collections were turned into specialist museums. A Royal Portrait Gallery was created and opened to the public at Frederiksborg Castle to form 'a kind of Pantheon for famous Danish men, who in chronological order were to surround the kings under whose rule each had excelled himself'. One of the museums even had the word chronological in its title: *The Chronological Collections of the Danish Kings at Rosenborg Castle*, which was opened to the public in 1833. Together these museums aimed at emphasising the progress of civilisation.

However, the flagship of Danish museums throughout the 19th century was the Museum of Nordic Antiquities, headed by the self-taught archaeologist C.J Thomsen, who laid down the principles of the so-called three-age system. His seminal arrangement of weapons and tools by Stone, Bronze and Iron Ages was to gain him world renown. Thomsen also demonstrated what museums could be used for. Once a week Thomsen himself conducted tours of the collection and he played a key role in the development of the Danish national museum until 1865, when

Worsaae succeeded him. In 1892, the Museum of Nordic Antiquities was renamed The National Museum.

During the Danish–German national conflicts, which dominated the years around the middle of the 19th century, the common Nordic past of Denmark, Norway and Sweden was stressed in the political debate in which museum curators played an important part, not least Worsaae himself. A new pan-Scandinavian identity was invented based on the Romanticist idea that folk groups with similar language, religion, culture and traditions should also be linked together politically. Arguments for a Nordic federation were put forward as a weapon against German influence and dominance. The term *Scandinavism* was first formulated in academic and literary circles in the 1830s to emphasise the similarities between Denmark, Norway, and Sweden.

This was when the Vikings became synonymous with the people who settled Southern Scandinavia about the time of the Anglo-Saxon invasion of the British Isles, and when the 'Viking Age' was first used as a period label. However, *Scandinavism* was, according to a present day historian, a kind of escapism, and the movement was put to rest after the Danish defeat in the second Schleswig War in 1864, when the two sister nations failed to deliver the promised assistance against Denmark's powerful southern neighbour.

Scandinavism was an ideological movement in which the Old Norse tradition had great symbolic value. It also encompassed contemporary 'folk life' research and an artistic programme. In 1844, Niels Høyen, an art historian and professor at the Royal Academy of Fine Arts in Copenhagen had given a lecture entitled: *On the Conditions for the Creation of a Scandinavian National Art*. Twenty years later, in another lecture more modestly entitled *On National Art*, he called on Danish painters to choose subject matter drawn from rural life. He encouraged the painters to go to rural areas of the country and paint the peasants in their traditional costumes, and engaged in their daily work. Høyen, too, was instrumental in instigating the systematisation of the so-called 'national costumes' of the different regions of Denmark. The same happened in Norway, both being a parallel to the elaboration on the myth of the clan tartan and the Highland dress, which took place at the same time in Scotland.

'All over Europe, everywhere there is a demand for the peculiarly national. Our paintings are admired at the exhibitions in London and Paris because they depict the national, the history of the people and contemporary folk life,' Høyen explained.[3]

One of the most powerful national icons created at this time was a painting entitled *Mother Denmark*, in which archaeology and folk culture form a symbiosis. It is significant that this painting personifying the nation was executed by a Polish immigrant artist in 1851 to commemorate the

Danish victory in the first Schleswig War. It shows a blond peasant woman walking through the cornfields wearing a nondescript national dress. She is clearly of Nordic extraction, and the jewellery she wears is a selection of museum pieces from the Museum of Nordic Antiquities: a Bronze Age collar adorns her long blond hair, whereas her bracelet is an Iron Age piece.

With her Bronze Age sword, another museum item, she is prepared to defend her country. Over her shoulder she defiantly carries what was to become the most potent emblem of nationality, the flag *Dannebrog*. At exactly this time, the old red-and-white Royal banner, dating back to the 13th century, was adopted by the Danish people as a popular national symbol, and every house had a flagpole erected to be able to boast the national sentiment of its residents.

Curiously enough, the admission of systematic archaeology at the beginning of the century did not ease the entrance of folk culture into the museums. However, the ethnographic viewpoint was stressed when presenting the Danish nation abroad. In Denmark, as everywhere else in Europe, the sudden interest in folk culture was partly aroused by the rapid industrialisation and the realisation that peasant culture was about to disappear.

The international expositions were a new means of mass communication of cultures across the borders. Here each nation presented itself as a cultural entity with its own distinctive features, using in Orvar Löfgren's words, 'an international cultural grammar of nationhood with a thesaurus of general ideas about the cultural ingredients needed to form a nation'.[4] National symbolism was inevitably found in the past, such as in folk art and historic building styles. Both at home and abroad, it was exactly at this point in time that the Vikings became synonymous with Scandinavia, and consequently provided the Nordic countries with their own distinctive national ornamental and architectural style: the 'Viking' or 'Nordic' style, with its dragon coils and interlace pattern.

At the international expositions, alongside the newest industrial products, national pavilions were erected and the exhibits displayed in an entirely new manner against a setting of each country's vernacular architecture. Presentation of farmhouse interiors, complete with furniture, fittings and utensils, formed the core of the display. Folk *tableaux* arranged as stage sets finished the display. In moving the museum object from the showcase into 'natural' surroundings, the Swede, Arthur Hazelius, pioneered this entirely new manner of heritage interpretation. When Hazelius opened the first Scandinavian Folk Museum in Stockholm in 1873, to become the Nordiska Museet in 1880, it took over the visual language of the international expositions.

In most cases, museum staff curated the international expositions, and the exchange of both staff and exhibits between expositions and museums was a characteristic aspect of this reciprocity between culture and industry. Thus the Museum of Nordic Antiquities supplied the exhibits for the Danish Pavilion at the 1867 Exposition in Paris. In 1879, the director of the museum, Worsaae, chaired the committee organising a gigantic Scandinavian Exhibition of Art and Industry in Copenhagen. A section of this exhibition was devoted to Danish folk culture. Subsequently, these elements were directly transferred to the new folk museums and open-air museums.

The first Danish Folk Museum opened in 1885. Around the same time, the Museum of Nordic Antiquities was organised to focus on the period from the middle of the 17th century to the middle of the 19th century. The objective of the museum was to show 'through a comprehensive and fascinating exhibition how the national peculiarities of the people has been formed by our climate and the nature of our country under the steady impression of European culture', and 'to imprint the image of how it was before the new times and the development have equalised all characteristics of class and place'. Furthermore, Bernhard Olsen, the founder of the museum, in a somewhat high flown manner envisaged a collection encompassing also material from former Danish territory 'in order to teach Danish youth what was once Denmark, to remember what was lost, and pave the way for a spiritual reunion of the scattered territories, which is the only way of re-conquest I can possibly see.'[5]

In the 1880s, Denmark was still licking its wounds after the disastrous outcome of the Second Schlesvig War, which in 1864 had reduced the country's territory by almost a third. The need for self-assertion was deeply felt, and the Danish Folk Museum was not the only museum established with the purpose of regaining national self-confidence.

In 1878, an ambitious museum project on an even grander scale had been launched. The creation of a Museum of Danish National History at Frederiksborg Castle was a therapeutic measure intended to awaken and teach historical awareness in the Danish people. In this museum, the nation's past was to serve the interest of the present and the future.

The situation of the museum was unique in that the architecture was part of the programme. A castle and former royal residence, where the Royal Portrait Gallery had originally been installed in 1812, was to be the home of this museum. In many ways, Louis Philippe's Versailles Museum of 1837 inspired the Danish museum. This was dedicated to *toutes les gloires de la France*, so as to remedy the identity crisis of the post-Napoleonic French Monarchy. Frederiksborg Castle, a vast Romantic early 17th century building, was to be the domicile for a type of museum called by a present-day German scholar: *eine Gesamtkunstwerk und Begehbares Lehrbuch* (a synthesis of the arts and a textbook to be walked through).[6]

Curiously enough the Museum of Danish National History was neither initiated nor supported by the government. The founder of the museum was J C Jacobsen, an industrialist and great patron of the sciences and the arts, who was convinced that knowledge of history, and especially the history of one's own country, was the way to attain a specific goal: namely, that of imbuing his countrymen with self esteem and a feeling of national loyalty. He outlined his motivation for the founding of the museum as follows:

> Living with the memories and mementoes of the past arouses and develops a nation's sense of history and strengthens its consciousness of the part it has itself played in the general cultural development of mankind. In thus, this fosters recognition of the obligations that this heritage imposes upon the present and coming generations. This form of consciousness and recognition cannot help intensifying a nation's self esteem and moral strength – things which a small nation like ours so definitely needs.[7]

The museum was far-sighted in several ways. Spanning the period from the introduction of Christianity in Denmark until the present day it was seen as a chronological continuation of the remit of the Museum of Nordic Antiquities. For the first time, the recent past was told as history. Besides, the museum was pointing forward, in that it had to be kept up to date continuously. In other words, it was a comprehensive illustrated history of Denmark with the aim of visualising, by means of art, the conception of famous events and remarkable personalities in Danish history.

This visual reconstruction of history was meant to arouse and nourish patriotism. Portraits of national heroes, role models past and present, were commissioned along with several sets of history paintings recreating the martial, cultural, scientific and literary achievements of the Danes. A deliberate omission of the less honourable episodes in Danish history, as they were not spiritually edifying, was part of the programme. Systematic archaeology was now superseded by an evocative populist presentation of images of key persons and major historical events.

The story of 19th century museology is a tale of how attempts were made to construct historical totalities. On the contrary, the 20th century saw the expansion of the concept of heritage in time and space within the context of museum policy and practice. New museums covering every aspect of human endeavour appear at regular intervals. It is no longer just a question of safeguarding the relics of the past. In anticipation of the future, evidence of present day culture and of contemporary life have found its way into museums. In an attempt to link together the fragmented museum landscape, the state acts as co-ordinator of collecting. Electronic central registers are established and the state legislates on museum matters.

Only museums of national history still attempt to synthesise, and Worsaae's assertion that small countries, and countries whose independence are threatened, have the need to create national museums as a manifestation of national identity still seem to be valid. This is clearly demonstrated by some recent examples.

Germany is a case in point. In 1987, only two years before the reunion of the country, collecting of material from scratch for a museum of the common history of the then divided nation was started. Christoph Stölzl, director of this new museum in Berlin, the *Deutsches Historisches Museum*, echoes his 19th century Danish colleague when he sees the establishment of the museum as 'therapy' and as 'a symptom of crisis'. In the debate that followed about history museums in general, two German scholars defined today's national history museum as 'laboratory, stage and identity factory.'[8]

Kenneth Hudson points out that 'there are no comparably national museums in France, England or the United States, because in these countries there is no common agreement on the interpretation of the nation's history.'[9] Or, one might suggest, great imperial powers have no need for national self-assertion, but smaller countries do. Would the story of Danish museology have been different, had the history of the country in the 19th century been a history of success?

Scotland is another case in point. Although the Museum of Scotland in Edinburgh has been under way for a long time, this ambitious project materialised at a crucial moment in the history of the country as a manifestation of specific Scottish identity. 'Why should there be an obsessive search to find a national identity?' David McCrone asks.[10] 'If we set out to look for what is distinctive in Scotland, we run the risk of focusing on the trivial and epiphenomenal, which will be found only in the past and in the museum.'[11]

So, according to the Scottish sociologist, museums and national identity are still inextricably linked. However, at a time when the concept of the nation state is undergoing drastic transformation in response to a rapidly developing modern pluralistic society, the concept of national identity in the Herderian sense is bound to change and make way for a broader and more complex interpretation of identity. Nationhood is made up of numerous interacting forces and hardly any nation today can claim ethnic homogeneity. This situation is mirrored in the definition of some of the principal objectives of the Danish National Museum, according to the Museum Act of 1984 and consolidation Act of 1989, which are:

1. to contribute to a knowledge and understanding of and respect for the diversity of cultures across national boundaries;
2. to contribute to an understanding of how a peculiarly Danish culture, history and identity are created in the historical context of constant exchange with other countries and peoples;
3. to contribute to an interpretation of Danish nationality which can also accommodate new population groups, and form part of their identity.[12]

In 1993, the Museum of Danish National History and National Portrait Gallery staged an exhibition that borrowed its title from the first line of a patriotic song written by Hans Christian Andersen in 1850. The exhibition, entitled 'In Denmark I was...', consisted of a series of 41 portrait photographs of personalities who had gained distinction within the field of art, science, humanities, music, theatre, business, journalism etc. in Denmark. None of these distinguished and well-known Danes were born in Denmark, the missing word in the title actually being 'born'. Subsequently, the series was bought by the museum and incorporated into the National Portrait Gallery.

So the relationship between the nation and its citizens is in constant flux. At the beginning of the 19th century, Denmark was a state encompassing Greenlanders, Faroese, Icelanders, inhabitants of the Danish West Indies, and the German speaking population in the Duchies of Schleswig-Holstein. The national symbols of the Danish 'mini' nation state of today, covering the territory left after centuries of defeats in wars with our neighbours, are still primarily found in the past. Cultural heritage and museums still play a role, not least in the territories that once formed part of the country.

In 1944, when the union between Iceland and Denmark was severed, and Iceland seized independence from Denmark, the new Icelandic Republic reclaimed its most precious national heritage. This was the Saga manuscripts, which had been collected by Icelanders and kept in Copenhagen since the beginning of the 18th century. Following an emotional debate and court battles, an Act of Parliament was passed in 1961, allowing most of the Saga material to be transferred back to Iceland. In anticipation of Home Rule for Greenland, enacted in 1979, the National Museum in Copenhagen has transferred material from its collections to the Museum of Greenland, which was established in the 1960s. These recent examples demonstrate that nations or communities within nations still see their identity as an historical condition rooted in their past, and that is why the physical remains of the past kept in museums are of paramount importance as items of national identification.

The Author

Mette Bligaard is Director of the Danish Cultural Institute in Edinburgh. She was born in Denmark and educated at the Universities of Aarhus and Copenhagen, and was a lecturer in art history at the latter before becoming a curator at the Museum of Danish National History at Frederiksborg Castle, serving as its Director 1989–97. She has curated exhibitions both in Denmark and abroad. Her special interest is 19th century architecture, and she is a prolific writer and popular lecturer.

References

1. Worsaae, J.J.A., *Om Ordningen af Arkaeologiske-Historiske Museer i og Udenfor Norden,* Nordisk Tidsskrift for Vetenskap, Konst och Industri, 7, 1884.
2. Nyerup, R., *Oversigt over Faedrelandets Mindesmaerker fra Oldtiden, Saaledes som Samme kan Taenkes Opstillede i et Tilkommende National-Museum,* 1806.
3. Høyen, N.L., *Om Betingelserne for en Skandinavisk Nationalkonsts Udvikling,* in Ussing, J.L. (ed), 'Niels Laurits Høyens Skrifter', 1871, pp. 351–368.
4. Löfgren, O., *The Nationalization of Culture,* Ethnologia Europaea XIX, 1, 1989.
5. Rasmussen, H., *Bernhard Olsen. Liv og Virke,* Nationalmuseet, 1979, p.132.
6. Boockmann, H., *Geschichte im Museum?,* 1987, p. 13.
7. Bligaard, M., *J.C. Jacobsen and Frederiksborg,* Det Nationalhistorisk Museum på Frederiksborg, 1997, pp. 16–32.
8. Kooff, G. & Roth, M. (eds), *Das Historische Museum. Labor, Schaubühne, Identitätsfabrik,* Campus Verlag, 1990.
9. Hudson, K., *Attempts to Define 'Museum',* in Boswell, D. & Evans, J. (eds), 'Representing the Nation: A Reader. Histories, Heritage and Museums', Routledge, 1999, p. 377.
10. McCrone, D., *Understanding Scotland. The Sociology of a Stateless Nation,* Routledge, 1992, p. 190.
11. Ibid., p. 194.
12. Nationalmuseets Virksomhedsregnskab for 1997, p. 14. (*The Principal Objectives and Responsibilities of the National Museum.*)

Further Reading

Birkebæk, F. & Lauenburg, M. (eds), *Danish Museums,* 1992.
Bligaard, M., *Die Gründung des Museums für Danische Nationalgeschichte in Schloss Frederiksborg,* in von Plessen, M.L. (ed), 'Die Nation und ihre Museen', Campus Verlag, 1992.

Georgel, C., *Le Musée, Lieu d'Identité* in Georgel, C. (ed), 'La Jeunesse des Musées. Les Musées de France au XIXe Siecle', 1994, pp. 105–112.

Jensen, J., *Thomsens Museum. Historien om Nationalmuseet*, 1992.

Lundbæk, M., *Organization of Museums in Denmark and the 1984 Museum Act*, in 'The International Journal of Museum Management and Curatorship', 1985, 4, pp. 21–27.

Rasmussen, H., *Dansk Museumshistorie*, Dansk Kulturhistorisk Museumsforening, 1979.

Stocklund, B. (ed), *Kulturens Nationalisering: Et Etnologisk Perspektiv på det Nationale*, Museum Jusculanums Forlag, Kobenhavns Universitet, 1999.

Vammen, H., *National Internationalism: The Danish Golden Age Concept of Nationality*, Thorvaldsen Museum Bulletin, 1997.

Østergaard, U., *Nationale Identitäten: Ursprünge und Entwicklungen, Deutschland, der Norden, Skandinavien*, in 'Wahlverwandtschaft: Skandinavien und Deutschland 1800 bis 1914', Deutsches Historisches Museum, Natiopnalmuseum, Norsk Folkemuseum, 1997.

'Mother Denmark' was painted in 1851 to commemorate the Danish victory in the Schleswig War, being the most powerful national icon created during the period of 'Scandinavianism'. *Courtesy Ny Carlsberg Glyptotek, Købehavn*

Britain's Princess Maud, youngest daughter of King Edward VII, photographed by K. Nyblin in Hardanger costume on her tour of the western fjords of Norway in 1893. This picture was brought to light and endowed with symbolic significance when she became Queen of Norway in 1905.
Courtesy Norsk Folkemuseum

24

NATIONAL COSTUME
A Symbol of Norwegian Identity

Anne Britt Ylvisåker

National costume is arguably one of Norway's oldest and strongest national symbols, in some respects even pre-dating the flag. As a concept of national identity, it goes back to the late 18th century when people began to develop an interest in what was perceived to be distinctively and genuinely Norwegian. This interest in both flag and costume was part of an upsurge in national assertiveness, prior to the dissolution of the union with Denmark in 1814.

A variety of campaigns have been pursued since, inaugurated by groups with different aims and views on the wearing of national costume, in attempts to unify the nation and provide it with a national symbol. For some, promotion of folk culture and national costume became an aim in itself, whereas others used it as a means of expressing their cultural, political or commercial identity.

As described below, national costume has played a unifying role whenever Norwegian culture has been promoted abroad. It has also functioned as a consolidating factor internally when the nation as a whole, or a particular district, has felt threatened from without, regardless of whether the 'enemy' was foreign intrusion, urbanisation, industrialisation, the global economy or, more recently, the European Union.

Townspeople and country folk have alternated between the active and the passive in their attitude to attempts at nation building around traditional modes of dressing. In the 19th century, national costume represented an expression of interest in romantic folklore among the urban middle class, but in the early part of this century rural communities began to assume ownership of something which really belongs to them, and the costumes have since then assumed a significant role in Norwegian national politics. Nowadays, the use of such costumes on festive occasions, both public and private, is common in both town and country.

Interestingly, the Norwegian costume and its accoutrements represent the equivalent of the kilt and tartans in Scotland, but in Norway each distinct pattern is associated with a geographical area rather than a family clan. Accordingly, Norwegians normally wear the costume of the region where they live, or the place their ancestors hail from.

THE CONCEPT OF NATIONHOOD

In order to develop national symbols, the concept of a nation must exist. Towards the end of the 18th century, the notion of a genuine Norwegian nation began to take shape. A wide range of national projects was promoted, some with clear political aims, others of a more cultural nature.

The focus of these projects varied according to the motivation and background of the various groups of people who provided leadership at different times. Still, all had certain features in common. They were rooted in contemporary European ideas, which were adapted to Norwegian requirements. One important influence was enlightened French ideas about democratic government. The other was emotionally laden national romanticism in Germany. Internationally, the proud and independent Norwegian farmers were idealised as the very personification of the nation's distinguishing characteristics.

Full political independence was a matter of vital importance to Norway, and in the course of one hundred years the country progressed from effectively being a part of Denmark, via union with Sweden, to gaining the status of a Sovereign State in 1905. The Constitution of 1814 and the introduction of parliamentarianism in 1884 were important political milestones on the road to independence. In parallel with this process of becoming a nation, steps were being taken to give substance to the 'essence' of Norway. But the question was: is there such a thing as a genuine and distinctive Norwegian national culture?

As elsewhere in Europe, the 19th century intellectual leaders of Norway set about the task of detailing and preserving popular culture. The aim was to uncover, piece by piece, the national cultural heritage, and in time the intellectual and political elite began to form a picture of what was truly Norwegian. Legends and folktales, folk dance, folk music and local customs and costumes were painstakingly recorded. The information thus assembled was then disseminated through books and illustrations. In the first half of the 19th century alone, a large number of paintings and prints were produced, along with several collections of colour plates featuring Norwegian national costumes.

Although showing strong interest in the historical evidence, there was never any question of the urban middle class adopting folk traditions to replace their own cosmopolitan culture. However, certain features were identified that might with advantage be 'refined' and used as national icons in their own right. Like other forms of folk culture, national costume was not considered to be a form of dress suitable for general use by the urban-based leaders who sought to build a distinct Norwegian nation. Such costumes were worn mostly at fancy dress balls and national pageants: in other words, purely for entertainment purposes.

Norwegian culture also proved to be of interest to others. In Britain and on the Continent, there was a widely held belief that the purest forms of national culture were to be found in the small communities tucked away in the folds of the mountains, and this enticed the first adventurous foreign visitors to Norway. Vivid and enthusiastic accounts of their travels encouraged a growing number of tourists, not least from Britain, to visit the country to fish for salmon, marvel at the majesty of the mountains and fjords, and to view Norwegian folk culture at first hand.

Before long, folk culture had become a 'commodity', and tourism began to be viewed as a market where cultural nationalism was a significant factor, and in which traditional costumes could play a leading role. Foreign tourists flocked to the Hardanger Fjord region of Western Norway, where national costumes were still in everyday use, and the visitors were captivated by what they saw. The tourism industry was quick to respond, and before long the Hardanger costume was promoted as a tourist attraction in itself. The girls who served at table in the local hotels were clad in costumes, and 'country weddings' were staged to entertain the tourists. They were encouraged to try on the bridal dress, and then to buy complete outfits as souvenirs of their stay. As a token of esteem, or as a marketing gambit, particularly distinguished visitors were sometimes presented with a local costume as a gift.

Hotels and tourist resorts all over the country soon followed the example of Hardanger. In many places local traditions and costumes had fallen into disuse, and the colourful Hardanger costume became the standard mode throughout the country. Soon it was a familiar sight abroad, and eventually it gained status as the national costume of Norway. Souvenir dolls in national costume began to appear, as did sets of colour plates and illustrated publications with explanatory texts in several languages, as well as a multitude of postcards featuring people in national costume. These were some of the ways in which the tourist industry chose to exploit the popularity of the costumes.

In retrospect, the 1893 tour of the western 'fjord country' by England's Princess Maud, youngest daughter of Edward VII, has come to be regarded as an event of national importance. The princess was among those who bought a Hardanger costume as a souvenir, and she wore it for a formal portrait photograph.

As a result of growing radical nationalism and political strife, Norway's uneasy union with Sweden since 1814 was dissolved in 1905. At long last, Norway was again a free and sovereign state. The throne was offered to and accepted by Prince Charles of Denmark, who assumed the name of Haakon VII of Norway and was married to the very same English Princess Maud.

There was a good deal of discussion as to whether heads of state with foreign antecedents could be truly Norwegian. However, this problem was largely overcome when the 1893 picture of Maud in her Hardanger costume was brought to light and endowed with symbolic significance. Norway's first queen for several hundred years, clad in the fledgling nation's national costume, instantly became 'one of us'. Furnished with the words 'Queen of Norway' and the date 1905, the picture was turned into a highly popular postcard.

Apart from the political struggle for independence under the slogan 'Out of the Union', members of the radical left harboured ambitious nationalist aspirations in the cultural sphere. They were not prepared to utilise only a fragment of folk culture to rebuild the nation: in their eyes the only 'genuine' national alternative to what they dismissed as a Danish-dominated, fashionable urban culture was a complete and 'living' rural culture. The campaign to create a Norwegian national identity was accordingly focused on reviving the folk culture that was rapidly disappearing in rural communities, and returning it to the districts in a new and enhanced state.

Central to this plan was the creation of a separate written language, referred to as 'New Norwegian', to be clearly distinct from the language in official use, which was a form of Danish. National costumes also found a natural place in this context. The entire movement was strongly influenced by the poet Arne Garborg (1851–1924) and his wife Hulda (1862–1934). He was the movement's leading ideologist and wrote in New Norwegian. She promoted genuinely Norwegian culture through theatrical productions, displays of folk dancing and the wearing of national costume. They were convinced that, if Norway's rural culture were to be viable, it must be regarded not as an archaic tradition, but as an essential part of the nation's living culture. With a firm foothold in what was truly national, the radicals looked outwards to the world at large: 'My aim is to clothe modern European cultural concepts in Norway's national costume', declared one editor and ardent exponent of New Norwegian. The intention was not to freeze the past but to remould it to accord with the Norwegian present, in conjunction with new ideas from abroad.

Hulda Garborg viewed national costumes in the same way. Although she felt that use of the Hardanger costume had got completely out of hand, she argued that people should be allowed to make minor alterations to make them more practical and more in tune with the times. 'I shall have to make minor changes where changes are needed, that will make it easier for me to retain the best of the old', she once said. Nor was she averse to the idea that a region that had no traditional local costume should be allowed to design one based on the costume of some other region. In other words, that features drawn from costumes in different areas could be combined, or that people might be permitted to choose the costume they liked best.

Nonetheless, it was felt that firm guidance would be necessary before country folk could be entrusted, little by little, with the task of undertaking such cultural transformations on their own. The fact remained that the intellectual urban elite, though many of its members may well have been born and raised in the countryside, still held the reins of power, and felt themselves entitled to distinguish between what represented value in folk culture and that which was deemed of lesser significance.

In the 1920s and 1930s, rural communities began to make their voice heard, and set out to assume a leading role in matters of folk culture. For who, it was argued, was better qualified to define folk culture than those who were a part of it? 'For townspeople to rule over folk art is a farce we would do well to rid ourselves of', proclaimed one staunch patriot. Country dwellers felt they had a 'right of ownership' to folk culture, and now they claimed that culture in support of their own political aims.

Rural Norway was exposed to the winds of change and felt itself threatened on many fronts. Young people were leaving in droves to find work in the towns, and industrialisation was continuing to spread across the country, bringing in its wake workers whose values were international. Farming methods were being mechanised, labour was becoming more expensive, and there was competition from cheap imports. A reactionary and protectionist agrarian nationalism began to gain ground. The pre-industrial and self-sufficient society was portrayed as the ideal, and this was being 'contaminated' by modern urban and industrial pressures.

Authenticity and age (that which is truly Norwegian) were the most important hallmarks of folk art, and the watchword was that the past should not be tampered with in any way. It should be merely replicated, and this also applied to the wearing of national costumes. The political initiative moved from the national level to the regional, and instead of the Hardanger costume prevailing throughout the country, regional costumes were introduced according to strict rules. Standardised features adjudged 'correct' by experts discouraged variations in any single regional costume, from which all traces of modern urban culture had been carefully removed.

This circumscribed and protectionist rural nationalism never achieved wide political support, but remained such a significant force in cultural affairs that its effects were still in evidence until quite recently. What many people regarded as a rather rigid attitude to the wearing of national costume was not appreciably relaxed until shortly before 1994, when it came to play such a prominent role.

NATIONAL COSTUME YEAR 1994

In February 1994, after several years of preparation, the XVII Winter Olympic Games in Lillehammer proved to all the world that 'little' Norway was fully capable of staging an international sporting event, and transforming it into a popular celebration the like of which had never been seen before. A parade of people clad in national costumes formed part of the impressive opening ceremony, and provided an opportunity to display costumes from all over the country. Even the young girl who sang the Olympic Hymn wore her own local costume.

The organisers felt it was important to demonstrate that the Games were not intended only for athletes, sports enthusiasts and the business community of Lillehammer, but were also intended to be a broadly based cultural event that embraced the whole nation. It was by our active participation and combined efforts that we, as patriotic Norwegians, were able to present to the world the best we had to offer. By incorporating national costumes, a deep-rooted and 'unifying' symbol designed to distinguish Norwegians from everyone else, our national sense of community was deepened and consolidated.

The other major event of relevance here, was the referendum held in the autumn of 1994 to decide whether Norway should join the European Union. Those in favour of remaining outside emphasised the importance of continuing to be master of one's own house. A prominent politician made a point of underlining the fact that Norway as a Sovereign nation has no need to submit to the whims and rulings of a European super-State, and would be safest standing alone. Those in favour of membership were sceptical about the wisdom of isolation, and opted for active participation in a shared European future.

The artist, Helland Githle, contributed to the debate with profound wit when he presented what he called his EU costume, on the front page of a local newspaper. The cut, embroidery and characteristic pleated head-dress were based on the traditional dress of his native Hardanger, which a century earlier had been proclaimed the 'most national' of all national Norwegian costumes. But Githle had played tricks with the colours: he had included the EU flag's circle of appliquéd yellow stars on a blue background, to many Norwegian people a provocative alien element. The embroidered roses on the bib had been replaced by a scattering of Norwegian flags.

The artist, tongue firmly in cheek, maintained that this would enable the bib to be changed to suit each member country, while the rest of the costume would be suitable for wear throughout the entire union. What Githle actually did was to create a symbiosis of the battle standards of both camps. He had also designed a costume that could be construed as suitable to wear by supporters on both sides of the conflict.

On 17 May, Norway's Constitution Day, three months after the Olympic Games and at a time when controversy over EU membership was at its height, there were more national costumes to be seen in the streets than ever before. What is more, dressmakers all over the country found themselves working to capacity, so much so that they were unable to meet the demand: everyone wanted a national costume, and soon waiting lists extended several years into the future. Indeed, new categories of customer were clamouring for outfits: an increasing number of people from towns and cities wanted to wear them, and men too, have begun to regard them as an acceptable substitute for formal evening wear on festive occasions.

A common feature of the 1994 events was the enormous cultural interest they aroused among broad segments of the population. They stimulated new interest in the wearing of national costume, but for totally different reasons. The ceremonial aspects of the Winter Olympics placed a strong emphasis on the cultural assets of the host country. Along with other characteristics of folk culture, the wearing of national costume was used as a branding tool for international promotion. At the same time, the division of opinion over membership of the European Union encouraged the growth of political nationalism, with the anti-EU campaign using the nation's political independence as its cornerstone. Likewise, the pro EU camp used cultural identity for its own purposes to good effect. The remarkable feature was that both sides used the wearing of national costume as a means of achieving their respective political aims.

CONCLUSIONS

These brief glimpses of Norway's history over the last 200 years show how costume has served as a symbol of national unity in widely differing ways. The national aspect has been the principal message of such costumes, but they have also conveyed other messages, depending on time, place and wearer.

As far back as the 19th century, costume served as a symbol of national identity in cultural, political and commercial contexts. The forces underpinning these widely differing contexts have subsequently lived on side by side, although they have not always carried the same weight. There have been times when wearing national costume has been regarded as both radical and forward looking. At other times, it has been regarded as something reactionary and conservative.

Perceptions have depended on how such costumes were used, and the causes with which they were associated. A deciding factor has been the degree of support the various movements have enjoyed, both at national and local levels. Furthermore, it has not always been easy to distinguish between the different factions. Cultural nationalism has sometimes enjoyed the status of a cause in its own right, but it has also been utilised to pursue political objectives, both having been exploited for commercial ends in certain contexts. Indeed, the value of costume as a significant icon in national branding seems to be generally recognised.

This being so, the author feels neither anger nor resentment at the sight of some gangling youth, all decked out with a punk haircut and rings in his nose and ears, wearing national costume on Constitution Day. However, one cannot help being curious: how is one to interpret the seemingly conflicting messages he conveys? Not very different from the editor's reactions to seeing youths of similar description sporting the kilt in the streets of Edinburgh and Glasgow on St Andrews's Day.

The Author

Anne Britt Ylvisåker is Senior Curator at the West Norwegian Museum of Decorative Art in Bergen, and was formerly Director of the Sogn Folk Museum. She graduated in art history at the University of Bergen, and has lectured on the subject at the city's College of Art and Design for the last eight years. She has written a series of articles on the issues of national identity and home crafts, and her books include *Home Craft: Living Traditions* (1994) and *Colour in Painting: Natural Colour Systems as Instruments in Analysing Paintings* (1996). More recently, she was consultant adviser to the Royal Ministry of

Foreign Affairs for their 1999 National Costume exhibition held in Edinburgh's Royal Museum.

References

Damm, A., *Glimpses of Norway (Gløtt av Norge)*, W.N. Damm & Norwegian State Railways, 1945.
Hanglid, R. (ed), *Native Art of Norway*, Dreyers Forlag, 1977.
Underdal, H.M. & Eldal, J.C., *Wooden Hotels of Norway: Living Legends*, Kom Forlag, 1996.

A hotel dining room at the end of the 19th century, with all the waitresses dressed in Hardanger costume. The wood carvings of the room was done by Lars Kinsarvik of Hardanger. *Courtesy Bergen Museum*

The 'EU Costume' designed by Helland Githle in 1994 and photographed by Øystein Klakegg.

Tore André Flo, the Norwegian football player with Chelsea,
photographed by Lars Chr. Solheim wearing local national costume on the
occasion of his son's christening in 1999.

The cathedral church in the Kremlin of the Solovetski Monastery, located in the archipelago of the White Sea, where Nikolay Nickishin once worked in the local museum. As the Christian outpost in the Russian North, its cultural significance goes back to early trading links with the West by sea, and more recently as the 'archipelago gulag' for prisoners after the Bolshevik Revolution.

25

THE MUSEUMS OF RUSSIA
Four Centuries of Development

Nikolay Nickishin and Magnus Fladmark

Alongside literature on the subject in Russian, western students can now turn to the two volumes of *Museums and the State's Power*, published by the Russian Institute for Cultural Research in 1991. As implied by the title, they focus on the relationship between the state and museums as the major factor in their development, still strong in our professional consciousness. Readers who wish to be acquainted with the subject in a wider cultural context will soon have access to *The Encyclopedia of Russian Museums*, which will contain a special part devoted to the history of Russian museums. It has already been compiled and edited, and is now awaiting enough sponsorship for publication.

What follows is an attempt to paint a picture of how Russian museology has evolved over the last 400 years. The main focus is on shifts in emphasis over time, and the analysis will hopefully be of comparative interest to fellow practitioners in other countries, whether their main concerns are seeking to make sense of the past or coping with new developments.

Museums are taken to be social institutions determined by ownership. It is assumed that they essentially exist to serve the person or group which founded, governs or supports the institution. There are four basic types or main levels: personal, dynastic (family or clan of families), territorial (local or regional) and national institutions. The long established Soviet tradition of neglecting privately owned collections has required a substantial adjustment in attitude to accept that personal and private collections are now to be considered in the same context as 'normal' museums. The reforms have now reached a stage where it is high time to start thinking about non-state museums, the number of which is rapidly growing.

It is also assumed that the museum is a special environment for cultural communication to counteract the tendency of some cultural values to be lost from a living culture, to serve as a channel for communicating values from both archaic and more recent cultures, to act as an instrument for borrowing and introducing the values of other contemporary cultures, and to provide a place for creative synthesis of newly generated cultural values with those of the old and the borrowed.

Communication in museums is centred on objects, and these represent signs and symbols of human relations which constitute a semiotic system that is intuitively used and understood. The museum is neither just a place where the collections (or the thesaurus for communication) is formed and conserved, nor is it simply a channel where the coded information is being transmitted. The museum is the place where somebody consciously formulates targeted messages based on objects and addressed to somebody else. In other words, the theory and practice of professional museum work is to achieve optimum accessibility to cultural assets by interpreting objects for an agreed purpose, using the objects as signs to reveal new meanings and understandings.

The following account is structured around the last four centuries. Although history is not ruled by the calendar, it is evident that the turn of a century always attracts the interest of thinkers and historians. Like the Roman god Janus, after whom the month of January was named, many of us tend to look behind and forward, trying to extract the lessons and conclusions from the experience of the previous century for the benefit of future action.

A century is the time span which is the most close to the length of the human life. The term in the Russian language for old age sounds like 'starost', meaning 'grown to a hundred'. Our eagerness to celebrate centenaries for everything demonstrates our attachment to what might be called the milestones of time, beside which we like resting to reflect upon our destiny.

THE SEVENTEENTH CENTURY

Russians usually start the history of the museum as an institution at the beginning of the 18th century, being the time when the first state owned museums appeared. The most important institution of this time was the Kunstkammer, planned for St Petersburg by the great Tsar Peter I, and founded in 1714. It was so significant that museum people now often forget the fact that it was fact not the first Russian museum.

The first type of early museum belonged to the ancient monasteries, usually called 'riznitsa', from the word 'riza', a garment worn by priests.

The riznitsas existed in almost all medieval monasteries. One of the most famous was the riznitsa of Pechersky Monastery in Pskov, where the old armament and artefacts associated with the Russian tsars were held. So, the riznitsas were repositories of the most important ceremonial clothes, icons, holy books and other ecclesiastical valuables, as well as some secular objects such as banners and armour.

Our earliest documented knowledge of riznitsas is in 17th century literature relating to the dramatic events of Patriarch Nikon's reforms of the Russian Orthodox Church. That is how we know about the riznitsa of one of the most northern monasteries called Solovetsky, located in the archipelago of the White Sea. The Solovetsky monastery was one of the centres of opposition to Nikon's reforms, and it was attacked in 1676 by state troops and forced to accept the new religious regime. It is assumed that the monastery's riznitsa suffered from this conflict more than other services, and we know that its chamber and collections had been entirely reconstructed by the year 1705. Like in other riznitsas, the old religious relics were used to show and interpret the spiritual origin of certain brotherhoods of monks to tell the story of the church with the help of old objects as symbols.

The collections found in riznitsas were accessible to the monks and to pilgrims, who were the principal target groups. The artefacts had been assembled to articulate the identity of the monastery itself and to provide symbols of the ideals, beliefs and traditions of the Orthodox Church. Like museums today, the role of riznitsas was to reflect the ethical code of communities and to conserve artefacts representing their spiritual heritage for future generations. In many ways, the riznitsas served the same function as private family collections, essentially instruments of self-identification and cultural conservation.

Indeed, the 17th century ritznitsas represent a cultural phenomenon reaching far back into the distant past of human history. They are also profoundly important today: both to Russians themselves, who are rediscovering their spiritual past, and to how foreign tourists perceive Russia. The souvenir industry, which developed in association with pilgrim sites in the 17th century and earlier, is today a significant factor in respect of both the cultural and economic well-being of the nation.

During this century there also began to appear private collections of ancient artefacts, pieces of art, family treasures, curiosities and other rarities. The most well known collections of this kind belonged to names such as Golitsyn, Nashiokin, Khitrovo et al. As in many other European countries, the famous collections of this time belonged to rich noble families and were used like present day museums to show off to others of their class, their genealogy, their tastes, the extent of their political influence and social status. Other motivations were accumulation of material and cultural wealth as inheritance for future generations. But not least, such collections also provided pleasant leisure activities for the owners and their friends, and for the education of their children. Like museums today, they served an important mission. They clearly served to interpret and to establish the owner's identity and individuality: 'Look at these things, now you can understand who I am, what my origins are, and what my social status is.'

THE EIGHTEENTH CENTURY

As Peter I grew to maturity at the turn of the century, he was not satisfied with the Tsar's collection of treasures and symbols of royal power, especially the Royal Armoury, which had been located in Moscow's Kremlin since the end of the 15th century. It contained not only symbols of royal power, such as the banners from the 12th century, but also items of clothing and natural history objects.

In the Kunstkammer of 1714, he began to implement his new vision. The main objects of the collection were exotic curiosities and rare foreign artefacts telling Russian visitors the story, not about themselves, but about the culture of other countries. The basis for interpretation changed. Rather than portraying themselves, it was now a matter of comparing themselves with others. Russia opened the window (not yet the door) to Europe and met the challenge to understand itself in comparison with others. The idea of Peter the Great was clear: to push the culture of his people towards Europe. Not a simple task, even if backed by the Tsar's order to present all visitors with a glass of vodka.

Thus, the 18th century saw the appearance of a new interpretive concept. The message could be expressed as follows: 'Examine how different and interesting they are, then attempt to understand and learn from them.' This approach, documented in the Tsar's decrees at that time, was a result of his rethinking of past museum practice. This philosophy was reflected in the next most significant museum initiative of the century: the Hermitage, started by Catherine II in the 1760s. It was she who continued Peter's attempts to shape her own country's image in the context of European culture.

The interpretive orientation of Hermitage was clearly illustrated by the range of Western art collections purposefully being acquired by the Empress, the most significant being: Johann Ernest Gotzkowski's collection (Prussia), Count Heinrich von Bruhl's collection (Saxon), Baron Pierre Crozat's collection (France), and Sir Robert Walpole's collection (England). In 1785, the Hermitage collections counted 2,658 pieces of art from Western Europe

Catherine's advisers for many acquisitions were Volter and Didro. They worked alongside Russian intellectuals like Count Musin-Pushkin, the Russian Ambassador in London, and assisted in her developing the Hermitage as an outstanding museum institution. It became the first modern Russian Museum, even employing professional curators. One of them was a Venetian artist by the name of G. Martinelly. The Hermitage was thus another step in the search for differences and similarities between Russian and European cultures. Furthermore, the collections of Kunstkammer and the Hermitage were supplemented with a large number of archeological and natural history objects gathered by academic expeditions to the Southern and Eastern regions of the country.

The first catalogue of the collection was published in 1793. It shows that the guiding principle of the Hermitage was radically different from the normal way private house collections of noblemen were presented. It was not purely a matter of inferior decoration; it was more a systematic way of interpretation and presentation for promoting better understanding of cultural assets.

Only 60 copies of the first catalogue were printed. This indicated the real size of the audience and shows that in the 18th century museums were not intended for the general public. They were designed to address a very narrow layer of small elite groups, such as members of the Imperial Court, nobility, academics, artists and members of the Academies of Sciences and Arts. Some of these were more interested in the Kunstkammer, which later inspired the development of several academic museums, one such being the Imperial Russian Art Academy, founded in the middle of the 18th century. Like for the others, there was only limited public access after the 1760s, it being open to ordinary people only one week annually.

Similar characteristics could be attributed to other museum institutions of the century, such as the 1709 Admiralty collection of models (formerly the private collection of Peter I), the future St Petersburg Military Marine Museum of 1805, the Hall of Memorials in the St Petersburg Arsenal (famous for its military trophy collection) and the future Central Artillery Museum. The Admiralty's Modelkammer was probably the most successful among Peter I's museum initiatives. It is generally recognised that his admiration for Dutch maritime culture almost succeeded in destroying the entire Russian shipbuilding industry.

Thus it can be seen that the 18th century was essentially a period of elite museums which functioned as national institutions, and the message of interpretation in their exhibitions was addressed entirely to the social elite on behalf of the Tsar and his court. In fact, these institutions articulated the unity of the Imperial Court and the nation state, both being shaped together.

Among those who contributed to rethinking of Russian museums practice in the 18th century were O. Beliaev on the history of the Kunstkammer in *Kabinet of Peter the Great*, I. Georgi on the history of the Hermitage in *Description of the Capital City of St Petersburg*, and A. Malinovsky on the history of the Moscow Chamber of Armaments in *Description of the Ancient Russian Museum Called the Masters and Armament Chamber, located in Moscow.*

Bieliev expressed the hope that his book would be available even for those were not allowed to visit Kunstkammer themselves. He clearly considered it desirable that museums should be given much wider public accessibility. This is indeed a sentiment felt by all the above mentioned authors. Their writings allow us to learn what was happening at the end of the century in the minds of people thinking about the future of Russian museums. It is evident that they dreamed about making the collections more open to public, and efforts to realize this idea started at the beginning of the 19th century.

The former Modelkammer of Agricultural Instruments in St Petersburg opened the doors to the public once a week in 1803. The former Modelkammer of the Admiralty collection was transformed into the Public Maritime Museum in 1805. The new building for the Moscow Armoury was completed in 1810, and was designed to be accessible by the visiting public. The Manufactures Museum, especially provided for landowners and business people, was opened in 1811 to promote industrial innovation.

The above examples bear witness to a conceptual shift at the turn of the century. The museums of the beginning of the 19th century inherited the innovative spirit of the previous 100 years, moving from family initiatives to real national institutions accessible to a wider public. Not just the Imperial Court and noble families, but the whole nation started to be identified and shaped in close relationship to other European cultures.

THE NINETEENTH CENTURY

The pressure for allowing easier public access to museums gathered momentum in the new century, but the idea of a more nationalistic approach met with a fair degree of resistance from the Imperial Court based on the Tsar's policy of absolute monarchic power. At the time of the patriotic wars in 1812, the Russian scientist and diplomat, N. Rumiantsev and his 'Scientific Circle', proposed the creation of a national public museum. This was resisted by the Tsar, as were similar proposals in 1817 by F. Adelung , and in 1821 by Vikhman. Only in 1931, after Rumiantsev had died, was the big collection gathered by him and his colleagues to be opened as a public museum in the former Rumiantsev house. The property was transferred into the ownership of the Court, and Nikolay I authorised its opening as a state museum. However, it was poorly funded, and the time had clearly not yet come for this type of state institution.

The same fate befell several proposals to found national art history museums. Many attempts were made both in St Petersburg and in Moscow in the middle of the century, but the Tsar rejected them all. This was mainly due to his concern that the art museum movement was too clearly associated with personalities who were known to have nationalist sympathies and interest in the problems and views of the common people.

Many projects of this period represented attempts to reorient Russian museums towards the country's own cultural and natural heritage. This stood in stark contrast to the western oriented museum initiatives of the previous century, still actively supported by the Russian monarch. Indeed, the Hermitage and the Royal Armoury remained virtually closed to the general public well into the second half of the 19th century in spite of numerous appeals to the contrary. They were managed as private collections, open only to members of the Court and their guests.

Although the Tsar's power was strong enough to control the process of establishing new museums in the main cities, it was not always so easily done in the provinces. The more democratic approach to public access and a strong interest in Russian culture and natural history met with more sympathy from local government. It was possible to realise such ideas with the support of local intellectuals and wealthy families. The intellectuals were mostly teachers and clerks of the local authorities. The wealthy people were usually local entrepreneurs and merchants interested in supporting enterprise and developing regional economies.

The first public regional museums were opened in the Crimean towns of Feodosia (1811), Odessa (1825) and Kerch (1826). Their opening was in part made possible because of collections built on artefacts from excavations of settlements dating from Greek antiquity, although it has to be said that the most valuable finds were immediately transported to the Hermitage.

Much more favourable conditions for the development of regional museums appeared after the bourgeois reforms in the 1860s and 1870s. According to D. Ravikovich, 45 regional museum complexes were founded between 1861 and 1905. Half of these were located in the distant Asiatic provinces where only one museum, Irkutsk, existed before. Most of these museums had no support from central government, and relied entirely on sponsorship from the local authorities and business people.

The economic reforms in the second half of the century stimulated the development of agricultural and industrial exhibitions and museums in the major cities. The causal effect was clear, and the most significant innovations were the Agricultural Museum in St Petersburg, founded in 1859, ahead of the most important agricultural reforms, which was followed in 1873 by the Moscow Polytechnic Museum. These were followed in turn by parallel initiatives in the provinces, and all these new museums reflected new activity and growth in the natural economy.

The freedom of museum activities in Moscow and St Petersburg was still constrained by government control, but the enthusiasts for major national museums gradually succeeded by means of subtle tactics. Construction of the Russian National History Museum on Red Square in Moscow began in 1875 on the initiative of the scientific community with support from the city government. From the very beginning of the project, the future museum was named after Great Duke Alexander, the future Emperor Alexander III, who accepted the office of Honorable Chairman. Following this, the Tsar's family made available a series of eighteen museums halls, specially dedicated to the history of the Romanov dynasty, and this large museum opened its doors to visitors in 1883.

The first public Gallery of Russian Art History was opened to the public in 1881 as a private initiative by the brothers Pavel and Sergey Tretiakov. After the death of his brother, Pavel gifted the Gallery to the City of Moscow, and in 1893 it was transformed into a state institution with free public access. This noble gesture by a private person provoked the Tsar to do likewise, and in 1895 Nikolay I founded an Imperial Russian Museum in St Petersburg named after Alexander III.

The above analysis can only be but fragmented and partial, but it depicts the main tendencies which were actively influencing the evolution of Russian museum practice at the turn of the century.

The role of the Imperial Court as instigator and author of museum messages still seemed to be dominating, with leanings towards the culture of Western Europe, but it was in reality being replaced by a new social and intellectual elite able to formulate messages more concerned with Russian identity and nationhood. This was sometimes done on behalf of the monarch, and sometimes it was done to manipulate his wishes so as to move his decisions in a new direction. Towards the end of the 19th century, museums had become more democratic institutions by having been made more accessible to the public, and those in power were beginning to understand how powerful museums were as a means of interpretation to govern the perceptions of national worth and identity.

THE TWENTIETH CENTURY

For the drama and complexity of museum development in the 20th century, there is space for only a brief synopsis of the principal changes in policy and practice. The period from the turn of the century to the October revolution of 1917 was part of what is regarded as the 'silver era' of Russian culture. Between 1905 and 1917, the number of museums increased to almost 300, the majority being run by local authorities. These enjoyed the support of educated local intellectuals who contributed to their creation and development. They ranged widely in both type and size, one category of special significance being the 'memorial museums' of outstanding cultural figures, such as Lomonosov, Tolstoy, Pushkin, Lermontov and Suvorov, which promoted and interpreted their contributions to the cultural life and image of the nation. This was the beginning of a process searching for national and international understanding of Russia's cultural heritage.

Many initiatives were taken in response to historical events. For example, at the height of The Russian–Japanese War in 1902, a decree was issued for the creation of a Russian Military History Museum. In 1913, the States Duma proposed a Moscow Museum of All the Russian People to be located 'in the cradle of the Romanov Dynasty', dedicated to the tercentenary of their Monarchy. Such proposals showed that museum interpretation was regarded as a means of implementing what can only be called overt cultural propaganda by the state.

This duplicitous approach was carried forward into the Soviet period, when ideological propaganda became a key function of the museum sector. In essence, there were two agendas. One was political and emanated from central government. It served as an artificial mask for promotion of the official party line, assuming the same role for the state as when the Imperial Court existed. The other agenda was professional and operated at institutional level, where the aspirations of the Russian people provided the driving force for cultural interpretation, but the content of this work was strictly controlled by ideological dictate from central authorities.

The creative development of museums as an interpretive communication system was prevented by the Bolshevik regime and all institutions were required to support the policies of the Communist Party. Museums which did not conform were closed or reorganised, as the sector was seen as one of the most effective channels of communication for propaganda purposes, and this was the reason for rapid growth in numbers. By 1941, there were about 1,000 museums.

The museum type to dominate were those concerned with the interpretation of regional and local culture, but their adherence to ideological party propaganda resulted in uninspiring conformity. The second largest group was those concerned with the history of the Revolution, and there were about 300 of these in 1985. Many were memorial museums, mostly devoted to Lenin and his cronies: Stalin,

Sverdlov, Kirov, Kalinin et al. There were over 40 museums in the USSR entirely dedicated to the story of Lenin. Indeed, they represented an almost unstoppable force, as Lenin museums were still being constructed into the late 1980s at Krasnoyarsk and Samara. The category to suffer the greatest neglect were those concerned with science and natural history, and they represented less than ten per cent of the national total.

So where do we stand today? In spite of all our economic problems, activities associated with museum development are at an all time high. During the most dynamic periods of the Soviet era, the number of new museums rose by not more than about 20 annually. The present growth rate is almost four times higher. Since 1991, the number of municipal museums has increased by 600 new institutions, and the total is now over 2,000. These are financed from the regional and municipal budgets. In the same period, more then 50 private museums and galleries opened their doors to the public.

The total number of visitors fell at the beginning of the Perestroika period, due to disenchantment with Soviet type museums, but the numbers have now started to increase again. The growth was especially significant in the distant provinces, where the inertia of dependence on central state support was not as strong as in the major cities and their surrounding regions. As a result, many new types of museums, with a variety of exhibitions and activities are now appearing. New models of cultural interpretation, public participation and partnership initiatives are being developed.

This includes new and creative approaches on the international front, such as the recent bilateral partnership with colleagues in the UK. At the time of writing, arrangements were in place for some of our St Petersburg collections to be on display in London. The positive response to this initiative has been a source of welcome encouragement, and few Russian museologists would have expected to read in *The Times,* where Simon Jenkins recently wrote under the headline, 'History is for sharing – Russia gives us lessons in unlocking the hidden treasures in our museums':

> This summer the sleeping giant of St Petersburg will awaken and amaze us all. The greatest art collection in the world, the Hermitage, will open a branch at Somerset House by the Thames to display some of its treasures in rotation. If art is the lasting measure of empire, the Hermitage still rules the world...The best thing about the Hermitage venture is the gauntlet tossed down to other museums with similar treasures in store. At issue here is not whether London needs any more Rubens, Rembrandts or Farbergé eggs. That, I admit, is moot. What the Russians are saying is that the walls of a museum do not a prison make. The trophies of

Russia's greatness are part of Europe's culture. Since the Winter Palace cannot display all of them, why not share? Ownership is not in question. But museums were created for appreciation and dissemination, not for hoarding. The Hermitage is not a shrine of holy icons. Take these works, London, and let us all enjoy them together...Britain's museums are going through what is popularly called a crisis...Most custodians are institutional snobs. Fiercely acquisitive and protective of what they own...Where the Hermitage leads, let others follow.

As far as this initiative is concerned, the context of cross-cultural exchange between Russia and Britain spans several centuries. As Shvidkovsky has documented, it was Charles Cameron who gave us much of St Petersburg's fine architecture, which now houses our historical collections referred to by Jenkins. The timeless symbolism of this cultural reciprocity between nations stands as a beacon of inspiration at the beginning of a new era in Russian museology. We are having to rediscover our identity, and find ourselves having to rethink human values, partly from our own past, partly from other cultures. Both the opportunities and constraints are great. We are having to cope with immense challenges in providing products that will make a positive contribution to the understanding of our own history, as well as to the perceptions of Russian culture by others in the global village of the future. The creative potential of Russian museologists was banished for many long years. Now we are free, and determined to make most of it.

The Authors

Dr Nikolay Nickishin has held the position of Head of Museum Planning and Design within the Russian Institute for Cultural Research since 1986, and was the Institute's Senior Research Officer from 1983–86. He was formerly Head of the Environment Department of the Solovetsky Museum, associated with the monastery on Solovki Island in the archipelago of the White Sea. A prolific author, he has published over 80 articles in various scientific journals, and has also been Chief Editor of more than ten collective papers dealing with issues of museology. He has a PhD in Cultural Geography, has led many national museum projects and cultural policy initiatives, and now lectures in museum planning on the cultural programme in the Moscow School of Social and Economic Sciences at the Russian Academy of National Economy.

For details on Magnus Fladmark see end of Chapter 20.

References

Alpatov, M.W., *Art Treasures of Russia*, Thames & Hudson, 1968.

Brown, C.M & Taylor, B. (eds), *Art of the Soviets: Painting, Sculpture and Architecture in a One-Party State*, Manchester University Press, 1993.

Beliaev, O., *Kabinet of Peter the Great*, 1800.

Cross, A.G., *Anglo–Russian Relations in the Eighteenth Century*, Norwich, 1977.

Dolukhanov, P.M., 'Archaeology and nationalism in totalitarian and post-totalitarian Russia', in Atkinson, J.A. et al (eds), *Nationalism and Archaeology*, Cruithne Press, 1996.

Georgi, I., *Description of the Capital City of St Petersburg*, 1794.

Gerhard, H. P., *The World of Icons*, John Murray, 1971.

Howard, N., 'The Hermitage: Exciting Times Ahead', in Europa Nostra: The European Cultural heritage Review, No 2, 2000, pp. 60-2.

Hyden, P., 'Imperial Culture at Pavlovsk', in *Country Life*, Vol CLXXXI, No 24, 1987.

Jenkins, S., 'History is for Sharing: Russians gives us a lesson in unlocking the hidden treasures in our museums', in *The Times*, 28 January, 2000.

Jettmar, K., *Art of the Stepps*, Methuen, 1967.

Kohl, P.L., 'Nationalism, politics and the practice of archaeology in Soviet Transcaucasia', in *Journal of European Archaeology*, Vol 1, 1991.

Lazarev, V.N., *Moscow School of Icon-painting*, Iskusstov, 1971.

Malinovsky, A., *Description of the Ancient Russian Museum called the Masters and Armament Chamber, located in Moscow*, Part 1, 1807.

Masleenitsyn, S.I., *Jaroslavian Icon-painting*, Iskusstov, 1973.

Russian Institute for Cultural Research, *Museums and the State's Power*, Russian Institute for Cultural Research, 1991.

Shvidkovsky, D., *The Empress & the Architect: British Architecture and Gardens at the Court of Catherine the Great*, Yale University Press, 1996.

Talbot Rice, T., *Russian Icons*, Spring Books, 1963.

Tolstoy, V., *Russian Decorative Art 1917–1937*, Rizzoli, 1990.

26

THE WAY OF THE PEOPLE
A New Museum of the American Indian

W. Richard West and Magnus Fladmark

> If the museum can do anything, it is to help prevent us from getting to the point where we have to go to a museum to learn about ourselves.

> Nelson Cordova, Taos Pueblo, New Mexico

The Smithsonian National Museum of the American Indian is dedicated to the preservation, study and exhibition of the life, languages, literature, history and arts of the Native Indians. Established by an Act of Congress in 1989, the Museum works in collaboration with the Native peoples of the Americas to protect and foster their cultures by reaffirming traditions and beliefs, encouraging contemporary artistic expression and empowering the Indian voice. *The Way of The People* was adopted as the talismanic title for this historic initiative.

The Museum will comprise of three main facilities, one of which is already established: the George Gustav Heye Center. It was opened in October 1994 at the historic Alexander Hamilton US Custom House in lower Manhattan. It serves as a permanent exhibition and education facility in New York City, hosting programs of music and dance performance, films and symposia. The aim is to explore the diversity of the Native people of the Americas, and to promote the strength and continuity of their cultures from the earliest times to the present. New York was an ancient place of exchange among Indians, and the Hopi of Arizona had a prophecy of a time when they would travel to the east to meet with nations of the world in a 'house of mica'. The Heye Center is today such a place, where people of any nation can come for knowledge and to enhance their understanding of Native American culture.

The other two principal facilities are the Museum on the Mall in Washington DC, and the Cultural Resource Center in Suitland, located in Maryland, about six miles away from the Mall. Construction of the latter was completed this year, and the former is scheduled for opening in 2002. The following gives an outline account of these two initiatives. They represent an attempt to bring to the surface a set of realities and world views completely apart from the experience of Western society in modern times. For this to succeed, the Native voice is an essential element in articulating the substance of a culture, which can bring spiritual enlightenment in an age when most of us are too busy to know ourselves.

For an understanding of the institutional strategy described below, it is important to be aware that the collections of the former Museum of the American Indian, funded by the Heye Foundation, form the cornerstone of the new Museum. Assembled largely by the wealthy New Yorker, George Gustav Heye (1874–1957), who collected thousands of North American masterpieces, including intricate wood, horn, and stone carvings from the north-west coast; elegantly painted hides and garments from the northern Plains; pottery and basketry from the south-west, as well as archaeological objects from the Caribbean; beautifully carved jade from the Olmec and Maya peoples; textiles and gold from the Andean cultures; elaborate featherwork from the peoples of Amazonia; and paintings by contemporary Native American artists.

The collections include materials not only of cultural, historical, and aesthetic interest, but also of spiritual significance. Funerary, religious, and ceremonial objects associated with living cultures, are displayed only with the approval of the appropriate tribe. Repatriation is another important concern being addressed by the Museum. Human remains and funerary objects, religious and ceremonial artefacts, communally owned tribal property, or any holdings acquired illegally are returned upon request to individual descendants or tribal groups who can demonstrate a cultural affiliation and factual claim to the property in question.

THE MUSEUM ON THE MALL

The new Museum will be located on the last available Mall site to the east of the National Air and Space Museum. This will be the primary venue for Native exhibitions, performances, conferences and related activities, and will be the pre-eminent setting for the presentation to the world of the cultural achievements of the past and present Native people who live throughout the Americas. The Museum will include indoor and outdoor programmed public spaces as well as work space for museum staff associated with the museum's public programs and collections care.

The design guidelines for the project are of interest. They called upon the architects and others involved in the design to understand and learn from the context of the site, to ensure that the Museum activities complement, rather than compete with, those of neighbouring institutions, to understand Native American cultural symbolism, to have due regard to the planning guidelines for the National Mall, to make a place for the presentation of Native American culture, and to create a welcoming place for people where Indian customs and etiquette govern.

The Museum's Board of Trustees was appointed and hired its first staff in 1990. They devised a consultation and design process which tapped the ideas and expertise of a wide range of Native and non-Native constituents in establishing operational goals and architectural design criteria for the building. Through this process, it quickly emerged that the Mall Museum would be the centrepiece of the programs for the general public. As such, it could become profoundly important nationally and internationally in promoting public knowledge of and respect for the indigenous cultures of the Americas, their historical achievements and contemporary realities. Such a museum would serve as a forum for promoting the exchange of ideas and goodwill among all peoples.

Many Native people view traditional Euro-American museums as suspect institutions, the practices and methods of which generally contradict Native American thinking about the preservation and presentation of culture and artefacts. As a consultee noted, 'My grandparents were my collection, my museum.' In many Native cultures, everyday objects are regarded and cared for as living things, made for specific uses, to be properly discarded or recycled when they outlive their purpose.

The museum as a vault chamber or temple glorifying objects out of context is not a place of learning. Ceremonial and sacred objects and their related songs, stories and dances, as preserved from generation to generation, are to be regarded as personal or communal property to be used and seen only for particular ceremonies by authorised people. Collecting solely for scientific research, financial gain or aesthetic enjoyment fails to consider the cultural and spiritual needs of the communities from which the objects come.

The Museum's main challenge is to create a place and an institution where cultures are presented by Native people to a diverse international public, in ways that reflect their values and viewpoints. The Museum must create this place within the physical and cultural milieu of the National Mall, a context that offers both enormous opportunities and considerable difficulties. The essence of this challenge was aptly described by Richard Guy Wilson in 1991:

The Mall's buildings, sculpture, landscaping, and space represents attempts to convey meanings about America – its history, culture, and civilization; some of its buildings are easily understood, others more difficult. Displayed on the Mall is history as symbol, a carefully chosen ensemble that has been revised many times and will be revised again...The Mall in the 20th century becomes the physical representative of American history as an ideal.

One can hardly imagine a more symbolically potent site for the Museum, on the National Mall at the foot of the Capitol amid the country's most powerful physical expressions of national aspirations. The Museum will be symbolic of a new relationship between the Federal Government and the Native American Indian: on a site representing the last significant opportunity in the foreseeable future to add to or change the Mall's idealised architectural embodiment of our history and cultural values. Equally important, this is the first opportunity to create in Washington a place that honours and concerns itself primarily with Native Americans.

The National Mall and the public buildings lining it have evolved, under the scrutiny of interested politicians and civic leaders, into the current form through a fascinating series of built and unbuilt interpretations of the original concept sketched by Pierre Charles L'Enfant. Many Mall visions have reflected orthodox views of their time, while others have been more daring. Both formal-classical and picturesque-romantic designs were proposed, and were on occasion played off against each other, especially by those seeking to incorporate images and experiences of the rural and wilderness aspects of the American landscape as a counterbalance and relief to the rigid formality of city life.

The vision of the Mall that has stuck, however, is the one represented by the Senate Park Commission Plan of 1901–02, usually referred to as the McMillan Plan after the senator who presided over it. This Plan is rooted in the 'City Beautiful' movement. It dominated urban design in US cities between 1893 and 1917, and marked the beginning of comprehensive city planning in the US. It is characterised by an emphasis on Baroque grand vistas and streets linking Classical architectural and landscape elements of the city on a huge and comprehensive scale. Ironically for this project, the McMillan Plan had as its catalyst the 1893 Chicago World's Columbian Exposition, a fair commemorating the 400th anniversary of Columbus' voyage. This exposition came at the close of the frontier era of American history and embodied a refocusing of energy on the nation's increasingly urban and industrial character.

These events came at the end of an era of political, military and cultural conflict that diminished the population of Indian people to its lowest point and culminated in Wounded Knee (1890). This was also a turning point in federal Indian policy, marked by the Dawes (Allotment) Act of 1887, when forced removal changed to forced assimilation.

Few projects proposed for the Mall have escaped controversy and redesign, and some never reached fruition. They were victims respectively of arguments about the appropriateness of architectural styles, financial hard times and political views on the intended purpose of buildings. For example, fear of the communist inspiration of contemporary art killed the Smithsonian's proposed modern art museum (1939) for the site later assigned to the National Air and Space Museum. The last significant above-ground construction project fronting directly on the Mall was the East Building of the National Gallery of Art. Its design was approved before trends emphasizing historical allusion and physical context and laws governing the preservation of historic landmarks emerged as the significant forces in the established design review and regulatory climate that exists today.

Average annual visitation at the Mall Museum is projected at six million visitors, after an initial five years during which that average is expected to be exceeded by up to 1.5 million. This compares with current visitation at the National Gallery of Art and the National Museum of American History and would be second only to the approximately ten million at the National Air and Space Museum. Programs and opening hours will be planned to even out the distribution of visitors throughout the day and week, and to provide for outdoor orientation, exhibition and performance. The audience will reflect local and tourist markets for Washington, which include a large number of foreigners. In addition to those visiting the Mall site, many Native Americans will be reached by the Museum through its community service programs. These will include off-site access to information in various media, co-operative cultural resource projects and travelling exhibitions.

Visitors will be predominantly tourists, coming for the most part for a one-time or rare visit to Washington and taking in a number of other historical sites and Smithsonian museums. Average stays of one and one half hours are expected, though lengths of stay may sometimes be shorter, given the projected capacity of the building.

Most visitors will not have extensive knowledge of Native American history and cultures and many may have major misconceptions. In consultations, Indians and non-Indians alike recognized the importance and potential of the opportunity the Mall Museum presents to broaden and inform a national sense of cultural heritage in ways that will make a difference far beyond Washington. The museum must first dispel stereotypes about Indians, Eskimos and Native Hawaiians.

INTERPRETATION AND PERFORMANCE STRATEGY

The Mall Museum includes in its program 52,000 square feet of interior exhibitions galleries plus additional circulation and lobby spaces, food service spaces and exterior program areas that will also include displays and demonstrations. This space, along with about 20,000 square feet of galleries at the Heye Center in New York and a travelling exhibition program will enable it to exhibit its large and outstanding collection of Native American artefacts.

Interpretation and presentation of the Museum's collection and of materials loaned by others will be planned in consultation with respective tribes, special regard being given to the exhibiting of sacred or sensitive material. Tribes will also be consulted in the continuing documentation of the museum's collections and exhibit narratives will incorporate their input. This process of consultation had been begun in the planning of inaugural exhibitions for the New York facility and in the preliminary planning for traditional care of collections at the Cultural Resources Center in Suitland.

Interpretation and exhibition planning at the Mall Museum will vary significantly, in content, thematic organisation and design, from traditional treatments of indigenous culture in museums settings. Anthropological divisions and historical chronology, while useful for many purposes, will probably not be the primary organising elements of the Museum's permanent exhibitions galleries. Themes and organising models derived from holistic, non-linear Native approaches that emphasise relationships rather than compartmentalisation will predominate, with respect paid to making these appropriate to the learning styles of a diverse audience. The themes adopted for strategic planning were:

> Origin stories
> Debunking stereotypes
> Languages
> Family relationships
> Relationships with the land and environment
> Relationships with federal government
> Significant individuals
> Contemporary art, linked to traditional artefacts
> Social, political, educational and environmental issues
> Tribal community profiles

Exhibitions are expected to communicate not only visually, but also through sounds, smells and touch and, in the food service areas, through the taste of Native foods. Interactive technologies will be used to tailor visits to individual interests, and virtual reality has the potential to provide a more profound sense of context than is possible through conventional exhibition techniques. Modern information technology offers the capacity to tell in depth the stories of the hundreds of tribes represented in the museum's collections.

The programme provides for large permanent exhibition galleries interspersed with small galleries and classrooms. The smaller galleries are to be used for changing displays that support the themes of the main galleries. The classrooms will be used for interpretative, exhibit-related presentations, in person or through audiovisuals and as staging areas for exhibit installation. Temporary exhibition galleries are located in proximity to the main public lobby and include space for museum-produced and community-produced exhibitions.

Performances by Native dance and theatre groups, storytellers and musicians will be central to the museum's public program and integrated with its exhibitions programmes. Urban and reservation-based performers will do much to communicate the vitality and variety of both traditional and contemporary Native art and culture. The oral traditions of Native peoples can best be appreciated through live encounters, and the use of Native languages will be an important part of what is presented. Moreover, presentations by contemporary artists will enhance public understanding and appreciation of the Museum's rich collection of clothing, musical instruments and props for ceremony and dance. Established companies may be invited for extended stays and new groups given opportunities to debut their talents. Resident companies may also develop at the Museum.

The word 'Potomac', used by tribes originally located in the Washington DC area, has the meaning of 'where the goods are brought in'. It has therefore been adopted as the name for the main gathering place within the Museum, around which will be located the restaurant and cafeteria, the museum shop, demonstration and membership information and a flat floor performance area open to the main circulation space. The resource centre, community-produced exhibition galleries and member's lounge overlook this space.

These spaces are grouped to connect the retail activities to its public programs by placing them in proximity to performance and demonstration spaces, with the intention of communicating to the visitor the sense of an Indian community, where activities and the spaces used tend to be more mixed together than in an average American suburban area. Many of these activities can benefit from the views of the Mall and the Capitol and can expand into related outdoor program space during the spring and summer months.

The self-service cafe will seat 365 and will incorporate a variety of Native foods served from five serving stations that represent the indigenous cuisine of five broad regions – the Great Plains, Meso-America, the Northwest Coast, the Northern Woodlands, and South America. At the Northwest Coast serving station there will be a firepit where visitors can view traditional methods of preparing salmon. Preparation can be observed by the visitor where it is aesthetically and educationally possible to prepare the selected menu items in public view. There will be opportunities for reinforcing the Museum's commitment to hospitality, informing the visitor about Native contributions to agriculture and world cuisine, and presenting contemporary issues related to species diversity and nutrition.

The Museum shop will include books, cards, posters and items made by Native people including jewellery, textiles, baskets, pottery, children's toys and contemporary art. It is planned as two spaces – one on the Ground Floor and one on the Second Floor – that are connected by a large opening in the Second Floor by a monumental stair. Development of specific marketing and inventory plans will determine the size of each area. Native areas view the Mall Museum as a tremendous opportunity for world exposure and a way to contribute financially to strengthening the outreach programming and the presentation of contemporary cultural vitality.

Demonstration areas will be located in proximity to the shop. These will serve many purposes, including the demonstration of techniques by artists whose works are sold in the shop. Indeed, the opportunity and challenges, both technical and political, of this project are enormous, as are the expectations of the many stakeholders in the Museum's success as a provider of services. This pivotal role as a cultural catalyst is greatly enhanced by the Museum's location on the National Mall, arbiter and projector of the USA's cultural values and self-image, to the world and ourselves.

THE CULTURAL RESOURCES CENTER

Located in Suitland, around six miles form the Mall, the Center provides for the transfer of the extensive and extraordinary collections which were held at the Heye Foundation's premises in New York. It will be complementary to the new Heye Center facilities in Manhattan and to the Mall Museum in Washington.

Although the Mall Museum will be the centrepiece of the outreach effort to the general public, the Cultural Resources Center will be the hub of exchange with its Native American constituency, as well as the home of its collections. The aims are to foster broad and balanced relationships with stakeholders in its collections, to encourage participation by communities and individuals, and to incorporate their viewpoints in policy decisions relating to collections, research, exhibitions and care of objects. To realise these goals, it is planned to take full advantage of available information technologies, to share collections and in-house expertise with others.

The new Center is located at the eastern end of the Smithsonian Institution's 100-acre Suitland campus, currently housing the Museum Support Center (MSC) and Garber facility, used primarily for collections storage, research, conservation and exhibit construction. Additional accommodation has been created for collections storage and related activities for many of the Smithsonian's museums and support offices. Shared amenities, including food service, child care, and possibly a residential conference centre and dormitories are planned for the future.

The existing collections being transferred from New York include artefacts from throughout the Americas, a 40,000-volume library, and archival, photographic, film, video and audio collections. The collections are expected to expand in accordance with the collecting plan, which emphasises expansion of contemporary and traditional art forms, preservation of oral histories, language and music. The plan also identifies acquisitions to enhance the range of ethnographic and archaeological materials, and to facilitate public access to important examples of Native cultural heritage.

The scale of the operation is enormous, as the entire collections amount to approximately 800,000 objects, ranging in origin from the Arctic to Tierra del Fuego. There are items from all major culture areas of the Americas, representing virtually all US tribes, most of those in Canada, and important tribal representations from Middle and South America, as well as the Caribbean. Chronologically, the collections include artefacts from Paleo-Indian to contemporary arts and crafts, and contain utilitarian objects, as well as those of great historical and aesthetic importance.

The ethnographic collections, considered the best of their kind in the world, have been housed in severely overcrowded conditions with poor environmental controls, limited space and capacities to respond to tribal and modern museological requirements for care, placement and access. Most ethnographic artefacts will be shelved in open high-density storage units, arranged by tribe within rooms representing culture areas. High-density storage systems result in substantial space and cost savings through movable shelving units that create aisles only where and when needed to access a particular part of the collection.

Sacred materials, portions of the archaeology collection and other objects not suited to these compact units will be in fixed storage equipment around the perimeter of the rooms. The Museum's collections staff will be

331

located mainly in Maryland, including the curatorial, repatriation, registration, collections management, conservation, film, video and audio, photographic services, archives and library departments.

Visitation research predicts approximately 1,500 visitors annually to the new facility. This is in addition to the daily population for all Maryland facilities, projected to be about 1,500, and composed of researchers, scholars, interns, fellows, graduate students and other official visitors. They represent unprecedented levels for a facility of this kind.

Visitors will come to conduct research, collaborate on exhibitions, films, oral history and collections documentation, find artistic inspiration in the collections, give and receive training through internship and fellowship programs. Thousands will participate from remote locations through electronic access to collections and other information via transfer of visual, audio and text information into computer data, video and other formats that can be distributed via phone lines, broadcasting, satellite or mail.

Other client groups will be reached through technical assistance projects and travelling exhibitions, as well as at tribal, cultural and educational institutions. The on-site electronic accessing system for the collections will also benefit the wider community of academics and museum professionals, and thereby facilitate a two-way transfer with constituency feedback.

The Museum is committed to assisting local Indian communities in their cultural development on their own terms. It will serve as a facilitator of programs, activities and resource sharing that will enable Native communities to determine for themselves what is the best relationship with museum staff to achieve their cultural, educational and artistic aspirations. Among the services available will be programs that help communities to preserve their languages and customs, and to learn from their own oral tradition. The services will also embrace bilateral educational training programs and facilities for interns, fellows and other visiting collaborators.

CONCLUSIONS

It is not for the museum to preserve culture; that is our job. The museum is an instrument to teach our view of ourselves, our understanding of what we are, and that which we are willing to share with the world outside.

Raymond Apodaca, Ysleta del Sur Pueblo

Like the Museum of Scotland and the reconstituted Scottish parliament, created in the same time period, the National Museum of the American Indian in its constituent parts represents a symbolic return of the nation's native soul to its people.

It can also be said that the Museum represents a turning point in the history of the Smithsonian Institution. The new approach enshrined in the chosen title, *The Way of The People*, redefines the role of Native Indians from being an audience of the Institution to being an essential part of its constituency. This fundamental change in museum relationships, together with active stakeholder participation, has generated the extraordinary vision the Museum is seeking to articulate.

The essence of this vision is that art is an expression of living culture, reflecting the spiritual ethos of Native peoples, present and future, rather than simply their reflections in the mirror of history. This implies a focus on the 'creation' of objects, overriding conventional preoccupation with historical objects for their own sake.

Central to the strategic philosophy is the objective of bringing to the surface a set of human values and perceptions of the world that are largely absent from contemporary Western experience. It seeks to reach beyond knowledge of territorial possessions and material objects, to a spiritual dimension of enhanced awareness and enlightenment that can be shared by both audience and constituents.

The challenges are daunting, as we are essentially concerned with a process of defining cultural identity in the 21st century. Legislation passed by Congress stipulated that the shape of the Museum should be governed by Native involvement to ensure an ultimate sense of ownership. This being so, the constituents themselves will define the interpretive voice. But viewed in a global context, the Museum is also intended to serve as a forum for multicultural dialogue rather than as a temple of singular truth.

Meanwhile, the challenge for visitors walking 'the way of the people' is to make sense of the conundrum that, on their way into the past, they will encounter ancestors on their way into the future.

The Authors

W. Richard West studied American history at Redlands and Harvard Universities, and then Law at Stanford. He has been an associate attorney and partner with different law firms, and was in 1990 appointed Director of the Smithsonian Institution National Museum of the American Indian. The major initiatives under his direction have been opening in 1994 of the George Gustav Heye Center in Manhattan, and planning of the Mall Museum in Washington

DC and the Cultural Resources Center in Suitland. Public service has included membership of the Board of Trustees for the Environmental Defense Fund, Ford Foundation, Bush Foundation, and the Native American Council of Regents of the Institute of American Indian Arts. He is currently Chairman of the Board of the American Association of Museums. His father is Southern Cheyenne and his mother a Macrae of Scottish descent.

For details on Magnus Fladmark see end of Chapter 20.

References

Cole, D., *Captured Heritage: The Scramble for Northwest Coast Artifacts*, Seattle, 1985.

Deloria Jr, V. and Lytle, C., *The Nations Within: The Past and Future of American Indian Sovereignty*, New York, 1984.

Eroders, R. & Ortiz, A., *American Indian: Myths and Legends*, Pantheon Press, 1984.

Haggard, K., 'Site Relationship of Four Pre-Columbian Cities in Mexico', in Brogden, W. & Hausler W. (eds), *The Student Publications of the School of Design*, North Carolina State University, 1964.

Hoxie, F.E. (ed), *Encyclopedia of North American Indians*, Houghton Mifflin, Boston, 1996.

Johnson, T. (ed), *Spirit Capture: Photographs from the National Museum of the American Indian*, Smithsonian Institution Press & NMAI, 1998.

Josephy Jr, A. (ed), *America in 1492: The World of the Indian Peoples before the Arrival of Columbus*, New York, 1992.

Roberts, D., *Once they moved like the wind: Cochise, Geronimo and the Apache Wars*, Simon & Schuster, 1994.

Tiller, V.E.V. (ed), *Tiller's Guide to Indian Country: Economic Profiles of American Indian Reservations*, BowArrow, 1996.

Turner, G., *Indians of North America*, Blandford Press, 1979.

Williamson, L., 'Sustaining Cultural Identities: Community Arts in the United States', in Fladmark, J.M. (ed), *Sharing the Earth:: Local Identity in Global Culture*, Donhead, 1995.

Young, N., 'Gamble for Survival' (Mashantucket Pequot Indians), in *The Scotsman*, 24 July, 1999.

Wooden dance mask of the Yup'ik Eskimos on the Kuskokwim River in Alaska, dating from around 1875–90. Such masks are danced to honour the spirit of the animals captured in the hunt.

The newly built Cultural Resources Centre of the Smithsonian National Museum of the American Indian, located at Suitland.

The main building which will occupy the last vacant site on National Mall in Washington DC.

27

DEVELOPED INDIAN IDENTITIES
Seeing the Stereotypes and Beyond

Richard Hill

The photographer, as a recording artist and image maker, has been a powerful agent in creating enduring stereotypes. This chapter is built around analysis of photographic material, combined with personal reflections on encountered stereotypes. The story starts with me looking through a stack of old postcards at a local flea market in search of stereotypical images of Indians that might be used in my university class.

There were plenty of items to choose from: cards of Pueblo Indians performing the Eagle Dance; Navajo Indians sitting in front of their weaving looms; colourful Plains Indians mounted on horseback; Great Lakes Indians dancing at a powwow; Seminole Indians sewing their colourful clothing. Then I came across a hand-coloured photo card of 'Chief Cornplanter and Wigwam, Allegany (sic) State Park, N.Y.' If I had not known who Cornplanter actually was, I would have assumed that he was a Plains Indian. He stands in front of a painted tipi, wears a feathered war bonnet, holds a peace pipe, and raises his left hand as if communicating through sign language. This little postcard represents centuries of stereotypical images of Indians, but what most intrigued me was the realization that even Indians began to live up to such stereotypes.

The scene in the Cornplanter postcard matches both the kind of image of Indians that might be held by tourists and the kind of cultural clichés that predominate American popular culture. Edward Cornplanter was one of many Iroquois Indians who performed for the public, usually by telling stories, demonstrating crafts, and singing and dancing. He travelled in his own version of a big top tent show, billing it as a 'Double Show – Indian and Minstrel Concert'. When I first began to attend the traditional ceremonies in the longhouses of the Iroquois, I was amazed to see that in the ritual dances some men wore this style of Plains clothing. The lead dancers wore war bonnets rather than the Iroquois-style head-dress. Ironically, many Iroquois Indians from upstate New York had participated in the Wild West shows and adopted the dress of the Plains Indians, partly because it is very impressive, but mostly because such clothing was ingrained in the way many Americans envisioned Indians. It brought the 'dress-up' Natives a good income by playing Indian.

This stereotype of the Plains Indians was so deeply ingrained in both Indian and non-Indian images that Iroquois performers, re-enacting a drama of their sacred history, wore Plains Indian head-dresses while depicting ancient Iroquois in the story of the formation of their Confederacy of Peace. There is a photograph of a performance, held in 1906 at the Cattaraugus Seneca reservation, south of Buffalo, New York, which shows the legendary Peacemaker being heralded by the assembled chiefs. Their clothing, moccasins, beadwork, and head-dress were influenced by what they had seen in the Wild West shows that had passed through the area. This 'Hiawatha' performance toured across the United States and went overseas as well.

The Plains Indian culture had become the superculture against which all Indians were measured. As a result of the famous battles in the West and the perpetuation of those images through Hollywood, all Indians were assumed to live in tipis, ride horses, wear full-feathered head-dresses, and be experts at Native crafts. Comic books, toys, games, television programs, movies, and country fairs perpetuated these images. For over a century the war bonnet remained an essential part of these public representations of Indians. In the 1800s, the popular notion was that the only good Indian was a dead Indian. By the 20th century, however, it was commonly believed that the only good Indian was a dancing Indian. To survive, many Indians latched on to these stereotypes. Many natives joined in as the larger society toyed with Indian images. To the outsider this all looked authentic; to the Indians it was just a show. It did not seem to matter that these displays perpetuated distorted images of Native culture.

In nearly every toy store in America, multicoloured 'Indian' head-dresses, rubber tomahawks, and plastic bows and arrows are on the shelves. Through these things children absorb and literally buy into national stereotypes of Indians. During the Civil War, brass bands became popular on Iroquois reservations. By the 1890s, these bands played all over the countryside, bringing together a strange juxtaposition of images. Indians in war bonnets marched as they played peppy tunes on their cornets, trumpets, trombones, and drums. They wore a stylized 'Indian' outfit of feathered bonnets and cloth shirts with fringe across the front, beaded belts, and collars. Seeing old photographs of these bands and watching their modern-day counterparts play, I cannot help but wonder just how the Iroquois and the general public came to adopt and accept such images.

THE PHOTOGRAPHED STEREOTYPE

The invention of photography in the mid-19th century introduced a new dimension to Native stereotyping. Indians became collaborators, captured for eternity in strange poses that were not always of their own making. Staged poses for the camera resulted in photographs that lacked cultural depth. They were unreal. Photography brought the wild Indian into the safe confines of the home, and in doing so tamed the savage beast. These Indians might have strange costumes and surroundings, but they never appear threatening. Instead, they are enveloped in a romantic stillness and removed in time.

One enduring stereotype is that of the stoic stare of the silent savage. The slowness of early photographic technology contributed to this. People had to sit still, and smiling was taboo for everyone, not just Indians. Nevertheless, the sternness seen in many Indian faces has been translated as stoicism. It could just as easily be the sitter's annoyance with the pose.

Photography came into use during a time of great turmoil for Indians. The camera witnessed the implementation of the whites' Manifest Destiny and their hope to subjugate the Indians. Photography permitted editorial comments about this demise. The Indian, posed in 'traditional' clothing with feathers, beads, and bones, and shown holding a weapon, embodies a cultural contradiction. Those attributes represent the past, yet the soulful gaze into the soft light seems to question the future. Until the Native American Citizenship Act of 1924, this was the dominant image created by non-Indian photographers. They were icons of the battle to win the West. They were the enemy, the victims, and the prisoners of that long war.

It is difficult at best to look beyond the surface of a photograph to comprehend what was going on in the lives of the Indians who are now momentarily frozen in time. Undoubtedly, some photographs were more a white man's fantasy than Indian reality. Lives of Native Americans have changed dramatically since the invention of photography, yet we are left to wonder whether these archival photographs are stereotypical images or true reflections of reality.

In most cases, these photographs 'document' Indians as they lived, worked, and played in their communities. Only by peeling back the veneer created by false notions of Indians can we appreciate what was actually happening in the image. Past tendencies were to look at such photographs either as factual records that preserve information on aboriginal lifeways or as evidence of cultural decay. To see beyond those two extremes, it is important to remember that different stereotypical notions about Indians are at work.

THE TAMING OF INFAMOUS INDIANS

One stereotype that predominates is that of the warring chief or chanting medicine man. Male leaders often gained notoriety through their confrontations with settlers or soldiers, or through their depictions of possessing dangerous spiritual powers. Among the most famous, or perhaps infamous, Indians today are Osceola, Tatanka Yotanka (Sitting Bull), Ta-Sunko-Witko (Crazy Horse), Mahpina Luta (Red Cloud), Goyathlay (Geronimo), Cochise, and Heinmot Toolalakeet (Chief Joseph). Through photography these 'wild savages' have been subdued and remade into icons of fighting Indians.

Sitting Bull's victory over George Custer at the Little Bighorn monumentalised the name of this holy man of the Hunkpapa Dakota. His image is etched in our collective memory, and photographs of him perpetuate notions about the sternness of Indians. Perhaps he wanted to be seen this way. He might well have collaborated with photographers to make himself seem larger than life. White bureaucrats also wanted photographs of Sitting Bull, but primarily so military officers could identify these Indian troublemakers in the field. Ironically, Crazy Horse, the man who actually led the warriors at the Little Bighorn, refused to have his photograph taken, while Sitting Bull apparently expressed few objections.

A hand-painted image of Sitting Bull is part of a larger set of postcards in the Photograph Archive of the National Museum of the American Indian. This portrait could hardly be called a stereotype, for there was no stronger Indian nationalist than Sitting Bull. Nevertheless, it is intriguing that his image became so popular among the very people he fought against. Major General O. Howard, himself an Indian fighter, represented the thoughts of many when he described Sitting Bull in 1908 as 'a famous brave and a cruel, bad Indian,' who had influence over the other chiefs because 'they had a strange fear of medicine-men'. Sitting Bull's naturally creased face was considered grim, and even proof of his supposedly angry personality. Many Indians have furrowed brows that give the impression of sternness, which sometimes is misinterpreted as an indication of their determination to resist the whites.

Even though he was feared, hated, and ultimately assassinated, Sitting Bull became a proud emblem for both Indians and non-Indians. Major General Howard greatly despised Sitting Bull and labelled him a 'coward', yet others called him a hero. Strangely, some whites admired him, an attitude fostered no doubt by his stint in Buffalo Bill's Wild West Show in 1865. Imagine fighting the US army one year, and then touring the country to re-enact those battles as a form of entertainment a few years later. Somehow, Sitting Bull's struggle for his people and his homeland had been transformed into the idea that he was a noble and powerful Indian chief. The popularity and profitability of photographs of such Indians grew so rapidly that photographers began to copyright their pictures.

Red Cloud, an Oglala, was another famous Indian whose reputation was transformed from that of a fierce war leader to an Indian celebrity who defended Native rights at a lecture given at the Cooper Institute in New York City. Famous for defeating the US army, Red Cloud used his military victories to retain the Black Hills and to secure a peace treaty in 1868 that forced the army to abandon its forts along the Bozeman Trail. He became a real hero to his own people and something of a nobleman to many whites.

Photographed as if he were some kind of Indian royalty, Red Cloud appears as a Shirt Wearer, a position of high esteem among his own people. In a photograph, taken by C.M. Bell in 1880 during one of Red Cloud's ten trips to Washington, DC, he is shown holding a white man's cane rather than a tomahawk or a peace pipe, perhaps to suggest his desire to blend the two cultures. The juxtaposition of the war shirt with its hair locks against the melodramatic fake rock and painted backdrop makes this a metaphorical portrait of the tamed, noble savage who has been made safe by a treaty, yet still retains his dignity. Unlike Sitting Bull or Crazy Horse, Red Cloud lived to become an example of pacification, a negotiator of change, and an advocate for assimilation in the areas of religion and education. How did his own people see him? Given a camera, would they have depicted him this same way? Was he a hero to them, or did his compromises turn him into an Uncle Tomahawk?

REDRESSING THE WILD INDIAN

Wearing traditional clothing remains an important way to express communal identity. Many Indians today refer to old photographs for design ideas for their own clothing or for models for their artwork about 'the good old days'. These historic photographs, however, cannot be read too literally. One example is a portrait taken in 1888 of an Onondaga man (perhaps Chief Frank Logan) and two young girls. Typical of so many archival photographs, this image is not in sharp focus, the subjects are stiffly posed, and no indication of surrounding events is given. The real question is, where did the man get the idea to pose in the leggings and

Plains-style head-dress, while his daughters wear everyday clothing? This is certainly not an expression of Pan-Indianism: the Huron, Iroquois, Micmac, Ojibwe, and other Great Lakes Indians were wearing stand-up feather head-dresses long before the Plains Indians adopted the style in the early 19th century. Such forms of dress were introduced into other areas mainly through the influence of Wild West shows, which featured re-enactments of battles fought by the Northern Plains Indians. These shows often employed Natives from other regions to play the Indian roles. Performers then took their Plains-style clothing back to their areas. In distant communities wearing these forms of dress became a way for Native Americans to express their 'Indianness'.

In one obviously staged photograph, anthropologist Frances Densmore sits near Mountain Chief, a Blackfeet elder, as he interprets in sign language a song that she has recorded. Mountain Chief was almost certainly asked to dress in his 'Indian' clothing on this occasion. The bow and arrow were purposely set next to the recorder to underscore the contrast in technologies and races. The scene was arranged out-of-doors so there would be sufficient light to take the photograph. Most likely, none of this would have taken place during the actual process of translating the song. Considering this, the photograph has little anthropological value other than to demonstrate how intrusive scientific enquiry can be.

Sign language was developed among the Plains Indians, whose many different dialects and languages made communication difficult at best. Still in use among the oldest Plains people today, such sign language has become a cultural cliché largely due to movies that utilised hand signals to animate the grunts of actors playing Indians. In a movie still from 'Susannah of the Mounties' (1939), a young Shirley Temple is dressed as an Indian and learns sign language from a Blackfeet Indian named Turtle. The first 'moving' picture made by Thomas Edison in 1892 featured documentary footage of the Sioux Ghost Dance. Even though Indians were no longer considered a military threat after the massacre at Wounded Knee in 1890, movie producers kept the image of the warrior alive for decades.

INDIANS AS ENTERTAINMENT

Wild West shows brought the drama of the white man's war with the Indians to audiences around the globe. One photograph of a sham battle was taken in 1891, one year after the massacre at Wounded Knee. What makes this blurry photograph so unusual is that it was taken in Munich, Germany. Amid the dead and dying, a warrior wearing a dance bustle brings his rifle down upon a wounded soldier. The Indians were played by actual Native Americans, but little attention was paid to cultural or historical accuracy. Providing exciting entertainment and fulfilling stereotypes were among the show's primary objectives.

Another scene seems to be a photo drama unto itself. Standing in front of what appears to be stage scenery, a dour-looking Long Wolf holds a pistol next to his equally glum wife. Only the expression of the baby, who happily smiles at the camera, belies the seriousness of the situation. Perhaps these Indians were just having their family portrait taken. Through the influence of the popular Wild West shows, Indians began to strike the stereotypical poses as they associated with those performances. It is an aboriginal form of 'mugging' for the camera.

In a photograph taken at the 45th anniversary of the Battle of the Little Bighorn, a Cheyenne named Porcupine plays the role of 'the fallen foe'. Annual gatherings to commemorate what was the greatest US military defeat in its time turned the site into a national tourist spot by the early 20th century. The area remains a popular tourist destination in Montana, and in recent years Indians lobbied successfully to change its name from the Custer Battlefield Monument to Little Bighorn National Monument. Some venerate the place as the heroic last stand of outnumbered soldiers, as in the movie 'They Died With Their Boots On' (1941). Others see it as the site of the Indians' heroic victory to defend their freedom in their own land. Such duality fills Indian history and complicates the contradictory nature of stereotypes about Indians.

Hollywood created its own versions of Indian adventures, and television brought the western into American homes. Tonto, as the faithful companion of the Lone Ranger, became the most famous Indian of his generation. Today, many Native Americans criticise the fictionalised character of Tonto, yet nothing had generated more positive feelings towards Indians since John Smith's account of Pocahontas. On television, Tonto was played by Jay Silverheels, a Mohawk actor who provided the only positive media image of Indians at that time. Interestingly, Tonto did not wear a war bonnet, swing a tomahawk, or scalp anyone. He spoke broken English, but he usually got the Lone Ranger out of trouble. He was a 'good' Indian.

This fascination with Indians has turned into a multimillion-dollar industry centred on cultural tourism in the Southwest, the Northern Plains, and the Northwest Coast. It has also created an economic reason to perpetuate the Plains Indian prototype. People have come to expect Indians to look a certain way, and many Natives willingly delivered that stereotype as long as they made money at it. This is why stereotypes are so deeply ingrained into both American and Indian popular culture.

Winhold Reiss, a German artist who immigrated to America primarily to paint Indians in the West, made the Blackfeet popular through his artwork, symbolizing the type of Indians that tourists wanted to see. Inspired by the German author Karl May and the American novelist James Fenimore Cooper, Reiss went out in search for 'noble savages'. On his first trip to Browning, Montana, Reiss befriended a Blackfoot Indian named Turtle. Reiss made a drawing of him in 1919, which started him on his artistic mission. 'What finer thing could one do for these brave fine people, who are rapidly disappearing, than to go out to their reservations, live with them, study them and preserve their wonderful features and types?'

The very first Indian Reiss ever met was Yellow Elk, a Blackfoot Indian and down-and-out circus performer who was riding a Manhattan elevated train in 1917. Reiss took Yellow Elk to the American Museum of Natural History, where he talked the curators into allowing Yellow Elk to dress in a Lakota beaded shirt so Reiss could paint his first 'real' Indian. Ten years later, in 1927, the Great Northern Railroad, which operated several hotels in Glacier Park, Montana, hired Reiss to paint portraits of the Blackfeet Indians who were employed at or lived near the park. These paintings were then used as the basis of posters and calendars to promote the park.

Reiss broke with tradition by depicting the Blackfeet as he found them. He painted many portraits of them in their everyday clothing, which made them look more like cowboys than Indians. Not surprisingly, only staged photographs and his paintings of colourfully dressed Indians were used for the park's advertising campaigns. By this time many Blackfeet had stopped wearing their traditional outfits, and the Great Northern had to pay Indians to make and wear them for the sake of the tourists.

Dancing Blackfeet Indians in beautiful war bonnets of eagle feathers and magnificent outfits of bright white leathers, colourful beaded strips, and white ermine tails greeted trains loaded with visitors as they pulled into the park's railway station. It made for quite an impressive sight. It would be unfair to say that these Indians eking out a living at the park were consciously promoting stereotypes. These stereotypes already existed in the minds of the tourists. The Blackfeet just gloriously epitomised what the tourists had come to expect. It is far less appealing to compare these idealised images of the entertaining Blackfeet to the harsh reality of life on the reservation. This romanticised image of Indians became so popular that Reiss set up an art school at Glacier and taught others how to make portraits of Blackfeet and Flathead Indians.

Calvin Last Star, one of the Blackfeet dancers at Glacier, recalled that they would invite tourists to join in their round dance. 'We had a little program for the tourists at 8 o'clock every night...The tourists would mostly ask you to take pictures with them...I think my father and the older people enjoyed it...It was just something to do that was enjoyable during the summer.'

Some Blackfeet objected that entertaining tourists was degrading. Others complained that those Indians who did work there often made up stories and were treated like noble chiefs, even though few actually were. The railroad made them 'chiefs' so they would be more appealing to the tourists, and many Indians went along with the sham. Some even asked for money before they would pose, a practice that continues today.

Performing for tourists has become an Indian tradition. Professional dance troupes and performers at cultural festivals provide some insight into diverse Indian cultures, but often crowds of onlookers gather just to see the colourful Indians dance. 'Medicine Man Nettamu in costume' typifies how Indians thought whites wanted to see and photograph Indians. Posing for the camera (another Indian tradition), Nettamu, an Ojibwe Indian, wears a buffalo-horn head-dress and shakes a 'medicine' rattle. He dances in front of a tipi from which hangs a curlyheaded doll in a cradleboard. This hodge-podge of images makes it difficult to judge Nettamu too harshly. For many Indians from the turn of the century to the 1950s, the economic reality was that dancing was the only way to gain respect and money. Concerns over cultural purity, artistic integrity, and the long-term effects of stereotyping were outweighed by tourist dollars.

PERPETUAL WARRIOR AND NAKED APE

Where there are dancing Indians, warriors must be near by. Perhaps the image of the warrior is the most pervasive stereotype of Natives. It appears in toys, games, films, books, and in logos of sports teams. This powerful image is a difficult stereotype to assess. Admittedly, most Indians venerate their warriors. To fight and kill the enemy often brought prestige and honour to warriors among their own people. In fact, much of the modern-day powwow celebrates warriors, and dances recall their exploits.

Photographs present different aspects of this warrior stereotype. In one photograph a warrior with a pistol in hand poses in a photo-studio to cater to one stereotype. Hundreds of such photographs demystify Indian warriors by making them safe through phoney poses and fake scenery. This image almost mocks the reality of the fabled warrior. Such images were intended to illustrate a universal melodrama that exists only in the viewer's mind, one created by reading about James Fenimore Cooper's Indians, Longfellow's Hiawatha, and the fall of Custer, and by watching too many westerns on television and in movie theatres.

In contrast, a 1924 photograph of a real Yaqui fighter with bandoliers of bullets strapped across his chest does not immediately appear as an Indian warrior. Instead, he might be interpreted as a 'Mexican' revolutionary.

This photograph was taken a year after the death of Pancho Villa, who had led the insurrection in Mexico. An Indian himself, Villa had fought for the liberation of Indians who were considered 'peasants'. We often stop thinking of Indians as warriors after the massacre at Wounded Knee, which is viewed as the end of the Indian Wars, yet conflicts continued well into the 20th century, particularly in Mexico and in Central and South America. Even today when Indians rise up against their oppressors, they are labelled revolutionaries, radicals, insurgents, militants, or terrorists. This photograph and countless other images in circulation still paint Indians as rebellious people.

Compare these images with that of Goyathlay (Geronimo) and other Chiricahua Apache 'prisoners of war' as they rested by the side of the transport train that was taking them from Fort Sam Houston, Texas, to prison at Fort Marion, Florida. This 1886 photograph of the Apaches, with three armed and smiling soldiers standing guard over them, creates a powerful statement about Indians. Goyathlay was one of the US army's most feared enemies. Yet here, the Apaches wear pants, shirts, vests, boots, and hats much like their white counterparts. Their clothing does not suggest that they were defending an exotic or even slightly different way of life. The faces of the Apaches do not express defeat. They do not appear defiant, but instead are resigned to the fact that they fought long and hard for themselves, their families, their land, and their heritage. Without guns, they still seem strong. Ironically, this photograph was taken not too long after they had surrendered and had agreed to board a train heading east, which they thought would reunite them with their wives in Florida. When they arrived, the Apaches were imprisoned instead. In that sense, the soldier's smiles are the most telling aspect of this image.

A photograph of San Carlos Apache scouts attests to the internal split that has always existed among Indians. Not all Indians look alike, live alike, or think alike. Many people hang on to stereotypes about Indians being an idealised people who live in harmony, peace, and unity. These Apaches led the US army against Goyathlay, and the government used photographs of these scouts as visual propaganda to reinforce their policies.

Most of us would prefer to see photographs of Indians wearing their buckskins decorated with colourful beads, quills, and feathers. That is what makes them Indian. The archive of the National Museum of the American Indian contains hundreds of photographs of the 'undressed' Indian wearing everyday street clothes like that of the whites. Many members of the Indian delegations that visited Washington wore their street clothes, dressing up only for formal presentations and official portraits.

Sometimes straightforward photographs were taken for scientific purposes. Physical anthropologists wanted to record facial types in an effort to develop a catalogue of measurements for each tribal group, much like a visual genetic database. Two photographs of Ada Brenninger, a twelve-year-old Ojibwe, were taken around the turn of the century. During that time, social scientists believed that racial determinants of intelligence were based upon the size of the skull and brain. They also hoped to define the physical characteristics that made Indians a separate race and to look at the ancient origins of Native cultures. Many Indian skulls and remains were collected, some from the bodies of Indians killed in conflicts with the army, and sent to Washington for study. This 'crania study' became the leading rationalisation for museums and universities to collect Indian remains. It also represents a different kind of racial stereotyping. Under 'social Darwinism,' Asians, Africans, and Indians became the objects of study, and a hierarchy of races was formed, with people of colour at the bottom of the intellectual ladder and Caucasians at the top. Many photographs of Indians were used to document genetic features and to illustrate how bloodlines were either maintained or 'contaminated' due to interracial breeding.

Numerous photographs were taken of Indians of whom we know virtually nothing. One has stuck in my mind since I first saw it in 1972. It is a simple image of a Mandan Indian named Estapoosta (Running Face) that was taken around 1874. He wears his white man's costume, but two long braids hang down on each side of his head. Large braids cover his ears while narrow braids strung with brass beads hang from his temples. I am not exactly sure what has attracted me to this photograph all these years, but it has something to do with the fact that despite his clothing, his hair became the expression of his identity. This portrait made me want to grow my hair long, too.

Much later I discovered this photograph's significance. Running Face was one of the few Mandan who lived through the disastrous smallpox epidemic of 1837. Only 150 survived the disease that swept through Indian Country several times. Now when I study his face, I cannot help but wonder what his eyes have seen. I find a trace of loss, but also a slight toughness that covers up his dreadful memories. To me, the stereotype represented by this photograph is the story that lies behind the image. Think for a moment about the Gulf War veterans who complain of recurring health problems that they feel derive from their service overseas. The military refuses to identify the cause, which might be the Iraqis' use of chemical weapons. Now think what it must have been like for Running Face to watch his friends and relatives die of smallpox. What a burden it would be to bear knowing that smallpox was spread among the Indians through the distribution of blankets infected with the disease.

Finally, one photograph that is especially important to me is a portrait of James Mye, a Mashpee Indian from Cape Cod. Along with the Wampanoag of Massachusetts, the Mashpee were the object of historical myopia. Part of the problem has been the American attitude toward race. Many of the Indians in New England were sold into slavery, decimated by war, and killed by disease. Scores became racially mixed with Indian, white, and African blood and were often viewed with disdain by both whites and Indians. Even today, some Indians in the West do not consider the Wampanoag or Mashpee Indians at all. They are now wrongfully judged by the tone of their skin, the texture of their hair, or the state of their lifestyle.

True, they have suffered a great deal, have sacrificed more than other Indians can imagine, and have lost much of their land base, their native language, and their traditional practices. I have spent some time among the Wampanoag and Mashpee, the Narragansett, and the Mohican, and I have to say that they remain Indians in their hearts. Their inherent 'Indianness' is conveyed through the eyes of Adrian Caesar and James Mye. An untold history fills their faces, which represents the hope of the Indians' future in New England. When we see a Plains Indian wear a top hat, we find it charming. When we see an Eastern Indian wear one, we assume he is the victim of acculturation. This form of stereotyping keeps us from seeing the real people in the photographs.

The Author and Acknowledgements

Richard Hill is a writer who was formerly Special Assistant to the Director at the National Museum of the American Indian and Professor of American Studies at the State University of New York at Buffalo. He is a leading authority on contemporary Native American art and Indian images in artworks and on film. Mr Hill has also worked as Museum Director and principal designer of the new Institute of American Indian Arts Museum in Santa Fe, New Mexico, and was Museum Director of the Native American Center for the Living Arts.

A version of the above text and the illustrations have already appeared in *Spirit Capture: Photographs from the National Museum of the American Indian*, and the editor is grateful to the author and the Smithsonian Institution Press for permission to use the material in this volume.

References

Bush, A.L. & Mitchell, L.C., *The Photograph and the American Indian*, Princeton University Press, 1994.

Clifford, J., *The Predicament of Culture: Twentieth-Century Ethnography, Literature and Art*, Harvard University Press, 1988.

Fleming, P.R. & Luskey, J., *The North American Indian in Early Photographs*, Barnes & Noble Books, 1986.

Hauptman, L.M., *The Iroquois Struggle for Survival: World War II to Red Power*, Syracuse University Press, 1986.

Howard, O.O., *Famous Indian Chiefs I Have Known*, University of Nebraska Press, 1998.

Hoxie, F.E. (ed), *Encyclopedia of North American Indians*, Houghton Mifflin, Boston, 1996.

Johnson, T. (ed), *Spirit Capture: Photographs from the National Museum of the American Indian*, Smithsonian Institution Press & NMAI, 1998.

Sitting Bull in 1882 photograph by R. L. Kelly, showing the enduring image of the stern and unsmiling noble savage. *Courtesy National Museum of the American Indian*

Red Cloud captured by C.M. Bell on one of his visits to Washington DC, conveying the tamed noble savage holding a white man's cane rather than a tomahawk. *Courtesy National Museum of the American Indian*

Long Wolf and his family in a staged setting which reinforces the image of a stern and severe people. The only inconsistency to flaw the stereotyping is the baby's half-smile. *Courtesy National Museum of the American Indian*

28

HOW REAL IS OUR PAST?
Authenticity in Heritage Interpretation

Stuart Hannabuss

Heritage is a concept to evoke contradictory images and meanings. There are things we associate with authenticity, like the nobility and order of the past, stately homes safely stewarded for future generations and our enjoyment now, the celebration of human ingenuity and craftsmanship and taste, the archaeology and archiving of the human story. On the other hand, there are things, equally real in modern life, which associate with the artificial and commodified: the marketing hype of modern consumerism, the nostalgia, the Disneyfication of social and cultural history, making no distinction between hard and easy, high and low taste, past and present, local and international. Even the history itself can be manipulated and unreliable, and this we associate with the heritage industry and its styles of interpretation.

Heritage is ambiguous in being managed and mediated; received, interpreted and consumed; needed and used; believed and fabricated; and served up as diversion and spiritual refreshment. This paper is based on a personal journey by the author to heritage sites in Scotland and England, talking to administrators and visitors, and asking what people think is 'really real' and where the real 'hooks' are in the heritage experience.

The issues of 'staged authenticity' and 'spurious identification' lie at the heart of heritage interpretation. It has always seemed an uneasy mixture between scholarship and marketing hype, fact and nostalgia, educating and entertaining, and monologue and dialogue. If it is all these things, then it is no surprise that issues of identity play a dominant part in the heritage experience. It includes what you are expected to know, and what the provider expects you to want to hear and like. As a visitor, it depends on what you understand, or what you are prepared to make the effort to understand. It is about who you are: a tourist or a local, a native Scot or an American with Scottish roots, a pilgrim in search of spiritual uplift or a scholar in search of facts?

The concept of postmodernism is relevant here. It is preoccupied with identity, but it problematises reality in a conventional sense. It examines the effects that late capitalism, urbanisation and global culture have had on lifestyles and aspirations. It has told us that culture presents us not just with the question of understanding, as in art and music, but with the problem of what is true, as in the work of Magritte. Indeed, part of the problem is with the process of mediating and signifying meaning, as in heritage interpretation, which often makes it difficult to know what is real or true. It can be argued that, given the 'multiple' personality, the bricolage of roles and intentions and self-awareness, which the current world encourages, a perceived unease leads people to become cultural tourists and search for the past. The extent to which this search in itself, serves to change the past and commodify the experience, is a critical dilemma in heritage interpretation.

The author argues that in the heritage experience, we have moved into and through postmodernism. Now the real discussion is how to be 'really real' in an age where everyone is used to consuming heritage, accessing culture and education as a universal democratic resource, and living in a global world where media and cyberspace are providing everything for everyone, and consequently giving everybody everyone else's experiences, and turning most events and experiences into spectacles. It suggests that cultural tourists see beyond staged authenticity to the real things beyond, that identification is a deeper search for identity which draws on the self-referentiality of postmodernism and accepts the ironies of it. Nevertheless, in personal and collective forms, the search continues as a spiritual pilgrimage until visitors find what is 'real' for them. We have arguably moved from postmodernism to neo-realism.

AUTHENTICITY AND INTERPRETATION

Observers come to believe that they are participants because the process of heritage interpretation implicates them in increasingly interactive ways: living history like Jorvik, dressing up at Archaeolink and the Gordon Highlanders Museum, historical re-enactments at Fort George, interactive Internet websites and in virtual tourism. A dichotomy occurs because the distinction between the real and the unreal is suspended. It is as if we are here in the now and so can not be in the then; we know we are dressing up, but we think we know what it was like to be a soldier at Corgarff Castle on a cold winter afternoon trying to stop whisky-runs over old drove roads. The various strands in this heritage experience give it a very postmodern feel: it is the *flâneur* of Baudelaire and Walter Benjamin, both watching and being watched, having a personal experience whilst also being part of a crowd. We are students and consumers, caught up in education and entertainment, outside as visitors but drawn inside as actors, buying a postcard at the shop and taking away a felt emotion of the past in our hearts, knowing we are in the tourism business, but handling a product which is also a process.

This is where identity kicks in, because heritage interpretation, itself a product as well as a process, deals with identity: whether personal, as a group, community, or a national citizen. The marketing icons of Historic Scotland, presented in a burst on television, challenge us to bring our imagination in order to see and feel that image and identity of Scottishness: not kilts and haggises, but history to be proud of and identify with in an age of economic realism, cultural imperialism and social conformism, a past with living iconic relevance to the nation's future.

The sentiments 'what it is to be a Scot' or 'what it is to have genuine links with Scotland' run side by side with questions about 'why did the Lindsays finally lose Edzell Castle to debt and the last laird end his days as a stableman at an inn?', and 'how would the laird have sneaked on the talk of his retainers through the laird's lug at Castle Fraser?', or 'why would the first marquis of Huntly have represented, on the splendid frontispiece at Huntly Castle, himself and his lady, above them the king, and above them divine powers and the final triumph of Good over Evil?'. We want to know what these people did, why, and what they believed in. While we ask these questions, the dead come alive. We empathise with them and wonder what we would have done in similar situations. We might bring prejudices: 'typical of the lairdly classes then!' or 'just what I'd expect of someone trying to justify the status quo!'. All these reactions demonstrate how powerfully we react as human beings, above all to the story aspects of the heritage experience.

The thoughts, feelings, and reactions generated here, point first to the way in which people want to know something of who was there, who did it, and who is knowable about it today. We identify with the identity of people in the past. They point, second, to the urge people have to define and enrich themselves against, or with reference to, such questions, because they are there, they are themselves as Scots or English or Canadians as well as tourists or visitors. At Furness Abbey, just south of the Lake District, and at Hailes Abbey in the Cotswolds, English Heritage has provided taped guided tours. Narrator and actors in dramatised extracts take the visitor round the site, from nave to chapter house, refectory to hospital, as if you are a pilgrim, a visitor from and in the past, going for safety and the consolations of the faith, rather than paying for access to another old building before going on to the next motorway service area. We stand where the monks, on cold dark mornings, hurried devotedly and perhaps reluctantly to Prime. We hear of the abbot's fear and anger at his armed Scottish visitors in the 13th century, and his frustration at the scheming of Henry VIII's commissioners in the downsizing of the monasteries.

Heritage interpretation provides us with an identity, a persona, more than just that of a visitor: like a good radio play, we are drawn into life as it was, we are beguiled into thinking it is 'really real', we temporarily forget that 20th century technology (in the form of a tape recorder) is hanging around our necks. The visitor route is clear to follow, it has an intuitive logic: it is as if we are walking around then, not now. What appears to be a medieval perspective (that of an authentic member of the community then) is enhanced and reinforced by a variety of story telling and imaginative techniques which cross time, help an understanding of the people and their concerns long ago, and enable visitors to project themselves temporarily into 'themselves-as-if-long-ago'. This is widely done on school visits, usually to make education live. Successful heritage interpretation for adults seems able to transcend the artificiality of the tourist visit now and tap into deeper sentimental and spiritual roots. This is the domain of real involvement with the *genius loci* of the heritage site, and the place of identity.

If 'heritage experience' is equated merely to a kind of cognitive PR intended to socially engineer tourists and visitors into particular kinds of appreciative understanding and consumption, then both the story and the complexity of response will be lost. After all, the 'Castle Trail', like the 'Whisky Trail', is as much a commercial activity as anything else. We then begin to ask what history really is. It has been much abused, it is often impartial, incomplete, and often, as Lowenthal says, used to exalt local or national identity, call for credulous allegiance, serve a nostalgic search for roots. 'To be a living force the past must be ever remade', he says; 'heritage declares faith in he past rather than being a testable or even plausible account of it'. These points encourage us to ask how authentic heritage can ever be, even though 'heritage producers and stewards…seem increasingly concerned to ground their goods and stories in verifiable evidence'. Elsewhere he speaks about wanting, then knowing, then changing the past.

THE NEW HERITAGE COMMODITY

Heritage, like tradition and identity, is not only a complex product or process: it has complex connotations. These are the subjective or ethnographic meanings and values which people bring to them. It is what makes writers like Cannadine distrust the view that, since owners of stately homes now often hold them 'in trust' for the nation, then in some tangible way the homes are, symbolically and actually, national property, like Hampden Stadium and the New Town of Edinburgh. Part of this distrust arises because the heritage, held in trust, has in part perpetuated and reconstituted the hierarchical and institutionalised structures that existed long ago. In consequence, heritage consumption can take on a latter-day reverentialism for past values and social structures. This includes the postmodern ability to tolerate ambivalence, which can make us naive consumers, in the sense that we perceive it as ours while it is not, that it symbolises historical privilege and exclusion that we can now enjoy.

Our understanding of heritage is complicated still further by the idea that everything appears to be heritage these days. A mine that closes yesterday becomes industrial heritage today. This recalls the well-rehearsed argument of Hewison that manufactured industry is replacing 'real' industry in Britain. Industries like agriculture and fishing are, as never before, creating heritage centres which preserve history and tradition and set out to hand it on, either a time-capsule or a living continuing entity, to current visitors and future generations.

Professional activities like industrial archaeology and social history have increasingly seen the commercial incentives of tapping into a growing, often media-led appetite for 'the way we lived then', as in Tony Robinson's television programme *Time Watch*. School curricula, emphasising local history and independent resource-based investigation, tap into this explosion of what might be called a democratic heritage industry based on industrial heritage, based on what ordinary folk did (and still try in many cases to do). At Aden Country Park, the museum of agricultural life in north-east Scotland, with its machines and explanations of cropping, harvests and 'drystane' dykes and 'kornkister days', sits side by side with a working farm with a 'genuine' 1950s farmhouse (transported stone by stone from nearby but elsewhere). Early photographs on display play the time machine between the old past, the new, and the new reconstituted past.

Speyside Cooperage near Dufftown provides a visitor centre experience, from watching casks genuinely being made for sale (as they always have) to helping to make demonstration casks and buying garden furniture made from casks. Many organisations in this field combine the heritage experience with the shopping experience, perhaps the most powerful combination of all in view of current lifestyle trends. Muncaster Mill, in the Lakes, is a heritage site which also provides kinds of flour for the connoisseur home baker. Baxters of Fochabers have a 'Mrs Bridges-style' olde-world shoppe to sell their very modern jams and other products and a quality assurance workplace tour that convinces the visitor that here we have a major economic player. The words 'genuine' and 'authentic' keep appearing, and this reflects the hybrid character of this form of heritage – both education and entertainment, scholarship and fun, both history and lifestyle, both getting an idea of the past and buying bygones.

Hunter Davies tells the tourist that the Bobbin Mill at Finsthwaite Stott Park 'really is a bobbin mill', and that it 'can sound like any other little craft gallery, but it is actually a major site of what used to be one of the Lake District's most important industries'. So for the visitor there is already the matter of balancing ideas of what the place 'really' is – real in the sense of being there in tangible form, really a craft gallery with things going on, not just a craft gallery, but a bobbin mill like they had in grandpa's days. It is a place where you can do some serious work on the history of the bobbin industry (it folded because of the introduction of plastics in the 1970s), and now a place where guides really know the machines and their history, how to demonstrate them in action, produce real bobbins, and allow you to take one away as a souvenir. You go away saying to yourself not so much 'How quaint', but' hey, those guys really knew how to run a business all those years ago, and they're not making such a bad job of it now.'

The key reason why this mill is 'genuine' is the result of historical chance: such companies usually fold and get dispersed. When this one closed in 1971, it was bought by English Heritage, and stayed as it was until opening again as a heritage site in 1983. The original machinery, including the old water turbines and steam engines, are still there and still work. More than that, the guides know how to explain them scientifically and simply, mediating the information on both levels, and demonstrating how and why machines work. This bridges the gap between history and the present, esoteric technology and fascinating gadgets. Some of the people working there are now older, but when younger worked authentically in the industry itself. The heritage experience there is one where a careful and plausible balance between the then and the now, the real and the staged, is successfully managed.

The historiography of heritage in the last few decades has tended to emphasise the artificiality of heritage interpretation. From Hewison on, the critique has run along the lines that, since Britain cannot keep its industry afloat in a modern competitive world, and one of its main strengths is its past, then it makes commercial and cultural sense to turn the country into a museum or a theme-park. The British ambivalence about tourism, in the sense of providing it as a service industry, and emergent nationalism and regionalisms, have added to the mix of contradictory emotions on the part of providers and consumers alike. Consequently, money is made from the Catherine Cookson and James Herriott country experience, in Liverpool the Albert Docks become a museum, working harbours turn into the Buckie Drifter and lighthouses into museums, like Scotland's Lighthouse Museum at Kinnaird Head.

The past is not just a place where things have happened: it is the domain of events in which we, individually or as communities, invest feelings of affection, sad memory, resentment, vicarious pride. Many local visitors have personal links with the collections, and so shrine and memorial are added to museum and archive to make it meaningful. So, at the Fraserburgh Heritage Centre we step back in time 'through the centuries' to the 'bustling quayside in the age of sail'. We also explore the contemporary achievements of fashion designer Bill Gibb and the growing electronic database of questions and answers available for local people and visitors to use and to add to. The Scandinavian tradition of the folk museum has been (re)discovered in Britain, changing the motivations and responses in heritage museology. The displays and the tales are of *quines* and *loons* with local roots, sources of local pride and sadness, and the heritage experience emblematises the experience of the local community, and is expressed in forms which visitors can share.

The past, then, is a commodity and a living process through, and in which, local people and visitors alike can access events and feeling far and near. As a commodity, however, heritage has been identified with a factitious product easily manipulated and shaped into something merely worth selling and providing to others, at times for nationalistic and political reasons (such as the Holocaust experience, heritage sites intended to propagandise on behalf of causes or indigenous peoples). Heritage is often the domain of nostalgia, where past glories are exaggerated, the disease and inequality of working class life mythologised, agricultural life sentimentally preserved in *Lark Rise to Candleford* and *The Tale of Peter Rabbit*, and in Mother's Pride bread adverts. The fine line lies where perceived authenticity (where we believe things are real) is to be found, and where what we believe we are prepared to believe about the past fits, if at all, to agreed historical fact.

PAYING TO SEE STEREOTYPES

Featherstone and Wernick have written about cultural tourism, and about the older tourist, many of whom go in for holidays representing 'affirmations of identity which deny novelty through the invention of tradition'. By denial of novelty they imply absence of historical authenticity. Such tourism options are selected by people experienced in choosing such holidays. They are and informed, but blasé about the 'experience packages' available and the chances they provide to transform

357

personal identity. By accepting the events and experiences of the holiday, but by not identifying with them in the knowledge that they are only events and experiences, such heritage consumers act in a postmodern way. They are accepting contradiction, placing value in the heritage product and knowing that it is only a form of product management, knowing that their feelings as well as their wallets will be massaged by the product providers, and knowing that their feelings are still very much their own.

Identity involves identification, and in a postmodern sense, knowingly accepts and rejects the process of identification. We might represent it like this: I know what I am, I know that this experience is changing me, I can control the change because I am paying for it, I can control the change because I can switch off my belief systems whenever I want, I think these guys can offer me what I don't know I don't know, so let's see how things work out. I can always go on another holiday. Gergen said that the saturated self was a multiple self, that of a social chameleon, a relational self ever seeking identity from new interactivities, seriously involved in life but also treating it like a game. They are caught in a consumerist process where gratification and individualism dominate, accepting incoherence in time and in their social lives, and developing many selves rather than a single ego. It is this kind of deliberate and often self-referential 'self-handling' that we see at work in these affirmations of identity through cultural tourism: however organised the heritage response seems to be, cultural tourists ultimately want to organise it for themselves.

It is then relevant to ask how far affirmations of identity really deny novelty. Postmodernism and our general knowledge of the media age would tell us that people know everything about everything, and particularly show familiarity with scripts and roles often far distant from their own (e.g. the jealous step-mother, the possessive wife, the man on the edge, the woman whose children don't come to see her any more, what Foucault and others have called reification or turning people into things, feelings and experiences into externally-considered events). Adorno's critique argues that, once experiences have been identified, they can be commodified, and then they can be sold. Often the heritage experience has the effect of linking personal to collective legacy (Lowenthal), my identity as a Garioch loon and as a Scot, a native American and an American, and this brings paradoxical baggage like all the stereotypes of national identity, emblems of past culture, with which we may know, or come to know, that we are seeking to identify in and through the heritage experience. We go looking for it and, whatever it is, want it to help define our own identity.

Cultural tourism consists of many willing buyers who know what they like, and know providers know what they know they like. If denial of novelty does indeed take place through the invention of tradition, it suggests a heritage industry set on inventing tradition where it does not exist, and reinventing it in the supposed image of tradition itself, where it does, so that it is acceptable and accessible merely to the consumer. Such heritage interpretation will be reductionism, retrospective, consumerist, centred on the cultural consumer at the expense of its own integrity. In other words, a Disneyfied version of the real world, where the eye and purse of the beholder is the dominant criterion of authenticity and value.

Postmodernist insights help us look, in analytical and sceptical ways, at many of the products and processes of heritage interpretation. For instance, they allow us both to laugh at and understand why Darcy's shirt, from the BBC television series *Pride and Prejudice*, attracted a high sum at auction. Such a response piquantly balances admiration for Jane Austen and the series, understanding of human affection and lust, the star appeal of the actor and his physique. He was interviewed frequently at the time, and we learnt what he ate, who he lived with, where he came from and whether he really liked the heroine. Marilyn Monroe artefacts are not just her dresses and shoes and photographs: she is now the commodity itself. So is Darcy. In that series, people wanted to know more about Jane Austen country, the houses where the series was filmed, so that they could visit them too.

Dalemain, near Ullswater, is another such house, not just a 'much loved family home, set against the grandeur and picturesque splendour of the Lakeland Fells and Parkland' but also the scene of London Weekend Television's production of *Jane Eyre*, its medieval courtyard and 16th century Great Barn providing the exteriors and interiors of Lowood Institution. There is also a historical connection: the Reverend William Carus Wilson (1791–1859), nephew by marriage of Edward Hasell of Dalemain (1765–1826), founded the Clergy Daughters' School at Cowan Bridge, and was the inspiration for the character of Mr Brocklehurst, the founder of Lowood Institution.

Such factors add to the experience of the cultural tourist, working simultaneously along several levels of relevance. Things that are really there become 'really real', because of what cultural tourists and heritage consumers are prepared to bring with them to the experience, and because of the chemistry between what they know and feel on the one hand and what they discover on the other. There are a number of further factors at work here which help to make heritage experience 'really real', and heritage interpretation has gone some way towards understanding them and getting them right.

What these factors have in common is 'a sense of story', and this is often the hook. Of all the ways in which people make sense of the world, the one we all learn early on is the story. 'Once upon a time...' it often starts, 'long ago and far away, there was a light princess who kept floating off into the sky, a sad dragon who thought he couldn't get his fiery flames right, a third brother who set off with his pig to market, a heritage manager who thought that it was about time the Celts were demythologised'. Story telling is a critically important way of making sense of the world: it allows people to represent events and states of mind in words and meanings, it incorporates consequential actions and moral issues of good and bad, it explains important things about the human condition.

Heritage interpretation has lots of good stories, because it relies on history, which is full of them. They are often shaped chronologically to make sense, with a cast of thousands of colourful and eccentric characters, packed with suspense and glory, envy and decay. As seen from the present, they offer a consoling enclosure and a sense of orderliness. They convey metaphorical meaning, tap symbolic archetypes, and bridge the past and the present.

It is easy to identify with people in such stories. There is the story of the last of the Lindsays at Edzell who ended life as a stableman in an inn, or the heroism of Jamie Fleeman the fool who rescued his lord's kist, or the covenanting bigotry of Captain James Wallace who defaced the frontispiece at Huntly Castle in 1640, or the many hands (represented as plaster casts) of mill workers at Borås in Sweden, or the personal histories of people who worked at Verdant Works, the jute mill in Dundee. These and many more are stories which people want, remember, and retell. Heritage interpretation, like good history teaching, has always had a eye for a good story, for a good story allows a lot of fact and understanding to come through in the telling. For these reasons, story is an important tool in ethnographic research.

In modern heritage interpretation, representing experience, meaning and knowledge in the form of story provides heritage interpreters with a flexible and inclusive vehicle for explanation. Explanations used in education and cultural tourism can accommodate postmodern factors like cultural relativism, the fragmentation of experience, notions of manufactured imitations, epistemological issues of when an experience is authentic.

Story telling is not just narrative, not just fiction: it can incorporate historical facts, sequences of reasoning and explanation, events and their causes and consequences, and mind-states of characters, their motivations and intentions. They allow for a variety of voices, like first and third person, and can move dramatically between the two, and across a range of voices. They can also become embodied, literally, in the person taking visitors around a heritage site, what Lowenthal called the 'curator as bard'. In these ways 'storying' (not just 'telling stories' but representing and sharing meanings and explanations in story) represents a unique and intuitive form in heritage interpretation. We can see this in the many initiatives in preserving and promoting oral history. Above all, story is interactive, impelling active listening, capable of the most beguiling invention and powerful effects.

Story can be a way of explaining difficult and contradictory issues, like heroism in war, in the Gordon Highlanders' Museum, for making the medieval church accessible (as in the tape tour at Furness Abbey), and for explaining why electronic lights have now superseded manned lighthouses. In each case 'a storying approach' has been used, focused on individual people who can easily be recognised, admired, identified with. At the Gordon Highlanders' Museum, a focus on the 'Jocks' as well as the top brass, and on men like Corporal Findlater who played the pipes through the thick of battle, though shot in both ankles, and won the VC. Likewise at Furness Abbey, you gain insight into the lives of abbot and monks and lay-brothers whose duties and quarrels come vividly through the narration and dramatisation on the tape.

An important aspect of story in heritage interpretation is its democratic appeal: story is a structure known to everyone, casual tourist and dedicated expert alike, and story can be constructed and mediated at any level of complexity. It can also indicate the logical structure of events and states of mind in history and heritage, explaining how and why certain things happen that led to other things, how and why the family died out and the castle was sold, why Archibald Grant of Monymusk planted trees and bred cattle, what effect being Roman Catholic had on the family at Traquair, why an English king put a regiment permanently in residence at Edinburgh Castle, how Inchcolm became a focus of pilgrimage, why General Wade built roads through Strathdon, and the strained story of the relationship between the owner of Duff House and the Adam family of architects and designers.

Story telling can be inclusive in another important sense, in drawing on reminiscence. One of the strongest connections to be found with a heritage site is personal – not just an interest in the people associated with the site but a family connection. So the visitors to the Gordon Highlanders Museum for whom the staged authenticity is least staged and most 'real', and for whom the spurious identification is least spurious and most authentic, are those with this connection: those who have served in the regiment, those whose relatives and friends have served or died in uniform. Indeed, all those who feel a strong community connection with the former regiment and its roots in the North East of Scotland. Interviews with visitors reveal that an important distinction should be made between people with this local and personal connection, and others for whom the museum is, gloriously or not, a presentation and representation of military history. What we connect into here is the authentic story of the regiment, felt by people about people, often the 'ordinary' visitor about the 'ordinary' soldier, who in being part of the regiment takes on extraordinary qualities of valour and meaning.

Indeed, issues of identification and the 'really real' take on a particularly interesting and self-reflexive form when heritage sites use former employees of the 'real' industry as guides or demonstrators. The guides have exactly that kind of elusive authenticity which have been discussed in the paper drawing on postmodern ideas. They are authentically part of the history on which the heritage is based, they are authentically actors in the modern heritage experience. Yet their discourse and actions, such as demonstrating the making of a bobbin or the harnessing of a shire horse, have been 'decontextualised' from the actually historical or industrial process which led originally to their creation. The bobbins are not used, the horses do not draw the plough. Lowenthal's 'curator as bard' fits perfectly, describing the attributed credibility of the mediator, attributed by heritage consumers who 'both believe and don't believe' but who have come ready to suspend disbelief.

THE SPIRITUALITY OF HERITAGE CONSUMPTION

It is valuable to explore whether and how heritage interpretation works when ways of by-passing stageyness and spuriousness are actually found. This depends, obviously enough, on what commitment the cultural tourist brings to the heritage experience. At its deepest perhaps is the commitment of the pilgrim, explored in such a timely way by Fladmark. Some travel writers show this determination to penetrate through to the mystery of people, time and place, and to understand their own relationship to that mystery: Marsden's quest for the real Armenia, Sepúlveda's re-evaluation of what Chile means to him, Wheeler's reflective and feminist journey to Antarctica, O'Hanlon's obsessive Congo journey, and Theroux' disillusioned voyage around the islands of the Pacific. These are articulate professional writers, of course, not cultural tourists. What appears to be missing, in the incomplete research on the phenomenological dimension of cultural tourism and heritage consumption, is making the spiritual dimension, the sense of intelligent quest, thoroughly explicit.

The spiritual dimension of heritage comes through vividly in Nicholas Luard's account of his journey to the shrine at Santiago de Compostela, in *The Field of the Star*. On one level this is a travel book, with the author walking through France and then Spain to his destination, describing sites and markets, churches and rough terrain, the train to Burgos and remembering Hemingway's interest in the bull-fight at Pamplona. On another level, Luard is a pilgrim, walking to make sense of his own life, and in particular his relationship with his daughter who dies during the course of his walk (which extends, in stages, over several years). There were, he says, two landscapes, inside his mind and the physical one without. He believed in God and his pilgrimage increased his faith, made him more certain and better able to deal with grief. He realised that life was the only chance to walk around the block.

Luard is well aware of the contradictions and tensions in such a walk. It is a private matter yet he writes a book about it. It is a travel book, full of roughing it and the realism of wayside hostels and crowds of other people, but it is also a private journey, a way of dealing with grief, of searching for consolation, expiation, grace. He is a pilgrim in a secular, post-Christian age, a successful writer and administrator looking for structure, a caring father facing his inadequacy. He is travelling a pilgrimage in the late 20th century which people do as tourists now but centuries before did as pilgrims. His journey is ostensibly spiritual but every step of the way is pre-planned by the London-based Confraternity of St James. At the end, he went to the pilgrims office to show their stamped passports, and collect the official certificates 'with our names recorded in medieval Latin showing we'd duly and properly completed the *Camino*'. Spontaneity suddenly gives way to a 'packaged experience'. Can spirituality be packaged? Postmodernism finds no difficulty with the ambivalences here. Overriding that in its turn, is the attitude of the tourist or pilgrim. For Luard, the ambivalences fade away in the face of achieving the spiritual destination.

So, when people mention heritage to the author now, he no longer reaches for his gun. He goes on talking, both in casual conversation and in formal research, to managers and guides and other visitors. He looks for the personal connection and what they most remember about a visit, whether it was made real by a peat fire in the grate at Corgarff or a piece of cake at Aden or the garden at Edzell Castle. When one member of staff was asked how he was able to make the garden look so good, he responded by saying that all it took was four hundred years of care, and that, in any case, he was just a steward. In this way, cultural tourism becomes simply life-enhancing rather than life-consuming, not a spectacle but an experience, because real people still live it and share it with real people who interpret it. We are able to experience reciprocity and feel enriched by it. This may sound rather self-conscious, and perhaps that is why authenticity in heritage interpretation is so elusive. It is something both provider and consumer should take more seriously as it sets signposts pointing toward the discovery of both reality and the spiritual meaning of identity.

The Author

Dr Stuart Hannabuss holds degrees from Oxford, London, Aberdeen and Heriot-Watt universities, and teaches in the School of Information & Media at The Robert Gordon University in management, communication, law and research methods. He contributes to the MSc in Heritage Management, and is research supervisor for several associated projects. He is author of four books, is a prolific writer with a focus on bibliography, literature, education, management, censorship and ethics, and he has had short stories broadcast on BBC Radio. He also writes poetry and is a certificated counsellor.

References

Cannadine, D., *The Decline and Fall of the British Aristocracy*, Yale University Press, 1990.

Cannadine, D., *Aspects of Aristocracy: Grandeur and Decline in Modern Britain*, Yale University Press, 1994.

Davies, H., *The Good Guide to the Lakes*, Forster Davies, 1997.

Featherstone, M. & Wernick, A. (eds), *Images of Ageing: Cultural Representations of Later Life*, Routledge.

Fladmark, J.M. (ed), *In Search of Heritage: As Pilgrim or Tourist?*, Donhead, 1998.

Gergen, K., *The Saturated Self: Dilemmas of Identity in Contemporary Life*, Basic Books, 1991.

Graesser, A.C. & Clark, L.F., *Structures and Procedures of Implicit Knowledge*, Ablex, 1985.

O'Hanlon, R., *Congo Journey*, Hamish Hamilton, 1996;

Hewison, R., *The Heritage Industry: Britain in a Climate of Decline*, Methuen, 1987.

Lowenthal, D., *Possessed by the Past: The Heritage Crusade and the Spoils of History*, The Free Press, 1996.

Lowenthal, D., *The Past is a Foreign Country*, Cambridge University Press, 1985.

Luard, N., *The Field of the Star: A Pilgrim's Journey to Santiago de Compostela*, Penguin Books, 1999.

Luard, N., 'To Santiago de Compostela: A Journey of Remembrance', in Fladmark, J.M. (ed), *In Search of Heritage: As Pilgrim or Tourist?*, Donhead, 1998, pp. 77–89.

Mandler, J.M., *Stories Scripts and Scenes*, Erlbaum, 1984.

Marsden, P., *The Crossing Place*, Harper Collins, 1993.

Pocock, D., 'Catherine Cookson Country: Tourist Expectation and Experience', in *Geography*, 77(3), 1992, pp. 236–43.

Samuel, R., *Theatres of Memory: Past and Present in Contemporary Culture*, Verso, 1994.

Sepúlveda, L., *Full Circle: A South American Journey*, Lonely Planet, 1996;

Spretnak, C., *The Resurgence of the Real: Body, Nature and Place in a Hypermodern World*, Addison-Wesley, 1997.

Theroux, P., *The Happy Isles of Oceania: Padding the Pacific*, Hamish Hamilton, 1992.

Toolan, M.J., *Narrative: A Critical Linguistic Introduction*, Routledge, 1998.

Wheeler, S., *Terra Incognita: Travels in Antarctica*, Cape, 1996.

Wright, P., *On Living in an Old Country: The National Past in Contemporary Britain*, Verso, 1985.

'*Oath of the Batavians*', painted by Rembrandt in 1661 for the new Town Hall in Amsterdam

29

HOW BIG IS IDENTITY?
The Mobile Co-ordinates of History

Duncan Macmillan

How big is identity? How long is a piece of string? When Louis XIV had himself painted by Rigaud, or indeed when he built Versailles, that architecturally monstrous extension of himself, he gave definitive expression to one vision of identity in the modern nation state: 'L'Etat c'est moi'. He enrolled in his person the identity of the nation, and so maybe identity was around five feet nothing with his heels on perhaps. Several centuries down the line, our own Queen is just another small lady in a hat. How far things have moved. Or have they? For the justification of her position is still ultimately as a function of our collective identity.

Louis's notion of kingship was adapted to quite new circumstances from much earlier concepts of the role of chieftains and kings. It is neat and serviceable and inspired a good many imitators among the monarchs of Europe, as did his palace of Versailles. It was designed to impress on the visitor the power of kingship, but did so by deliberately diminishing his or her sense of their own individual identity. Even the gravel in the entrance courtyards is out of scale. Such things clearly indicate how, though its origins are archaic, this is a notion of identity that leaves much to be desired, and that the principal one is its failure to accommodate all the other individual perceptions of identity that do actually constitute the nation. That in contrast, is the basic ambition of democracy. Indeed, the definition of democracy hinges on the idea of the equal rights of all individuals and so democratic identity is by its nature a compound. But many other notions of identity that are in this respect more recognisably modern than absolute monarchy had already served well in different circumstances long before Louis XIV and very often they had found expression in art.

For instance, 500 years before Le Roi Soleil, the Christian Catalans backed up against the Pyrenees by the Arabs and fighting back, produced some of the earliest and finest Romanesque painting, a style marked vividly by the individuality of the anonymous painters, but also by their respect for individuality in what they represented. However, it was also a style that became a European form of expression and so it reflects the way identity is porous and mobile. It can be both part and whole, or perhaps to return to the original question, it is more a piece of elastic than a piece of string.

Catalan Romanesque is vigorous, passionate and strikingly informal. The exact opposite of the court art of an absolute monarch, it appears in tiny churches high in the mountains where the congregation can never have been more than a few shepherds, but where it seems the need to maintain political and religious identity in a potentially hostile environment provided the defining pressure for this kind of expression. Fifteen hundred years before the Catalans, the Pergamenes had done something rather similar under pressure from the Celts and produced the 'Laocöon'.

One of the most enduringly effective expressions of the social construction of identity in modern Europe, the Catalan national dance, the 'Cerdanya', also has its origins in the same section of the eastern Pyrenees, taking the name of one of its loveliest high valleys, also home incidentally of the first cathedral of the reconquest, the 9th century foundation of Seo de Urgell. The Cerdanya is a dance that is performed usually in a town or village square and in an indefinitely extended circle. You join it as an individual where and when you will, linking hands with your neighbours and performing a complicated series of steps in unison. There is no dramatic movement. In fact, you more or less stay in the same place, but it is a moving celebration of the idea of community and the need for a balance between individual and group. As we perform it, as a kind of dance, 'Auld Lang Syne' maybe does something a bit similar.

Of course dance has always served this purpose in the past, and the modern practice of dancing virtually alone is a strange and disturbing one when seen in that perspective. In Ambrogio, Lorenzetti's fresco of *Good Government* in the aptly named Palazzo Pubblico in Siena, for instance, just such a dance as the Cerdanya is taking place at the centre of the town. The dance here is the epitome of social harmony.

In Scotland, David Allan's *Penny Wedding* and David Wilkie's reworking of the same theme were specifically celebrations of the same idea, a community in harmony with itself giving expression to that sense of harmony through music and dance. It was with these two painters, also part of the argument that these were natural forms of expression, the product, not of sophistication, but of its absence, of the spontaneous and untutored expression of natural feeling. Neil Gow, the great Scots fiddler, as he was painted by Raeburn, and also by Wilkie and Allan, actually leading the dance, was an intuitive musician, drawing music from within himself as he led the dancers. This is another example of balance between individual and community, and perhaps in this case also an epitome of the artist cultivating something in him or herself for the service of the group in its collective expression of identity. And here we must recognise the importance of belief, the Enlightenment belief in human nature and the resources for good that lie within us which nourish this spontaneous will to harmony as these artists express it.

But in Catalan, Romanesque belief in identity was subsumed into religious belief, and one does not need to look for long at the history of Europe to see the explosive nature of this mixture. Leaving aside Enlightenment optimism for a moment, the first problem one faces when trying to answer the initial question is how to define a notion of group or communal identity that does not fall back on the kind of tribal lines of demarcation expressed in the mutual religious hostility that still causes such terrible division and suffering in Europe?

That faces you directly with the question, is identity really this dangerous, atavistic thing? However you dress it up, is it really better simply suppressed? But to take that position as some Unionists do in Scotland would be deeply pessimistic. It would be to propose that human nature is incorrigible and its instincts best denied. For there can be no doubt that a sense of identity as individual, member of a family, group, community or nation, and we all regularly combine all of these, is instinctive, a fundamental part of human nature and a necessary part of the individual self-esteem of each of us. We need to know where we belong and here collective self-esteem, the self-respect that is the essence of a wider sense of identity is as important to the nation as it is to the individual.

This is something that Adam Smith recognised long ago. It is rooted in feeling, not reason, but he did not see that as a negative, as cause for alarm. It is our best feelings that bind us, he argued, above all sympathy, and sympathy is mediated by imagination, the primary human faculty. According to both Hume and Smith, it is the faculty that makes it possible for us to understand the world and each other within it. Thus it follows that morality itself is made possible by imagination, just as it is sympathy that binds us into communities. That is a great insight into human nature. It is also why culture comes before politics: no culture, no politics. Maybe you can have culture without politics, but unless it be the uncultured politics of tyranny where sympathy and imagination have no place, you cannot have meaningful politics without culture.

Profoundly shaped by Christian belief no doubt, Smith's insight is nevertheless one of the gifts that the Enlightenment passed down to us and one on which our attempt to build a humane modern society has to a large extent been constructed. At its heart is the recognition that society is itself a psychological construct, a product of feelings which also naturally find expression in our sense of identity. Thus it follows that it is in the cultivation of the imagination that our values are forged. Identity is one of these, or perhaps it is the vessel in which they are contained and in part articulated. Politics are simply the vehicle of their implementation. Politicians in their self-importance consistently forget that. They relegate culture to leisure and tourism whereas it is the partner, indeed the parent, not merely of politics, but of education too.

This raises, too, the whole question of the perception of culture in our society, a question addressed by the author in an earlier volume in this series,[1] which still needs to be addressed politically. Happily in her recent consultation paper, *Celebrating Scotland: A National Cultural Strategy*, Rona Brankin shows herself aware of this and willing to lead the debate.[2] She recognises that Scotland's identity is distinct, but also is a product of international exchange, but a key statement that she makes in the present context is: Scotland through the promotion of her culture can generate self-respect, win the respect of others and contribute to civilised living.

However, it is also important that this key statement is not overshadowed by an earlier remark: Scotland's culture will play an important role in the nation's economic and social development. The economic importance of culture is a vital part of it clearly, but it is vital that where reputation is a commodity that can be manufactured and marketed, witness Damien Hirst and the Spice Girls, that we do not allow our wider cultural values to be debased to the status of market-led commodities. Our cultural institutions must of course live in the market place. We all must. But they must not be forced to live by the market place. That would destroy what they stand for, part of the structure of our identity and so of our vital self-esteem, as touched on by the author in *Our Heritage: Not just an Armchair by the Fireside of History*.[3]

But here we come to another aspect of this debate: the role of education and the need to recognise that this question of identity, of the national frame of mind is not just a function of culture as entertainment. It is much more essential than that, for if the imagination is the faculty on which all this depends, then the cultivation of the imagination becomes an imperative, not merely a luxury. It should be at the heart of our education system. It is also this imperative, and the link between imagination and our moral and social natures, that underlies the evolution of modern art – and of course, we too easily forget, imagination is also the motor of science. And however much it may seem to have strayed from the point at times, from Blake to Andre Breton, to Eduardo Paolozzi's great exhibition, *Lost Magic Kingdoms*, or to Ian Hamilton Finlay's garden at Little Sparta, that link has remained central to the real artistic agenda all the same. That is the ultimate justification of our art institutions, including our museums. They represent resources for the imaginative life of the community, as it draws on memory to articulate its identity and seeks to develop self-awareness and self-esteem, just as we each do in our separate lives. This means that museums and other organisations for the care, interpretation and presentation of our heritage, mediate knowledge and information, but they do so in a context that is still essentially psychological, shaped by feeling, because that is the nature of the society that they represent.

Higher education is also part of this too, and one of the most damaging episodes in the recent history of the Scottish Universities was the way in which, in 1979, they came out against devolution. This might not at first sight seem important now, but it reflected how far they were out of touch with their social role, with their place in the cultural leadership of the community whose identity they share. Things perhaps are different now. This volume is the product of a partnership between the National Museums of Scotland and the Robert Gordon University. Dundee has embarked on an imaginative partnership with the city in the Dundee Centre for Contemporary Arts. Edinburgh has ambitious plans which could put the creative arts back at the centre of the humanities and create a new kind of access. Certainly, there is an opportunity as new agendas are set for the Scottish Parliament to look to bring the universities back to the role they once played, international certainly, but Scottish too, visible from afar but framed by identity.

To bring higher education into this discussion may startle some readers, but it is a reminder that it is essential to recognise that our concern with identity is legitimate. It should be part of our progressive understanding of the world, not something atavistic. Perhaps the best witness to the truth of that idea is found in the history of the intellectual freedom that has been essential to the construction of our modern society, as also of the science on which it depends, and the part that this imaginative identity has played there. Imagination is of course not only the province of art. It drives science too. One of the earliest and most powerful expressions of the connection between imaginative and intellectual freedom and the proper sense of both individual and collective identity that lies at the centre of the whole project that is modern society is found in Rembrandt. In it, he is engaging directly with the foundations of modern science as they were being laid by his contemporaries. It is a complex proposition to propose that all these strands come together. But Rembrandt saw how they do, so surely we can learn from him.

We go back to 1634, when Galileo was silenced by the Inquisition and compelled to recant his empirically established belief in the Copernican System – that the sun is the centre of the solar system and the planets

371

revolve around it, a shock to our human identity too, hence no doubt the Papal response. Two years later, to commemorate that turning point in modern history, Rembrandt painted the *Blinding of Samson* for his patron, Constantin Huygens, secretary to the Stadtholder of the United Provinces, William of Orange.

It is an extraordinarily graphic and violent picture, the mighty Samson betrayed by a triumphant Delilah and overcome and blinded by hideous pigmies. But Rembrandt, by implied contrast, identifies the humanity of his own community, through the person of Huygens, representing the freedoms enjoyed within the United Provinces. Collective identity of this kind needs freedom vested in a free community, the collective identity itself also being its guarantor. Above all, the American Constitution stands for this. The collective identity is the defender of that vital imaginative freedom, and by his gesture in presenting his picture to Huygens, Rembrandt proclaimed that fact, central to the development of modern society. That is identity through belief, being inclusive and not exclusive.

It is indeed a very modern concept, and those archaic tribal boundaries were no part of it. Rembrandt returned to this too, to articulate the values that he saw enshrined in the modern sense of identity in one of his grandest and late compositions, *The Oath of the Batavians*, a picture commissioned for the new Town Hall of Amsterdam, itself a monument to the successful defence of that freedom and so also a proud declaration of the independent identity of the United Provinces.

The picture celebrates the revolt of the ancient Batavians against Roman domination. Described by Tacitus, it was led by one Claudius Civilis. Rembrandt shows the conspirators swearing an oath of loyalty, or perhaps of defiance. But what is striking about the picture is the extraordinary grotesqueness of the characterisation, their bizarre individuality still further exaggerated by dramatic simplifications of strong light and shade. The expression of their collective identity is a product of the strength of their individual identity. Most striking of all is Claudius Civilis himself. Shown full-face beneath an extraordinary hat, he has only one eye. 'Borgne' is the French word for it.

The greatest ancient Greek painter, Apelles, was commended by Pliny for his sense of decorum in painting a certain North African king. He also had only one eye. He had lost it in battle, but Apelles painted him in such a way that the result of the injury, the defect as Pliny saw it, was not visible. Piero della Francesca followed Pliny's guidance in the rules of classical decorum when he painted the Duke of Montefeltro. Another one-eyed warrior, he painted him in profile from his good side so that his disfiguring war wound was not visible.

But it was also part of what distinguished him as an individual. In his Claudius Civilis, Rembrandt deliberately and explicitly defied those rules, taking the side aesthetically of the Batavians revolt against the tyranny of Rome, the tyranny of a classicism that is normative. Based on the rule of the general over the particular, it denies individuality. Rembrandt had no reason to suppose that his hero was one-eyed. In the brief account he gives of these events, Rembrandt's only source Tacitus, says nothing about it. Rembrandt was making a point that was both political and aesthetic and one that is fundamental to our modern idea of identity. The classical style was identified with Rome, in Protestant 17th century terms, enemy of freedom. Pliny's idea of decorum, being normative was inimical to individuality. Individuality, the central concept of the modern west, is irreducible. Burns makes the same point in the 'Jolly Beggars'. His marvellous company, 'the randy gangrel bodies' in the poem, is composed of just such grotesque characters as Rembrandt paints, all celebrating:

> Liberty, the glorious feast:
> Life is all a variorum,
> We regard not how it goes;
> Let them cant about decorum,
> Who have character to lose.

At the height of the Spanish Civil War, Miró reverted to just such an image of a community of grotesque individuals in a ringing declaration of identity, but they are all rolled into one. For the Spanish Pavilion at the Paris World's Fair in 1937, he painted the *Catalan Peasant in Revolt*. Miró's picture was lost and Picasso's *Guernica* is more famous, but Miró's image which also takes inspiration from Catalan Romanesque art is surely the more effective of the two in this context. His defiant peasant brandishing his sickle, the opposite of Louis XIV, is somehow both irreducibly individual and collective and he is rooted in the soil like an olive tree in Miró's native Catalonia.

From Rembrandt and Burns to Miró, it is surely clear that art has a role in the constant process of negotiation between individual and community, the tightrope walk between individual and collective that is modern society. Art can, as needs be, state both points of view, though in truth, perhaps through lack of awareness of the wider need, modern art is often reduced to no more than a solipsistic statement of individual existence. But all the same there have been few more penetrating investigations of the private experience of individual identity than the great series of Rembrandt's self-portraits.

Rousseau followed with his *Confessions*, his psychological autobiography, and when Ramsay painted him, he made the connection back to Rembrandt by using one of his self-portraits as the model for his picture of Rousseau. Thus he placed together at the centre, the Western tradition of concern with individual identity, elusive though it is when you try to pin it down as they did, but as Rembrandt certainly understood. But Rousseau, as he examined the nature of self, also explored the construction of community. Both are psychological, and that is why between the two there is a constant problem of negotiation, keeping the balance on that tightrope.

As art has so often had greatest success in focussing the idea of the uniqueness of individual experience, witness Rembrandt, it is interesting to look at the difficulty that the artist faces when he tries to represent collective action, the expression of a common will. Here it is interesting that while Rembrandt painted exactly that in *The Oath of the Batavians*, for some reason though we do not know what it was, he took the picture back from the Town Hall in Amsterdam where it was installed and cut it down from an enormous and grandiose canvas to what we have now – still big, but also in a strange way intimate. Perhaps it was because in the language of large scale painting that he had originally used, the collective action becomes generalised, no longer the sum of individual actions, but simplified and so diminished.

Totalitarian art falls over the other side of the same fence. Up to a point this is an aesthetic problem, but aesthetics do not exist in isolation. They typify that need for negotiation between the two points of view. If the individualism of western art is not the whole problem, perhaps the issue is that what is represented is an action. If an action defines identity, then identity itself is dynamic not static. It is a process not a state. Hence the value of the metaphor of the dance, the community in movement, again dynamic, not passive. It is a metaphor to which Miró returned, too, in the mosaic pavement that he designed for the Ramblas in Barcelona, the principal social artery of the city. In coloured brick set in the ground it is the circle of the Cerdanya.

The reason for invoking Miró here is not just that the Catalans with his help seem to have been conspicuously successful in negotiating their collective identity within the larger Spanish state and Europe beyond it. If it were as simple as that, then the answer to the opening question, 'How big is identity?', might be about five million people does just nicely, thank you. A handy figure for the Scots too, and there may be something to be said for it. But Miró comes in here, and with him his predecessor Gaudí, who created in the Sagrada Familia a spiritual expression for the collective identity of the Catalans to stand alongside those of the 12th century, because both Miró and Gaudí drew heavily on the inspiration of the Arts and Crafts movement of the late 19th century.

There the ideas of Owen Jones, Ruskin and Morris and the polemics of Walter Crane, gave powerful and influential expression to the notion of the psychological nature of collective identity, that it is the same kind of construct as individual identity, built up out of feelings, memory, experience, history in sum. Political identity is a cultural construct, but also a historical process. This view was pioneered and popularised by Walter Scott, giving it universal currency in Europe and beyond and making cultural identity as we are discussing it here a major force in modern history. But Scott himself was following Adam Smith and the men of the Enlightenment. It was given practical expression, or at least the theory of its practical expression through art was developed by the artists of the Arts and Crafts: a community in which, long before universal suffrage, men and women played an equal part, gender being another fundamental part of the construct of identity.

The principal organ of this expression of collective identity in which men and women shared, according to Crane's view especially, was to be public art, decorative art he called it, above all art incorporated into architecture and so permanent, monumental and common property. Implicit in this and developed significantly here in Scotland by Patrick Geddes was the idea that such forms of expression are just as important for the community as for the individual: that they are a vehicle of collective memory and an expression of the crucial role of imagination in the construct that is society, remembering the link between imagination and sympathy. It was a woman artist, one of the first major women artists in the country, Phoebe Traquair, who returned to a musical metaphor in one of the finest products of these ideas, the painted choir on the walls singing together with the real choir of boys and girls practising in the St Mary's Song School.

Building on Ruskin, but also on Darwin, Huxley and other students of the natural world, Geddes saw that society itself was not only a psychological construct, it was actually organic; that therefore it was capable of sickness and of health, but Geddes also saw how it follows that the collective mind, a society's consciousness, a community's sense of itself, needed cultivation just as much as the individual, that the collective memory, too, needs to be kept fresh. It is not surprising that Geddes was a champion of museums, but he was equally a champion of the place of the art of the present in all our lives, and so of the need to keep imagination fresh in all of us, not just because it is fun, but because it is essential.

One of the grandest and most moving expressions of identity was the Scottish National War Memorial, truly an expression of collective memory, and of shared feeling at the tragic losses of World War I: the nation mourning as a family and a team of artists working in co-operation to articulate that grief and the shared feelings of a common identity. It was a matter of pride, indeed it was a condition that it was built with money raised by public subscription in Scotland. It was a public act of the collective will and it is a moving testimony to the Enlightenment vision of society bound together by feeling and imagination, but also by collective memory.

Here, there is another pitfall to avoid. Collective memory can be manipulated as manufactured myth, only think of Hitler. But if there is a danger, myth and memory are not invalidated by it. Self-knowledge is the key. Hence the importance of museums, indeed of the whole care of our heritage, physical and intellectual, but perhaps especially of those institutions dedicated to the interpretation of our community's history, like the Museum of Scotland. Was Wallace really a red-herring when the museum opened and the press focussed on his absence, not Mel Gibson's blue-faced, cardboard *Braveheart*, but the real Wallace, signatory of that matter-of-fact letter preserved miraculously in Lubeck? That tiny fragment of truth inoculates against the infection of irresponsible myth.

Museums are repositories of memory, but as we explore that memory, they also remind us of the complex concentricities of identity, the links out of which it is built. As discussed by the author in *The Arts and Identity: From Pilgrimage to Grand Tour*,[4] Scottish art is part of European art. It takes part of its identity from that, but it also gives back in exchange part of the identity of that larger whole. In this exchange neither is weakened. Both are valid for one is a set of the other. For in the end there is no answer to the question. Identity is elastic, dynamic, constantly to be renegotiated, and in that renegotiation the museum has a central role to provide as honestly as possible the raw material of collective memory. No wonder Geddes was a champion of the importance of museums.

There is a series of magnificent gold torques or necklaces in the National Museum in Stockholm composed of a set of widening concentric circles, each set with rows of tiny figures. Ancestors, community or cosmology, we do not know and perhaps it does not matter. A metaphor, they seem to place the individual who wore them at the centre of the complex concentricities within which we know ourselves, another way of expressing individual in community, perhaps going beyond the local to the universal, from the human to the divine.

More mundanely, we all remember those addresses we wrote as children, from house to street to town, from county, to country, to continent, planet and universe. All valid co-ordinates, but such geographical measurements are mostly fixed and relatively simple. It is the others, the mobile co-ordinates of history – family, social group and nation – which are problematic. The lines between them have constantly to be mediated and redrawn. Identity is not a thing, but a process of navigation, and like any navigation it needs accurate instruments. Good museums, the whole articulation of our heritage, through education in school and university as well, and our access to it, are ways of providing them.

As time passes, the opening of the Museum of Scotland and a few months later the opening of the Scottish Parliament will not seem merely a historical coincidence, but the expression of a single wish. As John Smith put it so memorably, it was 'the settled will' of the Scottish people that their Parliament should be recalled, but that will was forged far more in felt cultural experience, in the consciousness of identity given expression in the Museum, than in empty political debate about taxation, profit and loss.

The Author

Professor Duncan Macmillan is an Honorary Royal Scottish Academician, Curator of the Talbot Rice Gallery, and Professor of the History of Scottish Art at Edinburgh University. He is the author of several books, including *Scottish Art 1460–1990*, the most authoritative work ever written on the subject. He is also Chairman of University Museums in Scotland, the Scottish Society for Art History and the Edinburgh Galleries Association.

References

1. Macmillan, D., 'Here Stand Our Cultural Heroes: But Have They Stood in Vain?', in Fladmark, J.M. (ed), *Cultural Tourism*, Donhead, 1994, pp. 75–87.
2. Brankin, R., *Celebrating Scotland: A National Cultural Strategy*, consultation document by the Scottish Executive, 1999.
3. Macmillan, D., 'Our Heritage: Not just an Armchair by the Fireside of History', in Fladmark, J.M. (ed), *Heritage: Conservation, Interpretation and Enterprise*, Donhead, 1993, pp. 285–299.
4. Macmillan, D., 'The Arts and Identity: From Pilgrimage to Grand Tour', in Fladmark, J.M. (ed), *In Search of Heritage: as Pilgrim or Tourist?*, Donhead, 1998, pp. 163–177.

Further Reading

Boardman, P., *The Worlds of Patrick Geddes*, Routledge & Kegan Paul, 1978.
Macmillan, D., 'Scottish Art', in Scott, P.H. (ed), *Scotland: A Concise Cultural History*, Mainstream, 1993, pp. 205–228.

30

THE POVERTY OF NATIONS
Should Museums Create Identity?

James Bradburne

In recent years it has become popular to laud museums for their role in creating, shaping, and sustaining culture. Much in the way that early feminists optimistically argued that dressing girls in blue would address the problems of gender asymmetry, it is now stridently claimed that museums define a nation's identity, contribute to a nation's pride, and play a role in shaping a nation's culture.

As I write this, the nations of an increasingly federal Europe are violently and unsuccessfully trying to intervene in the attempts of one Sovereign nation to suppress and ultimately crush the claims of another, not-yet-recognised nation in the former Yugoslavia. In this paper I will argue that the attempt to hitch museums and the culture they preserve to the cart of the shaping of nationhood is dubious, misguided, and possibly dangerous. Whilst the words 'museum' and 'culture' can of course, indeed should, be spoken in the same breath, the construction of national identity is a different responsibility.

Let us first look at the terms invoked in the key themes of this volume: museums, culture, and (national) identity.

What is culture? On the one hand, the word is over-used, almost devalued past recognition or redemption. After the recent shooting at Columbine High School in Colorado, the American press was filled with accounts of the failings of America's 'secular culture'. As Alan Gopnik writes, 'add the culture of violence, the media culture, kid culture, gun culture, and jock culture, and you've got more cultures in one country than would fit in a Petri dish'. How can we meaningfully look at the idea of culture, let alone the national culture that it is argued museums play a role in shaping?

When we roam the halls of a museum, or wander through a shop, or sit in a restaurant and watch young parents with children, we can actually see culture in the making. 'Don't run, speak quietly, let the grocer pick out the oranges for you, keep your elbows off the table, don't slurp your milk' – culture is all the instruction that becomes internalised to the point of invisibility. In a very serious Heideggerian sense, culture only comes into existence when it breaks – when it is confronted with that which it is not – otherwise it is completely invisible. Culture is like accent, it is a measure of distance: social, geographical and political. No one has an accent at home. The entire idea of accent, like culture, has meaning only when confronted with others who 'speak' differently.

While culture is notoriously difficult to define, according to Edward T. Hall, 'in spite of many differences in detail, anthropologists do agree on three characteristics of culture: it is not innate, but learned; the various facets of culture are inter-related – you touch a culture one place and everything else is affected; it is shared and in effect defines the boundaries of different groups'.

Nationhood is also difficult to define – in fact, the notion of the nation-state is a relatively recent construction, certainly as it is understood today. In the universities of the late Middle Ages and early Renaissance, students congregated in 'nations' of shared language and culture, but few would have understood the meaning of Germany, Austria, or Italy – let alone being Austrian, German, or Italian. Identity was on the one hand far more local, at best regional, and on the other, far more international, as religion, class and learning readily spanned the rudimentary borders between cities, provinces, and emerging states. Like culture, national identity is learned, complex, and shared.

The world of the late Renaissance court – from Ferrara to Florence and from Paris to Prague – was still largely defined by City-states, small aristocratic principalities, and loose and constantly shifting federations of interests that colluded and collided depending on territorial ambitions, religious convictions, and sheer opportunism. To call any of these groupings 'nations' in any but the loosest sense would be an anachronism. Ports such as Venice, Genoa, and Antwerp were at the centre of vast trading networks linking Europe with China, India, Africa, and later the Americas. In the late Renaissance, the banking system as we know it slowly came into being, and the notion of risk started to figure in the justification of exacting higher interest rates from princes than those permitted within the Christian definition of usury.

Despite the importance of trade, the economy was still largely based on agriculture, and the wealth of the aristocratic dynasties based on rents and taxes derived from their lands. The notion of 'capital' – at least as investment – had yet to be invented, and centuries were to pass before the

Industrial Revolution gave meaning to the term 'means of production'. As families and courts amassed wealth from their activities, they translated this wealth into patronage to guarantee loyalty, and into conspicuous display to instil fear and respect. Princely collections were one important way in which the ideology of power was communicated to those over whom the ruling classes wished to exercise dominion. However they exercised their power, their identity, and that of those over whom they ruled, was defined less by national identity than by dynastic, religious, and territorial considerations. A Habsburg, for instance, was a Habsburg first, a Catholic second, and an Austrian third – if at all. Domus Austriae was defined as Habsburg – certainly not the other way around.

Beginning in the late 18th century, a social and economic earth tremor transformed the nature of Western society and European economy: the Industrial Revolution. We should be cautious of over-rating the importance of this so-called revolution – European society had already been transformed by other revolutions – such as the introduction of separated script (9th century), the banking system (14th century), the printing press, and the discovery of the New World (both 15th century). However, coming as it did at a time when the prevailing magical description of the world was giving way to a mechanical, rational one, the harnessing of machines to create new products had an enormous impact on the organisation of European society and the national identity of its inhabitants.

Nationhood in the sense we understand it today – and in the sense in which it is being contested in Ireland, Québec, Tibet, and Kosovo – can really be said to date to the mid-17th century, and only really reached its full expression as a consequence of the Industrial Revolution and the increasing integration of politics and economics that characterised 19th century capitalism, which, as we shall see, also had an effect on the kinds of museums we were to plan, and on the uses to which they were put.

Museums are rather easier to define, although the history one writes depends on the definition one chooses. According to Joseph Veach Noble (Head of Education at the Metropolitan Museum of Art and later President of the American Associaton of Museums) the purpose of the museum is 'to collect, to conserve, to study, to interpret and to exhibit.' These, he said, 'are like the five fingers of a hand, each independent, but united for a common purpose. '

If one defines the museum largely as the first three fingers of the hand, its history is linked to that of the collection, and the museum has its roots in the Classical past. The earliest museum of which we can speak was actually a library: the 'mousseion' of Alexandria, the institutional sibling of the famous library that flourished three centuries before Christ. Since the Renaissance, the dominant model of the museum has been the collection, and the demands of the collection have taken precedence in the museum's organisation. For example, let us take Rudolph IIs Kunstkammer as a collection par excellence. Publicly, it was an instrument of power, and played an important role in legitimating the Habsburg's dynastic claims. As families and courts amassed wealth from their activities, they translated this wealth into patronage to guarantee loyalty, and conspicuous display to instil fear and respect. Princely collections were one important way in which the ideology of power was communicated to those over whom the ruling classes wished to exercise dominion.

If one puts the emphasis on the last two fingers, the museum's history can be traced to the late 18th century. By the end of the 18th century, the political situation was extremely volatile, and the demands for access to social, political and cultural machinery found decisive political expression. Following the French Revolution in 1789, the very existence of private collections was called into question. Out of the passionate defence of the need for collections to the Convention of 1793 and 1794, the first modern museums were born: the Louvre, the Museum de l'Histoire Naturelle, and the Musée des Arts et Métiers.

The Musée Français, (later called the Musée du Louvre), was a creation of the Convention of 1793, and was originally the repository of the fruits of the confiscation of works of art from the church and the aristocracy during the Revolution. Under the Directoire, the museum's collections were organised systematically according to 'schools', and most importantly, explanatory texts were placed with each artwork. In addition to explanatory texts, the Louvre, following its initial vocation as 'the people's museum', was open to the public free of charge, published a guide for visitors and sold an inexpensive catalogue.

The Museum de l'Histoire Naturelle was created primarily from the Cabinet du Roi and the Jardin des Plantes by the Convention of 1794. Lamarck was outspoken about the needs of those who were excluded from the cabinets, and went on to enunciate one of the fundamental principles of the modern museum: public admission – 'the museum should not only be open to the public during the afternoon, that is to say during the hours when passers-by and idle folk seek some relief from boredom; but during the morning as well, that time of the day so particularly intended for travail, above all in investigations relative to the sciences.'

Thus the arguments for founding museums were linked to their ability to teach new skills, not just convey information about the distant past or amuse idle time-wasters. Justifying the creation of the Musée des Arts et Métiers, arguably one of the first museums of applied arts, the Abbé

Gregoire summarised his proposal to the Convention by saying 'I have just disclosed to you the means of developing the national industry.'

The educational objectives of the Conservatory were clear from the outset. Faced with a substantial delay in catching up with English industry, apprentices were to be routinely brought to the Conservatory to study machines and working models of machines, in order to make up the French deficit in technology speedily. Moreover, the Conservatory became the depot of records for all inventions patented in France, the repository of the history of France's entry into the industrial world. The Convention was convinced, and the Conservatoire des Arts et Métiers in Paris was created on 26 September, 1794.

In the institutions founded in the turbulent years of the Convention, the principal institutional characteristics of museums had all been sketched. First, they should contribute to the advancement of knowledge. Second, they should be organised to some system of classification. Third they should not be administered by a single, private individual. Finally, they should be open to the public. However well-defined its principles, the full development of the museum had to wait until the 19th century, when the growing middle classes, enfranchised by the commerce made possible by the political and industrial revolutions, and the imperial ambitions of the growing European nation-states, were powerful enough for their voice to be heard as a group, demanding full access to the cultural resources they could not afford to have individually.

The need to find an appropriate vehicle for the display and promotion of such a vast quantity of trade goods found its expression first in national trade fairs, popular in France, Germany and Great Britain since the 1840s, and finally in the idea of an international exposition. Consonant with the century's fascination with collection, arrangement and display, which can be seen in the rise of the great museums and galleries, the *Great Exhibition of the Works of Industry of All Nations* was seen as a convocation of all the industrial wonders of the world, and a demonstration of their utility in all spheres both industrial and cultural. Held in Hyde Park, London, in 1851 under the enlightened patronage of the Prince Albert, the Great Exhibition was a huge popular success, and attracted millions of visitors to Joseph Paxton's *Crystal Palace*, itself a tribute to the industrial virtues of modularity, mass production and utility.

After the Fair closed, the profits were so substantial that in the coming years a concert hall, music scholarships, and three new museums – the Natural History Museum, the Science Museum, and the Victoria and Albert Museum – were founded with the proceeds. The barrier that separated the museum from the World's Fair in the late 19th century was extremely permeable. As early as 1876, the US government solicited the help of the Smithsonian Institution in developing the themes for the centennial exhibition in Philadelphia, despite the opposition of the research community, as the museum was seen as the single most important institution of public exhibition. In 1893, at the World Columbian Exposition in Chicago, the Smithsonian was again implicated in the organisation, as were other museums including the Peabody at Harvard.

The French Revolution had called for a broad and democratic participation in cultural capital – a radical demand on the part of representatives of the disenfranchised. Yet, as in the case of the earlier American Revolution, the benefits of the dispersion of the cultural and economic capital devolved largely on to the middle classes, and the lower strata of society, while able to participate in principle, were effectively denied access to the machinery of capital and culture alike. Large segments of society had to wait for benefits of public education, reduced working hours and wages sufficient to permit access to the great palaces of culture.

In America at least, the ideology of the Founding Fathers had tended to consider art in general as a sign of decadence, and saw the importance of art as a function of its utility. Benjamin Franklin wrote: 'one schoolmaster is worth a dozen poets, and the invention of a machine or the improvement of an implement is of more importance than a masterpiece of Raphael', while John Adams wrote: 'Every one of the fine Arts from earliest times has been enlisted in the service of Superstition and Despotism'. It is therefore not surprising that American museums, almost all of which had their origins in the last quarter of the 19th century, sought to define their goals in terms of utility: to provide models for American 'tawdry' manufacture, and to educate and refine the labouring classes. John Choate, trustee of the new Metropolitan Museum of Art, wrote that the museum's plan:

> ...was not to establish a mere cabinet of curiosities which should serve to kill time for the idle, but...to gather together a...collection of objects illustrative of the history of the arts in all its branches...which should serve not only for the instruction and entertainment of the people, but should also show the students and artisans of every branch of industry...what the past has accomplished for them to imitate and excel.

Nearly all the new museums had as their mission to educate the public, notably the labouring classes, often with the explicit expectation that an increased exposure to the arts would be translated into better products. Museums were no longer to be the preserve of the few – they were to open Sundays and evenings for the many. Workers newly sensitive to beauty would give industry the competitive edge. This was the Golden Age of the

Industrial Revolution, and industry needed a visually literate public – to buy its goods, and to produce them. The museum was an important part of a broad national social, economic, and cultural strategy. Since mid-19th century, the museum's political masters also had a strong interest in defining national interests, and in using the museum's pre-eminent position as a pulpit from which to proclaim the truths of national identity.

Traditionally, the museum has been seen to be neutral, and has thereby enjoyed the trust of its visitors. The modern museum preached the truths of the grand narratives – Manifest Destiny, the superiority of Western culture, the onward march of Progress, the Triumph of the Will. To visit a great museum was to situate oneself in a fabric of common achievements – and more importantly, common goals. There was perhaps, however briefly, a time when nation states and national identity meant something to nearly everyone. However, these are no longer modern times.

They are, if we must use a term, postmodern times. The 20th century has seen the compact of trust between society and its institutions violated, broken, and fragmented. The First World War washed away empires in a sea of blood, the Nazis used the narratives of nationhood in the service of unspeakable evil, and the past decades have given us Vietnam, Watergate, Monicagate, and recently Kosovo, undermining any remaining faith in the ability to articulate a common national identity. In a recent article, Peter Schjeldahl wrote of contemporary America:

> As a nation, the United States is a fiction that stands on three legs: a set of still contested 18th century documents; the cautionary example of the Civil War; and the daily consumption of mass culture. That's it. Everything else, however tremendous, is secondary.

As if to underscore this postmodern vacuum, he writes further: 'Americanness is nobodyness. Deep down, I feel like nobody.' In a Europe groping towards a new identity armed only with a common currency, I doubt whether Schejdahl's angst is uniquely American.

The question must be asked as to whether the notion of a national identity, or at least a national identity defined in terms of the traditional Sovereign state, makes any sense in an increasingly global society – a world made irretrievably interdependent by technology and commerce. If national identity does makes sense, who defines it, and how? What role does a museum play in defining, shaping, and celebrating the national culture – and which national culture?

I was born in Canada, a country where identity is both shaped and distorted by disagreement over which claims to sovereignty take priority. Is Québec a nation? The Dene people? The Inuit? If so, what is Canada?

Which museum celebrates what identity? The question would be even more vexed if we took the example of Serbia. Who is a national and who is a minority depends on the definition. A Kosovar is in the minority in Serbia, while a Serb would be in the minority in an independent Kosovo. What would a Kosovar Museum in Belgrade exhibit? Or a Serbian Museum in an independent Kosovo? As museum professionals, are we content if our museums are only instruments through which we trumpet jingoistic self-affirmations?

In many ways, the coupling of museums and national identity represents a dead-end – or at very best, a vicious circle. If museums are to shape national identity, nations must first have a meaning. However, as economic and political independence are eroded, and our world becomes increasingly global, the meaning of nationhood becomes increasing metaphorical and fragmented. It seems that in a matter of decades we will once again be using the term 'nation' as we did in the 13th century – unhooked from any notion of national sovereignty and geographical boundaries. In the 21st century, the very notion of the boundary is called into question.

Yet the idea that museums can shape national identity is an extremely seductive one, given the history of the museum. Originally, collections were the possession of an individual collector: Emperor, prince, or wealthy merchant, and their enhancement and interpretation were intimately linked to their owner's personality. Soon after the birth of the museum as a public institution, the burden of defining its mission passed to an elite group of specialists: the museum curators. Since the early years of the museum as a public institution, it was seen as a complement to the university – one an informal setting for learning, the other a formal setting for education, and often there was acrimonious competition between them. Despite this tension, the curator's mission was fundamentally seen as that of a professor, delivering the truth about the museum's objects from on high; a priest at the altar of art history, preaching to the unwashed masses. More often than not, curators would preach to each other, and exhibitions became a means for scholars to create and sustain reputations, further careers, and to impress other scholars.

When confronted with the collapse of the grand narratives, the museum's response to the postmodern dilemma has been to remain firmly 'top-down', and to address the content of the narrative, ever seduced by the desire to retain control over the narrative it presents. 'Bad' old grand narratives are to be replaced by 'good' new de-centred author-less narratives. Instead of museums of heroes, we now make museums of victims. Instead of museums that celebrate imperial identity, we make museums that trumpet new national identities. However, it is still the museum that calls the shots, and shapes the content. So, under pressure to affirm new national identities, we create new national museums with verve, enthusiasm and pots of public money, occasionally ignoring the fact that national identity is no longer necessarily the strongest defining feature of self-perception. However, if this is true, and the museum continues in its 'top-down' role, where does it end? Perhaps with a museum of the three flats next door, as our identity becomes increasingly fragmented. Where we stop if we follow this logic is only a matter of time and entropy.

To the author, the problem seems to stem from an unwillingness to re-examine the way in which museums have traditionally defined their own role, and what is called for is a total reappraisal of the notion that museums can and should have something to do with shaping national identity. By definition, the notion of nationhood is restrictive, historical, and constructed from the top-down. It is a part of the legitimation of political objectives on behalf of those who wield power, and part of the ideological armament of political action. Culture, on the other hand, is fluid, ever-changing, and almost always bottom-up – boundaries are only discovered through exploration. As long as the museum considers that its primary role is to define content – by definition a top-down approach – it must answer for the arbitrariness of the content it defines, regardless of its inherent 'correctness'.

Traditionally, museums have considered their visitors – when they considered them at all – as ignorant, or at best, as blank slates on which to write new information – whether the truths of taste or the truths of nationhood. In fact, the opposite is true. Far from being ignorant, our visitors are competent, intelligent and, more often than not, highly educated. They tend to know exactly who they are and where they belong. Far from being blank slates our visitors are already experts in some things, and come with existing experience, education and opinions. Visitors create their own understanding, and the museum gives them opportunities to create new knowledge during and after their visit. We cannot insist on dictating the specific new knowledge they create – a museum is an informal learning environment – not a school classroom.

The role of the museum is to create an informal environment where the visitors can explore the ways in which they can actively modify their relationship with culture, by enhancing their knowledge, piquing their curiosity, by honing their critical judgement. In the museum, visitors should be in control, and they should be encouraged to chart their own course. Given its history, learning in the museum should not be top-down, but bottom-up.

What does this mean in a museum? Surely the museum always plays a role in shaping the visitor's experience? Here are a few concrete examples that point to the museum's role of capturing identity from the bottom up – not imposing it from the top down. The Scottish Museum, under the leadership of its Director, Mark Jones, has already taken a step along this path, as witnessed by the fact that the majority of the objects in the museum's 20th century galleries have been chosen by the people of Scotland themselves. While the author still finds problematic the way in which national identity is the frame into which people's identity is squeezed, or if you prefer, the lens through which it is seen, certainly to involve the people of Scotland themselves in this process signals a far-ranging and courageous re-examination of the museum's 'top-down' role.

In 1994, the German Kunst-und Ausstellungshalle in Bonn hosted the exhibition 'Wunderkammer des Abendlandes', about the transformation of the private collection into Cabinet of Curiosities, and the Cabinet into the modern museum. Curated by Pontus Hulten, it was a breathtaking panorama of museum history, built around richly detailed settings of collections. As striking and provocative as the exhibition was, it would have remained a 'classical' exhibition had it not been for the addition of a collection of children's 'treasures'. In seven freestanding vitrines, were displayed objects collected by children, organised into the categories the children themselves used – treasures, toys, old stuff. Moreover, in order for the objects to qualify for inclusion in one of the large vitrines, the children had to undertake the work of a curator. They had to describe the object in material terms, date it, ascribe an insurance value to it, specify the conditions under which it could be displayed, and most importantly, assign it to a category. The children were thus introduced to the concepts of collecting, conservation, and curatorship. In this part of the exhibition, the children were in control of the definition of their own culture, and their identity was carefully preserved in the teeming binders full of 'curatorial' information.

Last summer, the San Francisco Exploratorium opened an exhibition on the theme of 'Memory'. While some of the exhibition looked at the neurophysiology of memory, large sections also looked at the subjective experience of memory – memories of childhood, memories of historical events, happy memories and sad. To fill a large wall, the design team proposed painting a timeline. Along the timeline, quite traditionally, were written important dates – at least dates that were important within a larger national narrative – the bombing of Pearl Harbor, the day Kennedy was assassinated, the date of the first moon walk, etc. One of the team members, Sally Duensing, suggested that they place pencils and 'post-it' notes either side of the timeline, in the hopes that visitors would contribute their memories.

Despite the success of earlier prototypes, no one expected the huge success that followed the exhibition's opening. Within days, the wall looked like a shaggy yellow-furred dog, as visitors filled the timelines with 'their' memories, and 'their' identities. Some of the dates had only personal significance: 'I was born', 'my Father died', 'my sister had a baby'. Others had broader significance: the founding of a local church, a downtown fire, the results of a local election. Unlike traditional museum displays, this exhibit registered and preserved culture as experienced by local actors, rather than imposing a new narrative in which they were expected to fit their own experiences.

Finally, let me add another local example, the Scottish Cultural Resources Access Network (SCRAN). Scotland has here taken the lead in the preservation and interpretation of its cultural resources. This project has the ambitious aim of digitising all known Scottish material culture – from sword hilts to chess men – and to making these resources available over the Internet to educational institutions. This project, under the Chairmanship of Lady Balfour of Burleigh, has already created rich interpretive resources to accompany the objects and their description. However, the potential of this project lies in its ability to be an instrument to gather 'soft' historical information – personal reminiscences, ephemera, accounts of events – and to post this information as part of a growing archive that defines identity from the 'bottom-up'. In doing so, it serves as a catalyst for a re-definition of the museum's role – or a strengthening of the museum's real mission to collect, preserve, study, interpret, and exhibit. The power of the SCRAN model is being used as an inspiration for other projects around Europe.

It can be seen from the above that a museum can continue to fulfil its goals of collecting, preserving, studying, interpreting and exhibiting, without necessarily shaping, constructing and creating all of the content. A museum's role can be to support – not to create. Of course it can be rightly argued that the museum is still playing an active role in creating certain possibilities and discouraging others – and indeed it is a necessary part of a bottom-up approach that the museum's agency be made visible, and not elided – nevertheless the qualitative difference between the bottom-up approach and the traditional top-down approach cannot be overemphasised.

Creating content, whether top-down or bottom-up, is not enough, however, if the society no longer has the skills necessary to reappropriate its own culture. As long as the museum continues to create content without placing an important emphasis on communicating new skills, then it contributes to the very 'dumbing down' of society that it purports to resist. As the technological means to preserve material culture increase, as they have with breathtaking speed over the past 50 years, then the importance of the skills needed to decode the preserved information becomes paramount. The more we store instead of learning, the more we need to ensure we keep and transmit the skills to unlock the stored information.

The past decades have seen European society transformed by a series of changes – each as revolutionary in its way as the revolution that swept across Europe when the printing press was introduced in the 15th century. As Neil Postman observed: 'Prior to the telegraph, information moved only as fast as a train could travel: about thirty-five miles an hour'. With the computer and the development of new global information networks, not only information, but massive amounts of currency moved around the globe in a fraction of a second, capital restlessly seeking greater return where it can find it – 24 hours a day. Time and space are transformed by information technology, and even our identity is now called into question. Who we are and where we are is one on the Internet – we are our address. In the virtual world of the Internet, the author is jamesb@museum-kunsthandwerk.de – no matter where he logs in.

With information playing an increasingly important role in delivering products more effectively and more efficiently, we have seen the European economy moving from a product-based economy towards a service-based economy – much as it earlier moved from an agrarian economy to an industrial one. In a sense we could describe this as a shift from a 'high-volume' economy, wherein industry makes a lot of products and selling them each at a profit – to a 'high-value' economy, wherein profit is made by being more flexible, more responsive, more creative. If we are to continue to justify our Euro-lifestyle – and pay our Euro-taxes – it is imperative that this shift towards a high-value economy be made as quickly as possible. Even now, new MBAs are taught that 'the only sustainable advantage is the ability to learn faster than your competitors'. We must become a learning society, and lifelong learning has to figure very high in our list of priorities.

Thus, the museum's assets must be seen to include not only its collections, but also its role as a privileged site for learning, and must therefore stress the acquisition of new skills, not just information. For the museum to play its role in this 'community of learners', it must take up the challenge of communicating the skills needed for the next century. At the end of the 19th century, these were the skills of industrial production. Now they are the skills of creativity and communication. These skills are largely shared by fine art, applied art, science and technology alike: creativity, collaboration, abstraction and critical judgement.

The common ground provided by putting the accent on skills has the effect of making less important the distinctions formerly made according to content: science, ethnology, history, fine arts. Naturally, information is still indispensable, but it must be linked to the skills of finding, using and appropriating that information. This strategy recalls the humanist education of the Renaissance, and prepares us to play our part in the community of learners. As Jonathan Miller once said, the museum must 'prepare us for a world in which the life of the mind is a pleasure.'

The museum is a public place, a 'piazza'. It is a place to wander, to stroll, to sit and to enjoy. It is, as Sherman Lee, former Director of the Cleveland Museum of Art once said: 'a permanent storage battery'. It is to the museum that we come to recharge our batteries after a long week at the office. It is to the museum that we bring our children to show them the richness of the world they will inherit and will soon help to create. It is to the museum we come to be with our friends, to explore, to discover, and to share new experiences. A museum and its collections help remind us of what all our money is for – making the world around us richer, more beautiful, and more dynamic.

It is in the spirit of the piazza that the museum must be a public forum, a place where all voices can be heard, differences explored, similarities compared. To fulfil its role in the next century, the museum must wean itself from the need to dispense the truth from on high – it must give up being top-down. The museum does not make culture, it does not shape identity, it does not have all the answers. The museum plays a potentially far more important role. It preserves culture, registers identity – it has questions.

The museum is an institution in which every voice can be heard, and by having a place, can define its own identity – national, regional, religious, or sexual. It is a place where supporting questioning and exploration is the prime goal. It is a place where we ensure that the past can continue to play a role in shaping identity, without being a place where identity is prescribed from the outside. It is a place where we all belong, where no one is excluded. Frank Oppenheimer often said: 'No one ever failed a museum'. He meant that the visitor can not 'fail' a museum in the sense of failing an exam. In an informal setting there are no tests and no conditions for participation. A museum can, and often does, fail its audience – it is the visitor who can not fail.

Museums are for all of us, but to be for all of us, they should not aspire to the role of telling us who we are. By making history accessible, and serving as a mirror of identity, they can be profoundly local. At the same time, by putting an emphasis on communicating the skills needed to appropriate culture, they can be profoundly global. Therein lies the future of our museums, our culture, and our identity.

The Author

Dr James Bradburne became Director of the Museum für Kunsthandwerk in Frankfurt am Main in 1999, following six years with the newMetropolis in the Netherlands. A British–Canadian architect, designer and museum specialist, his doctorial research was on the subject of creating effective educational strategies in informal learning environments. His work experience includes planning World's Fair pavilions, science centres, international art exhibitions, research projects and symposia for UNESCO, national governments, private foundations and museums worldwide. He currently sits on several international advisory committees and museum boards, and recently curated and designed exhibitions including Rudolph II (Prague, 1997) and Theatre of Reason/Theatre of Desire (Villa Favorita, Lugano, 1998). He lectures on new approaches to informal learning, and has published extensively. His books and papers have been translated into seven languages.

References

Allwood, J., *The Great Exhibitions*, Studio Vista, 1977.

Antonovich, F., *L' art à la cour de Rodolphe II Empereur du Saint Empire Romain Germanique, Prague et son rayonnement*, Le Louvre des Antiquaires, 1992.

Axelrod, R., *The Evolution of Co-operation*, Penguin, 1990.

Baudrillard, J., *L'effet Beaubourg*, Galilée, 1977.

Baxandall, M., *Patterns of Intention*, Yale, 1985.

Benassayag, D. (ed)., *Le futur antérieur des musées*, Editions du rénard, 1991.

Bennett, T., *The Birth of the Museum*, Routledge, 1995.

Bezombes, D., *La Grande Galerie du Muséum*, Le Moniteur, 1994.

Bourdieu, P. and Darbel, A., *L'amour de l'art*, Editions de minuit, 1969.

Brown-Goode, G., *Museum History and Museums of History*, Papers of the American Historical Association, Vol. III, No.1, Putnam's, 1888.

Chartier, R., *L'Ordre des livres*, Alinea, 1992.

Elsner, J. and Cardinal, R., *The Cultures of Collecting*, Reaktion, 1994.

Evans, R.J.W., *Rudolph II and his World*, Clarendon, 1973.

Findlen, P., *Possessing Nature*, University of California, 1994.

Georgel, C., *La jeunesse des musées*, RME, 1994.

Gopnik, A., *Culture Vultures*, New Yorker, 24 May 1999, pp. 27–28.

Grafton, A. and Blair, A. (eds), *The Transmission of Culture in early Modern Europe*, University of Pennsylvania, 1990.

Hale, J., *The Civilisation of Europe in the Renaissance*, Harpers, 1993.

Hall, E.T., *Beyond Culture*, Doubleday, 1976, p. 16.

Hooper-Greenhill, E., *Museums and the Shaping of Knowledge*, Routledge, 1992.

Hudson, K., *A Social History of Museums*, Humanities Press, 1975.

Hulten, P. (ed), *Wunderkammmer des Abendlandes*, Kunst und Austellungshalle, 1995.

Impey, O. and Macgregor, A., *The Origins of Museums*, Clarendon Press, 1985.

Lhotsky, A., *Die Geschichte der Sammlungen, Festschrift des Kunsthistorisches Museum*, Vols 1–2, Ferdinand Berger Verlag, 1941.

Lowenthal, D., *The Past is a Foreign Country*, Cambridge University Press, 1985.

Lumley, R., *The Museum Time Machine*, Routledge, 1989.

Mai, E., *Expositionen: Geschichte und Kritik des Ausstellungswesens*, Deutscher Kunstverlag, 1986.

Maland, D., *Europe in the Seventeenth Century*, Macmillan, 1991.

McClellan, A., *Inventing the Louvre: art, politics, and the origins of the modern museum in 18th century Paris*, Cambridge University Press, 1994.

Pomian, K., *Collectionneurs, amateurs et curieux*, Gallimard, 1987.

Pomian, K., *L'ordre du temps*, Gallimard, 1990.

Postman, N., *Technopoly*, Vintage Books, 1993.

Schaer, R., *L'invention des musées*, Gallimard, 1989.

Schejldahl, P., *American Pie*, New Yorker, 17 May 1996, pp. 94–95.

Schroeder-Gudehus, B. and Rasmussen, A., *Les Fastes du Progrès*, Flammarion, 1992.

Schwarz, M. (ed), *Wereld tenstoonstellingen*, KVGO, 1991.

Shapin, S., *A Social History of Truth*, University of Chicago, 1994.

Zacharias, W., *Zeit phänomen Musealisierung*, Hermes, 1990.